INTRODUCTION TO SATELLITE COMMUNICATION

SINTRODUCTION TO
ATELLITE COMMUNICATION

Bruce R. Elbert

Hughes Communications, Inc.

Artech House

Library of Congress Cataloging-in-Publication Data

Elbert, Bruce R.
  Introduction to satellite communication.

  Includes index.
  1. Artificial satellites in telecommunication.
I. Title.
TK5104.E43   1987   621.38'0422   87-27544
ISBN 0-89006-229-3

Copyright © 1987
ARTECH HOUSE, INC.
685 Canton Street
Norwood, MA 02062

International Standard Book Number: 0-89006-229-3
Library of Congress Catalog Card Number: 87-27544

10 9 8 7

In memory of Gregory Jarvis,
A spacecraft engineer and payload specialist
aboard the Shuttle Challenger,
Who definitely had the right stuff.

Contents

Preface

Introduction to Satellite Communication is a book designed to meet the needs of information industry professionals and students. Based on comments from many friends and associates over the years, it had become clear that a comprehensive, accurate, and understandable book on the subject of satellite communication systems did not exist. This has made it extremely difficult for new entrants into the field to gain a foothold in a relatively short time. Whether the reader is technically trained or not, the need exists for an indoctrination in the construction and usage of satellite networks.

The book that is in your hands will give you an understanding that should permit you to begin work as a satellite professional or as a user of satellite communication. However, this book is not a substitute for engineering texts and papers on the design of satellite communication equipment or the implementation of satellite links. To include such design information with the needed mathematical base would have rendered the book unreadable to the larger audience. So, we have included a selection of reference books in the bibliography to aid in the reader's study of the field. We have made every effort to simplify the technical concepts so that a person without a technical degree or background can grasp them.

Many classifications of professionals and students should profit from a significant portion of the material. A major group includes newly hired personnel working for satellite and earth station equipment manufacturers as well as operators of satellites and earth stations. Among operators of earth stations are TV and radio networks and affiliates that rely on satellite transmission, and communication service companies, which deal primarily in the video and international marketplaces. Large corporations employ professionals in telecommunication and data processing management, who work with terrestrial and satellite-based networks and therefore need to understand many of the principles outlined in this book. While not intended for engineering courses, the book would be useful for background reading by electronics and computer engineering students at the undergraduate and graduate levels. The book's explanatory nature and broad coverage make it suitable as a textbook for university programs in communication management and policy. Practitioners in associated legal and financial fields would find the book particularly helpful when they must deal with telecommunications projects and issues.

The information in the book has been drawn from the author's 18 years of satellite communication industry experience, which has involved assignments in engineering design, system implementation, program management, operations, and marketing of hardware and services. The companies that provided this experience include Hughes Aircraft Company, Communications Satellite Corporation (COMSAT), and Western Union Corporation. Many of the concepts which are used to explain the technology were introduced in seminars led by the author at the AIAA Communications Satellite System Conference and the Satellite Communications Users Conference.

The book is organized into nine chapters to correspond to the major areas of technological definition and application. These are summarized in the following paragraphs.

Chapter 1, "Introduction," identifies the key features of satellite communication, and reviews the origins and history of the technology. In Chapter 2, "Applications of Satellite Networks," the ways in which satellite links can be applied to practical communication problems are described in some detail. This gives the reader an appreciation for the variety of uses where satellites have gained a stronghold. Technologists involved with the spacecraft will find that this chapter explains many of the mysteries surrounding the business of using satellites. "Microwave Link Engineering," Chapter 3, gives the reader a basic understanding of the physics of the radio link between the earth station and the satellite, and covers those factors which are under the designer's control as well as those that are not. It is assumed that the reader has little or no technical training, so the only form of mathematics used is arithmetic. Chapter 4, "Multiple Access and Modulation," rounds out the basic theory of communication as it relates to efficient satellite transmission. This particular chapter is fairly compact, and it may be helpful for interested readers to supplement their study with a basic textbook in communication engineering.

Chapter 5, "Spacecraft Technology," is perhaps the first comprehensive tutorial review of the elements of a communication spacecraft and how they work as an integrated system. As is customary in the industry, the spacecraft is subdivided into the communication payload (repeater and antenna) and the spacecraft bus (the supporting elements). While this chapter is not essential to understanding how to use satellite communication, it will be of general benefit because the actual operation of a spacecraft will occasionally affect the performance of the services rendered. The complementary topics for the ground facilities used in conjunction with the satellite are covered in Chapter 6, "Earth

Stations and Terrestrial Technology." Care has been taken to include only the current classes of earth stations, particularly those used for broadcast and VSAT applications. This chapter will be useful to those who plan to use satellite transmission, since ownership and control of ground facilities are increasingly in the hands of the user, rather than the satellite operator.

Chapter 7, "Launch Systems and Orbital Operations," covers topics that have become of great concern to operators and users of satellites alike. We provide the reader with a thorough review of the alternatives for placing satellites into orbit. We emphasize in the chapter that particular launch vehicle choices change over time; however, because reliability is based on a consistent experience record, much of the change is evolutionary, rather than revolutionary. This chapter also discusses the planning and operation of the mission, which is the sequence of events of launch, placement into geostationary orbit, and control of the satellite during its useful lifetime.

In Chapter 8, "Economics of Satellite Systems," the underlying characteristics of the satellites and earth stations are related to the cost of implementing and operating a satellite network. The framework is useful for analyzing the economics of either a complete system or a portion of a system (e.g., one or a few earth stations).

The final chapter makes a reasonable projection into the future, using today's technologies and applications as a base. Therefore, Chapter 9, "Future Directions for Satellite Communications," is quite conservative, since we have not yet thought of some of the more important uses to come.

The book can be read sequentially from cover to cover because the material follows a consistent thread. All of the technologies of spacecraft and earth stations are covered. Chapters can be read out of sequence if necessary, since each explains the concepts relevant to it. References to other chapters are provided throughout. The material is completely current as of the time of publication (*circa* 1987), but care has been taken to emphasize concepts that are not likely to change quickly. Point-to-multipoint (broadcast) applications, like cable TV and two-way interactive applications using very small aperture terminals (VSAT), are stressed due to their dominance in satellite communication. Readers who work in certain fields covered in the book should find the other material useful in rounding out their understanding. Once read, the book can be used as a reference because most of the technical terms in current usage are defined and illustrated. The detailed index can be used as a glossary in that many terms and abbreviations are incorporated, and a separate glossary of acronyms is included as well.

ACKNOWLEDGEMENTS

I wish to acknowledge my colleagues at Hughes Aircraft Company with whom I have worked, studied, and traveled over the years. My first introduction to satellites, however, came at COMSAT Laboratories, where we examined many technologies and concepts well before they were applied commercially (and some are yet to be applied). Finally, I wish to acknowledge my wife, Cathy, who provided the support and motivation necessary to start and complete an individual project of this scope.

Chapter 1
Introduction

Satellite communication has evolved into an everyday, commonplace thing. Most television coverage travels by satellite, even reaching directly to the home from space. No longer is it a novelty to see that a telecast has been carried by satellite (in fact, it would be novel to see something delivered by other means). The bulk of transoceanic telephone and data communication also travels by satellite. For countries such as Indonesia, domestic satellites have greatly improved the quality of service from the public telephone system and brought nations more tightly together. A unique benefit has appeared in the area of emergency preparedness and response. For example, when the devastating earthquake of September 1985 hit Mexico City, the newly launched Morelos satellite maintained reliable television transmission around the nation even though all terrestrial long distance lines out of the city stopped working.

This book is about the technologies that comprise the field of commercial satellite communication, intending to provide a bridge between those who need a practical understanding and those whose business it is to develop and operate these systems. One of the main objectives in writing this book is to give the reader enough of this understanding to allow him or her to ask the right questions. The explanations and factual material provided here are directed toward that objective rather than offering a technical or historical reference. Within the context of this book, the term ''satellite'' means the actual communication spacecraft in orbit which relays radio signals between earth stations on the ground. Unfortunately, in the United States, common vernacular among telecommunication consumers applies the term satellite to the service rendered by the satellite in conjunction with the accessing earth stations. If this is the reader's frame of reference, please adopt that of this book, since much of what follows relies upon the proper distinction.

Rather than focusing on a particular aspect of satellite communication, all of the primary areas are covered in relevant chapters. Technical concepts are introduced as needed, without using detailed design information. It is hoped that this will keep the reader from getting lost in the "forest" of engineering equations and complicated diagrams that are found in other technically oriented text books and manuals. To provide an overview of the field, the remainder of this chapter describes the features of satellite communication networks as well as the principal elements of an overall system. The brief history at the conclusion of the chapter is intended to explain how the satellite industry developed and why things are the way they are. It may be read in sequence or deferred until other chapters have been read first to get a better feel for the technology and terms.

1.1   BASIC CHARACTERISTICS OF SATELLITES

A communication satellite permits two or more points on the ground (earth stations) to send messages to one another over great distances using radio waves. The class of earth-orbiting satellites that is the subject of this book consists of those satellites located in the geostationary orbit. As is discussed later in this chapter and again in Chapter 7, a satellite in the *geostationary earth orbit* (GEO) revolves around the earth in the plane of the equator once in 24 hours, maintaining precise synchronization with the earth's rotation. It is well known that a system of three satellites in GEO, each separated by 120 degrees of longitude, as shown in Figure 1-1, can receive and send radio signals over the entire globe except for the polar regions. A given satellite has a coverage region, illustrated by the shaded oval, within which earth stations can communicate with and be linked by the satellite.

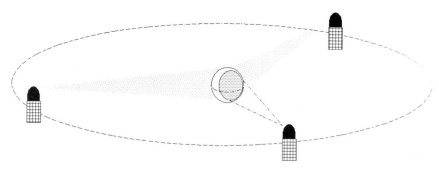

Fig. 1-1 A System of Three Geostationary Communications Satellites Provides Nearly Worldwide Coverage

The GEO (also referred to as the *geostationary satellite orbit (GSO)*) is the ideal case of the entire class of geosynchronous (or synchronous) orbits, which all have a 24-hour period of revolution but are typically inclined with respect to the equator. As viewed from the earth, a synchronous satellite in an inclined orbit will appear to drift during a day about its normal position in the sky. The GEO is not a stable arrangement and inclination naturally increases in time. As discussed in Chapter 5, inclination is controlled by the use of an on-board propulsion system with enough fuel for corrections during the entire life-time of the satellite. A synchronous satellite not intended for GEO operation can be launched with considerably less auxiliary fuel for this purpose. Orbit incli-nation of greater than 0.1 degrees is usually not acceptable for commercial service unless the earth station antennas can automatically repoint toward (track) the satellite as it appears to move.

The key dimension of a geostationary satellite is its ability to provide coverage of an entire hemisphere at one time. As shown in Figure 1-2, a large contiguous land area (i.e., a country) as well as offshore locations can simul-taneously access a single satellite. If the satellite has a specially designed com-munication beam focused on these areas, then any receiving antennas within the "footprint" of the beam (the area of coverage) will receive precisely the same transmission. Locations well outside the footprint will generally not be able to use the satellite effectively. The typical example in North America is the Galaxy I satellite (see Photo 1-A), which has 24 television channels with coverage throughout the 50 United States. These 24 channels are broadcast to more than 15,000 cable television systems and to over two million home backyard and rooftop antennas. In general, two-way (full duplex) communication is possible because the satellite's receiving beam will provide the same footprint.

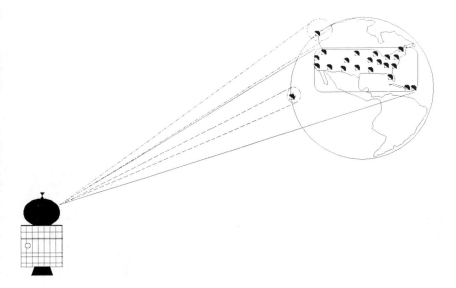

Fig. 1-2 Typical Footprint of a U.S. Domestic Communication Satellite Showing Coverage of Continental and Offshore Points

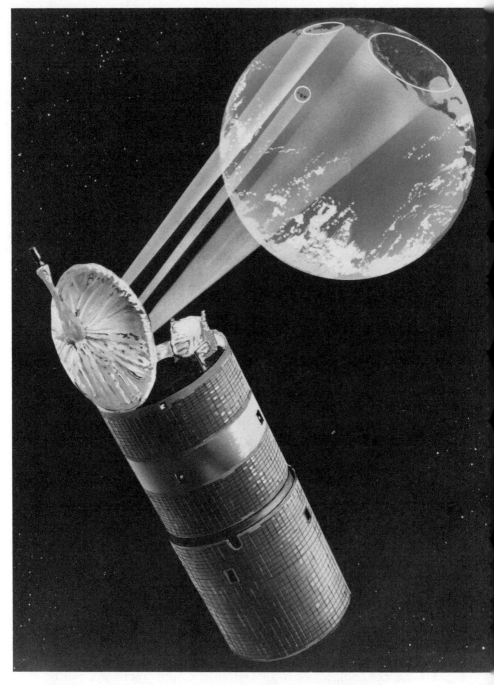

Photo 1-A. Typical Footprint of a Geostationary Satellite
(photograph courtesy of Hughes Aircraft Company)

The expansion in the use of satellites for communication has not occurred in a vacuum. Terrestrial communication systems, which include cable and point-to-point microwave radio, were around before satellites, are still around, and will be around long into the future (as will satellites). Technology is always advancing, and satellite and terrestrial communication will improve in quality, capability, and economy. As shown in Figure 1-3, however, terrestrial systems must spread out over a land mass like a highway network in order to reach the points of access in cities. The time, difficulty, and expense incurred are extensive; but once established, a terrestrial infrastructure can last a lifetime. Satellites, on the other hand, are designed to last about ten years in orbit due to the practical inability to service a satellite in GEO and replenish consumables (fuel, battery cells, and degraded or failed components).

Fig. 1-3 An Extensive Network of Cable and Microwave Links Would Be Required to Provide Wide Area Coverage Comparable to that of a Satellite Network

The term "bypass" is often used to refer to the ability of satellite links to step over the existing terrestrial network and thus avoid the installation problems and service delays associated with local telephone service. Figure 1-4 depicts the three means of long haul communication used to connect two user locations. Using the satellite in a duplex mode (i.e., allowing simultaneous two-way interactive communication), the user can employ earth stations at each end, eliminating any connection with the terrestrial network. In a terrestrial microwave system, radio repeaters must be positioned at intermediate points along the route to maintain line-of-sight contact. This is because microwave energy, including that on terrestrial and satellite radio links, travels in a straight line with a minimum of bending over or around obstacles. In the case of a long distance cable system, a different form of repeater is needed to amplify the signals and compensate for changes in cable characteristics. Therefore cable systems (coaxial and fiber optic) are probably the most costly to install and maintain. Only providers of local and long distance telephone services and major users of communication services (government agencies, multinational corporations, railroads, utilities, etc.) are able to justify the expense of operating their own terrestrial cable or microwave networks. Satellite networks, on the other hand, are well within the reach of much smaller organizations, since satellite capacity can be purchased or rented from a much larger company or agency. Examples of satellite operators include international consortia like INTELSAT, government-owned communications companies, and private companies like Telesat Canada and Hughes Communications, Inc., which construct the systems and operate them as a business. The availability of small, low-cost earth stations which take advantage of more sophisticated satellites has allowed the smallest potential users to apply satellite bypass networks to achieve economies and save time. The idea of a satellite dish on every rooftop is now possible.

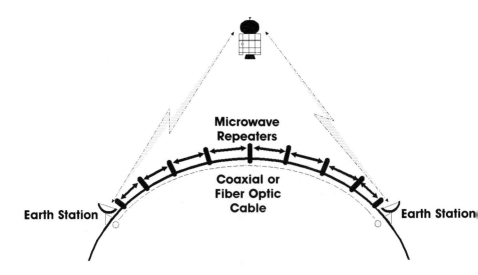

Fig. 1-4 Terrestrial Microwave and Cable Systems Require Multiple Hops While a Satellite System Provides the Same Capability with a Single Hop

1.2   SYSTEM ELEMENTS

Implementation of a communication satellite system is a major undertaking. Fortunately for the great majority of current and future satellite users, several systems are already in existence and are open for business in virtually every part of the world. In some cases the requirements may be so extensive that a dedicated satellite is justified. The purpose of this book is to define and describe all of the parts of such a system, since an understanding of satellite communication requires the development of a feel for the breadth of the technology. This section describes the system in terms of two major parts—the space segment and the ground segment.

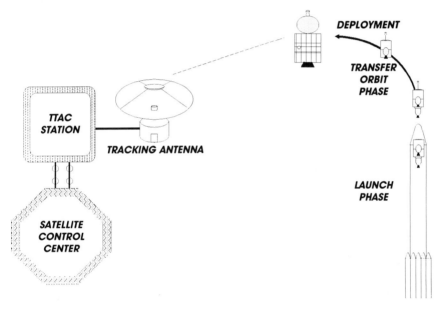

Fig. 1-5 The Elements Needed to Implement the Space Segment of a Geostationary Communication Satellite System

1.2.1   Space Segment

An overview of the main elements of the space segment is shown in Figure 1-5, demonstrating that placing a satellite into orbit and operating it for ten years involves a great deal. Placement in orbit is accomplished by contracting both with a spacecraft manufacturer and with a launch agency, and allowing them the 30 to 40-month period necessary to design, construct, and launch the satellite. Chapter 5 provides considerable detail on the design of a communication satellite, while Chapter 7 reviews the launch aspects.

After the satellite is properly positioned at its assigned longitude above the equator, it becomes the responsibility of a satellite operator to control the satellite for the duration of its mission (its lifetime in orbit). This is a fairly complex task and involves both sophisticated ground-based facilities as well as highly trained technical personnel. The tracking, telemetry, and command (TTAC) station establishes a control and monitoring link with the satellite. Precise tracking data is periodically collected via the tracking antenna to allow the pinpointing of the satellite's position and the planning of on-orbit position corrections. This is because the orbit tends to shift with respect to the ground due to irregular gravitational forces from the nonspherical earth, from the sun, and from the moon; more on this in Chapter 7. The second facility shown in Figure 1-5 is the satellite control center (SCC) which houses the operator consoles and data processing equipment by which the control and monitoring of the satellite or satellites are accomplished. Other common names for the SCC include Operations Control Center (OCC) and Satellite Control Facility (SCF). The SCC could be at the site of the TTAC station, but more commonly is located some distance away, usually at the headquarters of the satellite operator. The actual satellite-related data can be passed between the sites over low-speed data and voice lines (either terrestrial or satellite). As was mentioned previously, the level of training of the personnel at the SCC is quite high, involving such fields as orbital mechanics, aerospace, and electronic engineering.

Referring back to the launch phase, the satellite must be located and tracked from the ground beginning after it has been released from the last rocket stage. This tracking service can be provided by the launch agency, but more often than not, it is arranged separately with other owners of TTAC stations appropriately located around the world. The satellite operator could employ his own TTAC station to participate in transfer orbit maneuvers (actions prior to placement in GEO) and the station can be the point from which commands are transmitted to the satellite to deploy its antennas and solar panels.

Routine operations at the SCC and TTAC station are intended to produce continuous and nearly uniform performance from the satellite. Actual communication services via the microwave repeater aboard the satellite do not need to pass through the satellite operator's ground facilities, although the main TTAC station could serve as a communication hub for a large city. Often the TTAC station includes separate communication equipment to access the satellite repeater for the purpose of testing and monitoring its performance. One particularly nice feature of a geostationary satellite is that the communication monitoring function can be performed from anywhere within the footprint (Figure 1-1)—e.g., the SCC can have its own independent monitoring antenna not connected with the TTAC station. Having several monitoring antennas strategically positioned around the coverage region can be useful when measuring satellite repeater output and in trouble shooting complaints and problems (users often blame the satellite for poor or no reception when the difficulty lies with their earth stations).

Another problem area for which monitoring is essential is that of dealing with harmful interference to communication services. Also called "double illumination," it occurs when an errant earth station operator activates a transmitter on the wrong frequency or even on the wrong satellite. In the congested North American orbital arc, double illumination must be detected quickly and the source identified so that disruption of valid communication services is minimized. Such problems, while serious when they occur, are relatively infrequent, and satellite transmission is still perhaps the most reliable means of communication.

1.2.2   Ground Segment

The space segment provides a communication repeater at essentially a fixed position in space capable of linking many points on the earth. It is the function of the ground segment to access the satellite repeater from these points in a manner which satisfies the communication needs of users (telephone subscribers, television viewers, data communications servers, etc.) within the structure of the satellite system. A typical ground segment is illustrated in Figure 1-6; a satellite is shown only to indicate that the links are established through its repeater rather than directly from earth station to earth station. Incidentally, "earth station" is an internationally accepted term which includes satellite communication stations located on the ground, in the air (on airplanes), or on the sea (on ships). Most commercial applications are through earth stations at fixed locations on the ground; thus the international designation for this arrangement is the *fixed satellite service* (FSS). The *maritime mobile satellite service* has been in operation for less time, while the *land mobile satellite* and *aeronautical mobile satellite* services are still in the planning stages.

A single "integrated" network is illustrated in Figure 1-6, showing four relatively large earth stations and clusters of smaller ones. Connection of the satellite network with the outside (terrestrial) world is accomplished through larger stations which access the public switched network (the national telephone system) or an international gateway (allowing communication with foreign countries). The headquarters of a major user such as a corporation or government agency is also a logical location for a major earth station, since a large volume of traffic (i.e., telephone calls, demands for image or data transmissions, etc.) is likely to exist. Smaller stations, on the other hand, are inexpensive enough to justify their placement at points of low traffic demand such as small towns, commercial branch offices, or industrial suppliers. The term *very small aperture terminal* (VSAT) is used to describe a compact and inexpensive earth station intended for this purpose. The aperture is the surface area of the antenna which radiates or collects the radio signals on the satellite link.

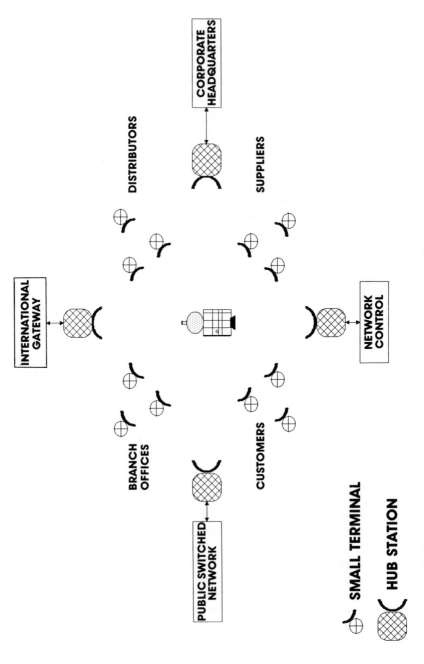

Fig. 1-6 The Ground Segment of a Satellite Network Providing Two-Way Interactive Services to a Variety of Locations

The ground segment, therefore, is not a single, homogeneous entity, but rather is a diverse collection of facilities, users, and applications. It is constantly changing and evolving, providing service when and where needed. One of the four large stations shown in Figure 1-6 would also control portions of the network or perhaps even the entire network. The use of a centralized network control point (called a network management center) is critical in networks where traffic flows are dynamic (i.e., changing with time) and where remote sites are unmanned. Using modern microprocessor technology, the network management center can measure and maintain service quality by remote control.

1.3   FREQUENCY BANDS

Satellite communications employ electromagnetic waves to carry information between ground and space. The frequency of an electromagnetic wave is the rate of reversal of its polarity in cycles per second (now defined to be units of Hertz). Alternating current in a copper wire also has this frequency property, and if the frequency is sufficiently high, the wire will become an antenna, radiating electromagnetic energy at the same frequency. Recall that wavelength is inversely proportional to frequency, with the proportionality constant being the speed of light (i.e., 300,000,000 meters per second in a vacuum).

A particular range of frequencies is called a frequency band, while the full extent of all frequencies for zero to infinity is called the spectrum. In particular, the *radio frequency* (RF) part of the electromagnetic spectrum permits the efficient generation of signal power, its radiation into free space, and reception at a distant point. The most useful RF frequencies lie in the microwave bands (between approximately 300 MHz and 300,000 MHz) although lower frequencies (longer wavelengths) are attractive for certain applications.

An RF signal on one frequency is called a carrier and the actual information that it carries (voice, video, or data) is called modulation. A carrier with modulation occupies a certain amount of RF bandwidth within the frequency band of interest. If two carriers are either on the same frequency or have overlapping bandwidths, then *radio frequency interference* (RFI) may occur. To the user, RFI can look or sound like background noise (which is neither intelligible nor particularly distressful), or it could produce an annoying effect like herringbone patterns on a TV monitor. When the interfering carrier is comparable in power level to the desired (wanted) carrier, the interference effect would be classed as harmful, a condition similar to the radio jamming encountered in the shortwave broadcast band.

Frequency bands are allocated for various purposes by the *International Telecommunication Union* (ITU), a United Nations agency which is located in Geneva, Switzerland. Members of the ITU include essentially every government on the planet, who in turn are responsible for making specific assignments of

RF carriers to frequencies within the allocated bands to domestic users. The ITU has allocated the same parts of the spectrum to many users and for many purposes around the world because of the fixed nature of the resource. The consequence of this is that users of radio communication always allow for limited amounts of RFI and must be prepared to deal with harmful interference if and when it occurs. When there are disputes between countries over RFI or frequency assignments, the ITU often plays the role of mediator or judge.

The spectrum of RF frequencies is depicted in Figure 1-7, which indicates on a logarithmic scale the abbreviations that are in common usage. The bottom end of the spectrum from 0.1 to 100 MHz has been applied to the various radio broadcasting services and is not used for space communication. The frequency bands of interest for satellites lie above 100 MHz, where we find the VHF (very high frequency), UHF (ultra high frequency) and SHF (super high frequency) bands. The SHF range has been broken down further by common usage into sub-bands with letter designations, the familiar C and Ku bands being included. It is interesting to note that these letter designations are of historical interest, since they formerly were classified designations for the microwave bands used for radar and other military or government purposes. Today they are simply shorthand names for the more popular satellite bands, all lying in the range of 1 GHz (1,000 MHz) to 30 GHz.

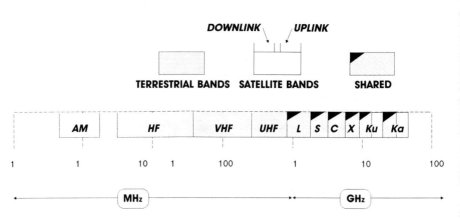

Fig. 1-7 The Radio Frequency Spectrum Identifying Commonly Used Frequency Bands and Their Designations

An important consideration in the use of microwave frequencies for satellite communication is the matter of *sharing*. Figure 1-7 indicates that most of the satellite bands (light shading) are "shared," which means that the same frequencies are used by terrestrial microwave links. Parts of the Ku and Ka bands, on the other hand, are not shared with terrestrial so that only satellite links are permitted. In most instances, the two services must coexist by virtue of a process called frequency coordination, where users who plan to use a given band for a given purpose work with current users to assure that harmful RFI will be avoided. A band which is not shared, therefore, is particularly valuable to satellite communication, since terrestrial microwave systems can be totally ignored. Frequency coordination, however, is often necessary to control interference among satellite systems which use the same frequency band and operate in adjacent orbit positions.

A typical satellite band is divided into separate halves, one for ground to space links (the uplink) and one for space to ground links (the downlink). This separation is reflected in the design of the satellite microwave repeater to minimize the chance of downlink signals being re-received and thereby jamming the operation of the satellite. By way of contrast, such a division is not provided for terrestrial systems, but considerable care must be exercised in assigning frequencies, since links can run in any direction between microwave relay towers.

Uplink frequency bands allocated by the ITU are typically slightly above the corresponding downlink frequency band to take advantage of the fact that it is easier to generate RF power within an earth station than it is on-board a satellite, where weight and power are limited. It is a natural characteristic of the types of RF power amplifier used in both locations that the efficiency of conversion from ac power into RF power tends to decrease as frequency is increased. Along with this, the output from the earth station power amplifier is usually greater than that of the satellite by a factor of from 10 to 100. Satellite systems of the future which make extensive use of VSATs will allow less uplink power, so that the cost of the earth station can be minimized.

1.3.1 C Band

The frequency band known as C band was the first part of the microwave spectrum to be used extensively for commercial satellite communication. Another common designation which we will use is 6/4 GHz, which identifies the nominal center of the uplink frequency band (5.925 to 6.425 GHz) followed after the slash mark (/) by the nominal center of the downlink frequency band (3.700 to 4.200 GHz). (The uplink-downlink convention is not an industry standard and others have reversed the order to express the numbers in ascending order.) To this day, C band remains the dominant frequency band for commercial satellite communication, even as the higher bands (i.e., Ku) come into greater use. What were the reasons for the selection of C band in the first place, and why does it remain so popular?

C band had at the outset a principal advantage over bands which are either higher or lower in frequency—hence, it represents an optimum. Figure 1-8 identifies the factor dealing with the level of radio noise which can disturb reception at a distant point. The simplest means of overcoming this noise is to increase the level of received signal power from the radio link, either by transmitting more power towards the receiving antenna or by increasing the size of the receiving antenna. Considerably more detail on the subject of radio link engineering is given in Chapter 3. As shown in Figure 1-8, C band lies in a range of frequencies near 1 GHz where the combination of natural and manmade noise sources is a minimum. Hence, all other things being equal, C band requires less signal level to provide good quality communication. Lower frequencies toward 100 MHz suffer from a high level of man-made radio noise due to electrical equipment, automobile ignition systems, and the like. Another disadvantage of lower frequencies is the meager bandwidth that is available (Figure 1-8 has a logarithmic scale, magnifying the width at the lower end). For example, assuming that a 10% block of bandwidth is being allocated, the corresponding available bandwidth at 0.1 GHz and 4 GHz are 10 MHz and 400 MHz, respectively.

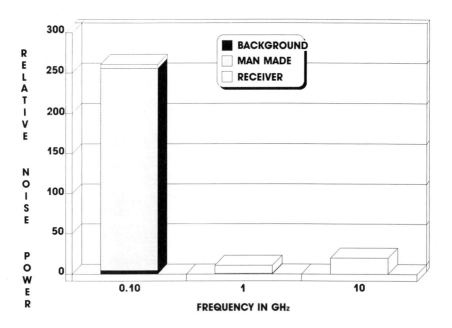

Fig. 1-8 RF Noise Power in a Receiving System as a Function of Frequency from Background, Man-Made, and Internal Sources

As one moves well above 1 GHz, the radio receiver itself produces the bulk of the noise which the signal must overcome. This type of noise can be heard in a TV set or FM receiver without an antenna connected (this demonstrates that the noise is in fact generated inside of the receiver). Receiver noise increases in intensity as frequency is increased, but is not the main detriment to operation at frequencies above 10 GHz, as is explained in the following paragraphs.

The principal factor which affects the performance of satellite links at frequencies above 10 GHz is the absorption of the RF carrier power by the atmosphere. The most detrimental atmospheric effect is rain attenuation, which is a decrease of signal level due to absorption of microwave energy by water droplets in a rainstorm. Due to the relationship between the size of droplets relative to the wavelength of the radio signal, microwave energy at higher frequencies is more heavily absorbed than that at lower frequencies. The following section on Ku and Ka bands will provide more background. Rain attenuation is particularly a problem in tropical regions of the world with heavy thunderstorm activity, as these storms contain intense rain cells.

Equipment technology and availability were factors in the favor of C band. In the early years (1965 to 1970), C band microwave hardware was obtainable from other applications such as terrestrial microwave, tropospheric scatter communication systems (which use high power microwave beams to achieve over-the-horizon links), and radar. No breakthrough in contemporary technology was necessary to take advantage of the technical features of C band. Today, the equipment has been made very inexpensive (relatively speaking) because of competition and high-volume production.

With all of the benefits, C band is still constrained in some ways because of the international requirement that it be shared with terrestrial radio services. Traditionally, C band earth stations were located in remote places where terrestrial microwave signals on the same frequencies would be weak. The potential problem runs in both directions—the terrestrial microwave transmitter can interfere with satellite reception (i.e., the downlink) at the earth station, and RF energy from an earth station uplink can leak towards a terrestrial microwave receiver and disturb its operation.

Shielding, illustrated in Figure 1-9, is the technique by which sharing can be made to work. A natural or man-made obstacle is located near the earth station antenna, but between it and the terrestrial microwave stations existing approximately within a 50-mile radius. As was stated in the beginning of this chapter, microwave signals travel in a straight line, and one would expect that an obstacle would block them entirely. Microwave energy will experience diffraction, however, since it is an electromagnetic wave. What diffraction does is to cause the wave to bend over (or around) an obstacle and thereby potentially interfere with reception on the other side. The amount of bending can be predicted and is a function of the distances between the source, obstacle, and receiver, as well as

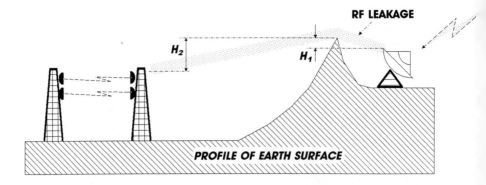

Fig. 1-9 The Use of Terrain Shielding to Block Radio Frequency Interference Between a Terrestrial Microwave Link and an Earth Station

of the height differences (indicated in Figure 1-9 by H_1 and H_2). If the height differences are large, causing all antennas to lie well below the top of the obstacle, then little signal will reach the receiver and good shielding is therefore achieved. Note that shielding is equal for both directions of propagation (i.e., from earth station to terrestrial microwave tower and *vice versa*).

A distance of greater than 50 miles usually provides adequate natural shielding from the curvature of the earth augmented by foliage and man-made structures. Obviously, if the microwave station is on top of a high building or mountain, then the earth station siting engineer will have to look long and hard for adequate natural shielding. Man-made shielding in the form of 30 to 60-foot metal or concrete walls has proven effective in such difficult situations.

Yet another aspect of sharing has to do with the ITU regulation which attempts to protect terrestrial radio receivers from direct satellite radiated signals. The level of such signals is low relative to that emanating from another line-of-sight microwave station; if satellite power is allowed to increase without bound, however, then it is theoretically possible to produce measurable interference into a terrestrial receiver. Figure 1-10 depicts the situation which has the greatest potential for such interference, i.e., where the antenna of the terrestrial station is pointing at another terrestrial station along the horizon but on a direct path to a satellite in orbit. To deal with this potential problem, the regulations limit the *power flux density* (power per unit area on the surface of the earth produced by the satellite) to an amount which would not cause significant interference to any terrestrial microwave receiver, no matter where it might be located. As with the shielding issue, this only is a concern in satellite bands which are shared with terrestrial services.

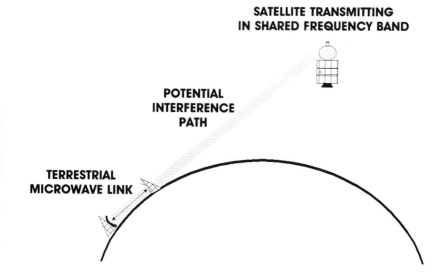

**SATELLITE TRANSMITTING
IN SHARED FREQUENCY BAND**

**POTENTIAL
INTERFERENCE
PATH**

**TERRESTRIAL
MICROWAVE LINK**

Fig. 1-10 The Potential for Direct Radio Frequency Interference from a
Satellite into a Terrestrial Microwave Receiver Where the Frequency Band is Shared

1.3.2   Ku Band

The frequency band that has done more to interest new users of satellite
communication is Ku band, a part of the spectrum lying just above 10 GHz (see
Figure 1-7). Portions of Ku band are not shared with terrestrial radio, which has
some advantages over C band, particularly for direct services using earth stations
with small diameter antennas. The precise uplink and downlink frequency ranges
allocated by the ITU vary to some degree with the region of the world. There
are effectively three sections of Ku band which have been allocated to different
services on an international or domestic basis. The most prevalent is the fixed
satellite service (FSS), which is the service intended for one or two way communication between fixed points on the ground. All of C band and the bulk of
Ku band are allocated to the FSS for wide application in international and
domestic communication. Sharing of these frequencies with terrestrial radio
services is mandated by ITU regulations, however, and consequently part of Ku
band is subject to the same coordination and siting difficulties as C band. The
particular part of Ku band thusly affected is referred to as 14/11 GHz, where
the uplink range is 14.00 to 14.500 GHz and the downlink range is 10.95 to
11.7 GHz (minus a gap of 0.25 GHz in the center). Only the downlink part of
the allocation is actually subject to sharing.

A portion of the Ku allocation for FSS which is not shared with terrestrial services is referred to as 14/12 GHz (uplink range again is 14.00 to 14.50 GHz and downlink range is 11.70 to 12.20 GHz). The availability of 14/12 GHz is limited to Region 2, which is composed of North and South America, and can only be used for domestic communication services. North America, in particular, has seen wide introduction of 14/12 GHz, while no such satellites are currently serving South America. Power levels from these satellites are not subject to the same restrictions as at C band, although there is an upper limit to minimize interference between satellites. Ku-band satellite operations in the rest of the world (i.e., Regions 1 and 3) are restricted to the 14/11 GHz shared allocation. In some instances, a Region 1 (Europe and Africa) or Region 3 (Asia) country can make 14/11 GHz appear like 14/12 GHz simply by precluding domestic terrestrial services from the band. Terrestrial radio services in adjacent countries are not under their control, however, and therefore international coordination must still be dealt with in border areas.

There is a third segment of Ku band, referred to as 18/12 GHz, which is allocated strictly to the *broadcasting satellite service* (BSS). As with the 14/12 FSS band in Region 2, the BSS band is not shared with terrestrial services. Its intended purpose is to allow television and other direct-to-home transmissions from the satellite. There are two regulatory features of this band which make direct broadcasting to small antennas feasible. The first is that, without sharing, the satellite power level can be set at the highest possible level. Adjacent satellite interference could be a problem in a common coverage area, but this is precluded by the second feature: BSS satellites are to be spaced a comfortable nine degrees apart. In comparison, while there is no mandated separation between FSS satellites, a two-degree spacing has become the standard in the crowded North American orbital arc.

The operational advantages of 14/12 and 18/12 GHz lie with the simplicity of locating earth station sites (without regard to terrestrial radio stations) and the higher satellite downlink power levels permitted. The latter results in smaller ground antenna diameters than at C band, all other things being equal. As was discussed in the section on C band, however, Ku band is subject to higher rain attenuation which can increase the incidents and duration of loss of an acceptable signal. Figure 1-11 gives an indication of the relative amounts of extra downlink power, measured in dB of margin, needed to reduce the outage time to a few hours a month. (An explanation of the dB term is given in Chapter 3.) Ka Band (30/20 GHz) is included for completeness, and is discussed later in this chapter. As shown in Figure 1-11, the amount of margin to overcome a fade is also a strong function of the elevation angle from the earth station to the satellite in orbit. A rain cell exists as an atmospheric volume which is wider than it is high; therefore low elevation angles force the radio signal to pass through a greater thickness of rainfall. Elevation angles of forty degrees or greater are consequently

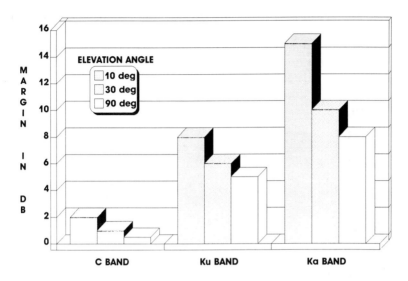

Fig. 1-11 Link Margin in dB Required in C, Ku, and Ka Bands for Satellite Links as a Function of Earth Station Antenna Elevation Angle

preferred for Ku-band frequencies and higher. Another important variable is the local climate, where desert regions are less affected than tropical. In general, the need for greater power margin at Ku band tends to reduce some of the benefits obtainable by virtue of the higher satellite powers that are permitted by the international regulations.

1.3.3 UHF and L Band

Even though the amount of available bandwidth below C band is diminished, these frequency bands are effective for providing rapid communication by way of mobile and transportable earth stations. With lower frequency of operation, the receiving antenna can be as simple as a small Yagi (TV type antenna) or wire helix. This is because the effective receiving area (discussed in Chapter 3) of a wire or rod antenna is inversely proportional to frequency. The use of relatively high power for each individual channel of communication (voice or data) also helps to reduce the size and cost of the receiving terminal. The tradeoff is in the number of voice channels per satellite: instead of being measured in the thousands for C- and Ku-band satellites, capacity of such lower frequency satellites ranges from tens to hundreds of channels. Figure 1-12 gives this tradeoff for a simple example of a relatively small satellite capable of delivering a total of 100 watts of RF power to its downlink antenna. At UHF or L band, ten watts per voice channel provides satisfactory reception by the type of antenna found on a ship or aircraft, but only ten such channels can be supported by this satellite at one time. A C-band satellite can deliver perhaps 10,000 voice channels because 0.01 watts per channel can be received properly by a fixed antenna as large as ten meters in diameter.

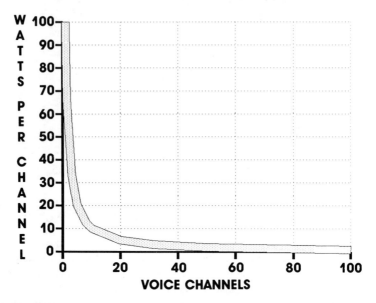

Fig. 1-12 Satellite Channel Capacity versus RF Power per Channel

    The use of such simple antennas on the ground, taking advantage of high power per channel in the satellite, also tends to restrict the total capacity of GEO in terms of the number of satellites that can operate at the same time. An earth station antenna has an angular range of operation, measured in azimuth and elevation, over which RF energy passes through at effectively its maximum level. In Figure 1-13 for a low frequency satellite system, satellite A is at the center (peak) of the oval-shaped antenna beam emanating from an earth station. Operation at a relatively low frequency causes this beam to be broad enough to interfere with the operation of a closely-spaced satellite at position B. The chords drawn within the beam show that the strength of the antenna beam (gain) in the direction of A is greater than in the direction of B, indicating that RFI would probably be harmful but not the maximum possible. A simple way to control RFI under this condition would be to use nonoverlapping bandwidths for the RF carriers of the respective satellite systems. More complex techniques which can "isolate" beams without separating the carriers in frequency are discussed later in this chapter and again in Chapter 3.

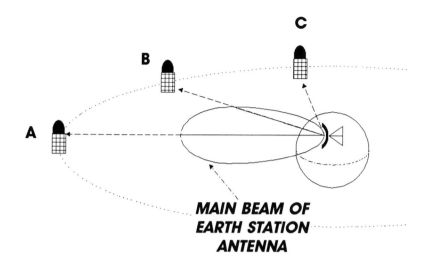

**MAIN BEAM OF
EARTH STATION
ANTENNA**

Fig. 1-13 Effect of Wide Beam Earth Station Antennas on GEO Arc Utilization

For the satellite at position C, the main beam of the ground antenna provides no measurable performance, and effective isolation is achieved. This means that satellite C can operate on the same frequencies as satellite A without causing or receiving harmful RFI. At higher frequencies and with higher gain ground antennas, illustrated in Figure 1-14, the main beam is significantly narrowed. This allows the three satellites to be moved closer together while maintaining the desired isolation, permitting more satellites to be accommodated in the orbit. Beam narrowing also happens when the diameter of the antenna is increased, as discussed in Chapter 3.

An example of a practical application of L-band ship-to-shore satellite communication is depicted in Figure 1-15. A commercial passenger ship is shown with a compact antenna mounted on a mast. The satellite used in this example is Marisat, first launched in 1976. Ships at sea have always had limited communication and the most important consideration is that message delivery be very reliable. A Marisat terminal typically can pass a single teletype channel along with a one-voice channel shared on a party line basis. The ship shown in the figure has a small directional antenna protected from the elements by an umbrella-shaped "radome." To compensate for rolling and pitching of the ship, the antenna is attached to a controlled mount which keeps the satellite more or less at the center of the antenna beam. The satellite completes the link to the shore via C band, accessing a conventional fixed earth station. Telephone calls and telex messages can then be routed to distant points over the public telephone and telex networks. The maritime mobile satellite system is being expanded,

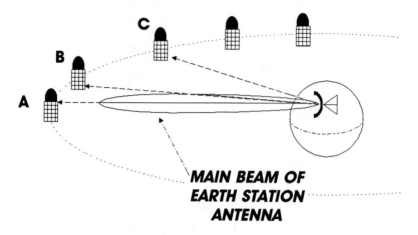

MAIN BEAM OF EARTH STATION ANTENNA

Fig. 1-14 Improved GEO Arc Utilization from Narrow Earth Station Antenna Beams

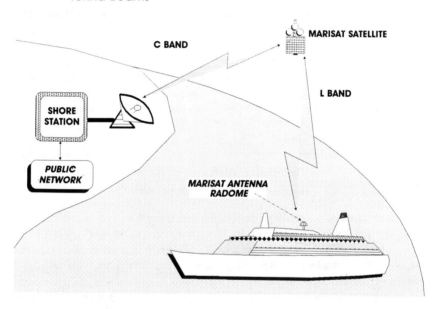

Fig. 1-15 Example of L-Band Service for Ship-to-Shore Communications Using the Marisat Satellite System

but the number of satellites which can simultaneously operate around the world is limited to fewer than ten. Such mobile services would provide reliable communication with ships, airplanes, and eventually vehicles, as they move at will. These possibilities are discussed further in Chapter 9.

1.3.4 S, X, and Ka Bands

The bands identified by S, X, and Ka in Figure 1-7 have been applied to geostationary satellites in varying degrees but generally not for commercial purposes. In this section, the current and planned uses of these bands are briefly reviewed, but the remainder of the book will emphasize C and Ku bands, because of their widespread use around the world.

S band, nominally centered at 2 GHz, lies just below C band and was actually the frequency range used for the downlink on the first experimental synchronous satellite, SYNCOM. It is even closer than C band to the optimum frequency for space communication, as outlined in Figure 1-8, and is one of the bands preferred by the US National Aeronautics and Space Administration (NASA) for communication with scientific deep space probes. However, the amount of bandwidth is much less than that afforded by C and Ku bands. Sharing with terrestrial services such as industrial and educational television and studio-to-television transmitter links makes it extremely difficult to accomplish frequency coordination for earth stations. NASA, in fact, has had to place their deep space tracking stations in very remote parts of the country and the world. Broadcasting services from S-band satellite transmitters are used in India and the Arab countries, but there are currently no plans to do so in other parts of the world.

Government and military satellite communication systems of the United States and some other countries employ X band and, on an experimental basis, Ka band. With an uplink range of 7.90 to 8.40 GHz and a downlink range of 7.25 to 7.75 GHz, X band is used extensively for military long-haul communication links much like C band is used on a commercial basis. In highly specialized cases, Ka band is being applied, since very narrow spot beams can be transmitted to and from the satellite.

There is a potential for the use of Ka band (30/20 GHz) for commercial applications in the decade of the 1990s when C and Ku bands may be fully occupied in some regions. During the 1970s, the Japanese space agency, NASDA, in conjunction with the government-owned telecommunications company, NTT, launched some experimental communication satellites which operate in the Ka band frequency range. The experimental links generally showed that the ample bandwidth that was allocated could in fact be used under certain circumstances. Severe rain attenuation at these high frequencies would require that a given earth station include two receiving sites separated sufficiently so that only one is heavily affected at a time. Reception would then be switched to the site with the acceptable signal. This works because the most intense part of the storm is within the relatively small volume of a rain cell, whose dimensions are smaller than the spacing between receiving sites. In the United States, there are currently no plans to use Ka band for commercial communication services; NASA, however, has been pursuing a precursor 30/20 GHz program called the *advanced communications technology satellite* (ACTS) to advance the technology base.

1.4   EVOLUTION OF SATELLITE COMMUNICATION

No book on the basics of satellite communication is complete without a review of the history of the technology and applications. Rather than going into the detail of every event and accomplishment, however, this section covers the highlights. A familiarity with the past satellite programs and applications will aid the reader in understanding why today's satellite systems and services are the way they are. To aid in providing the historical perspective, this presentation is given in chronological order. This section can be read in sequence or deferred until the basic concepts covered in Chapters 1 through 5 have been absorbed.

1.4.1   Source of the Original Idea

While various individuals of the early part of this century have recognized the existence of the 24-hour geostationary orbit, it is the eminent science fiction author Arthur C. Clarke who is credited with conceiving of the application to communication satellites. His article on extraterrestrial relays in *Wireless World* magazine back in 1945 specifically describes a three-satellite worldwide network, including a drawing like Figure 1-1. In recent years, some leaders in the satellite communication field have proposed that the GEO be renamed the Clarke Orbit, in recognition of Arthur Clarke's forethought. He knew at that time that the requisite electronic and spacecraft technology would take a few years to develop, and in fact it was not until the early 1960s that the first workable spacecraft was built and launched into GEO.

Following the launch of the Soviet Sputnik satellite in 1957, the United States accelerated its space program, and many proposals were developed for space relay satellites. The synchronous satellite was thought by many to be too speculative, and efforts were centered instead on low earth orbit passive reflector and active repeater technology. Such programs as Echo, Advent, Telstar, Courier, and Relay were pursued by NASA (and AT&T in the case of Telstar) in hopes of coming up with a viable system which would be competitive with terrestrial radio, buried cable, and transoceanic cable.

1.4.1.1   SYNCOM

In 1959 Harold A. Rosen and his two colleagues at Hughes Aircraft Company, Tom Hudspeth and the late Don Williams, identified the key technologies for a simple and lightweight active repeater communication satellite for launch into GEO. The basic concept used a drum-shaped spinning body for stability with tiny gas jets to alter the attitude (orientation) in space, as shown in Photo 1-B. This team, working at Hughes Laboratories in Los Angeles, California, built a working prototype in 1960 which demonstrated the feasibility of spin

Photo 1-B. The SYNCOM Spacecraft
(photograph courtesy of Hughes Aircraft Company)

stabilization and microwave communication. Supported by Allen Puckett, then Vice President and now retired Chairman of the Board of Hughes Aircraft, they convinced NASA and the Department of Defense to go ahead with the launch of SYNCOM, an acronym meaning "synchronous orbit communications satellite." On the second attempted launch of the Thor Delta rocket in July 1963, SYNCOM II became the first operational geosynchronous satellite providing intercontinental communication. The first transoceanic live television broadcasts ever were carried on SYNCOM, because undersea cables did not have the bandwidth to pass a television signal in real time.

1.4.1.2 COMSAT

The idea of going into the commercial communication business based on the use of satellites can be attributed to the administration of President John F. Kennedy, which issued ground rules in 1961 for the US operation of an international communication satellite system. President Kennedy favored private ownership and operation of the US portion of an international system which would benefit all nations of the world, large and small. The Communications Satellite Act of 1962 resulted from this initiative, establishing the charter for the Communications Satellite Corporation (COMSAT). This company developed a workable satellite system and helped to encourage worldwide expansion.

COMSAT raised money through the sale of common stock both to the public and to the US common carriers, particularly AT&T. At the time, it was assumed that sub-synchronous satellites would be used for basically two reasons. First, the US communication companies felt that the time delay associated with the propagation of radio waves which travel at the speed of light (approximately one-quarter second for the uplink and downlink combined) would prove to be unacceptable to a significant percentage of telephone subscribers; and, second, there existed a lingering doubt about the viability of the technology necessary to deliver and operate the spacecraft. All of these fears were substantially dissolved when SYNCOM demonstrated the feasibility and quality of synchronous orbit satellite communications.

1.4.2 The International System

Clearly the first and most demonstratable need for the commercial satellite was to provide international communication links. The term "telecommunication" is used internationally in reference to communication services offered to the public using electrical and radio means. Telecommunication companies in various countries can be privately owned or government controlled (which is usually the case as with the domestic postal service). The following paragraphs outline the evolution of the now well established international satellite system.

1.4.2.1 Early Bird

In March of 1964, COMSAT contracted with Hughes Aircraft Company for the construction of two spin stabilized satellites using C band (SYNCOM used S band which was authorized only for NASA experimentation). Early Bird, the well recognized name for this first commercial satellite, launched in the spring of 1965, worked perfectly for six years, well past its design life of two years. The second spacecraft was never launched and now resides in the Air and Space Museum of the Smithsonian Institution in Washington, D.C. Early Bird was positioned over the Atlantic Ocean and was first used to link stations in Andover, Maine, and Goonhilly Downs, England, providing voice, telex, and television service.

1.4.2.2 Intelsat

The intended international nature of the system led to COMSAT establishing a new organization called the International Telecommunications Satellite Consortium (INTELSAT). Later, the word "Consortium" was changed to "Organization", and INTELSAT grew to become the preeminent satellite operator in the world. In the discussion of generations of INTELSAT's satellites, only the first letter is capitalized (i.e., as in Intelsat I) to distinguish the name of a satellite series from the name of the organization.

Intelsat I, II, and III.

The formal name adopted for Early Bird was Intelsat I, being the first generation of satellite employed by INTELSAT. Generations II through VI are reviewed in the following paragraphs and Figure 1-16 illustrates the relative size of each design. Intelsat II and Intelsat III were precursors to the establishment of satellites as the primary means of international communication. NASA provided the motivation for the construction by Hughes Aircraft of the Intelsat II series to support the worldwide communication requirements of the Apollo Program, which placed men on the moon. The design of the spacecraft was similar to Early Bird with the exception that transmitter power was increased (supported by more solar cells and batteries—these aspects of the design are covered in detail in Chapter 5). Intelsat I and II employed a simple antenna which radiated the signal 360 degrees around the satellite as it spun, obviating the need to point or control the physical antenna structure in space. The first Intelsat II did not reach GTO because of failure of an internal rocket called the apogee kick motor; the remaining three were successful, however, and the satellites provided worldwide service for five years.

An innovation in the Intelsat III spacecraft, built by TRW of Redondo

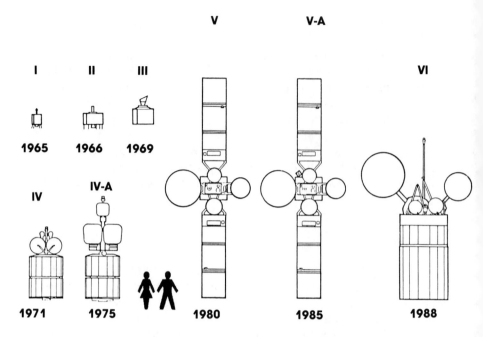

Fig. 1-16 Six Generations of INTELSAT Spacecraft

Beach, California, was the despinning of a directional antenna aboard the satellite so as to maintain a more intense beam on the earth. This type of global coverage beam, illustrated in Figure 1-1, allows access to the satellite repeater by any earth station which lies within the hemisphere facing the satellite orbital position. Eight of these satellites were built and launched, although the first launch failed and the apogee motor on the last malfunctioned. A common characteristic of Intelsats I, II, and III was their limited capacity in terms of the number of individual transmitters, since electrical power generated by their small solar panels could only support one or two power amplifiers.

Intelsat IV.

The big step up in satellite capability happened with the introduction of the Hughes Aircraft built Intelsat IV, a spacecraft many times larger than its commercial forerunners. A photograph of the assembled Intelsat IV spacecraft is presented in Photo 1-C. Intelsat IV employed the same basic spacecraft configuration as a military satellite called Tacsat, also built by Hughes Aircraft. A major innovation came in the way the repeater and antenna were attached. Instead of spinning the repeater with the spacecraft and despinning the antenna, the repeater with antenna were despun as a package. The configuration resulted from

Photo 1-C. The Intelsat IV Spacecraft
(photograph courtesy of Hughes Aircraft Company)

the work of Anthony Iorillo and is called the GYROSTAT (described in detail in Chapter 5). With considerably more power and communications equipment, the C-band repeater on Intelsat IV contained 12 individual channels of approximately 36 MHz each. The selection of the now standard 36-MHz RF bandwidth resulted from the technical tradeoff involving the bandwidth required for a single TV channel (using frequency modulation) and the maximum number of amplifiers that could be carried and powered. The term "transponder" has come into common usage to refer to the individual RF channel, typically of 36 MHz bandwidth. The first Intelsat IV was launched in 1971, and a total of seven have each provided ten or more years of service. Only one Intelsat IV was lost, and that was due to the failure in 1975 of the Atlas Centaur rocket to reach orbit. The Intelsat IV series became the backbone of international communication, and the last of the series was retired at the end of 1985. Furthermore, the transponder concept has been used in every subsequent commercial satellite.

INTELSAT saw the need to go beyond the design of Intelsat IV to match network growth in the Atlantic Ocean Region (AOR). The ideal solution in almost all cases is to have one large satellite at which all countries point their antennas. The 1970 traffic requirements of 50 earth stations, however, exceeded the capability of one Intelsat IV and INTELSAT needed a solution. Harold Rosen of Hughes Aircraft developed a practical approach to increase satellite capacity while retaining the basic configuration of the Intelsat IV spacecraft. The concept, called "frequency reuse," doubles the 500 MHz of allocated bandwidth at the satellite by directing two independent beams toward the visible face of the earth. Shaping of each beam causes the footprint to cover the landmass of the eastern or western hemisphere, leaving the open sea and some land extremities outside of the coverage area (this is necessary to isolate the signals in one beam from interfering with signals on the same frequency in the other beam). The redesignated Intelsat IV-A spacecraft design contained nearly 24 transponders of equivalent capability, with half connected to each of two hemispherical beams—one directed at North and South America and the other at Europe and Africa. This was the forerunner to satellite designs with several such beams (i.e., multiple beams), each narrowed sufficiently to cover a geographic region of high communication demand. A global coverage beam was retained to allow access by stations not within these "hemi" beams. (Bandwidth used in the global beam is actually not available for frequency reuse.) Additional improvements in solar cell and amplifier efficiency helped yield a spacecraft of the same size and design as Intelsat IV and able to do the job of two satellites.

Intelsat V.

Because of continued expansion of the INTELSAT system, both in terms of the number of member-users and of the traffic demands, Intelsat found that the problems of traffic overload in the AOR and also the Pacific Operating Region

(POR) required another doubling of capacity per satellite. The 14/11 GHz portion of Ku band was selected as the means of carrying heavy links in the two regions, freeing up C band for general connectivity among countries. A satellite with both C and Ku bands is generally referred to as a hybrid satellite. The Ku band transponders are connected to spot beams which point towards heavy traffic regions such as western Europe and the northeastern United States. The Intelsat V program was begun, with Ford Aerospace and Communications Corporation, in Palo Alto, California, winning the development and production contract. Ford chose the three axis approach (also called body stabilized), whereby an internal gyro is used in conjunction with small jets to keep the entire satellite pointed toward the earth (more on this in Chapter 5). With Intelsat IV and IV-A providing excellent service throughout the 1970s, the first Intelsat V was launched in 1980.

The C-band repeater on Intelsat V is very similar to that of Intelsat IV-A with the exception that frequency reuse was taken to another dimension with the use of polarization discrimination. In this approach, two signals on the same frequency and in the same footprint are isolated from each other by cross polarizing their electromagnetic waves. A more complete explanation can be found in Chapter 3. This allows a doubling of bandwidth in the Intelsat V's global coverage beam. Having a Ku-band repeater on board provides the extra capacity desired and even allows cross connection between stations using C band and those using Ku band. A modification to Intelsat V, called the V-A, added a payload package for maritime communication similar to that provided by Marisat. Altogether, 12 Intelsat V/V-A satellites were constructed, and these satellites have taken over the bulk of international satellite communication during the 1980s.

Intelsat VI.

Presented in Photo 1-D is a photograph of Intelsat VI, the largest commercial satellite ever built. Conceived in the late 1970s to provide for the widest possible expansion of international satellite services, the massive Intelsat VI spacecraft promises to continue the monotonic decline in cost per circuit. Hughes Aircraft won the contract in 1982 for the design and production of this very advanced satellite. Again, it is a hybrid design (C and Ku bands), but frequency reuse has been carried to an even greater stage in order to triple the capacity of the satellite as compared to Intelsat V/V-A. A new feature in the form of on-board switching of traffic is incorporated; this increases the efficiency of providing high capacity links and allows their reconfiguration with minimal effect on the earth stations. (A description of the technique can be found in Chapter 9.) The Intelsat VI program is the means for continued expansion of INTELSAT through the 1990s.

Photo 1-D. The Intelsat VI Spacecraft, Shown with Antenna Reflectors
Stowed for Launch
(photograph courtesy of Hughes Aircraft Company)

1.4.2.3   Alternatives to INTELSAT

The Soviet Union has used subsynchronous Molnoya satellites since the late 1960s for domestic communication and during the 1970s began to promote an international system called InterSputnik. Membership has nearly been limited to countries in the eastern block, and, over time, synchronous satellites named Statsionar have come into usage. Direct competition with INTELSAT is on the horizon in the form of private US companies which wish to offer trans-Atlantic and trans-Pacific services. As of 1987, none of these potential new entrants have begun operation, but some form of competition with INTELSAT is expected to appear.

1.4.3   Domestic and Regional Satellite Systems

The technology and economics of commercial satellite communication were established during the expansion of INTELSAT. The real opportunities for business development, however, appeared as domestic satellite systems came into being during the 1970s. The history and worldwide activity of domestic satellite systems are reviewed in Figure 1-17.

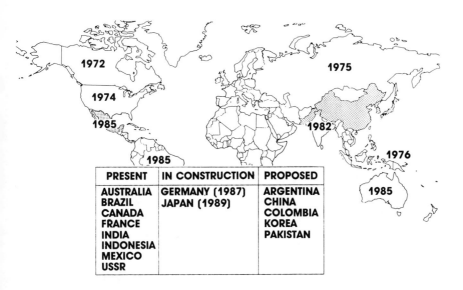

PRESENT	IN CONSTRUCTION	PROPOSED
AUSTRALIA	GERMANY (1987)	ARGENTINA
BRAZIL	JAPAN (1989)	CHINA
CANADA		COLOMBIA
FRANCE		KOREA
INDIA		PAKISTAN
INDONESIA		
MEXICO		
USSR		

Fig. 1-17 Progress in the Implementation of Dedicated Domestic Communications Satellite Systems

1.4.3.1   Canada

The first country to proceed with its own domestic satellite system was Canada, contracting with Hughes Aircraft for a 12-transponder satellite similar in capability to Intelsat IV but weighing half as much. The spacecraft, launched in 1974, had a beam which produced the type of footprint shown in Figure 1-2 but focused on Canada. A company called Telesat Canada was established in much the same way as COMSAT; its purpose, however, was to offer satellite communication services within Canadian boundaries. The system has proven useful in extending reliable communication into the remote and northern reaches of Canada as well as demonstrating the attractiveness of using a domestic satellite to distribute television programming. The name Anik, meaning "brother" in native Indian, was adopted for each of the satellites. Telesat went on to introduce Ku band into domestic service with Anik B, built by RCA Astro Electronics, and Anik C, built by Hughes Aircraft. The original Anik A satellites were replaced in 1983 with C-band 24-transponder satellites named Anik D, built by the team of Spar Aerospace Limited of Canada and Hughes Aircraft. The two Anik E hybrid C and Ku-band spacecraft, under contract to Spar and RCA Astro, will ultimately replace the current system composed of separate single-band satellites.

1.4.3.2   US Domestic System

The policy issues in the United States took longer to settle, and it was the administration of President Richard M. Nixon which allowed the industry to start through the "Open Skies" policy of 1972. This meant simply that any US company with the financial resources and demonstrable need for telecommunication could be granted the requisite authorization to construct a system and operate its satellites in orbital slots assigned by the Federal Communications Commission (FCC). The coverage foot print of most US domestic satellites is similar to that shown in Figure 1-2.

Westar and Comstar.

Six companies applied to the FCC under the Open Skies policy and one of them, the Western Union Telegraph Company, was the first to proceed. Their Westar satellites, of the same Hughes Aircraft design as Anik A, went into operation in 1974, augmenting Western Union's existing nationwide terrestrial microwave system. Only slightly delayed were COMSAT and AT&T with their

Comstar satellites, which provided 24 transponders using polarization frequency reuse and a spacecraft based on the Hughes Aircraft Intelsat IV-A. This system, also used by General Telephone and Electronics (GTE), provided long distance telephone circuits to expand the nationwide network and offered both diversity and flexibility in meeting a variety of future requirements. Replacement of three Comstars was accomplished in the early 1980s with satellites of the new Telstar 3 series, built by Hughes Aircraft, but owned and operated by AT&T alone. GTE went ahead with its own successor system, as discussed in a subsequent paragraph.

Satcom.

The polarization frequency reuse technology of Intelsat V and Comstar was adopted by RCA Corporation, now a subsidiary of General Electric Company, for their own domestic satellite system, which was to be owned and operated by their new American Communications subsidiary (RCA Americom). RCA had pioneered three axis stabilization for low earth orbit weather satellites and adapted the technology to a GEO communications spacecraft. Designed and built by RCA Astro Electronics, of Princeton, New Jersey, the spacecraft was particularly compact and efficient as it achieved the capability of Comstar with significantly less weight. The Satcom series of satellites, first launched in 1976, proved to be particularly popular for video programming distribution to cable television systems, a market pioneered by Home Box Office, a subsidiary of Time, Inc. RCA Americom has continued to launch satellites, including in 1985 two of their new Ku-band series (Satcom K), and is one of the most successful satellite operating companies in the United States. In 1987, the name of the company was changed to GE American Communications (GE Americom).

1.4.3.3 Indonesia

The year 1976 also witnessed the introduction of a major domestic satellite system; this time it was half way around the world, however, in the Republic of Indonesia. Implemented in only 18 months, it used two Hughes Aircraft satellites of the same design as Westar and Anik A. A 40 earth station network was installed and turned up in parallel, allowing President Suharto to demonstrate its operation to his people on the thirty-first anniversary of the independence of the Republic. The Light Traffic earth station which was installed on the Island of Bali is shown in Photo 1-E. The rapid introduction of such an integrated system providing telephone and television service throughout this archipelago

Photo 1-E. The Light Traffic Earth Station with 10-Meter C-band Antenna
on the Indonesian Island of Bali
(photograph courtesy of Hughes Aircraft Company)

nation spanning approximately 3000 miles would not have been possible without the use of satellites. Also, the cost of implementing and operating the system proved to be a small fraction of what it would have taken to do an even lesser job with terrestrial approaches. The Palapa System, named for a mythical fruit which an ancient king pledged not to eat until all of Indonesia was united, has expanded greatly to more than a thousand earth stations and also provides space segment services to neighboring southeast Asian nations. The system moved into its second generation in 1984 with larger Palapa B satellites, each with twice the capacity of the Palapa A. The second Palapa B failed to reach GTO, was recovered by the space shuttle (as discussed in Chapter 7), and subsequently replaced in 1987 by a similar spacecraft. Because of the success of marketing transponders to other southeast Asian nations, Palapa B incorporates improved coverage of neighboring countries.

1.4.3.4 Applications Technology Satellite

As the US government agency responsible for space system research, NASA has been involved in several geostationary communication satellite projects since SYNCOM. The Advanced Technology Satellite (ATS) series consisted of six satellites which were used for communication demonstrations throughout the United States and the world. Hughes Aircraft built ATS 1 through 5; some of these satellites were still providing limited service to remote islands of the Pacific as late as 1987. ATS 6, the most advanced and the largest of the six, was built by Fairchild Industries of Germantown, Maryland, and was launched in May of 1974 directly into synchronous orbit by a Titan 3C rocket. With its 9-meter unfurlable mesh antenna, ATS 6 was used in the first direct broadcasting experiments, with the emphasis placed on educational programming. After providing service in the United States to isolated regions, the satellite was moved into position to be used in India. These experiments were very successful in that the benefit of using satellites to reach remote areas with educational and public interest programming was clearly shown. After three years of operation, the satellite was retired from service in 1979.

Another NASA experimental satellite program called Communications Technology Satellite (CTS, but also named Hermes) was jointly undertaken with the Canadian government. Designed and built in Canada but launched in 1976 from the United States on a Delta, CTS operated at Ku Band (14/12 GHz) and demonstrated the capability of high-power satellite broadcasting in this new frequency band. One-way and two-way services were provided with small aperture ground antennas. Pioneering work was done in the area of new applications, one being the first experience by nontechnical users with interactive video teleconferencing. Of particular note is that CTS was used in the restoration of communication during the Johnstown, Ohio, flood disaster in 1977, proving the effectiveness of compact, transportable ground stations operating at Ku band.

1.4.3.5   Europe

Regional satellite systems have always been of interest to provide services within and between countries which could not individually justify a dedicated satellite system. The countries of Western Europe wished to pursue a regional system, both for the services that could be rendered and to provide markets for their own aerospace and communication industries. Programs such as OTS and ECS were initiated in the late 1970s, leading to the creation of EUTELSAT, a consortium similar in concept to INTELSAT. EUTELSAT purchases satellites from European industry and arranges for launch also within the European Community from the European Space Agency and subsequently from the French launch services company, Arianespace. The indigenous companies that have produced spacecraft for EUTELSAT, which were all three axis in design, included Matra of France and British Aerospace of the United Kingdom. These satellites have Ku band (14/11 GHz) communication systems and the users tend to be the domestic post, telephone, and telegraph (PTT) agencies of the respective governments. Since the first ECS satellite was put into service in 1982, EUTELSAT has expanded its capabilities to transmit video programming to cable television systems.

The French PTT is constructing a separate domestic system for France, using the Telecom satellites developed and built by Matra and first launched in 1984. The use of this hybrid C-X-Ku band satellite makes France the first country in Europe with its own domestic satellite system. Germany, Scandinavia, the United Kingdom, and Ireland are implementing their own domestic satellite systems primarily for TV broadcasting (BSS) but with FSS capabilities as well.

1.4.3.6   Japan

The Japanese government pursued several satellite projects for experimental and industrial development purposes. The Communications Satellite (CS) series, launched in the late 1970s, emphasized experimentation with Ka band, i.e., 30/20 GHz; many observers in the United States and Japan, however, feel that the economic viability of this band has yet to be established. Ford Aerospace built these spinning spacecraft, but most of the communication hardware was designed and manufactured by NEC and Mitsubishi Electric. A precursor Ku-band DBS satellite was developed for the national broadcast network, NHK, but the satellites did not prove very successful, primarily because of technical problems with the satellites themselves, which were designed and built by the General Electric Company of the United States. A follow-on DBS program in Japan includes satellites designed and built by RCA Astro Electronics, now called GE Astrospace. Satellite communication is now being privatized in Japan, as is discussed in a subsequent paragraph. Japan continues to play a very important industrial role in developing both ground and space hardware for international use.

1.4.3.7 India

The domestic satellite for India, called INSAT, was first launched in 1981 and performed the dual function of providing communication services at C and S band (for TV broadcast) and meteorological scanning. The first to be launched of these complicated three axis spacecraft, designed and built by Ford Aerospace, reached orbit but experienced technical problems with deployment of antennas and operation of propulsion. A modified second spacecraft was launched in 1983 and has met its service objectives.

1.4.3.8 Arab Countries

After many years of planning and discussion, the Arab League countries embarked in 1981 on a regional system called Arabsat. Design and construction of the satellites were contracted to Aerospatiale of France, with a significant portion of the three axis technology provided by Ford Aerospace. The satellites, first launched in 1985, have communication capability similarly to INSAT in that C and S band services are possible.

1.4.3.9 Latin America

Mexico and Brazil initiated their satellite systems in 1982 using Hughes Aircraft designs. In the case of Brazil, the two satellites were constructed in Canada by Spar and provide 24 C-band transponders each. The Mexican Morelos satellites incorporate a hybrid C and Ku-band payload, intended to provide the widest possible variety of communication services to large and small diameter earth stations. Both countries were successful in implementing their space segments in 1985.

1.4.4 Advancing Technology and Markets

The proven spacecraft technology and innovations in communication services provided the base for evolutionary change and expansion during the late 1970s and 1980s. In the following paragraphs, this meshing of technology and markets is analyzed.

1.4.4.1 Satellite Business Systems

An important chapter in the commercial satellite industry was written in the United States during the late 1970s and early 1980s. Satellite Business Systems (SBS), originally a partnership of COMSAT, International Business

Machines Corporation (IBM), and Aetna Life and Casualty Company, started fresh in 1978 to implement an advanced, digital communication system with Ku-band (14/12 GHz) satellites. By using this nonshared frequency band and applying digital technology, SBS could offer private communications networks for voice and data to major US corporations and government agencies. The market was too slow to develop, and by 1985 the company was merged into MCI Communications Corporation, the second largest long distance common carrier in the United States. SBS demonstrated, however, that Ku-band satellites were very effective for introducing new communication services on a nationwide basis. Other companies which have imitated SBS include GTE Corporation with their GStar system and Southern Pacific Communications Company, which was later merged into GTE, with their Spacenet satellites. In 1987, there were a total of 30 domestic satellites serving the United States at both C and Ku band.

1.4.4.2   Galaxy System

Perhaps the most successful commercial satellite venture in the United States is the Galaxy System, owned and operated by Hughes Communications, Inc., a subsidiary of Hughes Aircraft. After the third RCA Satcom satellite failed to reach orbit in 1980, a shortage of transponders developed to the point that potential users became concerned about obtaining long term commitments for satellite capacity. Hughes Communications began to offer transponders for sale individually on a condominium basis, and essentially all 24 transponders were sold by the time the satellite was launched in 1983. The Galaxy II and Galaxy III satellites were also very successful according to industry standards, with most of the transponders sold on a bulk basis to MCI and a relatively new data networking company called Equatorial Communications. Hughes Communications has also joined with C. Itoh and Mitsui and Company to implement a two-satellite Ku-band (14/11 GHz) system to serve the Japanese domestic market. This was historical since, prior to 1985, no company except the government owned communication company, NTT, was allowed to offer communication services of any kind in Japan. Also, the satellites themselves do not contain Japanese elements, as was always required in past Japanese satellite programs.

1.4.4.3   INTELSAT Transponder Leases

In the early 1970s INTELSAT began to rent (and eventually sell) transponders to member nations for domestic communication purposes. The first such lease was signed with Algeria in 1974, and the demand for this type of service has grown at an impressive rate. By 1984, 27 countries were leasing transponders for domestic purposes. INTELSAT domestic leases have been attractive to countries that need to expand or improve their domestic public communication networks but which do not require the capacity of an entire satellite or pair of satellites. Conversion of INTELSAT's marketing to transponder sales (for the life of the satellite) occurred in 1985, in response to the buildup of some excess orbital capacity and to the threat of competition from privately financed international satellite systems.

1.4.4.4   Earth Station User Community

A last note in this section on history has to do with the expanding community of satellite users, which are companies and agencies which obtain satellite transponder capacity from the space segment providers. The users then in turn add their own ground facilities and offer more complete services to the public. There effectively were no satellite users prior to 1975, with the exception of the members of INTELSAT throughout the world. In the United States, the satellite user industry is at least as large as the satellite operator industry, and new applications are appearing all the time. Users can be broken down into two categories: video-broadcasting and telecommunication service. In the first category you will find the cable-television programmers like HBO, the television networks such as CBS and NBC, and TV and radio stations that rebroadcast programs delivered by satellite. The telecommunication category contains MCI, which purchased transponders for use in a C-band telephone trunking network. Companies like Arco and Citicorp own transponders to interconnect points around the country in their internal corporate networks. Earth stations called teleports have been opened up as businesses to provide local access to domestic and INTELSAT satellites. These facilities are attractive to users of video and telecommunication services who do not wish to make the associated capital investment.

Chapter 2
Application of Satellite Networks

The purpose of operating a satellite in orbit is clearly to provide connections between earth stations which in turn deliver or originate various types of communication services. Applications of such satellite networks are broken down into the broad categories of video, telephone, and data. The first part of this chapter reviews the features and generic arrangements of networks independent of the specific use. This provides a cross reference with regard to the applications which are reviewed in detail at the end of this chapter.

2.1 GENERAL FEATURES

2.1.1 Connectivity

The manner in which points on the earth are linked between each other is called "connectivity." There are three generic forms of connectivity: point-to-point, point-to-multipoint, and multipoint-to-point. Each of these connectivities, reviewed in the following paragraphs, can be established through one satellite and two or more earth stations. Comparisons are made with implementations of the same connectivities using terrestrial communication technology. It is shown that while terrestrial systems compete favorably on a point-to-point basis, satellite networks have a decided advantage whenever a multipoint connectivity is needed.

2.1.1.1 Point-to-Point

The simplest type of connectivity is point-to-point, illustrated in Figure 2-1 with two earth stations both transmitting simultaneously to the satellite. A pair of earth stations transmit RF carriers one to another (and receive each other's carriers), creating what is called a duplex link. The parties being served can thereby talk or transmit information in both directions at the same time. The uplink section of the satellite repeater receives both transmissions and after translation to the downlink frequency range, transmits them back toward the ground. Reception by an earth station of the opposite end's transmission completes the link. In most cases, transmissions between earth stations through the satellite repeater are continuous in time. If the satellite provides a single footprint covering both earth stations, then a given station can receive in the downlink its own information as well as that of its communicating partner. This supplementary ability provides a unique way for stations to verify the content and quality of satellite transmission.

A typical network of several earth stations and a satellite provides many duplex point-to-point links to interconnect the locations on the ground. There are many possible circuit routings between the locations. In a fully interconnected "mesh" network, the maximum number of possible links between N earth stations is equal to $N(N-1)/2$. To prevent harmful RF interference, all stations cannot be on the same frequency at the same time. The technology which allows the needed simultaneous transmission without RFI through the satellite repeater is called *multiple access*, which is covered in Chapter 4.

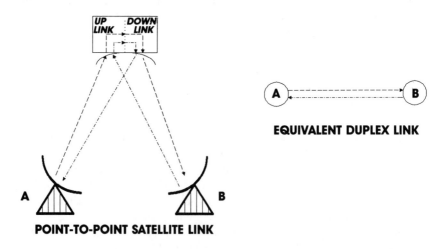

Fig. 2-1 Point-to-Point Connectivity Using a Full Duplex Satellite Link

2.1.1.2   *Point-to-Multipoint*

While point-to-point links are easily achieved by satellite, it is the point-to-multipoint link which takes full advantage of the wide area coverage of the satellite's footprint. Figure 2-2 indicates how satellite broadcasting is accomplished with one transmitting earth station (called the *uplink* in common practice) and many *receive-only* (RO) earth stations. The satellite repeater retransmits the single RF carrier containing the information to be distributed. It is usually advantageous to use the highest satellite transmit power possible, because this allows the use of smaller diameter (less expensive) RO antennas on the ground. As the number of ROs increases into the hundreds of thousands or millions, the optimum transmitter power to use in space becomes much larger than that permitted at C band by the ITU. The BSS segment of Ku band is available for such high-power broadcast applications, as discussed in Chapter 1. The cost of the more expensive BSS satellite is shared among more and more users, who then save substantial amounts on the cost of their ground equipment. This is an economic tradeoff between the cost of the satellite and that of the ground segment, as discussed in Chapter 8.

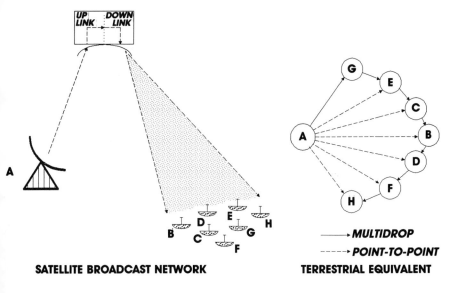

SATELLITE BROADCAST NETWORK   TERRESTRIAL EQUIVALENT

Fig. 2-2 Point-to-Multipoint Connectivity Providing a One-Way Broadcast Capability

Achieving point-to-multipoint connectivity with a terrestrial network is extremely expensive, since the cost of adding cable or microwave facilities to reach service points is roughly proportional to the number of points. In contrast to satellite broadcasting, there is usually no economy of scale in delivering broadcast information terrestrially. There is a cheaper terrestrial approach, wherein the receiving points are chained together. This tends to be less reliable on an overall basis because users are delivered the signal along the route of the system (i.e., a chain is no stronger than its weakest link). The first use of terrestrial microwave for TV distribution was accomplished in this manner. In data communication, a terrestrial chain of this type using telephone circuits is called a multidrop line.

2.1.1.3   Multipoint-to-Point

A multipoint-to-point satellite network compliments the broadcast approach by allowing remote stations to send information back to the central station. As shown in Figure 2-3, this type of connectivity provides two-way communication because the remotes receive the broadcast from the central station and can transmit back over the same satellite. It is different from a point-to-point network because the remote stations cannot communicate directly with one another but must do so through the central station, commonly referred to as the *hub*. In Figure 2-3, the remotes efficiently transmit packets of data toward the satellite on the same frequency but timed such that the packets do not overlap when they enter the satellite repeater. Multipoint-to-point networks are an important extension of point-to-point because of the relatively small antenna size and simplicity of the remote stations. These are afforded by using a more sophisticated hub station with a large-diameter antenna. Many commercial applications can effectively use this type of connectivity where subscriber response is necessary. Modern digital technology has supplied the low-cost means of adding the necessary intelligence to the remote stations while keeping the overall network cost competitive with modern terrestrial networks. As was mentioned in Chapter 1, the very small aperture terminal (VSAT) is this type of inexpensive earth station used in large multipoint-to-point networks.

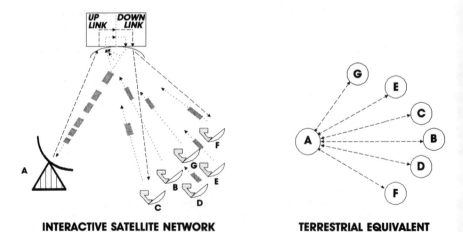

INTERACTIVE SATELLITE NETWORK   **TERRESTRIAL EQUIVALENT**

Fig. 2-3 Interactive Satellite Network Using Multipoint-to-Point Connectivity

2.1.2 Flexibility

A satellite-based network is inherently very flexible from a number of perspectives, which are described in the following paragraphs.

2.1.2.1 Implementation of Satellite Networks

To begin with, the implementation of the ground segment of a satellite network is relatively simple primarily because the number of physical installations is minimal. To put in a satellite network, a planner need only consider the sites where service is required. Installation of a fiber optic cable system requires first that the right-of-way be secured from organizations such as governments, utility companies, and railroads. Hundreds or even thousands of sites must be provided with shelter and power (and even access roads in the case of terrestrial microwave). After the entire system is installed and tested, all of the equipment must be maintained to assure continuous service. Even still, one outage along the route will probably put the entire chain out of service until a crew and equipment can arrive on the scene to effect repair.

In contrast, the time to install an earth station network is relatively short, particularly if the sites are close to where service is provided. This assumes that a space segment already exists. In the past, implementation times for earth stations were lengthened, not because of site construction, but rather because electronic equipment had to be special ordered and then manufactured. The low production volumes (because satellite communication requires less equipment in general than terrestrial) discouraged manufacturers from mass producing standardized equipment and holding inventory for future sales. In today's larger and more competitive earth station equipment market, higher manufacturing volumes along with the arrival of more standardized digital systems have allowed equipment suppliers to reduce cost and maintain on-the-shelf inventory. The time to implement satellite networks and add stations has been reduced from one to two years down to from one to two months. In contrast, a terrestrial fiber network is like a major highway project and will take years to design and construct.

2.1.2.2 Expansion of the Network

With a proper network architecture, new earth stations can be added without affecting the existing stations. This reduces the expansion timeframe to a few months or weeks, since all that needs to be done is to purchase the equipment, prepare the site, and then install the stations. Increasing the number of ROs is particularly easy and economical, and operation of existing stations is not affected. Satellite networks of the 1970s providing point-to-point links could not be modified easily because of the old, inflexible analog technology employed.

To add an earth station to an old analog point-to-point network would require dismantling the equipment at each old station to be linked with the new station. This major drawback of the older systems has been eliminated with programmable digital technology. These more flexible digital approaches, described later in this chapter, can now be assumed in virtually every future application involving two-way communication.

2.1.2.3   Simplification of Network Routing

Rather than purchasing new long distance facilities for their exclusive use, many users lease voice and data circuits from terrestrial network operators (called *common carriers* in North America). Therefore, the "backbone" network would already exist, and the only time necessary for implementation of such a private network is that needed to run local cable loops or to make appropriate wiring changes in the telephone offices. Time delays of many weeks to months are still involved, however, beginning from the moment when service orders are placed. The common carrier must then perform the network engineering, install equipment if necessary and make the required wiring changes, and then test the resulting circuits for proper operation. If the circuit or circuits cross the boundaries between the terrestrial networks of different service providers, then the process must be run simultaneously by the various organizations and coordination between them must be handled in some manner. (The reliability aspects of this particular problem are discussed in the next section.) In a modern satellite network, only the end connections are involved, because the satellite itself provides all of the intermediate routing.

Terrestrial networks must deliver a multipoint connectivity by extending terrestrial links to each and every point to be served. There are terrestrial radio techniques which mimic satellites by placing omnidirectional (i.e., wide, circular area coverage) repeaters on towers or mountain tops. Broadcast radio and TV work on a point-to-multipoint basis, and cellular mobile telephone is an excellent multipoint-to-point system. All such terrestrial techniques, however, are severely restricted as to range because of line-of-sight radio propagation. To extend well beyond this geographical limitation, less reliable point-to-point links must be established between the radio towers to chain the broadcast or cellular stations together.

2.1.2.4   Introduction of New Services

Expansion of a satellite network can add new services, many of which cannot currently be accommodated by terrestrial. Perhaps the clearest example is the long distance transmission of full motion color television, which, as noted earlier, could not be carried over transoceanic telephone cables. It was not until the advent of terrestrial microwave radio in North America that coast-to-coast TV transmission was possible. Satellite repeaters in the FSS have sufficient bandwidth to carry several TV channels along with an array of voice and data traffic. On a local level, the local telephone loops which bring voice and low-speed data services into the office and home are currently very limited in their capacity. Home cable television service is made possible only with a separate coaxial cable, and interactive two-way video teleconferencing is only provided on a very limited basis over terrestrial systems. Any and all of these services can be included in, or added to, the current generation of small earth station, particularly the VSAT operating at Ku band. Therefore, flexibility of satellite communication takes on added dimensions with new services which cannot currently be offered on a single terrestrial network.

The three generic types of connectivity were covered in the previous section. It is very noteworthy that a given satellite network can achieve these connectivities individually or simultaneously, while a terrestrial network is usually restricted to a point-to-point capability. It is not uncommon for a user to implement a point-to-point satellite network involving from 10 to 50 earth stations and then add a broadcast capability to extend the network to hundreds or even thousands of receiving points. Any one of the point-to-point stations could then be used as an uplink site to broadcast digital information or video programming on an occasional basis. The multipoint-to-point capability can be installed in the future by adding a transmit "retrofit" package to many of the smaller receive-only stations.

2.1.3 Reliability

The remaining features to be described are more difficult to explain and quantify; they can, however, ultimately be the factors which decide in favor of satellite transmission over terrestrial. The mere fact that a satellite link requires only one repeater hop, or a maximum of two in the case of international services, tends to make the satellite connection extremely reliable. The engineering of the link, described in Chapter 3, must properly take into account the frequency band and fade margin requirements. When this is done and an established satellite is employed, the link will be up and usable for well in excess of 99% of the time. In fact, satellite engineers normally talk of link reliabilities of 99.99%, which equates to an outage or downtime of nine hours in an entire year. Normally, this outage is segmented into durations of a few minutes distributed mainly through the rainiest months.

Long distance terrestrial systems normally provide reliabilities in the range of from 95 to 98%, where outage can be produced by fades on any of its radio paths (in the case of terrestrial microwave) and by equipment outage at any of the hundreds of repeater sites along the route. Cable systems are susceptible to accidental breakage or deterioration of the cable itself, and outages of several hours or even days at a time do occur. A single buried cable or microwave system is relatively unreliable due to the inevitable breakage or failure. Therefore, proper terrestrial system design requires that diverse routes be provided. Buried cable with diverse routing and automatic switching can provide an extremely reliable means of communication, although the cost of implementation would only be within the range of relatively wealthy organizations (AT&T, governments, and major industrial corporations).

Equipment failures on satellite links do occur, and for that reason backup systems are provided. As discussed in Chapter 5, a communication satellite contains essentially 100% backup for all of its critical subsystems to prevent a catastrophic failure. The individual transponders or transmitters within the repeater section will usually not be spared 100%, so that a fractional loss of capacity is possible at some time in the useful orbital life. Experience with modern commercial satellites has been excellent, and users have come to expect near perfection in the reliability of these spacecraft. The principal cause of communication outage is not failure of satellite hardware but rather is due to the double illumination problem described in Chapter 1. Harmful radio frequency interference (RFI) is a fairly routine occurrence and satellite operators are reasonably well equipped to respond to and identify the source of the problem (which is almost always accidental and of short duration).

The reliability of satellite communication is enhanced by the fact that virtually all of the ground facilities can be under the direct control of one using organization. If a problem occurs with equipment or its interface with other facilities such as telephone switches or computers, the user's technical support personnel can easily identify and reach the trouble spot. Restoration of service can thus be accomplished conveniently and quickly. Terrestrial linkups can involve many organizations which provide services in sections of the country or city, complicating the necessary troubleshooting and follow-up. For example, the former AT&T Bell System was broken up in the United States in 1983, resulting in the creation of seven independent corporations, each controlling roughly one-seventh of the local telephone service of the country. AT&T continues to be the largest long distance service provider as the regional Bell companies are currently restricted from this type of business. To reach customer locations in two different regions requires that the facilities of three different companies be used: two regional Bell companies and AT&T. A competing long distance company such as MCI may provide a more advantageous service at perhaps a lower cost and can be used in lieu of AT&T. The facilities of the regional Bell companies, however, must still be arranged for and used. Any type of reliability problem with one element of the end-to-end service will be amplified in time duration as the three entities work to locate and rectify the problem.

2.1.4   Quality

The following paragraphs identify different approaches to measuring quality of transmission. Emphasis is usually placed on human perception, which is particularly valid for analog signals such as voice and video. Quality in data communication boils down to the quantity of valid data which reaches the distant end.

2.1.4.1   Signal Reproduction

For a single point of transmission, a satellite is nearly ideal for delivering a signal of the highest quality. Modern satellite systems radiate sufficient power into the geographical footprint to be received by ground antennas of diameters in the range of 0.8 to 10 meters (3 to 32 feet). Because satellites use line-of-sight transmission in directions nearly perpendicular to the atmosphere, the frequency and duration of link fades are reduced as compared to terrestrial microwave. Many terrestrial networks suffer from man-made noise and various kinds of short interruptions (''glitches''), while satellite links experience primarily receiver noise (explained in Chapter 1) which is constant and easily compensated for with power. All of these factors allow the satellite communication engineer to design links of the highest possible circuit quality and to select equipment which will provide this quality with confidence. The communication application where these aspects of quality play the greatest role is in point-to-point and point-to-multipoint video. As was stated earlier in this chapter, essentially all video programming destined to North American homes is carried long distance by satellite. The perceived quality of the delivered video signal is for all practical purposes identical to that of the signal created at the studio or played from the originating video tape machine.

2.1.4.2   Voice Quality and Echo

The issue of quality of voice transmission has received a lot of attention, particularly in the United States where many large communication companies compete for customers. As was discussed in Chapter 1, the use of the GEO for communication relays was a controversial topic prior to the first use of SYNCOM in 1962 because of the delay of one-quarter second introduced by the long transmission path. The impact of this delay on voice communication continues to be debated even today, particularly as high-capacity fiber optic systems are installed in the developed world. Voice communication over satellite can be made acceptable to over 90% of telephone subscribers, as has been proven by numerous quality surveys. Terrestrial systems do not suffer as much from delay and hence are potentially more desirable, other facters being equal.

The mechanism that produces echo, which can be the most objectionable result of delay, is illustrated in Figure 2-4. Echo is present in any terrestrial or satellite telephone link, because electrical signals are waves and thus are reflected by the far end back over the return path. Echo becomes objectionable, however, when the talker hears his own speech delayed by more than a few milliseconds. Shorter delays produce a hollow sound, like that heard in a long hallway or tunnel. At the left of Figure 2-4 speech from a female talker is converted into electrical energy in the voice frequency range (300 to 3400 Hz) by the handset and passes over the single pair of wires to the telephone equipment used to connect to a long distance circuit. The same pair of wires allows the speech from the distant end (where the male talker is listening at the moment) to reach the female talker. In contrast, the long distance circuit breaks the two directions in half, segregating the sending and receiving wire pairs. The device that routes the energy properly between the two wire (local loop) and four wire (trunk) lines is called a *hybrid*. The typical configuration has a hybrid on each end; Figure 2-4, however, shows that the male talker is connected through an undefined terrestrial network within which several hybrids could exist. The echo path is produced within one or more of these unseen hybrids, allowing some of the female talker's speech energy to make a U-turn and head back towards the female talker. Since the echo is the result of uncontrollable factors in the terrestrial network, it must be actively blocked or else a negative impact on quality will result. Obviously, a satellite circuit with its one-quarter second (250 ms) delay is subject to an echo which occurs approximately one-half second after the talker utters his or her first word.

The simplest and most effective type of echo control is to use a voice activated switch, as shown in Figure 2-4. Whenever the female talker is speaking, the control circuitry of the switch detects the presence of the incoming speech on the upper wire pair, and the switch on the lower wire pair is opened. When she stops talking, however, the switch closes automatically, and the male talker is free to speak and be heard by the female talker. A similar switch would have to be placed on the female talker's end to protect the male talker from his own echo. This basic type of echo control device is called an *echo suppressor* and has been used on terrestrial and satellite circuits for decades. Other features are necessary to make the switch respond to characteristics of human conversation, such as when one party needs to interrupt the other. One of the biggest problems with satellite voice circuits of past years has been the difficulty of getting these old-fashioned echo suppressors to work correctly.

With the advent of high-speed digital circuitry and microprocessors, a much superior echo control device has appeared. This is the *echo canceler*, which works the way the name implies. Instead of switching in or out, an echo canceler works with the digitized version of the speech and mathematically eliminates the echo from it. It is an active control device and has the ability to

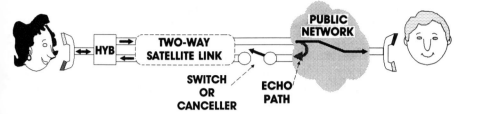

Fig. 2-4 Telephone Echo Over a Satellite Is Caused by Electrical Reflection at the Distant End where it Can Be Eliminated by an Echo Canceler

characterize the echo path through the hybrid or terrestrial network. From this information, the canceler determines how to subtract a sample of the incoming speech from the return path to the distant talker. The details of how this technology works are beyond the scope of this book. The important point, however, is that there is strong evidence that an advance digital voice communication link with modern echo cancellation will be rated higher in quality by telephone subscribers than a traditional analog voice link on a long distance terrestrial network.

2.1.4.3 Data Communication and Protocols

Data communication is an area for which satellites are beneficial if the right steps are taken in preparing the data for transmission. The key to successful computer-to-computer communication over satellite is to employ the right protocols and coding schemes. Computers which communicate over terrestrial links transmit data in relatively short bursts called "words," as shown in Figure 2-5. A protocol is a set of rules that the two ends follow in assembling the words for transmission and determining if the received words are valid. Provision is also made automatically to request retransmission if an error is detected at the distant end. The "conversation" illustrated in Figure 2-5 shows what happens when the receiving end detects an error and requests retransmission from the sending end (on the left). The sequence starts at the upper left and moves right to left and left to right, following the direction of the arrows. Introducing satellite delay would force the sending end to halt the transmission of new data for two seconds at least as the necessary requests and retransmissions are executed.

Terrestrial circuits normally produce a lot of noise spikes and short disruptions called "drop outs." Older protocols like IBM Bisync transmit relatively brief words, forcing the distant end continually to acknowledge that reception was good. Unfortunately for satellite links, the sending end using one of these old protocols will wait for this acknowledgement each and every time. Even without errors, this will slow transmission over a satellite link down to a fraction of what happens on even a noisy terrestrial link. This problem was corrected in early satellite data links by giving the sending end the acknowledgement that it expects even before the distant end has received the group of words. The piece of equipment which accomplishes this task of fooling (*spoofing*) the sending end is called a *delay compensation unit* (DCU). Errors are corrected by the DCU at the other end using special error correcting bits which are included by the transmitting DCU. The topic of error correcting codes is reviewed in Chapter 4.

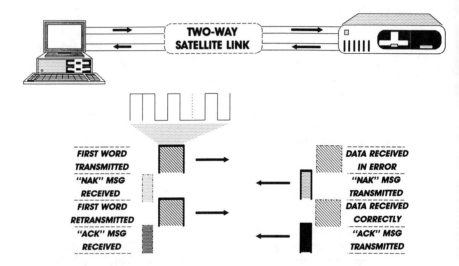

Fig. 2-5 Inefficient "Word-Oriented" Data Protocols Are Subject to Greater Delay on a Satellite Link When Experiencing Errors in Transmission

Recognizing that the DCU approach was only a provisional fix, IBM and other computer manufacturers have now adopted standard computer protocols which do not use repeated acknowledgement messages. For example, the IBM SDLC protocol transmits a long series of blocks of data words before expecting an acknowledgement. Any request for retransmission will be for a specific block. Such modern protocols make satellite links essentially as efficient as the best quality terrestrial links for the transmission of high-speed data.

Another data communication system uses packets of data which identify both their origin and destination. The X.25 packet protocol has been adopted on an international basis and will probably find widespread use in terrestrial and satellite networks. The first packet protocol specifically designed for satellite links is called ALOHA (discussed in Chapter 4), developed by Norman Abramson of the University of Hawaii.

2.1.4.4 Quality Appraisal

The issues of reliability and quality can in balance weigh in favor of satellite communication when the engineering, installation, and operation are done properly. The difficulty often is that the terrestrial network exists first, and transferring service over to a satellite network becomes a complex and difficult task. In cases where terrestrial service did not exist first, or was totally inadequate, the new satellite network was very well accepted (INTELSAT and the Indonesian Palapa system are good examples). In the United States, satellites have become the unchallenged champion in the distribution of television programming and subsequently in data broadcasting; terrestrial telephone communication has always been very good, however, making it more difficult for satellites to gain wide acceptance. It is anticipated that the breakup of the Bell System and the advent of advanced digital communication technology will tend to give satellites a new attraction, particularly with widespread use of VSATs operating at Ku band. Being able to control the entire satellite network, therefore, allows the service provider or user to render this high quality of service for a greater percentage of time and at a substantial savings in cost.

2.2 SATELLITE VIDEO APPLICATIONS

Television or video service, which are one and the same, is perhaps the most popular source of entertainment and information for the public. The broadcasting industry has embraced satellite communication as the primary means of carrying programming from the program originator (TV Networks, cable TV programmers, and program syndicators) to the final point of distribution (broadcast TV stations, cable TV system operators, and home dishes). In this section, the way in which programmers and distributors use satellites in their business is explained in some detail.

2.2.1 TV Broadcasting

To explain the importance of the current role of satellites, this section begins with a review of the general characteristics of the TV broadcasting industry as it exists in North America. Table 2-1 summarizes the participants in the US broadcasting industry. Broadcasting is the commonplace medium whereby local TV stations employ VHF or UHF frequencies to transmit programming to the community. The range of reception is usually limited by line-of-sight propagation to approximately 50 to 100 miles. To conserve frequency channels, the same channel is assigned by the government to another station some safe distance away. Individuals use directional antennas (yagis and reflector dipoles) to maximize signal strength and to suppress reception of unwanted distant stations operating on the same or adjacent channels. A given station only transmits a single channel and hence is constrained to offer only one program at a time.

PART OF INDUSTRY	EXAMPLES
COMMERCIAL NETWORK	ABC, CBS, NBC, FOX
NETWORK AFFILIATE STATION	WABC, KCBS, KNBC, KTTV
INDEPENDENT STATION	WWOR, KTLA, WGN
PUBLIC BROADCASTING NETWORK	PUBLIC BROADCASTING SERVICE
PUBLIC BROADCASTING STATION	WNET, KCET, WGBH
SYNDICATION COMPANY	BUENA VISTA TELEVISION
SYNDICATED PROGRAMMING DELIVERY	WOLD, SYNSAT

Table 2-1 Comparison of Programming Services in Use for Over-the-Air Television Broadcasting in the United States

2.2.1.1   Networks, Affiliates, and Independent Stations

There are national television Networks (ABC, CBS, NBC, and Fox in the US) to provide programs to affiliated TV stations for broadcast over their assigned frequency channel either in real time or by replay from video tape. The term "Network" in this context is capitalized to distinguish it from the generic term. Independent stations (i.e., those not affiliated with Networks) can also obtain programming from the outside from syndication companies which sell programs either individually or as packages. While most syndicated programs are in fact old network programs (reruns), syndicators often deliver new programs and movies. For example, "Wheel of Fortune" and "Entertainment Tonight" are two very popular syndicated programs not offered by the Networks. Network affiliates also obtain much of their programming from syndicators.

All stations operate their own studios so that they too can originate programs, particularly local news, special events, and most importantly to the success of the station, advertising. In North America, the revenues of the stations and the Networks are derived from the sale of advertising, because individual viewers do not pay for the right to watch over-the-air television (except of course when they buy the advertised product or service). Subscription television (STV), an exception to this rule, employed scrambling to control viewing of the broadcasts and assure that monthly fees were paid. In the United States, however, STV was only successful for a short while between 1980 and 1982 until competition from video cassette recorders and cable television undermined their profitability.

Networks offer the advertiser the important advantage over the local station of being able to deliver a nationwide audience, which is important to products like GM automobiles and *Time Magazine*. The revenues of the stations and Networks are tied to the relative size of their respective audiences, which is evaluated by respected polling organizations such as A. C. Nielsen Company. Therefore, the programmers need to deliver programming of sufficiently high quality to attract the largest possible audience. Their profitability is constrained, however, by the cost of producing this programming and of delivering it to the affiliated stations.

2.2.1.2   Satellite Program Distribution

This then brings us to the importance of satellites in providing the needed low cost and highly reliable means of delivering the programming. A single satellite can employ point-to-multipoint connectivity to perform this function on a routine basis. To receive programming, every TV station in the United States owns and operates at least one receiving earth station and many own earth stations usable as uplinks. To achieve very high reliability during an extremely high value (in terms of advertising dollars) event such as the Olympics or the Super Bowl, a Network will "double feed" the program on two different satellites at the same time.

In the United States, there exist public television stations which are neither operated for a profit nor obtain income from advertising. The Public Broadcasting Service (PBS) is the nonprofit television Network which distributes programming to these public television stations. Most of the funds for PBS and the stations are raised through individual and corporate contributions rather than advertising.

Stations also pay PBS and each other for program production and rights for broadcasting. This has allowed the development of a narrower slice of programming (i.e., not of mass appeal) which caters to an audience more interested in education, public affairs, and classical culture. Because of budget constraints, PBS was the first to adopt satellite delivery in 1976, using the Westar 1 satellite. The benefits of satellite delivery having been demonstrated, the commercial Networks then began to move quickly in the same direction during the following years. As indicated previously, by 1984 all Network programming and most syndicated programming was being delivered by satellite. Prior to that, the Networks had used satellite links over the INTELSAT system for providing coverage of overseas events.

The technical means by which the TV broadcast industry uses satellites is illustrated in Figure 2-6. The predominant frequency band employed is C band for the simple reason that more ground antennas and satellites are available than at Ku band. The program distribution satellite shown on the left is used to broadcast the edited program feed on a point-to-multipoint basis. The downlink is received at each TV station by its own receive-only earth station and from there it is either transmitted over the local TV channel or stored on video tape. In the case of a live broadcast from the Network studio, the signal is connected from the camera to the uplink earth station and over the program distribution satellite. A video switching capability in the studio and at each TV station allows technicians to insert taped advertising and computer-generated graphics. Even though most programs are played from video tape, it is generally more economical to distribute taped programs by satellite to the TV stations where they are again recorded rather than mailing the tapes (a process called "bicycling") around the country. Whether the programs are live or taped, the local TV stations are able to insert their own paid advertising in time slots left for that purpose by the Network or syndicator.

2.2.1.3   Backhaul of Event Coverage

All sports events and much news coverage is brought back to the studio over a separate point-to-point satellite link called a "backhaul." In the case of football games, for example, stadiums in North America have access via terrestrial microwave to a local earth station which can uplink the telecast to the backhaul satellite, illustrated in Figure 2-6. The Network or stations pay for the use of the satellite and uplinking earth station by the minute or hour. The Galaxy satellite system, owned and operated by Hughes Communications, Inc., is used extensively for this purpose and calls its occasional use business the Video Timesharing Service. Anyone with a receiving earth station can pick up the backhaul, which does not yet include the "commentary" and advertising spots that are inserted at the studio prior to reuplinking to the program distribution

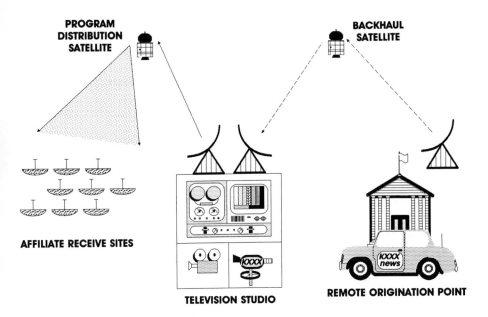

Fig. 2-6 The Use of Satellite Transmission in the Commercial Television Industry for Backhaul of Event Coverage and Program Distribution to Affiliates

satellite. If coverage is of a one-time event such as a natural disaster or Olympic race, then a truck-mounted transportable earth station is driven to the site and erected prior to transmission. The use of a Ku-band (14/12 GHz) backhaul has become particularly attractive for this type of rapid deployment service, and is called *satellite news gathering* (SNG). A Ku-band SNG transportable is much more compact and mobile than its C-band equivalent and can be operated almost immediately after it has been parked on location. In addition, the use of non-shared Ku-band frequencies eliminates any need for prior frequency coordination. Whether C or Ku band, the time demands and economics of event coverage can mean that a backhaul satellite link will be attractive where the distance to the studio is anywhere from 50 to 5000 miles. For example, a backhaul was used during the Los Angeles Olympics of 1984 to reach from Lake Casitas to Hollywood, a distance of approximately 60 miles.

2.2.1.4 Ground Antenna Utilization

A Network affiliated TV station will use one fixed-mounted earth station antenna to receive full-time Network programming from the point-to-multipoint program distribution satellite. In addition, some "roving" among other satellites can be done with a movable antenna to pick up special programs provided by syndicators and to receive live coverage of sports events of interest only to the local community (for example, when the local baseball team is playing an away-from-home game in another city). Antennas used by the Networks in backhaul service would therefore need to be movable, since events and satellites change from time to time.

2.2.2   Cable Television

The cable television medium has achieved widespread acceptance in North America with about half of all households subscribing to cable service. Originally a means to bring over-the-air broadcasts into remote areas with otherwise poor reception, a local cable TV system uses coaxial cable to connect to each home through a point-to-multipoint distribution network. The programming material is collected at the "head end" which has the necessary high-gain receiving antennas to pick up TV signals of reasonably good quality. In fact, the original name for cable TV was CATV, standing for community antenna television. A studio may be provided at a point between the head end and the cable distribution network. Unlike over-the-air broadcasting, viewers, called subscribers, pay a monthly fee for reception of the several TV channels delivered by the cable (many of which are "free" advertising-supported local and distant TV stations).

In the mid-1970s Home Box Office (HBO), a subsidiary of Time, Inc., experimented with a closed programming service which was made available to cable TV systems on a subscription basis. The key to the success has been the control that cable programmers and the cable system operators have over the delivery of the program "product" to the home. As was mentioned in Chapter 1, satellite distribution was adopted because of its low cost of making the program channel available throughout the country. Today, approximately one-third of all US domestic satellite transponders are employed for cable program distribution, which is by far the largest single application. Cable systems have their receiving earth stations located at the head end.

2.2.2.1   Classes of Cable Programming

There exist several classes of specialized cable programming, as summarized in Table 2-2. The satellite-delivered channels are each focused into particular niches. HBO established the most lucrative niche, that of recent movies. In fact, prior to widespread use of VCRs, HBO and Showtime, a service of Viacom International, provided the principal means to watch recent movies uninterrupted by commercials on home TV. To receive this service continuously

TYPE OF SERVICE	EXAMPLES
PAY MOVIE	HBO, SHOWTIME
SUPER STATION	WTBS, WWOR
NEWS	CNN, CSPAN
SPORTS	ESPN
MUSIC	MTV, NASHVILLE
CHILDREN	NICKLEODEON, DISNEY
RELIGIOUS	CBN, ETERNAL WORD
SCIENCE/EDUCATION	DISCOVERY
HOME SHOPPING	HOME SHOPPING NETWORK SKY MERCHANT
ADULT ENTERTAINMENT	PLAYBOY

Table 2-2 Comparison of Cable TV Programming Services Available in North America

along with the regular channels, subscribers pay an additional monthly fee which is shared between the programmer and the cable system operator. The revenue of the programmer is then used like the advertising revenues of a Network, paying for the acquisition of programming and for its distribution by satellite.

Because of the marketing strategies of the movie studios which produce most of the product offered by the pay services (HBO, Showtime, etc.), there still exists a time delay (*release window*) of one year or more between when a movie is first shown in movie theaters and when it is made available to cable. Furthermore, the time delay is somewhat shorter with regard to the availability to the public of video tapes for home VCR usage. A new form of cable service called "pay-per-view" has appeared, wherein the subscriber places an order to receive a specific movie broadcast at a scheduled time for a fee. The administration of this type of service is considerably more complicated, because the telephone order desk can anticipate thousands of calls for a particular movie. The delivery of the product into the home is controlled with decoders which will allow the scrambled picture to be received only when authorized.

In addition to the pay services, there is a wide variety of "free" services which are delivered by satellite exclusively to cable systems. Ted Turner, chairman of Turner Broadcasting in Atlanta, Georgia, pioneered two of these services. The first is called a *super station*, his SuperStation WTBS being the best known. A super station originates from a major independent over-the-air broadcast TV station in a large city and is uplinked to the cable distribution satellite. This is useful to the TV station because it increases its audience in size and scope, making it more attractive to advertisers. The cable systems usually pay a relatively low fee per subscriber. The other service invented by Turner is the 24-hour news channel, exemplified by the highly successful Cable News Network (CNN). Essentially all of its audience is via cable systems, and it is supported both by advertising and small subscription fees.

Up until 1985, only independent TV stations were being used as super stations; however, a new cable programming service from Satellite Broadcast Networks has begun to uplink Network affiliated stations for reception primarily by home antennas. Called Prime Time 24, the service is scrambled and subscription fees are collected from individuals who wish to watch Network programming delivered by a C-band satellite.

Another innovative cable service is the video music channel. MTV, a very popular and successful music TV channel owned by Viacom International, is supported in the same manner as CNN and plays music videos 24 hours a day. This type of programming is popular among young people (but probably watched by few people over the age of 30). The Disney Channel from Walt Disney Productions and Nickelodeon from Viacom have gained acceptance among the younger generation. Other cable channels offer religious programming, science, education, sports, shopping and adult entertainment. The mix keeps changing all of the time in the United States as new programmers experiment with format and content. Many of these innovative concepts catch on and are adopted by the more established pay services and by the Networks. As a general comment, the audience enjoyed by the Networks has declined significantly in recent years due to inroads of cable TV and VCRs; the Networks, however, still attract the largest audiences for successful programs and earn many times the revenues of the cable programming services.

2.2.2.2 *Satellite Utilization in Cable TV*

The satellite delivery system used by cable is essentially identical to that employed by the Networks. As shown in Figure 2-6, program distribution satellites are used to carry the cable programming channels to the cable system head ends. A typical cable system head end in the United States will continuously receive from 10 to 30 satellite-delivered channels, coming from one to four different satellites. This means that multiple receiving antennas are usually required. The cost of the receiving antenna is relatively low because of the small reflector size required (12 to 18 feet). Expense can sometimes be minimized by using a single reflector with several feeds, each aligned for reception of a different satellite. In actuality, it is the cost of the indoor receivers and considerations as to physical space for antennas that dominate the economics of the cable head end.

To control access to their product better, the cable programmers have begun to scramble the programming at the uplink using the Video Cipher II system developed by M/A-Com and sold by General Instruments. The receiving site at the cable head end then requires a descrambler for each channel being recovered. This approach allows the programmer to certify the particular downlink because the descramblers can be turned on (*addressed*) individually. The video part of the signal is distorted with a random sinewave while the audio is encrypted digitally. Scrambling also allows the programmer to reach the backyard dish owner and collect a monthly subscription fee, as if he or she were connected to a cable system.

Some cable programming services cover remote events and therefore employ satellite backhaul just like the Networks. CNN relies heavily on backhaul to provide nearly around-the-world news coverage. Also, WTBS broadcasts the away-from-home games of two of the main Atlanta professional sports teams and is a major user of backhaul links. An important requirement in the use of satellites for cable is that the backhaul (which is occasional) be separate from the program distribution (which is full time and continuous). Cable systems themselves generally do not alter the programming coming from the satellite and many cannot handle a break in transmission the way TV stations are equipped to do.

2.2.2.3 Direct to Home

The use of improved C-band satellites with increased downlink power like Galaxy I has reduced the size of the receiving antenna needed to obtain an acceptable picture. A new industry appeared in the early 1980s to manufacture and sell inexpensive receiving systems to the public. The attraction at the time was the cable programming available for free that the satellites delivered. By 1985, over one million "backyard dishes" were installed at homes, making the concept of direct broadcasting a reality. The pay cable services began to scramble their signals in 1986, and a new phase of industry development was underway. Individuals can buy a Video Cipher II decoder and pay a monthly or annual fee to the cable programmers so that their decoder would be authorized to unscramble the signals. By 1987, more than two million backyard dishes have been sold, and penetration of the home Video Cipher II has accelerated. The development of this new (but not unexpected) market will be important, both to the near-term success of cable TV programming and also to the ultimate success of the direct broadcast satellite concept itself. The successors to this "grass roots" service will be the ambitious direct broadcast satellite systems using the BSS allocations discussed in Chapters 1 and 9.

2.3   TELEPHONE SERVICES

Telecommunication facilities used to provide telephone service can be divided into essentially three parts: subscriber loops, switching, and transmission. A telephone subscriber has on his or her premises one or more subscriber units, which can consist of telephones, facsimile equipment, data terminals, and video teleconferencing equipment. The common denominator is that any of these instruments can send and receive via a telephone line with three kilohertz of bandwidth (300 to 3400 Hz frequency range). The subscriber unit is connected to the local telephone switch by a single pair of wires called a subscriber loop. In specialized cases requiring maximum transmission performance, the loop can be provided over a four wire line (two for send and two for receive). The telephone switch accesses other local subscribers as well as more distant subscribers which are not directly connected to the same local switching office. Transmission facilities provide the point-to-point links (trunks) which are used to carry the calls between switches.

Public telephone systems connect the switches together according to a five-level hierarchy to allow a subscriber to place calls to any destination in the region, country, or the world. The smallest local switch is designated level 1, while the toll switches are designated 2 through 5, depending on their capacity and location (level 5 being reserved for the largest long distance switching offices). In contrast to this, private line service is implemented by fixed point-to-point circuits which do not pass through switches. The implications of switched *versus* private line services are very important both to the user and to the service provider. Satellite communication can and has been applied to both applications. The basic arrangements for switched and private lines are shown in Figure 2-7.

2.3.1   Switched Telephone Service

Switched telephone service is an effective and economical means of allowing individual subscribers to communicate by telephone or other voice bandwidth techniques over a single subscriber loop. As shown at the top of Figure 2-7, a telephone instrument is connected to the local switch which provides access to the national telephone network. Other local subscribers can be called typically with only seven digits because of the limited number of separate loops served by the same or other nearby switching offices. To place a long distance call, another series of digits is required to indicate the region of the country or other country to be called. These "area code" digits are passed to the toll switch which has available to it dedicated point-to-point transmission facilities called trunks reaching a variety of distant toll switches. By interpreting the area code, the toll switch can connect the call through on the proper trunk and notify the toll switch on the other end that a circuit is to be established. The call may be routed through more than one toll office, depending on the availability of direct trunks from the originating toll office. The distant local switch receives the seven dialing digits and rings the telephone of the subscriber being called. The end-to-end circuit is established and maintained until either party hangs up, at which time the local loops and trunks are made available to provide other service.

**SWITCHED LOCAL AND LONG DISTANCE
SERVICE**

PRIVATE LINE SERVICE

Fig. 2-7 Commercial Telephone Service Can Be Obtained Either Through Public Switching Facilities or Through Dedicated Private Lines

The long distance trunks between toll offices use either terrestrial or satellite links. As was explained in Chapter 1, terrestrial facilities predominate in all developed countries, particularly in populated regions such as the eastern United States. Satellite trunks are attractive for economic reasons when covering distances greater than 500 to 1000 miles or if large bodies of water must be spanned.

When properly engineered, satellite trunks cannot be distinguished from long distance terrestrial trunks by most telephone subscribers. When the circuit is to pass voice band data in both directions, the delay from satellite transmission can disrupt the performance of the connection, unless an appropriate protocol is used. This was discussed earlier in this chapter in the section on quality.

2.3.1.1 Standard Message Telephone Service

Public switched long distance service in the United States is provided under two schemes: standard Message Telephone Service (MTS) and Wide Area Telecommunication Service (WATS). Any individual or company with a telephone number can use MTS by dialing the digit "1" to reach the standard access to long distance. While AT&T had traditionally been the long distance service accessed this way, the competing carriers have recently been allowed to offer the same service through the local telephone companies. Subscribers pre-select the particular long distance carrier that they would reach by dialing "1." Alternatively, subscribers can use the competing carriers by dialing a special local access number which connects the call to the carrier's toll switch. Tolls for using MTS are charged by the minute, with the rate being more or less proportional to distance. Volume discounts have also become available.

2.3.1.2 Wide Area Telecommunication Service

The other alternative for switched long distance is WATS, which is used primarily by business and the government. The long distance carrier provides a direct tie line from the subscriber to his toll switch, and the user can place and receive long distance calls directly. While WATS tie lines cannot be used to place local calls, distant parties can access the user from their respective local switch by prefacing a seven digit number with the universal "800" area code. All billing for the use of the particular WATS number goes to the subscriber, not to the distant caller. Businesses use WATS to engage in what has become known as "telemarketing," where customers call in toll free by dialing an 800 number. The charge for using WATS is also by the minute and distance within wide ranges called "bands" emanating from the subscriber. Advancing digital technology is allowing carriers to offer other innovations of MTS and WATS.

2.3.1.3 Terrestrial and Satellite Trunking

Essentially every long distance service provider in the United States has used or is using satellite trunks to interconnect their most distant toll switches. The advent of digital fiber optic links between major cities, however, has reduced the attractiveness of satellite trunks for the heaviest routes. The future use of satellite trunks will probably be limited to what are called thin routes, where it is not economically attractive to install fiber. Later on in this section, the use of very small aperture terminals (VSATs) at Ku band will be reviewed. It is widely believed that VSATs will play an important role in handling thin-route traffic for business and government users.

2.3.2 Private Line

In North America, private line refers to the provision of point-to-point circuits for use in special applications, i.e., without using public telephone switching. The typical example is shown at the bottom of Figure 2-7. The satellite circuit is exactly the same as in the case of long distance trunking; the difference is that the lines are not connected between the toll switches of the public telephone network. Whether by satellite or terrestrial means, a private line is installed whenever the volume of calls and average usage of the public telephone system between two specific points is very large.

2.3.2.1 Private Line Circuit Operation

If telephones were connected at both ends of the private line, the circuit operation would be as simple as an intercom: party A picks up the telephone, causing the telephone of party B to ring (or *vice versa*). Once both parties have their telephones "off hook," the conversation may commence. It is usually more advantageous to connect the private line to a privately owned switch called a *private branch exchange* (PBX). Private local switching can also be obtained as a service from the telephone company called Centrex. Calls can be placed between location A and location B by any party with access to either private switch. Access to the public network (at the lower right of Figure 2-7) is also possible because most PBXs have subscriber loops from the local telephone company. Private lines therefore can potentially provide convenient bypass of the public long distance telephone system, provided that permission to do so has been obtained from the proper authority. Often, the local telephone company installs the tie lines needed to connect from the subscriber location to the private line carrier. Local bypass can be accomplished if the user is willing to install local area transmission facilities such as cable or microwave.

2.3.2.2 Traffic Engineering for Private Lines

To determine if a private line is economically justified, it is necessary to study the actual calling patterns and costs of current usage of switched long distance service. The total number of paid minutes for telephone calls between specific locations is compared to the monthly lease rate of point-to-point private lines. Traffic engineering principles can be used to estimate the number of private line trunks which would be required. For example, Figure 2-8 presents the traffic handling capability of point-to-point trunks between a pair of locations as a function of the number of trunks. To compile the graph, it was assumed that for every 20 attempts at placing a call over the trunks, one attempt failed because all trunks were busy (occupied). The ratio 1 in 20, or 0.05, is called the "grade of service." Traffic handling capability is measured in terms of the average number of simultaneous calls that can be carried. Owing to the statistical pattern of subscribers placing calls, there will be times when usage is less than the average, and other times when it is greater. From Figure 2-8, it is clear that the more trunks are included in the point-to-point group, the greater will be the efficiency of usage. The minimum effective usage is 5% for one trunk increasing to 60% for a bundle of 10 trunks.

The implication of traffic engineering is that if calling patterns show low usage between specific locations, then private lines are probably not attractive. Heavy calling and long call durations, such as would be required for data transmission, suggest the need for private lines. Another factor is the distance between locations. Satellite links cost the same to implement, no matter the ground distance. Therefore, the economics of long distance can be swung towards private lines with low-cost earth stations, as discussed in the following section.

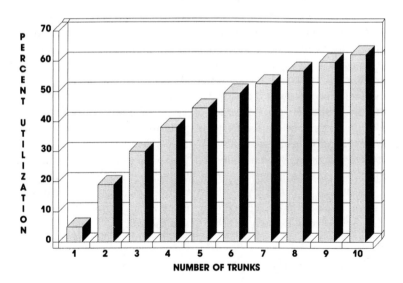

Fig. 2-8 Average Utilization of a Bundle of Trunks Between Two Points Expressed as a Percent of the Number of Trunks (Erlang B Equation)

2.3.3 Very Small Aperture Terminals

The features of satellite networks outlined at the beginning of this chapter can be used to the fullest advantage in telephone service with very small aperture terminals (VSATs). The type of earth station called a VSAT is typically inexpensive and easy to operate, justifying its use on the customer's premises. Figure 2-3 shows how a VSAT is used in a multipoint-to-point network and Chapter 6 contains a detailed discussion of VSAT equipment configuration. With a typical antenna size of 1.8 meters (6 feet) and a purchase price comparable to that of a small business computer system, a VSAT gives full access to a private switched network involving hundreds or thousands of locations. Such networks would be prohibitively expensive if implemented with dedicated point-to-point private lines, whether terrestrial or satellite. In a VSAT network, a user can view the satellite as a toll switch in the sky, eliminating the need for local loops, toll switching, or even PBXs in some cases. The key to the effectiveness of a VSAT network is its interactive nature, allowing two-way communication from remote locations in the same manner as the terrestrial telephone network.

2.3.3.1 VSAT Network Architectures

The network architectures available to VSATs are not new because similar concepts have been used by INTELSAT in the SPADE system and by Hughes Aircraft in the Palapa A *demand assignment multiple access* (DAMA) system. These earlier thin-route systems operated at C band, however, and required large diameter earth stations. The use of medium-power Ku-band satellite transponders and true VSAT ground facilities makes bypass of the terrestrial network more attractive.

Two network architectures are effective for VSATs: the *star* and the *mesh*, illustrated in Figure 2-9. Each interconnection, shown as a double-ended arrow, is actually a point-to-point satellite link. The connectivities illustrated in Figure 2-9 are not permanently established; instead, they are only set up for the duration of a call. The process of DAMA by which this is actually done is discussed in Chapter 4. Satellite capacity (power and bandwidth) necessary for each call is assigned from a "pool" by a network control system of some type. Using modern computer technology, the satellite network responds to calls placed by subscribers in the same manner as a conventional telephone switch.

Star networks are easily implemented using VSATs, because the low sensitivity of the small dish is compensated for by the high sensitivity of the large antenna and high-power amplifiers at the hub. This is why the first VSAT networks to be introduced in North America all employed hubs in a star architecture. As will be discussed in the next section, star networks are satisfactory for one-way and interactive data communications. Conventional switched telephone service requires a mesh architecture, because the VSATs must be able to communicate directly with each other without a double hop through a hub.

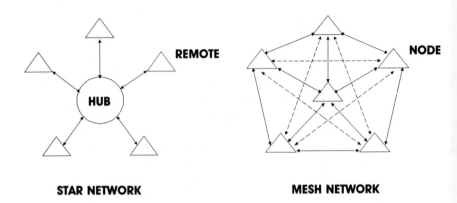

STAR NETWORK   **MESH NETWORK**

Fig. 2-9 Full Connectivity in a VSAT Network Is Achieved with Either the Star or Mesh Configuration

2.3.3.2   Efficiency of VSAT Usage

The efficiency of utilization of a VSAT is potentially greater than that of a private line, shown in Figure 2-8, because of the inherent flexibility of the DAMA network. Specifically, it takes several point-to-point private lines to connect one location to a number of other locations of interest. A single VSAT in a satellite network accomplishes the same thing, because the satellite channel is switchable on demand to any location in the satellite footprint. By picking up the low-traffic demands to several destinations and aggregating them in one satellite channel, the VSAT achieves much higher average utilization than could a network of private lines. A VSAT can also pay for itself in a traffic engineering sense by savings in long distance calls made over the satellite network instead of through a switched long distance common carrier.

The VSAT has other dimensions which are outside of the current capabilities of the terrestrial network. Video teleconferencing has been gaining acceptance as a valuable business communication service, rendered through the TV receive-only feature of the VSAT. Also, the VSAT is capable of receiving and transmitting high-speed data at transmission rates considerably in excess of what can pass through the 3 kHz bandwidth of the telephone local loop. Many of the features of the ISDN concept, including simultaneous voice and data communication, are accommodated through a VSAT. For many users, these added dimensions provide justification for employing VSAT technology as the centerpiece of their private telecommunication systems.

2.4   DATA COMMUNICATION

The purpose of data communication is to link computers and other centralized data processing facilities with remote users or with other computers. Among the very first data communication networks was the SAGE system developed for the US Air Force by IBM in the 1950s. Its purpose was to gather radar tracking data from remote early warning radar sites, process the data to identify friendly and possibly unfriendly aircraft, and display the results on CRT screens for use by aircraft control personnel. Another such early network was American Airlines' first computerized reservation system called SABER. In the 1980s, data communication networks have been applied in nearly every business imaginable, from grocery store inventory control systems to automated teller machines at banks.

The volume of data along a given path is measured in kilobits per second (kb/s). Low speeds ranging between 1.2 and 9.6 kb/s can pass through a telephone circuit and have generally been served by both the public switched network and by private lines. The special circuits which are required to conduct medium speeds up to 56 kb/s have been difficult to obtain even in North America. Analog transmission systems, which currently predominate, were designed to carry voice band frequencies which are too narrow for data rates higher than 9.6 kb/s. Satellite links, however, can support any speed, including rates of 1000 kb/s (i.e., 1 Mb/s) and higher. Terrestrial networks are being upgraded around the world to provide direct digital connections which are capable of the highest rates, also. With the increasing number of alternatives, it becomes a complex task to identify the specific data communication needs of the particular application and then compare the approaches offered by satellite and terrestrial networks.

In using the terrestrial telephone network, data communication users find that they are forced to pay high monthly lease rates for private lines. Organizations such as stock brokerage houses, airlines, department store chains, oil companies, and car rental agencies must maintain nearly continuous data links with hundreds or thousands of branch offices and stores, even though only a small amount of data is being sent to one specific site at one time. In addition to cost, the critical problems in making a data communication system work properly have been the reliability and throughput capability of the interconnecting telephone lines. Satellite links are attractive for data communication because of recognized strengths in all of these areas. Because of high performance to cost ratios, a great deal of emphasis is now being placed on using VSAT networks.

As was stated earlier in this chapter, modern data protocols allow satellite links to achieve the efficiency formerly possible only on high-grade terrestrial lines. The star network using VSAT technology has proven particularly valuable for thin-route data communication. As performance and cost of digital ground equipment improve and as Ku-band satellites with advanced features become available, interactive VSAT data networks will become widespread. To provide background for this evolution, the following paragraphs explain satellite data communication applications in terms of the three generic connectivities (i.e., point-to-point, point-to-multipoint, and multipoint-to-point).

2.4.1 One-Way Data Broadcast

The most common data communication application implemented by satellite is data broadcasting, illustrated in Figure 2-10. Point-to-multipoint connectivity is used to deliver information in digital form (numbers and characters) to numerous receiving ground antennas. The data are typically transmitted in fixed blocks called packets, since customers can segregate their own data to be delivered like letters. Each packet is "addressed" to certain receivers and even coded so that only authorized users can gain access to the information. Full access to all information in the broadcast is provided in the case of a news wire service such as the Associated Press.

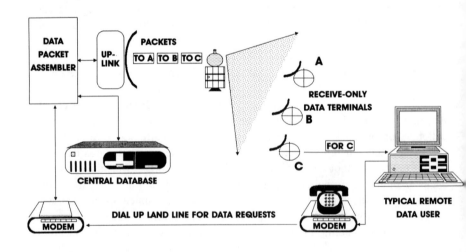

Fig. 2-10 One-Way Data Broadcasting to Low Cost Receive-Only Terminals, Illustrating Terrestrial "Dial-Up" Response

2.4.1.1 Data Broadcast Network Arrangement

A central hub earth station, shown at the upper left of Figure 2-10, uplinks a nearly continuous stream of packets to the satellite. Information to be transmitted as packets originates from a central database located at the hub or connected to it by a private line. A data packet assembler (upper left of Figure 2-10) is a digital processing device that takes the information to be sent, organizes it into packets, and places appropriate address bits at the beginning of each packet. Since each packet is self-contained with source and destination addresses, it can be routed in any way over the satellite and ultimately through a terrestrial packet switched network.

The data broadcast reaches receive-only terminals, shown as sites A, B, and C in Figure 2-10, which are all within the satellite footprint. Receiver C, for example, contains digital processing electronics which can identify the packets addressed to it and recover the data for delivery to the user terminal or storage device. In the illustration, the user at site C has a personal computer to view the data and store it for analysis or later use. Also, the modem and telephone instrument allow the user to reach the hub station or data base to request that certain additional data be transmitted over the satellite. With this dial-up capability, the broadcast network can perform as if it were a multipoint-to-point network.

2.4.1.2 Spread Spectrum Feature

Equatorial Communications Company of Mountain View, California (now a subsidiary of CONTEL/ASC), was the first to offer data broadcasting with receive-only VSATs approximately two feet in diameter. An antenna of this size has a beamwidth of nine degrees, which is broad enough to allow RF signals from several satellites to enter the ground receiver. To visualize this situation, examine Figure 1-14, which shows closely spaced satellites and a large ground antenna with an appropriately narrow beam. Imagine how the situation would look if the broader ground antenna beam of Figure 1-13 were employed with these closely spaced satellites. With multiple satellites transmitting signals potentially on the same frequency, the ground receiver must have some means of selecting the signal from the right satellite and suppressing the rest. The technique exploited by Equatorial is called *spread spectrum*, which is explained in Chapter 4. With spread spectrum, the digital demodulator of the VSAT is able to separate the desired data broadcast from the adjacent satellite interference (and terrestrial microwave interference as well).

Spread spectrum, which is inefficient in its use of transponder bandwidth, is not needed if ground receiving antennas of sufficiently narrow beamwidth are used. A C-band antenna of approximately 12 feet (not exactly a VSAT) would discriminate adequately against adjacent satellite signals. On the other hand, Ku-band VSATs of four to six feet can also perform adequately without spread spectrum, because the beamwidth is approximately one-third that at C band for the same diameter of receiving antenna. A data broadcast on an RF carrier without spread spectrum modulation is said to employ the single channel per carrier (SCPC) technique, which is also used to distribute audio services as discussed at the conclusion of this chapter.

2.4.1.3 Data Broadcasting with Video

Data broadcasting has also been applied as an adjunct to video transmission, which is convenient to do because the video signal requires a lot of power and bandwidth, while the data requires very little (assuming a data rate of 56 kb/s or less). The cost of reception is relatively low, because the data terminal can use conventional video receiving equipment of the type in mass production for industrial and consumer markets. In one common technique, a low-speed data stream is inserted into the vertical blanking interval of the video transmission. (The vertical blanking interval is the horizontal black band which is visible in a gently rolling television picture.) The data is removed from the video signal by a special decoder unit to which the display terminal or data recorder is connected. Another approach employs a separate baseband "subcarrier" onto which is modulated a low or medium-speed data stream. The receiving earth station will require a separate subcarrier receiver and decoder to recover the data; the subcarrier approach can potentially carry much higher data rates, however, and does not interfere with the video signal in any way. For these reasons, data subcarriers can be found on a large percentage of video carriers used for full-time delivery of cable TV programming. Alternatively, broadcast data service is being provided on subcarriers without the video as a means to optimize the link for reception by the smallest possible receive-only antenna.

2.4.2 Interactive Data

While data broadcast has a variety of uses, most data communication applications require that the remote terminals be able to respond back to the central site. Also, the remotes may need to transmit information between one another.

2.4.2.1 Network Architecture for Interactive Data

Figure 2-11 shows an interactive data network where the remote stations can transmit information to the hub over the same satellite that delivers the data broadcast. This is obviously more convenient for the remote station than using a dial-up line as suggested in the previous section. However, there is a significant trade-off between the money saved by using the same satellite transponder and the money spent to add the transmitting capability to every remote station. In cases where the remote stations transmit infrequently (once per day, for example) but need to receive data continuously, the point-to-multipoint broadcast network (Figure 2-10) will probably be the lowest in cost.

The principal advantage of an interactive VSAT network is that no terrestrial facilities of any kind are required, as is shown in Figure 2-11. The hub's large antenna allows remote stations to uplink with the lowest RF power possible, usually less than ten watts. Even still, transmissions from remotes will be at significantly lower data rates than originate from the hub. It is usually advantageous to share a VSAT among several users, such as would be the case at an airline reservation office. The data concentrator shown at the lower right of Figure 2-11 combines (multiplexes) the data flows from the three terminals and inputs a single stream of bits to the VSAT indoor electronic unit. Conversely, the data broadcast from the hub is demultiplexed by the VSAT for delivery to the individual user terminals. To maximize the efficiency of satellite transmissions, the RF electronics are mounted in close proximity to the VSAT antenna feed horn (more detailed information on earth-station design can be found in Chapter 6).

CENTRAL DATA PROCESSING FACILITY

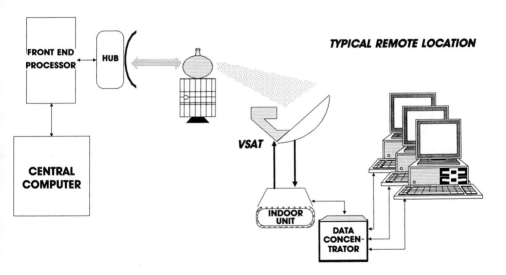

Fig. 2-11 Interactive Data Communications from a Shared Very Small Aperture Terminal

2.4.2.2   Network Management

The hub station has many of the same elements as shown for the broadcast application. The necessity of controlling the transmissions from numerous remote stations, however, adds another level of complexity. This function is accomplished by a *network management system* (NMS), which is incorporated into one of the hub stations in the VSAT network. Since VSATs are usually unmanned (in the same sense as a PBX or minicomputer), the NMS automatically interrogates each VSAT on a routine basis to determine its operating status and past history of usage. A given VSAT which has failed and cannot transmit to the satellite could still reach the NMS over a dial-up telephone line. This results in a powerful and resilient network where faults in remote VSATs can be isolated and even corrected. If human intervention is required to restore service at the remote location, then the operator on duty at the NMS can notify the appropriate field maintenance person. The integrity of the interactive satellite network is particularly strong, because the failures are limited to accessible sources within the hub, the VSAT, the satellite transponder, and possibly the NMS itself. As was mentioned previously, satellite links are extremely reliable and yield error rates which are lower (i.e., better) than those achievable with terrestrial private lines. The earth stations in the network are subject to equipment failures and software problems, which will cause outages on occasion. Experience has shown that such outages can be minimized in frequency by using field-proven electronics and in duration by providing standby (redundant) equipment which can be activated by remote control from the NMS.

2.5   INTEGRATED DIGITAL SERVICES

The expansion of high capacity digital communication systems is causing the dividing lines between telephone, data, and video transmission to blur. In fact, as discussed below, it is possible to convert any and all of these services into a digital format and thereafter utilize common terrestrial and satellite links. New standards and equipment are being developed under the name of *integrated services digital networks* (ISDN), by which many applications would be digitized essentially at the source and combined together (integrated) for efficient routing and transmission. When implemented on the user side of the typical local loop, ISDN is expected to provide such capability as two separate telephone lines plus an independent digital data line. This is referred to as 2B + D, which stands for two bearers (channels) plus data.

Advances in digital bandwidth compression are allowing the multiple channels of voice, data, or video to be carried over a link which could previously only carry a single channel. This is accomplished by high speed programmable digital processors which remove blank time and redundancy from the signal information coming from the source. Users cannot usually detect compression, because the equipment at the distant end reconstructs the signal adequately for its intended purpose. A rather fundamental way of combining digital signals together is called *time division multiplexing* (or simply *multiplexing*), which is described in Chapter 4. The reverse process of splitting out the individual data channels is called *demultiplexing*.

In a major advancement of the last decade called *statistical multiplexing*, the combining of input data channels is done in response to the time varying (*dynamic*) demand for transmission. The sum of data rates of the input channels would exceed the capacity of the output transmission link, except that only those channels with data to be sent are passed through. From the user perspective, a full-time data link is provided and the dynamic switching of the statistical multiplexers at both ends is transparent, i.e., it can be totally ignored by the user. Blockage of users when the outbound link is overloaded is automatically signalled to terminal equipment through the data transmission interface, which is discussed in Chapter 6.

As a precursor to full implementation of ISDN, the *time division multiple access* (TDMA) networks pioneered by COMSAT Laboratories of the Communications Satellite Corporation (discussed in Chapter 4) required digitization and multiplexing of voice and data channels before uplinking to the satellite. This technology, proven out in the early 1970s, became the driving force for developing signal processing techniques and for proving that digital systems can work reliably. Digital transmission facilities did not become commonplace, however, until the mid-1980s, delaying commercial development and marketing of associated ground equipment.

2.5.1 Digital Hierarchy

Once the user information in whatever form is digitized and multiplexed, it can be viewed as a single stream of data. It is a common practice to classify data streams according to the amount of transmission capacity or bandwidth that is required. The digital hierarchy established in the 1960s for the Bell System uses standard levels designated by DS-0, DS-1, DS-2, . . ., DS-*n, et cetera* ("T" can be substituted for "DS" in the naming convention). Table 2-3 summarizes the basic transmission rates and applications for the levels of the hierarchy currently in use. Perhaps the most common transmission speed for integrated digital services is DS-1 (1.544 Mb/s), because a link of this capacity can support a variety of different services even at the same time. Levels of the hierarchy above DS-3 (45 Mb/s) carry such large amounts of information that they are not generally available for resale. In terms of ISDN (mentioned at the beginning of this section), DS-0 (64 kb/s) is seen as the basic user interface rate on the local loop and DS-1 is the level used for most trunk transmission. In the ISDN form of the DS-1 link, there are 23 bearer channels plus one data channel, i.e., 23B + D. There is currently some difficulty in reconciling ISDN standards with the digital hierarchies in North America, Europe, and Japan. This is because European countries have adopted different digital rates for their hierarchy, making it somewhat inconvenient for them to interface with North American and Japanese digital transmission facilities.

DEFINED LEVEL	RATE	RELATED TO OTHER LEVELS	TYPICAL USE
DS-0	64 kb/s	(Root)	Voice,56kb/sData
DS-1, T-1	1.544 Mb/s	24 × DS-0	Voice, Video Teleconferencing
DS-2	6.0 Mb/s	4 × DS-1	High Capacity Trunking
DS-3	45 Mb/s	28 × DS-1	High Capacity Trunking, Video

Table 2.3. The Digital Multiplexing Hierarchy Currently in Use in North America

2.5.2 Combining of Digital Services

The multiplexing and transmission of integrated digital services is illustrated in Figure 2-12. On the user side (shown at the left) are three possible applications: telephone, video teleconferencing, and high speed data. A high-level multiplexer is located at a point of service aggregation to combine and route traffic to the digital transmission network. On the right, high-speed digital streams (typically DS-1) reach other locations over various point-to-point transmission systems, which can consist of satellite links, terrestrial microwave systems, and fiber optic cables. An example of this type of multiplexer is the Integrated Digital Network Exchange (IDNX) developed and marketed by Network Equipment Technologies, Inc., of Redwood City, California. An IDNX would be located at each major user location to establish a network node. Traffic routing between nodes is programmed in a routing pattern which can be altered at any time by an operator using a computer terminal connected to any IDNX in the network. Another important feature of this class of equipment is that it provides statistical multiplexing efficiently to squeeze together smaller streams of data traffic.

2.5.2.1 Digital Telephone Services

For telephone service, modern local switches and PBXs digitize the incoming voice frequency information (including voice band data and facsimile) and connect users to each other and to those at distant locations. The trunk side of the switch would be at the DS-1 level, providing 24 digital voice channels each at the DS-0 (64 kb/s) level. With digital compression, the number of voice channels that can be carried by a DS-1 channel is in the range of 44 to 90, depending on the mathematical process (algorithm) employed. This increased telephone capacity shows the effectiveness of digital compression of maximizing the use of the transmission facility.

The digital switch shown at the top of Figure 2-12 provides access to a private or public long distance network utilizing digital transmission at a high level of the hierarchy. Users are connected to the switch by local loops within the same building or by terrestrial tie lines. The interface device at the switch which determines the type of subscriber service is called a ''port.'' A standard telephone instrument or voice band data modem accesses the switch through a two-wire analog voice port. Analog four-wire trunks can be connected to the switch through a tandem port. Some switches allow direct digital connections at 9.6 kb/s and even 56 kb/s through a digital data port. Lower-speed devices can be combined together using a statistical multiplexer, as discussed in previous paragraphs. Finally, in the case of ISDN, digital switches will be modified to provide greater capability and to accommodate DS-0 ports and other port configurations which result from current efforts to standardize the user interface.

2.5.2.2 Compressed Video Teleconferencing

The video teleconferencing system shown at center left of Figure 2-12 can establish a two-day video link with one or more distant locations. Again, thanks to digital compression, a full-motion color TV signal with sound can be transmitted at the DS-1 rate or even lower. The device which digitizes and compresses the video signal from the camera is called a video *codec* (coder-decoder). Devices of this type have existed for ten or more years, but companies like Compression Laboratories, Inc., of San Jose, California, have caused the cost and size of

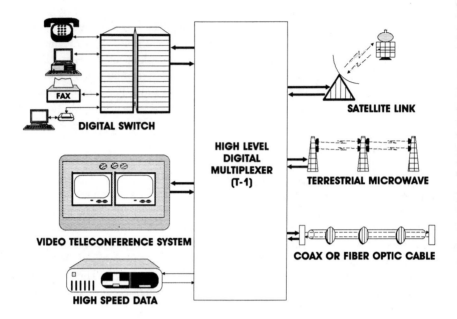

Fig. 2-12 Integrated Digital Services Using a High Level Multiplexer with Connections to Satellite and Terrestrial T-1 Transmission Facilities

codecs to decrease greatly. The quality of this type of video is adequate for business meetings showing "talking heads" and presentations consisting of color slides or computer graphic images. It is common to operate the video teleconferencing system at one-half the DS-1 rate (called half T-1) and use a high-level digital multiplexer to introduce other services into the outbound DS-1 stream. When 56 kb/s compression produces picture quality comparable to current T-1 codecs, it is expected that there will be a significant rise in the use of the technology. In contrast to video teleconferencing, a broadcast-quality picture requires a rate of 90 Mb/s or greater with existing equipment. However, broadcast-quality TV at the DS-3 (45 Mb/s) rate is gradually being adopted for point-to-point links via fiber optic cable systems.

2.5.2.3 Digital Data Service

The last type of user access shown in Figure 2-12 is high-speed data on a point-to-point basis. This type of service could be required to interconnect two or more large computer systems, each capable of transmitting at 56 kb/s, 256 kb/s, or even DS-1. These high rates would be required when a large file of data must be transferred. Another application for such high speeds is for digital facsimile such as that used to reproduce newspaper or magazine pages. With rates up to T-1, an entire newspaper can be transmitted with absolute clarity in under one hour. In general, high-speed digital access can be required in special cases, and, therefore, it is difficult to establish standards. The advantage of using digital integration is that such unusual requirements can be easily accommodated with a more conventional network composed of DS-1 transmission facilities and high-level digital multiplexers. Port configurations for any of these rates are available from the suppliers of high-level digital multiplexers.

2.5.3 Digital Integration with TDMA

Modern TDMA equipment can perform the function of the high level multiplexer, making TDMA particularly attractive for private digital networks with large and diverse service requirements. An important benefit of TDMA is that it can make use of the point-to-multipoint capability of the satellite and thereby reduce the number of individual transmission links that would otherwise be required with point-to-point DS-1 channels. This aspect is covered in greater detail in Chapter 1.

The various technologies and transmission facilities for digital integration are evolving at a rapid rate in North America, Europe, and parts of the Pacific region. This will ultimately mean that all communication services will be processed, switched, and routed in a digital format. At present there is a lack of standards within and between countries and regions, making it extremely difficult to join systems except on an analog basis. Since it is theoretically possible to adapt any format to any other, it will probably not be long until standards either exist everywhere or are made unnecessary by advances in signal processing.

2.6 HIGH FIDELITY AUDIO SERVICES

The delivery of high fidelity audio services by satellite to broadcast radio stations represents an effective although relatively small niche in the telecommunication business. Sound quality is excellent because of the wide audio bandwidth (specified anywhere between 5 and 15 kHz, depending on the application) and low noise provided over the satellite link. Using point-to-multipoint connectivity, either monaural or stereo sound is uplinked to the satellite typically with the single channel per carrier technique. The audio information can be sent in either analog or digital form, with the receive-only station performing the necessary conversion. One audio SCPC transmission occupies only a narrow slice of bandwidth in a transponder; therefore, a given transponder can carry one hundred or more audio signals. In another approach, several high fidelity audio channels are digitized and multiplexed together into a high speed stream of data. This transmission is uplinked to the satellite on a single carrier, and received at the radio station where the desired audio channel is demultiplexed.

2.6.1 Audio Network Arrangement

The network arrangement is nearly identical to that shown in Figure 2-6 for broadcast TV. An affiliated radio station would use one antenna to receive a continuous or scheduled network feed containing music, news, and national commercials. Local commercials and information are inserted at the radio station in the same way a TV broadcast station adds to its network feed. A second, roving antenna is used for sports events and for syndicated programming such as a nationwide talk show. Uplinks at every Major League baseball stadium in the US are operated by IDB Communications Group of Culver City, California, offering local radio stations convenient access to the away games of their home teams. In one business approach in the western United States, one particular radio station originates from Salt Lake City and is delivered by satellite to stations in several western cities. The main announcer is located in Salt Lake City, while the local stations only insert their specific call signs, weather forecasts, etc.

2.6.2 Alternative Delivery Concepts

Using satellite, it is possible to have private radio networks which are never actually broadcast over the air. The Supermarket Radio Network (SRN) of Atlanta, Georgia, provides individualized ''radio stations'' for supermarket chains. As shoppers stroll through the aisles, the specific SRN station is played over the store's audio system. The signal, received by a rooftop C-band antenna, contains popular music with a disc jockey who reads commercials targeted towards products which are already in the store. Rather that using SCPC, the radio channels are uplinked as subcarriers on a wideband carrier similar to the type used for video transmission. Satellite transmission is particularly valuable for this application, because the point-to-multipoint transmissions go directly from the studio to the store without passing through any (uncontrollable) terrestrial lines or tie points.

Chapter 3
Microwave Link Engineering

Microwave link engineering is the branch of communication engineering which deals with the analysis, design, implementation, and testing of radio paths which operate at frequencies above 100 MHz. Satellite and other microwave radio links obey certain rather predictable laws of nature, allowing engineers to design satellite networks on paper (or more likely on computer) with good accuracy. Said another way, after the satellite and earth stations are put in place, the links will almost always work as expected.

Understanding the fundamental principles of microwave link engineering is not difficult because of similarities with many aspects of common life. Microwave energy travels in straight lines through space in the same manner as a light beam. This should not be a surprise, since both light and microwaves are forms of electromagnetic energy, light being at much higher frequencies. Radio waves in general and microwaves in particular can propagate through space like light and heat, spreading out as they move further and further from the source. The waves travel through a vacuum at the universal speed of light, the same for all forms of electromagnetic energy. Microwaves can be kept from propagating by forcing them to travel within a closed metallic pipe called a *waveguide*. The physical similarity to common household pipes has led to the use of the term "plumbing" when referring to the waveguides found in earth stations and satellites. At the input end of the waveguide would be found the transmitter, the electronic device which generates the microwave energy on the proper frequency.

Microwave power levels and link effects are almost always expressed in terms of the decibel (dB), which is why it is important to introduce the concept early in the discussion. Converting a quantity to dB simply means taking the logarithm to the base 10, or common logarithm, and multiplying the result by ten. (As an historic note, the original unit of the Bell was found to be too large when applied in audio power measurement; hence, the tenth of a Bell or decibel was adopted.) Since the logarithm of the number 1 is equal to zero, a zero dB change simply means that there has been no change in the power level of the signal. You may recall that logarithms are exponents and in the case of logarithms to the base 10, they are exponents of the number 10. A 3-dB difference in power level is nearly equal to a factor of 2, while a factor of 10 is exactly equal to 10 dB (i.e., 10 log (10) = 10). When dealing with factors in an equation that multiply each other, it is convenient first to convert each factor to dB. Then the equation can be solved by summing the dB values instead of having to resort to multiplication. This is the basis for the link power balance calculation, reviewed later in this chapter.

The following sections review the propagation, generation, and reception of microwave signals, in preparation for studying unique aspects of satellite communication which are presented in Chapters 4, 5, and 6.

3.1 RADIO WAVE PROPAGATION

The process by which radio signals reach us from the transmitting station is called *radio wave propagation*. As was mentioned previously, radio waves represent a part of the electromagnetic spectrum, which encompasses radio, infrared, visible light, ultraviolet, and X rays (given in increasing order of frequency or decreasing order of wavelength). The reasons for selecting the microwave portion of the spectrum for satellite communication were presented in Chapter 1. All radio waves behave similarly in free space, but various forms of matter will produce interesting results when placed in their path. This is because this type of energy can be absorbed, scattered, bent, or reflected.

A question that comes to mind is, "How does such a wave, travelling at the speed of light, come into existence in the first place?" Since space consists of nothing, a radio wave does not propagate like the crest of a wave in the ocean. Instead, it is usually the result of the high-frequency vibration of electrons in a piece of wire or other conducting material of appropriate dimensions. Alternating current from a transmitter causes the electrons to vibrate back and forth, and by not flowing continuously in one direction, the electrons lose most of their energy by throwing it off into space. Energy which is not propagated into space is dissipated in the antenna structure in the form of heat. The same type of radiation goes on in a microwave oven which cooks food by exposing it to microwave energy given off by electrons in motion in the oven's microwave vacuum tube. Such intense radiation around a high power microwave transmitting station can "bake" you if you come too close. At sufficient distance from a transmitting antenna, the microwave energy will safely decrease in density. In fact, it will keep on decreasing in intensity by the inverse of the square of the distance from the source. This particular concept is the basis for link design, as discussed in subsequent paragraphs.

3.1.1 Isotropic Radiators in Free Space

The most fundamental type of radio antenna is the *isotropic source*, which is analogous to the light bulb illustrated in Figure 3-1. At a fixed radius from an isotropic source, which defines a sphere, the energy intensity is constant. The area of this sphere of uniform received energy is equal to the constant π (3.14159 . . .) multiplied by four times the square of the radius. It is the common practice to measure the intensity at the particular radius in units of watts per square meter, calculated by dividing the power of the isotropic source by the area of the sphere in square meters. RF power driving the isotropic source produces a constant power density at a fixed distance, and this density decreases as the point of reception moves further away from the source. Ignoring losses, it is theoretically possible to capture all of the transmitted power by collecting it with a closed surface around the source, regardless of distance.

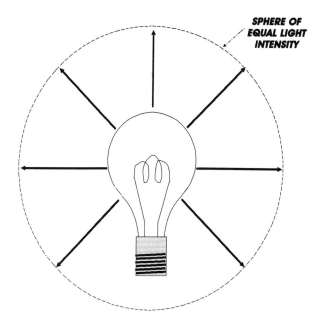

Fig. 3-1 An Isotropic Source Can Be Represented by a Light Bulb Radiating Energy in All Directions with Equal Intensity

Receiving antennas, therefore, work by way of the area that they expose to the RF energy radiating from the source. This is illustrated in Figure 3-2 by an isotropic source which radiates energy, shown as equally spaced rays, towards two antennas of equal area. One antenna surface (at distance D_2) is further away from the source than the other (at distance D_1). Notice how the closer area intercepts considerably more power than the more distant area. This is the reason why a radio signal becomes weaker as the receiver is moved further away from the transmitter. It also demonstrates the important concept of capture area, i.e., the relationship between the effective area of an antenna and the strength of the signal received by it. For example, the efficiency of a dish antenna is defined as the ratio of the effective area (i.e., the area that would perfectly capture the same amount of energy) to its physical area. Typical values of dish antenna efficiency are between 50 and 80%.

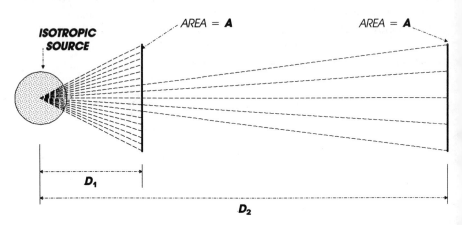

Fig. 3-2 The Radio Energy Captured by a Fixed Antenna Area Decreases as the Distance to the Source Increases

3.1.2 Directional Properties of an Antenna

The simple picture of the isotropic source does not represent most situations in satellite communication, because transmitting antennas are directive. The concept of *directivity* simply means that the antenna has the ability to focus the energy in specific directions, thereby increasing the effectiveness in a point-to-point link. Energy which would have been radiated in the other directions around the sphere is concentrated by the structure of the antenna and redirected so as to increase the intensity in the desired direction by many times. Another important property of an antenna is its transmit-receive capability at a given frequency, which is called *reciprocity*. This allows it to receive with precisely the same directional characteristics as it transmits. Figure 3-3 illustrates a simplified antenna gain pattern for transmission or reception with a main beam (the region of maximum directivity) oriented towards the right. The uniform pattern of an isotropic source is superimposed to scale on this directional antenna pattern for comparison. In addition to a main beam, every real antenna will operate in undesired directions, shown in the figure as a pair of sidelobes and a back lobe.

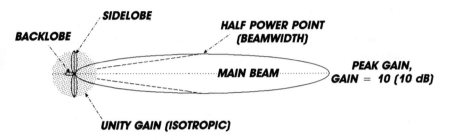

Fig. 3-3 Gain of a High Gain Antenna Expressed as a Power Ratio and Presented as a 360° Polar Plot

3.1.2.1   Antenna Gain

The gain of an antenna is the most important measure of its performance. It is customary in commercial satellite communication to define the gain in a specific direction by taking the ratio of intensity of the radiated energy to that of an isotropic source. Of course, both the antenna and isotropic source would be driven with the same amount of RF power. In Figure 3-3, the main beam of the antenna has a peak gain (i.e., in the direction of maximum radiation) of ten (10). This simply means that the antenna produces a signal ten times as strong as an isotropic source with equal input power and located the same distance away. The gain of an ideal dish antenna with a fixed effective area increases as the square of the frequency. Since antenna gain is a ratio of powers, it is a common practice to express it in dB. At microwave frequencies, gains of between 40 and 60 dB are typical for earth station antennas.

3.1.2.2   Antenna Patterns

There are a number of other useful definitions of antenna performance besides the peak gain. The half-power beamwidth (often called simply the *beamwidth*) is the angular width of the main beam measured between the points where the intensity is one-half that of the peak. An equally accurate name which is often used is the three-dB beamwidth, since the half power point is where the

intensity is three dB down. Assuming that the microwave link can accept a three-
dB decrease in signal strength, the half power beamwidth defines the range of
antenna pointing (alignment angle) over which the antenna or satellite can move
without causing the link to collapse. It is a common practice to allow only one
dB (25%) drop in signal power, which demands tighter antenna pointing accuracy
or satellite position control.

Presentations of antenna performance are called antenna patterns, illustrated in Figures 3-3 and 3-4 in terms of relative power and dB, respectively.
The sidelobes shown in the figures happen to have intensities equal to isotropic,
which means that their gain is one (i.e., 0 dB). Almost every antenna has a
backlobe in the opposite direction from the main beam. As shown in Figure 3-
3, however, the gain of the backlobe can be made to be less than unity, in this
case producing a negative gain of −3 dB (Figure 3-4). Sidelobes and backlobes
are those characteristics of earth station antennas which cause interference; therefore, much attention has been focused in recent years on reducing the gain of
these undesirable aspects. Isolation from interference is discussed in the following
paragraphs.

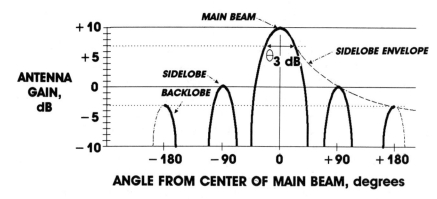

Fig. 3-4 Gain of a High Gain Antenna in dB for All Angles with Respect
to the Peak of the Main Beam Indicating the Worst-Case Envelope of Sidelobes

3.1.3 Isolation

The directive property of an antenna determines how effective it will be
for getting signal power from the source to the receiver. Any link can be degraded,
however, by signals on the same frequency which enter the receiving antenna
from a direction other than along the main beam. Likewise, a transmitting station
can cause degradation to other systems by sidelobe radiation. Any undesired

signal which can potentially degrade reception is called RF interference (RFI). There is a whole field of engineering study which is focused on the identification of sources of RFI, the establishment of criteria for acceptable operation in the presence of RFI (there is no such thing as RFI-free operation), and the development of techniques for countering its effects. Techniques such as beam shaping, cancellation, and shielding are effective in this regard.

All radio communication systems reuse frequencies; that is, there will be more than one radio station operating on any particular frequency at any particular time. To dedicate a frequency to one transmitter would be very inefficient, particularly because RFI can be controlled with practical means. This often requires cooperation among users (called *frequency coordination*) because, "one user's radio link is another's RFI." As was discussed in Chapter 1, several satellites can operate in the geostationary arc in the same frequency band, because each directional ground antenna can focus on one particular satellite, suppressing the RFI produced by adjacent satellites. This is made possible by antenna gain and directivity, illustrated in Figure 3-4. If, for example, the interfering satellite is located 45 degrees away from the satellite which we wish to receive (the "desired" satellite), then this particular antenna would suppress the RFI by at least 20 dB as compared to the desired satellite located on the peak of the main beam. Actual antennas used in satellite links provide 40 to 60 dB of peak gain with suppression at 45 degrees of 50 to 70 dB, which is adequate to allow satellite spacings as small as two degrees. There are usually several sidelobes in a real earth station antenna pattern. The first sidelobe is the strongest, being typically 15 to 20 dB down from and within one degree (more or less) of the peak gain. The control of these sidelobes demands careful design and installation of such antennas. A useful specification in this regard is the side-lobe envelope (shown in Figure 3-4), which defines the worst-case potential for RFI.

3.1.4 Polarization

Up to this point, we have dealt with radio propagation as if it were pure energy. There is a property of an electromagnetic wave called *polarization*, however, which depends on the orientation (or angle of rotation) of the transmitting antenna. You may be familiar with polarization as it relates to light. For example, three-dimensional (3-D) movies utilize vertically and horizontally polarized light to project appropriate left and right images on the screen simultaneously. The images are separated by invisible polarizing grids imbedded in the lenses of the viewer's glasses, where one lens is aligned vertically, while the other is aligned at a 90 degree angle (horizontally). Vertical and horizontal polarization can therefore "reuse" (i.e., use twice) a transmission path, such as the projection of a movie on a screen, or, as described below, a radio path.

3.1.4.1 Linear Polarization

The concept of polarization discrimination in radio communication is illustrated in Figure 3-5. Shown at the top is a type of simple wire or rod antenna called a *dipole*. Electrical current from the transmitter flows along the rods first upward and then downward, oscillating at the frequency of transmission. At C-band downlink frequencies, the rate of oscillation is 4,000,000,000 times per second (i.e., 4 GHz). As discussed previously, the alternating current in the rods produces an electromagnetic wave which propagates off into space. A dipole is not a true isotropic source, since there is no radiation along the direction of the rods. Instead, what is formed is a doughnut shaped pattern which is aligned horizontally. The electrical currents in the rods cause the electromagnetic wave to have its electric component lined up in the same direction, which is vertical for the illustration. This type of polarization is called *linear polarization* (LP), because the electric component has a fixed orientation. Horizontal LP is obtained when the dipole is rotated 90 degrees, so that the direction of the electrical current is also horizontal. Reception occurs when the electric component of the incoming wave produces a current in the receiving antenna, which cannot occur if the conductors of the receiving antenna are improperly aligned. In the lower half of Figure 3-5, horizontally polarized transmitting and receiving antennas provide for the maximum amount of power to be carried ("coupled") between them. This pair of antennas is said to be *co-polarized*. A vertically polarized receiving antenna, which is perpendicular to and therefore *cross-polarized* with the transmitter, will minimize the amount of coupled energy.

Microwave antennas make use of waveguide structures and solid reflecting surfaces, because they are much more efficient and predictable than wires and rods. The relationship between antenna orientation and wave polarization is shown in Figure 3-6 for a waveguide horn, which is nothing more than a slighty flared end of a piece of waveguide. Instead of electrical currents, the waveguide carries a tightly focused electromagnetic wave with the electric components extending between the parallel walls. Creation of these guided waves in the first place is accomplished with a radiating element (not shown) composed of one-half of a dipole inserted into the waveguide at the input end. Note how the electric components vary in intensity along the width of the horn, being a maximum at the center and dropping to zero at the edges. This particular natural property of a simple horn is used effectively in the design of reflector antennas. In any case, the radiated electromagnetic wave is linearly polarized, just like that from a dipole.

As with wire antennas, maximum coupling occurs when the transmitter and receiving horns are co-polarized. If one horn is rotated 90 degrees with respect to the other, then minimum coupling results, and they are cross-polarized.

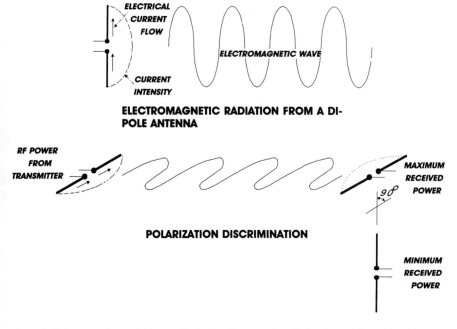

Fig. 3-5 Properties of Linear Polarization as Radiated and Received by Dipole Rod Antennas

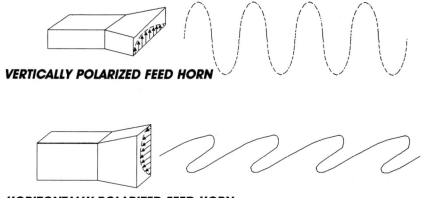

Fig. 3-6 Linear Polarization of Microwave Radiation from Vertically and Horizontally Polarized Feed Horns

The performance of LP at intermediate points follows a simple law: the relative energy coupled is equal to the square of the cosine of the angle. This characteristic is plotted at the left of Figure 3-7 for the co-polarized case, i.e., for the level of signal received as the receiving antenna is rotated from maximum coupling to minimum coupling. An ideal LP wave and antenna are assumed, for which the coupling goes from a maximum of one to a minimum of zero. Maximum coupling will always occur at some angle and minimum coupling will be as close to zero as physically possible. Properly designed and installed antennas can deliver minimum coupling values of 0.0001, or −40 dB.

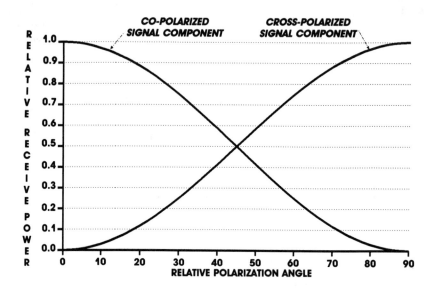

Fig. 3-7 Relative Receive Power as a True Ratio for the Co-Polarized and Cross-Polarized Signals in a Linearly Polarized Link as the Polarization Angle of the Receiving Antenna Is Rotated

Probably the most important application of polarization is in *frequency reuse*, where two cross-polarized signals are transmitted at the same time on the same frequency. The right-hand curve in Figure 3-7 shows how the level of the cross-polarized signal increases as the receiving antenna is rotated from zero to 90 degrees. Notice how at 45 degrees, both signals are at the same level. Figure 3-8 plots coupling in dB, termed *polarization isolation*, between the desired and undesired polarizations. Maximum isolation occurs at zero offset angle, i.e., where the receiving antenna is aligned in polarization with the transmitting antenna and the undesired polarization is "nulled" out (minimized). Alignment for maximum coupling is not particularly critical (plus or minus five degrees of error introduces very little loss of signal); the cross polarization isolation is extremely critical, however, and precise alignment is a necessity. The maximum value of isolation of 40 dB in Figure 3-8 corresponds to the typical value described in the previous paragraph. All modern satellite communication systems use polarization isolation to increase the capacity of the particular orbit position. Therefore, users must employ antennas on the ground which meet polarization requirements and which can be adjusted from time to time by rotating the feedhorn for minimum RFI.

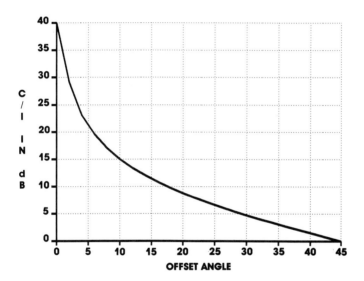

Fig. 3-8 Polarization Isolation in dB for a Linearly Polarized RF Signal as a Function of the Offset Angle from Maximum Isolation

3.1.4.2 Circular Polarization

Another type of polarization which is used in INTELSAT and broadcasting satellites is *circular polarization* (CP). To understand the composition of CP, first observe that linear polarization can be represented in the form of a vector, where the direction of the vector is in line with the electric component and its length is proportional to the power of the signal. This vector is always perpendicular to the direction of propagation. Circular polarization is a particular combination of two equal LP waves which are cross-polarized with respect to each other. Normally, the vector sum (resultant) lies at a 45 degree angle between the two equal magnitude perpendicular vectors and has a power which is the sum of the two powers. However, in CP, the same two vectors are out of phase with each other by 90 degrees. This is accomplished by first splitting the transmit signal in two at the source and delaying one component by a quarter period before radiating them through a dual-polarized antenna element. What is produced is a resultant vector which rotates like a corkscrew, illustrated in Figure 3-9, as it propagates through space. The sense of polarization is either rotating to the right (right-hand CP) or to the left (left-hand CP), determined by which linear component is delayed with respect to the other. Frequency reuse is possible, because left-hand and right-hand CP waves are cross-polarized with respect to each other, just like vertical and horizontal LP waves.

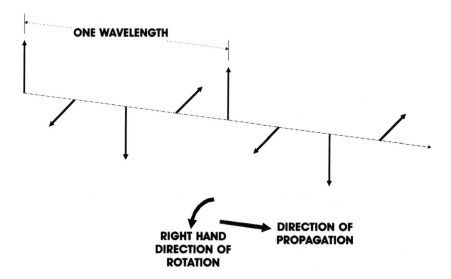

Fig. 3-9 Rotation of the Electric Component During the Propagation of a Circularly Polarized RF Signal

The advantage of CP is that the receiving antenna does not need to be aligned in polarization, since the electric component rotates 360 degrees at rate equal to the frequency of transmission. A receiving antenna would consist of combined vertical and horizontal LP elements, allowing the components to be coupled and recombined with the proper phase relationship. The sense of combining determines whether right-hand or left-hand CP will be recovered. The amount of polarization isolation thus obtained, however, is not as high as that achieved by LP because of the complexity of the microwave hardware design.

3.1.5 Propagation Losses

The free-space path between transmitter and receiver passes through a combination of atmospheric phenomena which can be divided into those which are constant and those which are both time variant and random. Taken together, these losses reduce the strength of the received signal and can cause its level to vary over time even to the point where the signal fades away. This is illustrated in Figure 3-10, which shows received signal strength (*signal level*) as a function of time during a period of rapid variation (*fading*). The mean-signal level results from the constant and predictable losses on the link; the random losses cause the level to decrease and occasionally drop below the acceptable level. When the signal dips below *threshold*, it is unusable for communication purposes because of excessive noise and, in the case of digital links, a loss of synchronization as well. The difference in dB between the mean level and threshold is called the *link margin*, which is discussed at the end of this chapter.

Summarized in Table 3-1 are the primary losses which must be determined and accounted for in any microwave link design. Certain of the losses are critical in all satellite systems while others will only be of concern in specific cases. Each is described in the following paragraphs.

PROPAGATION MODE	IMPORTANCE TO SATELLITE	TYPICAL dB
FREE SPACE	DOMINATING	200
ABSORPTION	NEARLY CONSTANT	0.5 to 2
RAIN ATTENUATION	SEVERE AT TIMES	2 to 10
REFRACTION	LOW ELEVATION ANGLES	0 to 3
SCATTERING	LOCAL INTERFERENCE	
DIFFRACTION	LOCAL INTERFERENCE	
MULTIPATH	OCCASIONAL WIDE SIGNAL VARIATIONS	0.5 to 6

Table 3-1 Comparison of Significant Propagation and Fading Modes Which Affect Microwave Links Over Earth-to-Space Paths

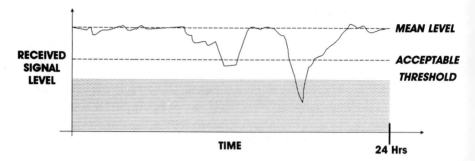

Fig. 3-10 Variation of the Received Carrier Power on a Microwave Link
During a Period of Severe Fluctuation (Fading)

3.1.5.1   Free-Space Loss

We have already covered in some detail the mechanism for free-space loss
which diminishes signal strength due to distance alone. For one square meter of
antenna area, the captured energy is simply

$$E = \frac{P_t}{4 \pi R^2} , \; \text{W/m}^2$$

where

P_t = the radiated power in watts(W),
R = the distance in meters(m).

Typical distance from a point on the earth to a satellite in GEO is 35,890
kilometers or 22,300 miles.

This relationship, which should be recognized from the previous discussion
on isotropic radiation, does not depend on frequency. It is a common practice
to introduce frequency into the equation by splitting apart the propagation loss
from the gain of the receiving antenna (here assumed to have an effective area
of one meter). The free-space path loss, which would be in the denominator of
the previous equation, is

$$a_0 = 1755 \, F^2 \, R^2 ,$$

where

F = the frequency in GHz.

The lower case *a* is used here to indicate that it is a factor and not expressed in dB. For a satellite in geostationary orbit at a distance of 22,300 miles and for frequencies in GHz, the free-space path loss in dB is approximately

$$A_0 = 184 + 20 \log F.$$

3.1.5.2 Absorption

RF energy will be absorbed to some extent (and converted into heat) as it passes through clear air, water vapor, and smog. The absorption is essentially constant, amounting to under one dB at C and Ku bands. As frequency increases above 15 GHz, the constituents of the atmosphere reach individual points of resonance and absorption can become very high and even total. The bands of frequencies around 22 and 60 GHz correspond to resonances for water vapor and oxygen, respectively, and are not employed for either uplinks or downlinks. Direct links between satellites, called *intersatellite links*, will bypass the atmosphere and hence may utilize the absorptive bands.

3.1.5.3 Rain Attenuation

After free-space loss, the most detrimental effect on commercial satellite links is rain attenuation, which results from absorption and scattering of microwave energy by rain drops. This loss, which increases with frequency, was discussed in Chapter 1 in the comparison of frequency bands and presented in Figure 1-11. Rain attenuation is not predictable with great accuracy, but estimates can be made which allow links to be designed. Obviously dry seasons and regions of the world with low rainfall would not suffer greatly from this phenomenon. Links to regions with heavy thunderstorm activity, however, should be provided with greater power margins or else service will not be maintained with sufficient reliability to satisfy commercial requirements. Because of rain cell geometry, the lower the elevation angle from the ground the greater is the amount of attenuation from a given amount of rainfall. Heavy rainfall will also alter the polarization of the signal (because raindrops are not spherical), tending to reduce isolation between cross-polarized transmissions. This phenomenon is called *depolarization*. For example, the maximum isolation in Figure 3-8 will decrease at Ku band in heavy rain from 40 dB to approximately 20 dB. This would not be detrimental to most transmissions, if appropriate adjustments are made in the link design. Depolarization in rain is not particularly harmful at C band and the lower parts of Ku band, but can greatly reduce isolation at frequencies above 15 GHz. Raindrop geometry causes depolarization of CP transmissions to be more severe than for LP.

3.1.5.4 Refraction

The lower portion of the atmosphere, called the troposphere, decreases in density upward from the earth's surface. Electromagnetic waves are bent by *refraction* as they pass through this medium, as illustrated in Figure 3-11; the satellite appears to have a different or *virtual* position lying along a slightly different path than that to the true position. This characteristic is taken into account in terrestrial microwave system design by slightly decreasing the curvature of the profile map used to plot the line-of-sight path. In satellite links, the bending is less significant because of the higher angle through the atmosphere.

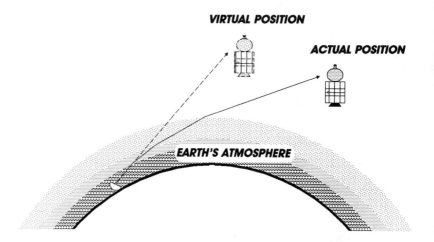

Fig. 3-11 Refraction Is the Bending of a Microwave Signal as it Passes Through the Layers of the Atmosphere

Unstable atmospheric conditions like temperature inversions, clouds, and fog produce discontinuities and fluctuations in what would otherwise be a uniform air density distribution. The consequent random, temporary bending can cause significant signal fading akin to rain attenuation. The effect is more pronounced for paths which are nearly parallel to the earth (line of sight microwave and satellite links at low elevation angles from the earth). Generally, refraction by itself will not impair typical satellite links, since the amount of bending is small relative to the beamwidth of the satellite and earth station antennas.

The phenomenon of *multipath*, discussed in a subsequent paragraph, is the result of refraction in the ionosphere, which is the layer of ionized particles at around 100 miles altitude. The ionosphere will completely reflect frequencies between 0.1 and 30 MHz under certain conditions, producing the "sky wave" effect which allows short-wave transmissions to cover long distances. In addition to refraction, the ionosphere will rotate the polarization of microwave transmissions (*Faraday effect*), although this can be compensated for by the appropriate adjustment of feed-horn angle at the receiving earth station. One of the reasons why CP was first used in satellite communication was to avoid the need for adjusting feed polarization angles to compensate for Faraday effect.

3.1.5.5 Scattering and Diffraction

It was mentioned that water droplets scatter microwave signals. This would reduce the direct path power level, spraying some of it back toward the source. At an earth station site, the occasional scatter can place RFI in the direction of terrestrial microwave receivers which otherwise would have been adequately protected. *Diffraction*, on the other hand, occurs when microwaves encounter and bend over a physical obstacle such as a building or mountain. This topic was discussed in Chapter 2 in relation to sharing of frequencies between satellite and terrestrial radio services. Frequency coordination of earth stations takes rain scatter and diffraction into account by requiring additional protection margin against such random RFI. Otherwise, the effects of scatter and diffraction can largely be ignored in commercial satellite communication.

3.1.5.6 Multipath

Also referred to as *scintillation*, multipath is the result of the same RF signal taking both a direct path and a slightly longer refracted path, the latter arriving at the receiving antenna delayed in time from the former. This is illustrated in Figure 3-12 for refraction caused by discontinuities in the ionosphere (i.e., ionospheric scintillation). The twinkling of a star is a multipath phenomenon, where two light rays, one direct and the other bent back in the troposphere, reach the eye and combine to produce a variation in light intensity.

In the RF transmission case, the direct and refracted paths combine using vector addition, illustrated in Figure 3-13. Shown at the top are the two signal paths reaching the same antenna, wherein they combine to form a resultant signal (this is because both paths contain the same signal, although the refracted path, being longer, introduces a delay or phase shift). The two drawings at the left of Figure 3-13 represent the extremes: minimal effect at the top and maximum effect (cancellation) at the bottom. The direct path is shown as the vertical signal

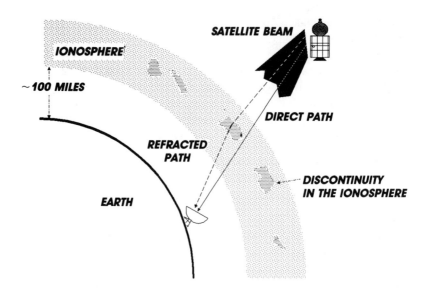

Fig. 3-12 Multipath Propagation Caused by Ionospheric Scintillation

vector of constant length. Added to this on a vector basis is the refracted signal (dotted vector) which can arrive at any random relative phase angle as indicated by the circle about the tip of the direct path vector. The resultant received signal vector, shown as a heavy arrow, is only slightly affected by the weak refracted signal. An increase or a decrease in strength occurs, depending on the relative phase angles.

If the refracted signal is comparable in strength to the direct path, then cancellation can occur when the relative phase is approximately 180 degrees. There can also be significant amplification (up to 6 dB) when the two vectors instantaneously combine in phase. Fortunately, the unstable conditions that produce this in the ionosphere only occur twice annually and only for relatively short periods of time. Earth stations near the geomagnetic equator experience the most severe scintillation fades during these periods of activity.

Tropospheric multipath works on the same principle and can be significant on line-of-sight microwave paths and on satellite links at low elevation angles from the ground. It is a common practice to assume that power margin provided for rain attenuation will satisfy requirements for both types of multipath fading as well.

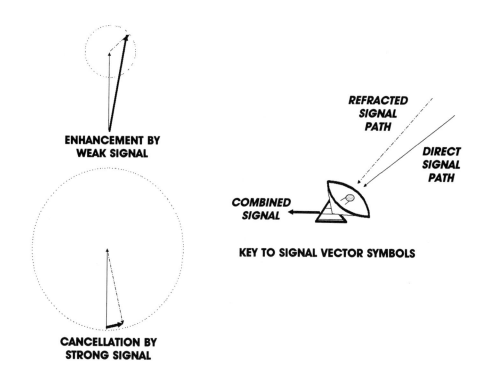

Fig. 3-13 Multipath Signals Produce Enhancement or Cancellation of the Direct Path Signal When Received Through a Common Antenna as Illustrated by Vector Diagrams

3.2 RF POWER GENERATION AND RECEPTION

The entry and exit points to the propagation medium are provided by the transmitting and receiving stations whose principal elements are reviewed in this section. The antenna, as previously discussed, is the means of converting electrical energy at microwave frequencies into electromagnetic waves, and *vice versa*. A transmitting station consists of equipment which impresses (modulates) the information to be sent on an RF signal called the *carrier*, places it on the appropriate frequency, and amplifies it to a high enough power level to reach the distant end. A receiving station works in the exact opposite direction and has the additional requirement to minimize the RF noise which enters the link both externally and internally to the receiving site. Deferred to Chapters 5 and 6 are detailed descriptions of the electronics of the satellite and earth station, respectively. All discussion is around the simplified block diagram of the respective station, showing a single chain of key components.

Figure 3-14 portrays a single transmitting chain of a microwave station, with the signal input at the left and the RF output from the transmitting antenna at the right. The signal to be transmitted consists of information in electrical form, such as one or more voice channels for telephone service, digital data in the form of a high speed bit stream, or a composite video signal such as that delivered from a video tape recorder.

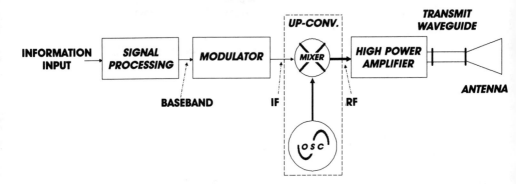

Fig. 3-14 Simplified Block Diagram of a Microwave Transmitting System Capable of Baseband Signal Processing, Modulation, Frequency Translation, and High Power Amplification

3.2.1 Transmitting Station

3.2.1.1. Signal Processing and Modulation

Within the signal processing element of the station (the first element to be encountered), the signal format is changed in some manner to prepare it better for transmission through the link. *Analog* processing used in earlier equipment usually introduced frequency compensation called *preemphasis*; also, the *Dolby noise reduction* (DNR) audio technique, used in cassette tapes and on FM radio broadcasts, is a form of signal processing which dynamically modifies the audio volume. Both preemphasis and DNR processing must be reversed at the receiving station or else the distant user will be delivered a distorted signal. In the last several years, *digital* signal processing has become widespread because of its ability both to improve quality and to compress the bandwidth of transmission. If the signal input is analog in form, then such digital signal processing must include the conversion from analog to digital (*A/D conversion*), wherein the signal becomes a bit stream.

The analog or digital output of the signal processing stage is referred to as the *baseband*. It is the purpose of the *modulator* to take the baseband and add it to an RF carrier. This process of *modulation* is also what goes on within a data modem used to interface a personal computer to a telephone line. The type of modulator used in a microwave station, however, handles a wideband baseband input such as that obtained from either a high capacity data stream measured in Mb/s or an entire video signal. The opposite of modulation is simply *demodulation*, which is the process whereby the baseband is removed from the RF carrier. More explanation of the characteristics of the baseband and the quality of demodulation is provided in the last section of this chapter and in Chapter 4.

3.2.1.2   Baseband to RF Chain

The RF carrier coming from the modulator is typically not at microwave frequencies but rather is centered within a standard frequency channel called the *intermediate frequency* (IF). Most transmitting and receiving stations use 70 MHz as the IF, allowing modulators and demodulators to be conveniently interchanged and interconnected by patch cords and coaxial switches. RF bandwidth is proportional to baseband bandwidth in most linear analog and digital modulation systems. In frequency modulation and other nonlinear modulation systems, the RF bandwidth is not simply proportional to the baseband bandwidth but rather will follow a complex mathematical law. Another point is that there are cases where the RF bandwidth is larger than 70 MHz, making it infeasible to use 70 MHz as the IF frequency. This can be overcome by directly modulating a carrier at the microwave frequency of transmission or, more likely, by using an adequately high IF such as 140 MHz.

The function of the *upconverter* is to translate the carrier without modification from IF to the desired microwave frequency of transmission. Within the upconverter is a microwave mixer and a *local oscillator* (LO). Translation is governed by a simple mathematical relationship which states that the output frequency equals the sum of the input IF frequency and the frequency of the

LO. For example, if the IF is at 70 MHz and the LO is at 6030 MHz, then the output RF frequency is 6100 MHz. From a practical standpoint, the RF frequency is usually assigned by someone else and the IF is fixed. Therefore, the LO frequency must be selected properly in order to put the RF carrier in the right place. Modern upconverters are *frequency agile*, which means that the LO can be tuned from the front panel much the same way as a TV set or car radio. The most convenient and versatile type of agile LO employs a digital *frequency synthesizer*, allowing any frequency to be chosen from the front panel or even by remote control.

3.2.1.3 High Power Amplifiers

The last active electronic element of a transmitting station is the *high power amplifier* (HPA). Because all processing and frequency translation has been accomplished by prior stages, the only function of the HPA is to increase the power of the microwave carrier from the low output of the upconverter to the power level needed to achieve satisfactory link operation. The HPA must operate at the assigned microwave frequency and cover sufficient bandwidth to accommodate any anticipated carrier type. Examples of typical C and Ku-band HPA devices and their power capability are shown in Figure 3-15. Practical commercial HPAs which do not require water cooling have been chosen for this presentation.

Power levels in the thousands of watts can be provided by the *klystron power amplifier* (KPA). Within the klystron microwave vacuum tube there is a resonant waveguide cavity which must be tuned to the specific frequency of operation. The operating bandwidth of a KPA is in the range of 50 to 100 MHz, making it necessary to retune the internal structure when changing transponders. This difficulty is overcome with the *traveling-wave tube amplifier* (TWTA) for which bandwidths as wide as 1000 MHz are possible. Because TWTAs are used extensively in satellites, a detailed discussion of their design and properties is included in Chapter 5. Practical TWTAs can be found with power outputs of from 10 to as much as 600 watts, although 10 kW water-cooled TWTAs were used in early INTELSAT earth stations. Both the TWT and klystron are vacuum tubes which require sophisticated high-voltage power supplies, and both employ heated cathodes to emit electrons for use in the process of amplification. In the case of HPAs used in earth stations, it is unavoidable that both types of high-power tube will wear out and need to be replaced after a few years of operation. TWTAs used in satellites operate at lower powers and are designed somewhat differently to have lifetimes in excess of ten years.

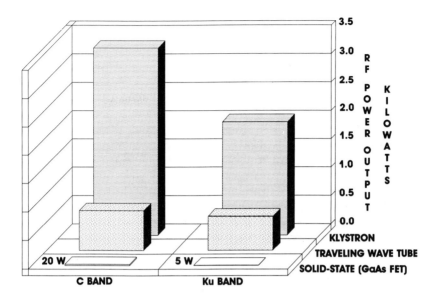

Fig. 3-15 RF Output Power Capability at C and Ku Bands of Standard Microwave Power Amplifiers

In low-power applications such as for VSATs, *solid-state power amplifiers* (SSPAs) can be employed. A detailed discussion of SSPAs can be found in Chapter 5. Figure 3-15 presents SSPA power levels available in 1987: up to 20 watts at C band and 5 watts at Ku band. It is always the case that technological advancement and business motivation lead to the availability of higher powered solid-state devices within just a few years.

3.2.2 Receiving Station

The reverse process found in the receiving station is illustrated in Figure 3-16. Since the microwave signal collected by the receiving antenna is very weak, it is first necessary to raise the power to a level which can be accommodated by the processing elements. This is performed by the *low-noise amplifier* (LNA), whose gain must meet the requirements described above. However, the internal noise contribution of the amplifier must be held small enough or else the weak signal input literally can be buried in noise.

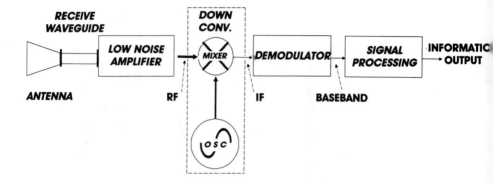

Fig. 3-16 Simplified Block Diagram of a Microwave Receiving System Capable of Low Noise Amplification, Frequency Conversion, Demodulation, and Baseband Signal Processing

3.2.2.1 Low-Noise Amplifiers

It is possible to express noise in terms of an equivalent noise temperature in kelvins (K). This scale begins at the noiseless state of absolute zero and measures the average random energy of motion of electrons within the receiver electronics. According to the theory, the random energy of the electrons is proportional to the noise power which overlays the desired signals within the passband of the amplifier. A super-cooled device is ideal because it will not contribute noise to the system.

Figure 3-17 compares the internal noise level of three classes of common LNAs, indicating that C-band noise temperatures are lower than those obtainable at Ku band. The amplifier with the lowest internal noise and, unfortunately, the highest price, is the *parametric amplifier* (PARAMP). In addition to being costly, the PARAMP is also considerably more complicated electronically and tends to have the greatest chance for failure. Most ground stations and satellites now utilize solid-state low-noise amplifiers using *field effect transistors* (FETs) manufactured from gallium arsenide (GaAs) semiconductor material. GaAs FET amplifiers are almost twice as noisy as PARAMPS, but the solid-state devices are extremely rugged and reliable. Some noise reduction can be accomplished, as shown in Figure 3-17, by lowering the physical temperature of the FETs using a device called a *Peltier cooler*. This confirms that noise temperature is not just a measure of noise power but is also directly related to how physically hot the amplifier actually is.

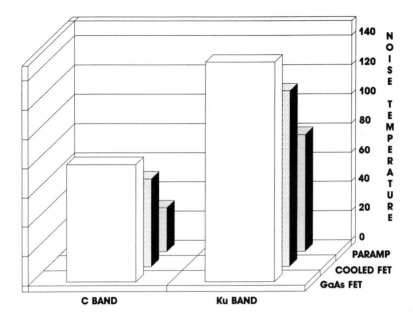

Fig. 3-17 Effective Noise Temperature in Kelvins at C and Ku Bands of Standard Microwave Low Noise Amplifiers

3.2.2.2   RF to Baseband Chain

The remaining electronic elements of a receiving station work to reverse the process of the corresponding element of the transmitting station. Frequency translation from microwave to IF is accomplished by the *downconverter*, with the LO appropriately tuned again to the difference frequency. As discussed in Chapter 1, the satellite's downlink frequency is offset from its uplink frequency. Hence, to receive the same carrier, the frequency of the LO of the downconverter would differ from that of the upconverter by the fixed frequency offset (2225 MHz for C band) introduced by the satellite repeater. To complete a previous example, the downconverter LO should be set to (6100–2225)–70 MHz, which is equal to 3085 MHz. After demodulation and baseband signal processing, the information is rendered suitable for delivery to the user.

In general, integration of two or more of these functional elements into a single package is a trend in commercial satellite communication. Low-cost receive-only earth stations and VSATs economize on electronics by combining the LNA and downconverter into an integrated unit called an LNC (*low-noise converter*) or LNB (*low-noise block converter*). A transmit package containing a signal processor, modulator, and upconverter is called an *exciter*.

3.2.3   Link Budget Analysis

The key station elements and propagation phenomena having been described, it is now possible to review the analysis and prediction of link performance. Figure 3-18 shows a simplified microwave link with a key parameter indicated for each element. The transmitter can be characterized by the HPA power output, with the transmitting waveguide introducing some loss as it carries the power to the transmitting antenna. The electromagnetic wave propagates outward from the antenna into the medium where it is subjected to various losses, the free-space loss being dominant. The small amount of signal power gathered by the receiving antenna is carried through waveguide to the LNA of the receiver. It is possible to characterize the receiver by the minimum acceptable power level, which takes into account the RF noise as well as the quality desired by the user.

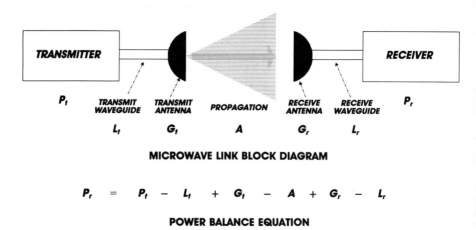

MICROWAVE LINK BLOCK DIAGRAM

$$P_r \;=\; P_t \;-\; L_t \;+\; G_t \;-\; A \;+\; G_r \;-\; L_r$$

POWER BALANCE EQUATION

Fig. 3-18 The Relationship Between the Critical Elements of a Microwave Link and the Power Balance Equation

3.2.3.1 Power Balance Equation

The simple mathematical relationship shown at the bottom of Figure 3-18 is the power balance equation. As stated above, the parameters of the link are actually multiplicative factors in an equation. It is a common practice, however, to express all of them in dB, because this reduces the analysis to addition and subtraction. The power balance in dB can be stated simply: the power received equals the power transmitted plus all gains and minus all losses. Transmitter power is expressed in dB relative to one watt, or dBW. For example, 1 watt is by definition 0 dBW; 2 watts is 3 dBW; 10 watts is 10 dBW; 100 watts is 20 dBW; and so on. The power balance equation is usually arranged in a table called a *link budget*, in which each parameter of the link is provided with its own explanation and quantity.

3.2.3.2 Typical Link Budget (Ku Band)

A typical link budget for a Ku-band satellite downlink is presented in Table 3-2. The first entry is the RF power output of the transmitter, expressed first in watts and then converted into dBW. Transmit waveguide loss of one dB (25% power reduction) is subtracted while the gain of the spacecraft antenna in the direction of the receiving earth station is added. A detailed discussion of spacecraft antenna design and performance is given in Chapter 5. It is customary to show a subtotal at this point called the *effective isotropic radiated power* (EIRP), indicating how the satellite is performing as compared to an isotropic source with one watt of RF drive power (i.e., 0 dBW). The value of 45 dBW shown in the table is typical for current medium-power Ku-band satellites in the fixed satellite service (FSS). By expressing this EIRP as approximately 31,600 watts of power (i.e., $10^{4.5}$), the effectiveness of spacecraft antenna gain is clearly evident.

The link budget contains a single entry of -205.6 dB of free-space loss for the 12 GHz path of 22,300 miles between satellite and earth station. Path losses such as rain attenuation which are random in nature are evaluated separately against the overall link margin. The next two items relate to the receiving earth station—the peak gain of an assumed 2.5-meter antenna and 1.5 dB of waveguide loss. The combined power balance yields a received power of -114.7 dBW at the input to the earth station LNA and receive electronics. For this hypothetical link, assume that we have determined ahead of time that the required power at the entry point should be greater than -121.6 dBW. This happens to represent the power needed to produce a visible TV picture and is referred to as the

PARAMETER	VALUE	UNITS
Transmit Power	40	W
	16.0	dBW
Transmit Waveguide Loss	-1.0	dB
Transmit Antenna Gain	30.0	dB
Effective Isotropic Radiated Power (EIRP)	45.0	dBW
Free-Space Loss	-205.6	dB
Receive Antenna Gain, 2.5 m	47.4	dB
Receive Waveguide Loss	-1.5	dB
Received Power	-114.7	dBW
Threshold Power	-121.6	dBW
Link Margin	6.9	dB

Table 3-2. Typical Link Budget for a Ku-Band Satellite Downlink

threshold. The difference in dB between the actual and threshold received powers is the link margin (6.9 dB in this example). This "bottom line" of a link budget indicates if the received power is adequate to meet user requirements in the face of rain attenuation and other variable and uncontrollable effects.

Actual link budgets include the effects of RF noise by computing the ratio of carrier power to noise power, called the *carrier to noise ratio* (*C/N*). The carrier power is determined exactly as shown in Table 3-2. As discussed in the section on LNAs, the main source of noise is the receiving system of the earth station. The total system noise temperature is equal to the sum of the equivalent receiver noise temperature (Figure 3-16) and the background antenna temperature, which is typically 40 K. Uplink noise within the spacecraft receiver contributes a lesser amount to the total link noise and is ignored in the present example.

Figure 3-19 presents the noise power in dBW as a function of frequency and bandwidth, assuming a standard GaAs FET type of LNA. The noise power in the bandwidth of the RF carrier in question is equal to KTB, where K is Boltzmann's constant, T is the receiving system noise temperature in kelvins and B is the bandwidth in Hz. It is convenient to express the result in dBW to facilitate computing the *C/N* in dB by subtraction from the carrier power in a link budget. Relating Figure 3-18 to Table 3-2 and assuming an RF bandwidth of 36 MHz, the threshold value of *C/N* in the example is equal to -121.6 dBW

$- (-131.6 \text{ dBW}) = 10 \text{ dB}$. The threshold C/N of 10 dB for analog FM video is adequate to produce a picture of acceptable quality with only slight impairment from impulse noise (visible occasionally as short horizontal streaks in the picture called *sparkles*). The following section expands on the topics of threshold performance and margin.

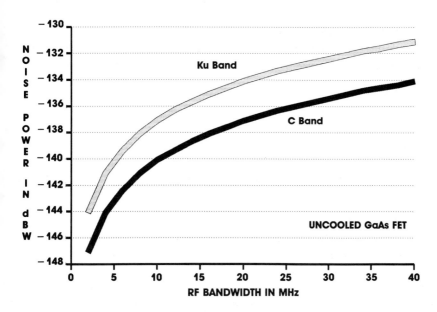

Fig. 3-19 Receiving System Noise Power versus RF Bandwidth and Frequency Band

3.3 OVERALL LINK QUALITY

The elements of the link and the power-balance equation are useful concepts for doing a preliminary link evaluation. As explained at the conclusion of the last section, noise from the receiving equipment is relatively easy to consider if the threshold is already defined. One of the more complex problems in microwave link engineering is to predict how a particular signal will be effected by the noise, which is random in nature, and by interference from other radio carriers. This section reviews some of the factors which determine the actual quality and threshold for digital and analog receivers. A clear understanding of the threshold of the link allows the engineer to predict how much margin will be available to overcome fading from the various sources discussed at the beginning of this chapter.

3.3.1   How Noise and Interference Affect a Microwave Link

Both noise and interference will degrade service quality and if not controlled will at times render the link unusable. Interference, as explained previously, is often due to the RF transmission of someone else. On the other hand, noise is totally random in nature, because it results from the random motion of electrons or other elemental particles in the environment or within the receiving equipment. Pure *"white" noise* is most common on satellite links and produces random voltage fluctuations which follow a normal (Gaussian) distribution. The term "white" refers to the fact that the frequency spectrum does not have discrete components at specific frequencies but rather is a continuum of frequencies like white light. Ideal white noise, running from zero to infinite frequency, is physically impossible, since it would represent infinite power. Noise is sufficiently white if it is constant over the bandwidth of the signal in question. The density of the noise power (*noise power density*) in watts per Hertz is equal to an equivalent noise temperature in kelvins times Boltzmann's constant (− 228.6 in dB terms). This simple relationship demonstrates why the noise performance of a LNA of a receiving earth station is rated in terms of an equivalent noise temperature.

As an example, the effect of white noise on a modulated carrier containing binary data can be shown using time waveforms, presented in Figure 3-20. The noise-free case is shown in (a) in the form of digital information impressed on a carrier. The transition from binary "1" to "O" occurs where the phase of the sinewave reverses. This type of modulation is called *phase-shift keying* (PSK, discussed in Chapter 4) because the shifting (flipping) of phase by 180 degrees is the means by which information is transmitted. It is the job of the demodulator-signal processor to detect this phase reversal in order to convey to the user the proper bit sense. The PSK signal is sent through the link and enters the receiver along with white noise inherent in the electronics. This noise is depicted in Figure 3-20 (b), where the mean voltage is zero and the standard deviation of the noise is approximately one-half of the carrier amplitude. Since power is proportional to the square of the voltage, the true ratio of carrier power to noise power is 4, or equivalently 6 dB. This rather high relative-noise (low C/N) level yields the sum of carrier plus noise shown in Figure 3-20 (c), where the carrier appears to be somewhat obliterated by noise spikes. A well designed demodulator and digital signal processor can, however, detect the transition from the "1" to "O" state in most cases. Since noise is random and can statistically reach a voltage greater than the signal amplitude, there will be occasions when the demodulator will be confused and make the wrong choice. The assumed binary digit will then be incorrect (i.e., a "1" instead of a "0" or *vice versa*, depending on what was sent). It should now be possible to visualize that the strength of the signal relative to the noise will determine the rate at which these errors in detection are made. This is a significant area of engineering study in the communication field and some of the most important breakthroughs in digital technology allow sending and receiving equipment to identify errors and reverse them prior to delivery to the user.

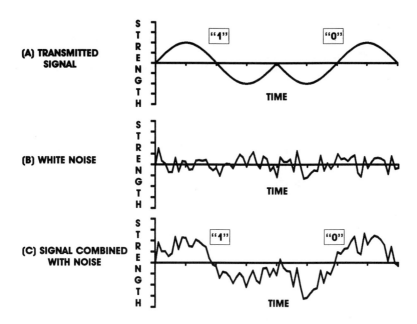

Fig. 3-20 A Digital Phase-Shift Keyed Signal Combines with White Noise to Produce a Distorted Signal Waveform Which Must Be Detected by the Receiver

Wideband interfering signals can be treated as white noise and often are. If the interference is narrower in bandwidth than the desired signal, however, then more sophisticated analysis techniques or even direct measurement must be employed.

3.3.2 Carrier to Noise Ratio

As discussed in the previous section, the strength of the carrier relative to the noise is what determines the quality of transmission and not the absolute level of what comes out. This can be understood by realizing that the power level of the baseband signal from the receiving station's signal processor can be raised by simple power amplification. The noise that is present, however, will also be amplified. Only by suppressing the noise at the input to the receiver can the quality of transmission be improved. This is why the true performance of the link is measured by the ratio of RF carrier power to noise power.

A receiving system showing a carrier, white noise, and a single source of interference is presented in Figure 3-21. The frequency spectrum in Figure 3-22 is similar to the display on a microwave *spectrum analyzer*, a very useful piece of test equipment. The figure shows a constant spectrum of white noise, providing what is referred to as a *noise floor*. The vertical scale is linear, measuring power density in terms of watts per Hertz. The symbol N_0 is used to refer to the constant power density of the noise floor. Piercing through the floor are the desired carrier occupying bandwidth BW_c and centered at frequency F_c, along with an interfering carrier at frequency F_i. The total noise power, N, over the bandwidth of the carrier is the product $N_0 BW_c$. An actual spectrum analyzer would have a vertical scale measured in dB to simplify the measurement of carrier-to-noise ratio. In this case, the ratio in dB is equal to the difference between the measured dB levels of total carrier power and noise density. While bandwidth can be taken into account by subtracting the quantity 10 log BW_c from the spectrum analyzer reading, it is also possible to preset the spectrum analyzer's measurement bandwidth to eliminate the need for manual correction.

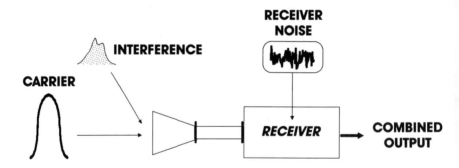

Fig. 3-21 RF Interference and Receiver Noise Usually Accompany the Desired Carrier in a Microwave Receiving System

The type of interference shown in Figure 3-21 is not noiselike and therefore cannot be analyzed in a straight forward manner. The ratio of carrier power to interference power can be taken from the spectrum analyzer display, but its effect on the reception process also depends on the frequency offset $(F_c - F_i)$ between the two carriers and their relative bandwidths. In real world situations, the

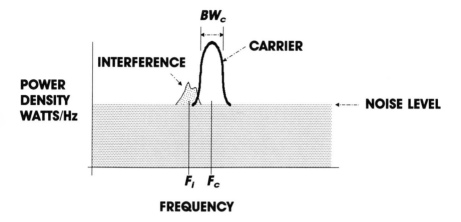

Fig. 3-22 Frequency Spectrum Showing the Desired Carrier, an Interfering Carrier and White Noise, as Seen on a Spectrum Analyzer

interference may rove through the bandwidth of the carrier, affecting it as well as other carriers on adjacent frequencies. Spectrum analysis is vital to microwave communication, since it provides a user-friendly "window" for viewing the reception process.

3.3.3 Baseband Quality and Signal-to-Noise Ratio

The output of the receiver demodulator contains the information along with baseband versions of noise and interference picked up over the link. Figure 3-23 depicts the type of baseband output that would be obtained in an analog microwave communication system using *frequency division multiplex* and *frequency modulation* (FDM/FM), which is discussed further in Chapter 4. Individual baseband information channels, which were multiplexed together at the transmitting end, are shown riding on top of a noise floor. Because the floor rises steadily with increasing baseband frequency (a normal property of FM demodulation), a compensating upward gain tilt called preemphasis (mentioned previously) was applied within the transmitting station's signal processor. The ratio of signal power to baseband noise power, or signal-to-noise ratio (S/N), is the final measure of user quality in analog transmission.

In most analog transmission systems, the process of modulation and demodulation causes the S/N to be significantly greater than the C/N by a fixed amount called the *modulation improvement factor* (MIF). For example, in FM TV transmission, the MIF is approximately 35 dB, yielding a S/N of 50 dB from

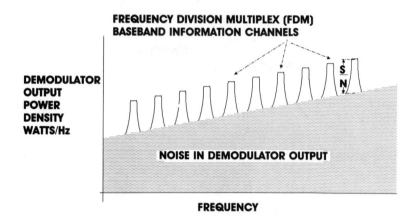

Fig. 3-23 Received Baseband Signal from an FM Demodulator Showing Frequency Divisioı Multiplex Channels and Triangular Noise Spectrum

a C/N of 15 dB. With operation above threshold, a one dB change in C/N produces a one dB change in S/N in the same direction. In most digital transmission systems, the baseband and RF power ratios are almost identical because actual demodulation usually occurs in the signal processor. The quality of a digital link is measured by the *bit error rate* (BER), which is the ratio of the number of bit errors (improperly detected bits) over a sufficiently long interval of observation. The key relationship is between the power ratio on the link and the bit error rate coming out of the signal processor. In typical cases the bit error rate decreases one order of magnitude (e.g., from 10^{-6} to 10^{-7}) for one dB increase in C/N.

3.3.4 Link Margin

The final and perhaps key concept in microwave-link engineering is that of link margin, which is nothing more than the excess power in the carrier relative to the minimum allowable (threshold) value. It is possible to measure the threshold in the laboratory under controlled conditions. The link performance under normal conditions can be determined using the power balance equation and spectrum analysis. Then, the margin is the difference in dB between the minimum value and the expected value. After the link is operational, margin can be verified by manually decreasing the transmit power to the point where the received baseband signal is barely acceptable. The recorded change in transmit power in dB is essentially the link margin.

Adequate link margin will allow the link to deliver exceptionally good quality (high *S/N* or low bit error rate) under mean signal, clear weather conditions. When either the uplink or downlink is experiencing heavy rain or multipath fading, however, the available link margin will determine how often and for how long the link will drop below threshold. The criterion often used is called *availability*, which is the percentage of time that the link is above threshold. Typical satellite links operate in the range of 99 to 99.95%, demonstrating the high reliability of line-of-sight paths between the satellite and its associated earth stations.

Chapter 4
Multiple Access and Modulation

The topics of multiple access and modulation are important to the efficient and effective use of communication satellites. In most networks, the efficiency of transmission is increased by combining several channels of information with a process called *multiplexing*, creating a baseband before transmission takes place. Modulation is the process by which this baseband in electrical form is then impressed upon a carrier. In Chapter 3, we touched on the role of modulation in transmitting user information on a microwave link, the principal importance being in maintaining circuit quality. The type of modulation as well as the specific parameters employed also determine how much traffic the satellite transponder will carry in aggregate. Also, the types of connectivity and flexibility achieved will depend in some degree on the modulation system. These aspects of RF transmission and link connectivity are referred to as multiple access.

4.1 MULTIPLE ACCESS METHODS

The basic concept of multiple access, illustrated for three forms in Figure 4-1, is that earth stations transmit to the same satellite without interfering with one another. RF carriers can be maintained separate in frequency, time, or space, indicated in the figure by three perpendicular axes. Hence, the use of the terms, respectively, of *frequency division multiple access* (FDMA), *time division multiple access* (TDMA), and *space division multiple access* (SDMA).

4.1.1 Frequency Division Multiple Access

The FDMA technique is traditional in radio communication, since it relies on frequency separation between carriers. All that is required is that the earth stations transmit their traffic on different microwave frequencies and that the

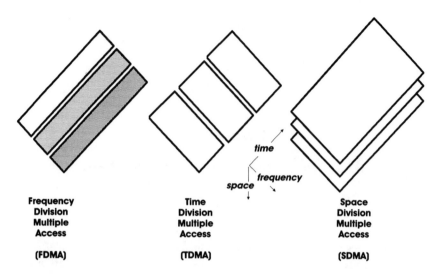

Fig. 4-1 Generic Multiple Access Methods Using the Three Dimensions
of Frequency, Time, and Space

modulation not cause the carrier bandwidths to overlap. Three such independent
transmissions are indicated at the left of Figure 4-1 by long rectangles extending
along the same "time" dimension but on different frequencies (indicated by
different shading). A constraint in FDMA is that the sum of the bandwidths of
the individual carriers cannot exceed the satellite's available bandwidth. Consequently, all three carriers in the uplink pass cleanly through the satellite repeater
and are radiated toward the area of coverage on the ground. If all carriers pass
through the same transponder, then the sharing of RF power among them must
be carefully balanced.

4.1.2   Time Division Multiple Access

Earth station transmissions in TDMA are all on the same frequency and
each employs the full bandwidth of the RF channel, which may consist of an
entire transponder. In the center of Figure 4-1, the wide rectangles represent full
bandwidth transmissions from earth stations within the same satellite coverage
beam. Jamming is prevented by sequencing the transmissions in time so that
they do not overlap. This can be a more complex process than FDMA, because
a common system of timing or control must be employed by the earth stations
sharing the same satellite channel. Individual earth stations, therefore, transmit
their traffic in the form of bursts of information, necessitating compression of
the traffic in time at the transmitting end and the complementary expansion at

the receiving end. The most appropriate modulation is digital in nature, as this is compatible with the compression and timing requirements of burst transmission. A similar technique is in use in computer-based *local area networks* (LANs), allowing several personal computers to "talk" to one another on a common cable loop.

A variant of TDMA called Aloha greatly simplifies the control of a digital satellite network, although at a cost in efficiency. Developed at the University of Hawaii, this is basically the technique illustrated in Figure 2-3 for multipoint-to-point connectivity. Stations transmit packets of data only when they need to communicate; therefore, there is no system of synchronization and the packets arrive at the satellite at random times. On occasion, two packets will overlap in time and therefore will interfere with each other. The use of an area coverage satellite allows every station to receive its own transmission after being relayed from space. Detection of interference results in the two stations automatically retransmitting their packets but only after different time delays to preclude a second incident of interference.

In terms of efficiency or percentage of data throughput, TDMA can achieve greater than 90%, approaching 99% in networks with elaborate terminal equipment. An Aloha network, which employs very simple earth stations, runs at approximately 20% efficiency primarily due to the time delays introduced by the automatic retransmission process. No such automatic retransmission is needed in TDMA, since the timing is fully controlled by a central station. The efficiency of Aloha has been improved by allowing stations which have large blocks of data to pass that data in a preassigned block of time using a *reservation* mode. A central control station can be added to establish a timing reference and make noninterfering time slot assignments. The more advanced TDMA architectures for VSAT networks incorporate features of standard TDMA, Aloha, and the reservation mode in order to provide the greatest flexibility and efficiency of bandwidth utilization for extremely large numbers of accessing terminals.

4.1.3 Space Division Multiple Access

The third generic multiple access method, SDMA, is nothing more than making physically separate paths available for each link. Transmission can be on the same frequency and at the same time, as illustrated at the right in Figure 4-1. Land-based SDMA networks can use separate cables or radio links; but on a single satellite, independent radio paths are required. The frequency reuse technique described in Chapter 3 is effectively a form of SDMA which depends upon achieving adequate beam-to-beam and polarization isolation. Multiple spot beams are the fundamental way of applying SDMA in a large system. In using SDMA, either FDMA or TDMA are needed to allow earth stations in the same satellite beam or polarization to enter the repeater. Advanced concepts for interconnecting beams within the repeater are described in Chapter 9.

4.1.4   RF Bandwidth Utilization in Multiple Access

The manner in which the three generic multiple-access methods use the bandwidth of the satellite is illustrated in Figure 4-2. Across the top are shown five transponder channels with the one in the center expanded to display occupancy. The channel bandwidth and spacing apply for the particular frequency band (C band, Ku band, etc.) and may also be arranged differently for a specific satellite design. A detailed description of the design of the repeater and transponders is covered in Chapter 5. We can assume that for the purpose of this example the channel bandwidth and spacing are 36 MHz and 40 MHz, respectively, which are typical of C-band domestic satellites operating in the North American arc.

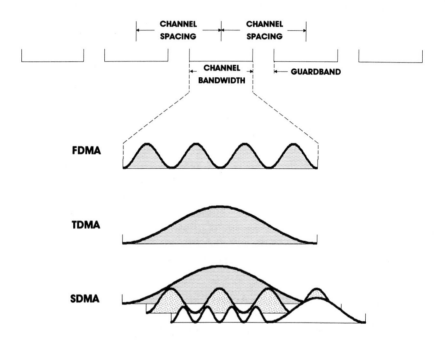

Fig. 4-2 Bandwidth Occupancy of the Satellite RF Channel Using Frequency Division, Time Division, and Space Division Multiple Access Methods

The example of a transponder used for FDMA shows four separate RF carriers of equal power and bandwidth. Each would come from a different earth station and contain multiple information channels in either analog or digital form. There is no reason to maintain constant bandwidth and power and most FDMA transponders contain a variety of carrier bandwidths and power levels. Between each carrier there is a small bandwidth opening called *guard band* to allow the earth stations to separate the carriers effectively. The satellite downlink contains all of the carriers and any particular one could be selected for reception at any earth station located in the coverage beam. To prevent the carriers from interfering with one another, the power and bandwidth are distributed by using an engineering process called *frequency planning* or *transponder loading*. This process considers the impairments and distortion effects, which are briefly reviewed at the end of the present chapter.

In the case of full transponder TDMA, all stations transmit bursts in the uplink, producing equal power as received at the satellite. A single wideband carrier transmitted by one station exists in the transponder at any instant in time. There would be brief blank periods of time (not visible in a spectrum) between station transmissions because full utilization is nearly impossible to achieve in practice. Called *guard time*, these intervals are needed to prevent overlapping of transmissions. The criteria which determine the shape of the digital carrier are covered later in this chapter. It is also possible to use TDMA with a lower data rate which uses less RF bandwidth to permit the sharing of a transponder on an FDMA basis. Networks of inexpensive earth stations with limited uplink power (e.g., VSATs) can utilize narrow-band TDMA because the power required is proportional to the bandwidth of the carrier, all other things being equal.

The display for SDMA in Figure 4-2 indicates three independent transponders with different carrier content. This is because in SDMA there are two or more transponders which actually operate over the same bandwidth. To separate the carriers, which can now overlap in frequency and time, the satellite must have multiple beams or dual polarization capability. The amount of isolation which SDMA can provide is of the order of 25 to 30 dB, which is adequate for proper operation with the modulation methods described in the following section.

To summarize, multiple access is the process by which several earth stations transmit to a common satellite and thereby share its communication capacity. Selection of the most effective multiple access method for a particular network will help to determine the ultimate success of its operation. The capacity and connectivity achieved also depend upon both the multiplexing and modulation formats of the individual transmissions as well as the multiple access method employed. In the following section, these important concepts are presented in greater detail.

4.2 MODULATION TECHNIQUES

Many of the purposes and concepts relating to modulation and its reverse process, demodulation, were covered in Chapter 3. Therefore, we need only review the important aspects as they relate to the efficient accessing of a communication satellite. The various approaches for multiplexing many information channels together for efficient transmission are also covered. Each of the methods is reviewed in Table 4-1, which also identifies the relationship between multiplex and modulation for analog and digital information signals. The reverse processes are called demultiplex and demodulation, respectively.

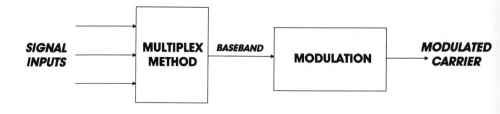

● **ANALOG SIGNALS (VOICE AND VIDEO)**

FREQUENCY DIVISION MULTIPLEX (FDM)

   —**AMPLITUDE MODULATION (AM)**
   —**PHASE MODULATION (PM)**
   —**FREQUENCY MODULATION (FM)**

● **DIGITAL SIGNALS (CODED INFORMATION)**

TIME DIVISION MULTIPLEX (TDM)

   —**FREQUENCY SHIFT KEYING (FSK)**
   —**PHASE SHIFT KEYING (PSK)**
   —**HYBRID MODULATION**

Table 4-1 Multiplex and Modulation Methods for Use with Analog and Digital Information Channels

4.2.1 Analog Signals

Information in analog form is continuous in time and represents, as closely as possible, the detailed nature of the source. For example, analog voice information, or simply voice, contains all of the true frequency components along with the amplitude variations associated with speech. Analog information is generated by and recognized by us humans, but it also can be used for the precise control of machines and vehicles.

A device called a *transducer* converts some type of sound, light change, or motion into analog electrical impulses which are carried to the radio facility by wire. The electrical impulses can be converted back into the original physical

form with reasonable fidelity by a transducer at the distant end. Perfect reproduction, however, is neither practical nor, in most cases, necessary. Diminished
quality of reproduction results from restrictions on the bandwidth of transmission
as well as the distortion of the amplitude and phase characteristics of the analog
information, which is discussed in a subsequent section.

4.2.1.1 Signal Conditioning

One of the simplest ways to minimize the demands on a satellite link is
to reduce the bandwidth of the analog information. The resulting signal will still
be understandable (intelligible), although some of its subtler aspects may be lost.
Bandwidth is reduced by filtering, effectively chopping off the higher frequency
components. In voice communication, human speech can be sent with nearly
perfect fidelity over a frequency range of 100 to 10,000 Hz: a bandwidth of
approximately 10 kHz. Most telephone systems filter this down to a bandwidth
of approximately 3 kHz, covering 300 to 3400 Hz. A similar process applies to
audio broadcasting, television, and scientific measurement using telemetry. The
important reason for filtering is that it reduces communication occupancy, permitting the efficient stacking of many channels together.

In addition to simple filtering, the signal can be prepared by altering its
voltage level or volume (in the case of audio). The preemphasis technique
mentioned in Chapter 3 introduces an upward tilt to the input signal spectrum
as a way of compensating for a similar tilt of the receiver noise coming out of
the distant demodulator. Another type of analog signal conditioning is *companding* (a contraction of compressing-expanding), which, like preemphasis, is
a way to overcome noise. In this case, the compressor at the sending end
automatically amplifies the input signal when it is weak and attenuates it when
it is strong, responding in real time to the rapid variation of the audio level. The
expandor at the receiving end works in an opposite fashion to restore the proper
audio response. The benefit comes when the expandor automatically attenuates
the noise in compensating for what was originally a weak audio input at the
transmitting end. The operation of the compandor is undetectable to most lis-
teners, and the effect is to enhance the signal to noise ratio by 15 to 20 dB. All
modern telephone transmission systems, be they analog or digital, now employ
companding in one form or another. The Dolby Noise Reduction system mentioned in Chapter 3 is particularly effective, because it incorporates features of
both preemphasis and companding.

4.2.1.2 Frequency Division Multiplex

The most common analog multiplexing scheme is *frequency division multiplex* (FDM), developed in the 1930s to reduce the number of wires needed to

connect two telephone switching offices together. Later, FDM found application in microwave radio links, since without it a separate transmitter and receiver pair would be needed for each end of a voice path. The term "frequency" in FDM is used because each individual information channel is assigned its own unique frequency, much like TV channels and AM radio broadcast frequencies. The bundle of FDM frequency channels follows a single transmission path between terminal stations. The incoming channels themselves can either originate from the same signal source or could have been tied together at a communication node.

A simplified block diagram of the FDM transmit equipment chain is shown in Figure 4-3, while frequency spectra corresponding to the intermediary points are shown in Figure 4-4. The number of channels to be multiplexed can be as few as two or three (as shown) or as many as 3600. Each channel is taken from its normal frequency range (300 to 3400 Hz in the case of voice) and translated to an assigned frequency channel by a mixer-local oscillator combination. This is the same technique as that used in an upconverter, discussed in Chapter 3. In this case, the multiplexed signals remain within the baseband section of the transmitting station. The mixing process in Figure 4-3 causes channel 1 to appear just above frequency F_1, channel 2 just above F_2, *et cetera*, as illustrated at the center of Figure 4-4. Being on separate frequencies, the channels can be safely added together in the summing amplifier (shown as a box with a plus sign) without causing interference among them. This FDM baseband spectrum would then be modulated on the IF carrier (indicated at frequency F_c in Figure 4-4).

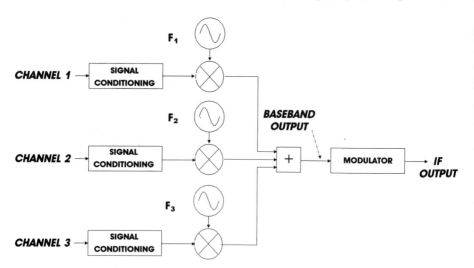

Fig. 4-3 Block Diagram of Equipment Used to Generate a Three-Channel IF Carrier Using Frequency Division Multiplex and Frequency Modulation (FDM/FM)

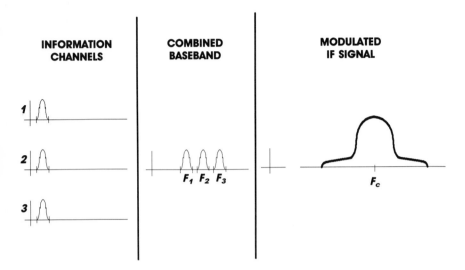

Fig. 4-4 Assembly of a Baseband Using Frequency Division Multiplex and Generation of an IF Signal with Frequency Modulation

In real telephone FDM equipment, the translation is done in multiple stages so that the baseband can be made from building blocks. In North America, the basic block is the *Group*, which consists of 12 channels spaced 4 kHz apart, lying between 12 kHz and 60 kHz. Using successive frequency translations, five Groups are multiplexed to obtain a 60-channel *Supergroup*. A *Mastergroup* consists of ten Supergroups and covers a baseband bandwidth of approximately 2.5 MHz. FDM equipment also includes facilities for maintaining constant signal levels and for detecting any fades or equipment failures. Different standards apply around the world to the the specific frequency ranges and groupings of channels, so the numbers cited above should only be considered examples.

For analog TV, audio channels are usually multiplexed with a video channel using FDM. In this case, the video is not translated from its nominal range between zero and approximately 5 MHz. The audio is not directly translated, but rather is modulated on a distinct baseband frequency called a *subcarrier*. In the case of stereo, the two audio channels would normally by sent on separate subcarriers at different baseband frequencies. Other subcarriers containing additional audio channels or even data can be added to the baseband for innovative broadcast applications (presented in Chapter 2). The modulation process shown at the right in Figure 4-3 operates on a composite baseband consisting of the video with audio and data subcarriers (if present).

4.2.1.3 Modulation

An RF carrier at a specific frequency can be modulated by varying either its amplitude or phase. Frequency modulation, it turns out, is a special case of phase modulation. The following explanation of these methods will be brief because many excellent discussions of modulation theory have been published over the years. (In particular, see M. Schwartz, *Information Transmission, Modulation, and Noise* in the Bibliography.)

Amplitude Modulation.

Amplitude modulation (AM) is in widespread use for radio broadcasting and also finds application in high-frequency radio communication. The basic form of AM is generated by varying the amplitude of the RF carrier in accordance with the level of the modulating signal. In terms of the frequency spectrum, the unmodulated carrier is still present at the center frequency and sidebands are visible above and below the carrier. The upper sideband is an exact replica of the modulating baseband spectrum while the lower sideband is its mirror image. Because both sidebands contain the information, it is possible to communicate effectively by transmitting only one sideband without the carrier and other sideband. This technique, called *single sideband* (SSB), requires specialized radio equipment and therefore is not used for monaural AM broadcasting.

The frequency translation process used to assemble an FDM baseband generates SSB signals which contain the information channels. Because SSB reproduces the baseband signals at RF almost directly, it employs a minimum of bandwidth. This makes it useful in cases where radio spectrum is limited. However, AM and SSB are very susceptible to nonlinear distortion (produced in most satellite transponders) and it is easily disturbed by link noise and interference. Consequently, AM and SSB are not used extensively as direct modulation techniques in satellite networks.

Phase and Frequency Modulation.

Phase and frequency modulation are used heavily in satellite communication systems because of their ability to deal with nonlinear distortion, noise, and interference. In both systems, the amplitude of the carrier is held constant so that there is no change in the power level. Most nonlinear distortion is the result of amplitude variations on the carrier, and therefore PM and FM will perform better in this environment than AM.

To introduce phase modulation, the unmodulated carrier is delayed in time (plus and minus) in proportion to the amplitude variations of the information being sent. Delaying of a carrier causes the angle of its phase to change, which can be detected at the receiving end and converted back to the original form.

Frequency modulation is easier to comprehend, because it is produced by varying the frequency of the carrier in proportion to the amplitude of the information. The carrier effectively swings back and forth in frequency; the amount of swing (*deviation*) is determined by the loudness of the information (in the case of audio), while the maximum range of the swing (i.e., the *peak to peak* deviation) establishes the bandwidth of the modulated carrier. As was mentioned previously, FM is directly related to PM. It turns out that the change in frequency is equal to the rate of change of phase (the first derivative of phase). An electronic device called the *phase-locked loop* (PLL) is very handy for demodulating PM and can also demodulate FM with additional components to perform the mathematical transformation.

The bandwidth of a PM or FM carrier is not a constant, due to its dependence on the amplitude variations of the information. Generally speaking, RF bandwidths for these modulation types are many multiples of the baseband bandwidth. For example, in conventional wideband FM, the RF bandwidth is approximately equal to the peak-to-peak frequency deviation plus twice the highest baseband frequency. Called Carson's Rule, this approximation generally gives a somewhat larger bandwidth than would actually be used. The benefit of bandwidth expansion in FM comes about after demodulation, where the narrower baseband bandwidth is restored with only a corresponding fraction of the RF noise accompanying it. This is because the PLL type of demodulator has an effective bandwidth closer to that of the modulating signal rather than to that of the RF carrier. Stated another way, the PLL tracks the deviation of the carrier, recovering only a portion of the RF noise and interference.

A familiar concept in FM radio communication is the *threshold effect*. As discussed in Chapter 3, the *signal to noise ratio* (S/N) from the demodulator follows the change in link carrier to noise ratio (C/N) dB for dB as long as the power level is above the threshold of the demodulator. If the C/N is at or below threshold, the demodulator delivers a degraded signal because random noise spikes will be stronger than the carrier at times. The further below threshold, the more frequent the disruption until the point is reached where the signal is totally useless.

Typical threshold values of C/N for FM are in the range of 6 to 10 dB, where the lower end of the range is obtained with the more modern PLL type of demodulator. With sufficient margin above threshold, the baseband noise level will be very low and noise spikes will be extremely infrequent. This is a particularly desirable situation for voice channels carrying low-speed data, since the noise spikes will almost always introduce bit errors. In the case of analog color video transmission, noise spikes near threshold appear as short horizontal lines called "speckles," mentioned in Chapter 3.

4.2.2 Digital Signals

The transmission by satellite of digital signals involves the process of *encoding* in addition to multiplexing and modulation. Generally speaking, RF transmission is an analog process, since a carrier is a continuous signal. Analog information is also continuous in nature, and hence the carrier can be modulated directly. Digital modulation, on the other hand, is discrete in nature in that a limited number of possible states such as "1" and "0" (as shown in Figure 3–20) are used. This requires that the carrier's amplitude, phase, or frequency be shifted a fixed amount in response to the digital code.

Examples of digital modulation are provided in this section. The design of the modulator-demodulator (*modem*) needed to perform this translation between digital modulation and analog carrier is quite complex, and the equipment has in the past been difficult to build and maintain. Fortunately, advances in microcircuit technology have yielded chips which simplify the design and manufacture of the requisite modems and associated ground equipment. An important physical law in digital transmission is that the RF bandwidth of the digital carrier is proportional to the rate at which the binary data is being transmitted. Also, the required RF power increases in direct proportion to the rate.

4.2.2.1 Encoding

The process by which a continuous information signal is converted into a stream of digital data is called analog to digital conversion (A/D conversion). Quite obviously, the reversal of digital data to analog information is D/A conversion. Many user devices such as digital PBXs and video codecs perform this function prior to delivery of the information to the earth station, as discussed in Chapter 2 and shown in Figure 2–12. In some applications, the earth station must perform A/D conversion. The digitized form in either case contains a stream of coded numeric values, each corresponding to a voltage level which was measured ("sampled") at a particular instant. Electronic devices that perform this measurement and conversion operate at extremely high rates. For each analog sample, the voltage range is divided into narrow bands called *quantization levels*. When a particular voltage lies in a specific range, the electronic "smarts" of the A/D converter put out a numerical code typically in binary system.

The fidelity of channel transmission results from the number of samples taken per second (the *sampling rate*) and from the number of discrete levels into which the signal's voltage has been divided (the *quantization*). A basic theorem in communication engineering is that the sampling rate must be greater than or equal to twice the highest baseband frequency of the information signal. For example, the standard sampling rate for telephone service is 8 kHz (8000 times per second), which is slightly more than twice the highest signal frequency (i.e., 3400 Hz). With regard to quantization, good telephone quality is obtainable with 128 levels (seven bits when coded in binary). Standard *pulse code modulation* (PCM) adds an eighth bit for synchronization, yielding a transmission speed of 64 kb/s per telephone channel. The receiving end is uncertain as to where exactly in the quantization range the actual signal was, causing slight distortion of the audio quality. Companding in the form of nonequal levels is used to help overcome some of the quantization distortion and channel noise.

Compression

The number of bits per sample can be reduced by taking advantage of predictable aspects of a particular signal type such as voice or video. After encoding, the removal of excess bits in the sample effectively compresses the signal bandwidth by allowing the resulting data to be sent at a lower speed. This requires that the compression equipment have intelligence in form of a micro-computer and an algorithm for controlling it. *Adaptive-differential* PCM (ADPCM), one such algorithm, is gaining wide acceptance as a standard voice encoding technique, since it cuts in half the number of bits per sample while maintaining the quality of voice nearly undisturbed. There does appear to be a trade-off in that the speed with which inband data can be sent is reduced: 9600 bps for PCM *versus* 4800 bps for ADPCM. Improvements in voice-band modem or ADPCM technology will eventually eliminate this disparity.

The situation with regard to video encoding is much more complex, since there are many uses and standards for signal quality. With more and more compression, the picture quality can look choppy, particularly when there is rapid motion. In video teleconferencing applications, compression down to 750 kb/s is usually acceptable. Broadcast video standards are very demanding, however, and little reduction from 45 Mb/s can be tolerated using currently available processing algorithms. Colors can be reproduced with excellent quality, no matter how much compression is used, simply because hue information occupies very little bandwidth to start with. Advances in the compression of full-motion video are anticipated as faster microcomputers and more sophisticated algorithms are developed. This topic is discussed further in Chapter 9.

Error Detection and Correction

Noise, interference, and distortion on a digital communication link will on occasion confuse the receiving data processing equipment, causing bits to be misread. The effect can be relatively minor, as in the case of voice communi-cation, or catastrophic, if the bits represent numerical data such as computer programs or important statistics. To control errors in the communication link, there are techniques for preparing the data prior to transmission. In particular, data can be coded to expand the number of bits and a sophisticated decoder used to reverse (correct) errors which occur along the link. This is a difficult concept to explain or understand without resorting to the mathematics of statistical communication theory and information theory. Nevertheless, the following paragraph reviews a simple example which would not actually be used in practice, but which identifies some of the concepts.

Suppose that the transmitting end codes the binary "1" into the four-bit sequence "1111" and the binary "0" into the sequence "0000". The four-bit sequence is called a code word. This simple code increases the data transmission rate by a factor of four, since the same information must get through the channel per unit time. The receiver is designed to be able to recognize that any of the following sequences probably started out as "1": "1111", "1110", "1101", "1011", or "0111". It would then deliver a "1" to the user. A zero bit being coded and sent would work in complimentary manner. This coding scheme can handle one bit error per code word. If a received code word has two 1's and two 0's, then there were at least two errors in reception. In this case, the coder cannot determine the correct bit sense. The way to handle this in the decoder would be to make a guess, recognizing that the choice would have a 50% chance of being correct. This code is a simple example of error correcting codes which are more powerful in their ability to correct errors caused by the link. Also, actual codes are more efficient in their use of the channel, increasing the data rate by a factor of two or less.

The performance of the RF channel in digital transmission is measured by the bit error rate, which is the average number of bits in error at the receive end. For data communication, a typical objective is one bit error per million bits transmitted, expressed as 10^{-6}. The channel efficiency of error correcting codecs (often included in the high speed modem in the earth station) is specified by the *coding rate* (R), which is equal to the ratio of information bits to coded bits on the channel. Also, the sophistication of the codec determines by how much the error rate on the channel is improved (reduced). For example, a rate $R = 3/4$ codec using what is called a "convolutional code" can reduce the error rate on a typical satellite link by two orders of magnitude (e.g., from 10^{-4} to 10^{-6}) which is equivalent to a 2 to 3 dB reduction in the demodulator threshold for a constant error rate. The only penalties with using this type of coding are the increase in bandwidth on the RF channel (because the data rate on the satellite is increased by a factor equal to the inverse of the coding rate) and the complexity and cost of including a codec in the RF modem. Contemporary microelectronic technology has essentially eliminated the later penalty.

Spread Spectrum Processing.

Processing of a digital bit stream using the spread spectrum technique can make the carrier more tolerant of RFI. The baseband bandwidth of the input data is expanded (spread) by mixing in a sequence of essentially random bits which is delivered at a much higher rate than the data. The random bits comprise what is called a *pseudorandom noise* (PRN) code that is generated electronically and can be independently replicated at the distant end with the same type of generator. By transmitting the combined stream (data plus PRN code) at the high rate with a conventional phase shift keying (PSK) modulator, the bandwidth of the RF carrier corresponds to that of the higher rate (wider) PRN code. After demodulation, the PRN sequence is electronically subtracted from the recovered digital stream, making the original data available for conventional processing and delivery to the user. Despreading of the carrier will only work properly, however, if the PRN generator at the receiver is synchronized with its counterpart at the transmitter.

Spread spectrum, which could be classified as either a coding technique or a modulation technique, provides two important benefits for commercial satellite communication. First, the high speed PRN code spreads the carrier over a relatively wide bandwidth, reducing the potential of RFI caused by the earth station transmission. This is important in siting of the earth station and in dealing with closely spaced satellites. Second, the recovery process at the receiving earth station can suppress almost all external RFI which is located in the RF bandwidth of the spread carrier. The important data is obtained by de-spreading the carrier, but this causes any nonsynchronized RF signal to undergo spreading after mixing in of the PRN code at the receive end.

4.2.2.2   Time Division Multiplex (TDM)

The multiplexing system which combines digitized information channels by time sequencing them is called *time division multiplex* (TDM). The topic of TDM was introduced in Chapter 2 since it is used extensively in digital telephone networks. Figure 4-5 contains a simplified block diagram of a transmit terminal capable of digitizing and multiplexing four independent analog information channels (sources). Each source can be continuous in nature and must occupy a specified baseband bandwidth (e.g., 300 to 3400 Hz for telephone and 0 to 5 MHz for video). In this illustration, the information is first converted to digital data in a PCM encoder, whose output would run at a continuous data rate (64 kb/s for telephone, 1.544 Mb/s for compressed video). Direct digital inputs can be accommodated by bypassing the A/D conversion elements. The function of the TDM multiplexer at the center of Figure 4-5 is to compress these rates in time (retaining the same number of bits per sample) and to output them sequentially as a single stream of data at a rate which is equal to or greater than the sum of the individual channel data rates. Some equipment designs reverse the sequence of encoding and multiplexing by using one high-speed coder to convert a TDM stream of analog voltage pulses (often referred to as pulse amplitude modulation) directly into binary data.

The building blocks in TDM which are analogous to the Group, Supergroup, and Mastergroup of FDM were briefly reviewed in Chapter 2. Table 2-3 contains a summary of these blocks in the form of the digital hierarchy used in North America. In terms of standard PCM voice channels (64 kb/ps), the digital group ("Digigroup") supports 24 channels using the 1.544 Mb/s T1 or DS1 channel. With the advent of ISDN, the Digigroup will continue to employ a T1 channel but will provide 23 channels at 64 kb/s plus one additional data channel (termed "23 B + D"). There is a big jump to the next standard block in digital transmission; the digital mastergroup uses a full DS3 to provide 672 channels. Conversion of multiplexed FDM channels directly to TDM is now possible with a device called a *transcoder*. The algorithm employed by the transcoder can interface a 24-channel Digigroup with two 12-channel FDM Groups.

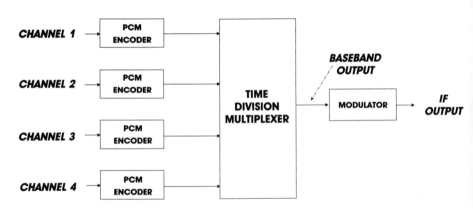

Fig. 4-5 Block Diagram of Equipment Used to Generate a Four-Channel IF Carrier Using PCM Time Division Multiplex and Phase-Shift Keying (PCM-TDM/PSK)

The signal conditions at the various intermediate points of a simple TDM terminal are shown in Figure 4-6. Time waveforms are indicated for each analog input: these are sampled and digitized into four bits per sample, as shown at the center of the figure. As discussed in the next section, the baseband spectrum of the TDM data stream starts with a maximum near zero frequency, decreases to zero, and then rises again in the form of a sidelobe. There is a similarity to the sidelobe of an antenna because both are governed by the same mathematical law. Sidelobes occur because the input has limits (a fixed bit time period for data and a fixed reflector size for an antenna). In theory, the sidelobes continue to infinity, decreasing in strength more or less exponentially. When modulated on a carrier using PSK, the baseband is reflected into a symmetrical IF spectrum, occupying roughly twice the bandwidth.

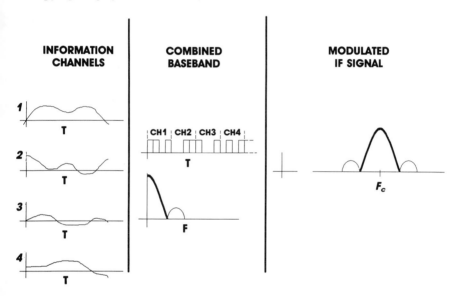

Fig. 4-6 Assembly of a Baseband Using PCM Time Division Multiplex and Generation of an IF Signal with Phase-Shift Keying

4.2.2.3 *Digital Modulation*

Nearly all digital modulation relies upon the basic characteristic of a pulse, shown in the time and frequency plots in Figure 4-7. The pulse has a fixed duration of length T seconds, which means that a continuous stream of such pulses would have a rate $1/T$ bits per second. If $T = 0.001$ seconds (one millisecond), then $1/T = 1000$ bits per second (1 kb/s). The frequency spectrum of this pulse, shown below in the figure, is a maximum at zero frequency and passes through the X axis at a frequency equal to the bit rate ($1/T$, or 1000 Hz for the previous example). Successive sidelobes have zero values at multiples of $1/T$. The bandwidth of the main lobe therefore is proportional to $1/T$, the bit rate, as mentioned previously. The formula for this spectral shape is simply the ratio

$$\frac{\sin (\pi F T)}{\pi F T} .$$

This formula is plotted more precisely in Figure 4-8 and converted to relative power in dB in Figure 4-9. The short-hand way of refering to this formula is $\sin (x)/x$. Substituting zero for f or x is misleading, since it results in the ratio 0/0. The value at zero frequency is actually one (1), however, since for small angles the sine of the angle equals the angle in radians. The important relationship here is that a fixed pulse length produces an infinite frequency spectrum.

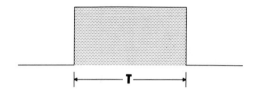

TIME WAVEFORM OF A SINGLE RECTANGULAR PULSE

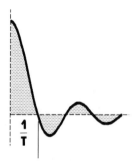

BASEBAND FREQUENCY SPECTRUM OF A RECTANGULAR PULSE

Fig. 4-7 Characteristics of a Rectangular Pulse in the Time and Frequency Domain

The baseband and IF bandwidths of signals follow these direct relationships, whether *frequency-shift keying* (FSK) or PSK is employed. It seems logical, then, that the spectrum of the pulse should be filtered to minimize the occupied bandwidth. This is illustrated in Figure 4-10, where the attenuation characteristic of a low-pass filter is shown superimposed on the spectrum of a rectangular pulse. After filtering (the heavy line), the output spectrum is confined

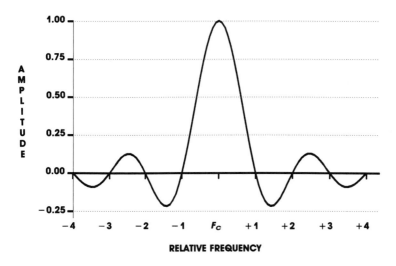

Fig. 4-8 Amplitude Frequency Spectrum of a PSK Carrier with Rectangular Pulse Modulation

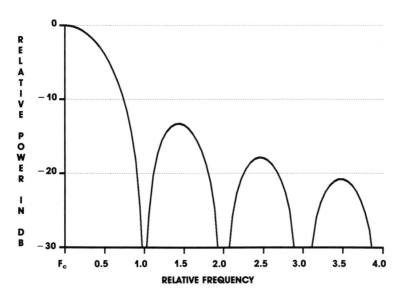

Fig. 4-9 Power Spectrum of Rectangular Pulse Modulation Shown on a dB Scale

within the bandwidth of the pulse spectrum's main lobe. Due to the same mathematical relationship which causes a rectangular pulse to have an infinite spectrum, a limited spectrum gives a pulse with infinite time duration. Instead of a rectangular shape, a filtered pulse has a time waveform with an oscillating tail much like the spectrum illustrated in Figure 4-8. A stream of filtered pulses, such as one would obtain in a real digital radio link, contains residual tails which increase the chance for errors. This is comparable to increasing the link noise level or adding interference; hence, the presence of tails is called *intersymbol interference*.

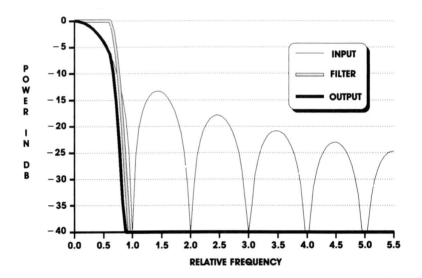

Fig. 4-10 Baseband Frequency Spectra of a Rectangular Pulse Before and After Filtering to Reduce the Transmission Bandwidth

The error-causing effect of intersymbol interference can be reduced by aligning the pulse tails so that their zero crossings occur at times when the pulse main lobes are at their peaks. This can be done by proper filter design and demodulator timing. Figure 4-11 shows an ideal rectangular spectrum and a spectrum shaped like a cosine curve (called the *raised cosine*). Both occupy approximately the same bandwidth. The corresponding pulse waveforms in time are plotted in Figure 4-12, clearly showing the reduction in the oscillating tail produced by special filtering. Both pulse waveforms have zero crossings at the times corresponding to main lobe peaks $(-3, -1, -1, 0, 1, 2, 3, \ldots,$ etc.), thus precluding intersymbol interference. In addition, the raised cosine spectrum pulse has a much weaker tail, making it less sensitive to timing errors in the demo-

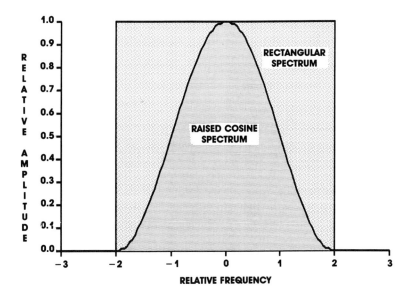

Fig. 4-11 Frequency Spectra of Bandwidth Limited Pulses Using Rectangular and Raised Cosine Shaping

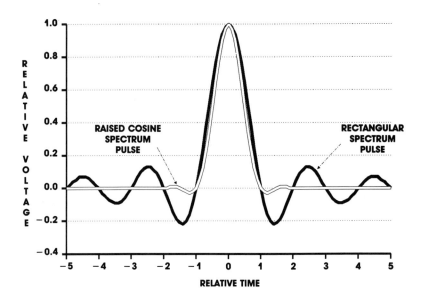

Fig. 4-12 Comparison of Pulse Waveforms with Limited Bandwidths for Rectangular Spectrum and Raised Cosine Spectrum Shaping

dulator. This type of shaping is one example of the techniques which are used to reduce the modulated bandwidth of a digital carrier efficiently. Typically, the necessary RF bandwidth of a properly filtered pulse is approximately equal to the bit rate expressed in hertz instead of bits per second.

Frequency Shift Keying (FSK).

   The earliest form of digital modulation to be used in radio communications was FSK. Illustrated in Figure 4-13, it is obtained by switching between two discrete frequencies in direct correspondence to the bit being sent. The carrier frequency in the figure jumps back and forth between F_1 and F_2, producing the dual spectrum shown at the right. In effect, two different modulators are being employed—one to transmit binary "1" and the other to transmit binary "0". This aspect forces FSK to consume twice the bandwidth of PSK, as will be shown in the next paragraph. The principle advantage of FSK was historically that simple hardware could be used in the modulator and demodulator. This lack of sophistication also means that FSK requires more signal power for the same performance in terms of error rate, which would have to be reflected in the link budget analysis.

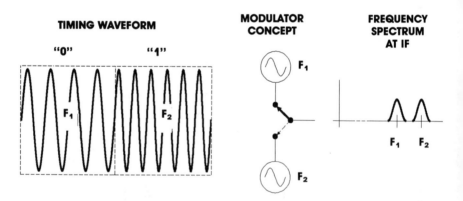

Fig. 4-13 Frequency-Shift Keying (FSK) as Shown in Time and Frequency Can Be Generated from Two Oscillators on Different Frequencies

Phase Shift Keying (PSK).

   The technique of PSK, discussed in Chapter 3 and illustrated in Figure 3-20, is the most common system for transmitting and receiving high-speed digital information. PSK modems operate at rates between 56 kb/s and 1000

Mb/s. Biphase PSK (BPSK) uses two phase states: 0 and 180 degrees. Quadraphase PSK (QPSK) uses four states split into pairs: 0 degrees and 180 degrees (the in-phase or "I" component), and 90 degrees and 270 degrees (the quadrature or "Q" component). In both techniques, a phase reversal is used to transmit the transition from binary 1 to binary 0. A property called *orthogonality* is used in QPSK, wherein the I and Q components are separated by 90 degrees from each other. This is similar in effect to the use of cross-polarization isolation to achieve frequency reuse (see Chapter 3). Both BPSK and QPSK are very efficient in the way bandwidth is used. In addition, present-day advancements in digital hardware and software have pushed the performance very close to that which is theoretically possible. This reduces the amount of power needed to obtain a satisfactory operating link.

BPSK modulation is employed with spread spectrum in such a manner as to multiply the RF bandwidth. The power density is reduced substantially by the inverse of the expansion of bandwidth. Multiple spread spectrum signals can actually be transmitted one on top of another as long as the PRN codes are not synchronized. The undesired spread spectrum carriers appear like noise to the demodulator and PRN despreader. The term *code division multiple access* (CDMA) has been used to describe this application of spread spectrum. Capacity of the RF channel is determined by how much the noise floor from the extra spread spectrum carriers can increase and still provide adequate link margin.

Hybrid Modulation.

A modulation method which combines PSK with either PM or AM is called a hybrid modulation method. The purpose is to increase the transmission speed in a limited bandwidth. For example, the I channel described in the previous paragraph could be used in BPSK to represent the coarse quantization level and can be transmitted with relatively few bits per sample. The Q channel would then carry the quantization error in analog PM form. Since there is no quantization error in the resulting modulated signal, reproduction can essentially be perfect. Noise and interference on the channel are still a factor, however, particularly with regard to the Q channel which carries an analog signal. A higher capacity digital modulation system uses the I and Q channels as in QPSK, and adds a third dimension by shifting the amplitude of the carrier (*amplitude shift keying*, ASK). The ASK channel thereby adds a few more bits to the possible sequence of binary data.

Because of the higher data rate per unit of bandwidth, the signal-to-noise ratio on the channel must be significantly higher than would be acceptable for PSK or FSK. In addition, the RF channel must be linear to allow the complex modulation format to pass unimpaired. Most applications are in telephone channels and in high frequency radio rather than on commercial satellite links. Future improvements in satellite channel performance, however, could make hybrid modulation more popular.

4.2.3   Single Carrier Impairments

The general topic of impairments relates to the distorting effects (exclusive of noise and external interference) that the communication channel has upon the information. This section reviews those impairments which involve the transmission of one carrier through the channel at a time. Treatment of multiple carriers such as are used in FDMA is reserved for the next section. An example of typical single carrier impairments is presented in Table 4-2 from the standpoint of both the *cause* and the *effect*. Along the left of the table are the impairing characteristics of the empty channel, i.e., those that can be measured without the desired information present. Among these causes are variations in the amplitude *versus* frequency response (i.e., bandwidth limiting) and the phase *versus* frequency response (also called delay distortion: the rate of change of phase is equal to time delay). Also of interest are two forms of gain nonlinearity: amplitude nonlinearity (AM-to-AM distortion) and phase nonlinearity (AM-to-PM distortion).

| | | EFFECT ON THE TRANSMISSION OF VARIOUS SIGNAL TYPES | |
		ANALOG SIGNAL (FDM/FM)	DIGITAL SIGNAL (TDM/QPSK)
CAUSE WITHIN THE CHANNEL	AMPLITUDE VERSUS FREQUENCY	*INTER- MODULATION DISTORTION*	*I TO Q COMPONENT COUPLING*
	PHASE VERSUS FREQUENCY	*INTER- MODULATION DISTORTION*	*INTERSYMBOL INTERFERENCE*
	AMPLITUDE NONLINEARITY (AM-TO-AM)	*NO EFFECT BY ITSELF*	*NO EFFECT BY ITSELF*
	PHASE NONLINEARITY (AM-TO-PM)	*INTELLIGIBLE CROSSTALK*	*NO EFFECT BY ITSELF*

Table 4-2   Matrix of Transmission of Impairments from the Standpoint of Either Cause or Effect

Shown across the top of Table 4-2 are two columns: one for an analog transmission system and the other digital. The impairments identified below are effects which are actually visible in an information signal or modulated carrier after it has passed through the channel. For an FM carrier containing an FDM baseband (FDM/FM), amplitude versus frequency variation (also called gain slope) causes interference frequencies to appear in the baseband. *Intermodulation distortion* (IMD) is the process by which these interference frequencies are caused in the FDM baseband. As explained in the next section, a different process called RF IMD occurs in the transponder bandwidth due to amplifier nonlinearity. The baseband variety, however, is the result of an FDM/FM carrier being swept back and forth across the gain slope and delay distortion characteristic of a transponder.

Impairment of digital data modulated on a carrier with QPSK (TDM/QPSK) typically results in an increase in the bit error rate. The "eye opening" is a useful measurement of the data signal before detection of the ones and zeros. Using an oscilloscope, the eye opening displays the extraneous pulse tails, providing a relative measure of intersymbol interference. Recall from a previous discussion that intersymbol interference raises the frequency of errors in detection when random noise is present. Intersymbol interference by itself will generally not cause errors. Specifically with regard to some varieties of QPSK modulation, amplitude versus frequency impairment transfers energy from the I component across into the Q component (and *vice versa*), producing real interference and increased bit errors.

The previous discussion was meant to give the reader an idea of the types of factors that are taken into consideration when a channel is analyzed in detail on a single carrier basis. Most of these impairments, while important, affect the performance to a lesser degree than the parameters which are taken into direct account in a link budget. If more background is desired, the reader can review the textbooks and technical papers which have been published on the subject.

4.2.4   RF Intermodulation Distortion

The gain nonlinearities (AM-to-AM and AM-to-PM) of satellite power amplifiers tend to produce unwanted interference to the output carriers by the process of RF IMD. This interference occurs when the carrier or carriers entering the amplifier have amplitude variations when viewed in aggregate. IMD appears as unwanted interfering carriers which produce the same type of signal degradation as RFI and noise. A single unmodulated carrier has a constant amplitude and therefore IMD will not occur, no matter how nonlinear the amplifier may be. Harmonics produced in a nonlinear amplifier are distortion products which lie at integer multiples of the input frequency. They are located way outside of the downlink band, however, and are easily removed by the output filters of a satellite transponder. In the following paragraphs, the considerations for multiple carrier IMD in FDMA and single carrier IMD for TDMA are reviewed.

4.2.4.1 Multiple Carrier IMD

The most basic type of IMD comes from two or more carriers which share the same nonlinear amplifier. To see how two unmodulated carriers produce the amplitude variations needed to generate IMD, examine the time waveforms in Figure 4-14. Illustrated at the top are a sinewave of amplitude 1.0 at frequency F_1 and another sinewave of one-quarter this amplitude at a slightly lower frequency, F_2. The algebraic sum of these two waveforms added point by point is shown below in the figure. Amplitude modulation of the carrier at frequency F_1 caused by the weaker carrier is clearly evident. It turns out that the AM is periodic with a frequency equal to the difference $(F_1 - F_2)$.

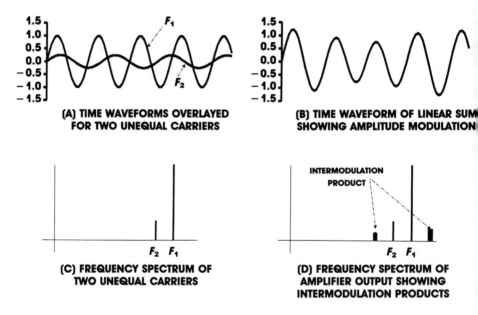

(A) TIME WAVEFORMS OVERLAYED
FOR TWO UNEQUAL CARRIERS

(B) TIME WAVEFORM OF LINEAR SUM
SHOWING AMPLITUDE MODULATION

F_2 F_1

(C) FREQUENCY SPECTRUM OF
TWO UNEQUAL CARRIERS

INTERMODULATION
PRODUCT

F_2 F_1

(D) FREQUENCY SPECTRUM OF
AMPLIFIER OUTPUT SHOWING
INTERMODULATION PRODUCTS

Fig. 4-14 Amplitude Modulation from Two Carriers Results in Intermodulation Products in the Output of a Nonlinear Amplifier

The gain nonlinearity of the amplifier responds to both the degree of the AM and to its frequency. If the nonlinear characteristics and input signal parameters are known, then the IMD can be predicted with accuracy sufficient to design the link. The IMD products occur at frequencies which are arithmetic sums and differences of the input carrier frequencies. For example, the two carriers in Figure 4-14 will result in the strongest intermodulation products being located at frequencies $(2F_1 - F_2)$ and $(2F_2 - F_1)$, illustrated at the lower right.

The power level of these products will be determined by the relative input power of each carrier into the amplifier, the total output power relative to the maximum capability of the amplifier (the "operating point"), and the particular nonlinear characteristic of the amplifier. With two equal amplitude carriers operating at the maximum power point of a typical TWTA (the point of "saturation"), each product will be approximately 10 dB weaker than either carrier. This level of interference is unacceptable for most transmission modes, although the products do not fall directly on top of the carriers in this example. As the total input power is reduced (i.e., as the input is "backed off"), however, the level of the products also decreases but at a somewhat greater rate. For example, with the total input power backed off by 10 dB from the point of saturation, the level of the IMD is approximately 18 dB below the carrier level. The fact that downlink carrier power drops at the same time means that an optimum point of link operation is reached where the sum of link noise and IMD is minimized.

The principle of how gain nonlinearity acts upon FDMA is shown at the left of Figure 4-15. The typical FDMA system illustrated occupies a single transponder and consists of four equal amplitude carriers with rectangular-shaped modulation, each transmitted from a different earth station. The amplitude and phase nonlinearity of the satellite power amplifier respond to the rapid amplitude fluctuations of the composite signal. The output spectrum, shown at the lower left of the figure, contains IMD products in the form of small carriers with triangular-shaped modulation. Each such product is the result of the interaction of combinations of either two or three of the input carriers, according to the following algebraic relationships:

$$F_{(2)} = 2F_a - F_b,$$

and

$$F_{(3)} = F_a + F_b - F_c,$$

where F_a, F_b, and F_c are the frequencies of different carriers in the input.

The combinations on the right side of the equations are frequencies in the same band as the carriers themselves and can overlap useful information. The degree of overlap depends upon the number of carriers and their placement in the RF channel, as governed by the formulas. It is important to note that the modulation on the IMD products is a combination of the modulations on the generating carriers; IMD products will therefore occupy a greater bandwidth than any one of them. With enough input carriers and wide enough modulation, the spectrum of the IMD appears as a noise floor almost like white noise. Most of the time, IMD can be treated like white noise over the bandwidth of the carrier in question and analyzed in that manner in the link budget calculation. However,

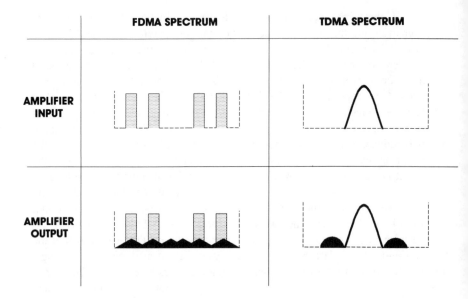

Fig. 4-15 RF Intermodulation Distortion Products Generated in a Non-linear Amplifier by FDMA and TDMA

IMD products which fall back on one of its generating carriers include the original modulation. FM is particularly susceptible to this, and the IMD product can track the carriers' frequency deviation, causing more harmful baseband interference.

The particular IMD products described in the previous example are called third-order products, indicated by the sum of the absolute values of the frequency terms (i.e., $2 + |-1|$ and $1 + 1 + |-1|$, both of which are equal to 3). Fifth-order terms, such as $3F_a - 2F_b$, also fall in band and would need to be included in the analysis, since they can add a significant although lesser amount of interference. Generally speaking, only odd-numbered orders fall in band and diminish in their power level and effect as the order increases. For frequency planning purposes, the design engineer determines and accounts for the order, location, and power level of IMD products by using sophisticated computer programs.

4.2.4.2 Single Carrier IMD

A single carrier operating at or near saturation is usually not expected to experience detrimental effects from IMD. It will be shown, however, that digital transmission using QPSK is often subject to IMD particularly, when pulse shaping such as was described previously in this chapter is employed. Referring back to Figure 3-20 (a), a PSK carrier (or either the I or Q components of a QPSK carrier) has a reversal of phase at the transition from one binary state to the other. Rectangular pulses would cause the modulated carrier always to maintain a constant amplitude, which eliminates the possibility of either AM-to-AM or AM-to-PM conversion in a nonlinear amplifier. As was explained previously, rectangular pulses have infinite bandwidth of the form shown at the bottom of Figure 4-7.

Since pulse shaping is employed in all digital transmission systems to minimize RF bandwidth, the carrier will have AM in conjunction with PSK. Figure 4-16 displays the familiar BPSK carrier with a binary transition from "1" to "0" indicated by the phase reversal. The rise and fall of the sinewave corresponds directly to the raised cosine spectrum pulse, illustrated in Figures 4-11 and 4-12. Note the similarity to the two-carrier AM example shown in Figure 4-14. Therefore, the output of a nonlinear amplifier will include intermodulation products which are interactions of the upper and lower halves of the main lobe of the PSK signal. The carrier component in this case is actually not present because the phase reversals have cancelled it out on average (another name for this technique is double sideband suppressed carrier).

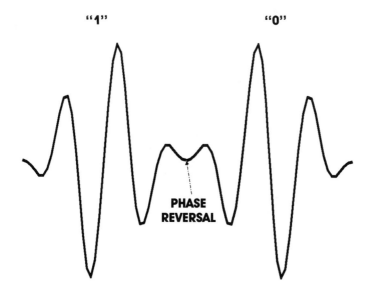

Fig. 4-16 Amplitude Modulation on a BPSK Carrier Produced by Raised Cosine Spectrum Pulse Shaping

The input and output spectra for a TDMA system using PSK with raised cosine spectrum pulse shaping is shown at the right in Figure 4-15. At the top, the ideal raised cosine shaping is evident and no sidelobes are present. After passing through the nonlinear amplifier, however, the sidelobes reappear, having been regenerated in the form of intermodulation products. Another way of viewing this is that the saturation of the amplifier flattens the tops of the AM pulses and the resulting re-squared pulse modulation has an infinite spectrum of the form $\sin(x) / x$.

The new sidelobes of the digital carrier defeat the purpose of shaping the pulses in the first place. Sidelobes are approximately 14 dB down from the carrier and can cause interference to carriers operating in adjacent transponders. By backing off the input drive to the amplifier by a few dB, it is possible to reduce the sidelobe level greatly and make adjacent transponders more compatible with one another. Once again, there is a trade-off in total link performance, since backing off the input will reduce the downlink power. Fortunately, the appropriate amount of back-off will only reduce the downlink by one dB or possibly less.

When operating several narrowband TDMA carriers in the same transponder, sideband regeneration will be nearly insignificant, and hence the carriers can be packed tightly together in frequency. Multicarrier IMD would have to be carefully considered in setting the operating point of the transponder, since there will be several carriers transmitting at the same time. This is the case for VSAT networks using the various TDMA and FDMA modes, demanding that the operation of the transponder be carefully examined before full-scale operation is commenced.

Chapter 5
Spacecraft Technology

The purpose of the following discussion is to explain how a satellite works and to review the critical factors in its design. This should familiarize the reader with the key concepts and terminology which are common in the satellite industry. Most of the emphasis is placed on the communication function as well as the other aspects of the spacecraft which affect it. The term *spacecraft* refers to the actual piece of hardware which is launched into geostationary orbit to become an artificial *satellite* for the purpose of providing a radio repeater station.

5.1 OVERVIEW OF COMMUNICATION SPACECRAFT

The hardware elements that comprise a communication spacecraft can be divided into two major sections: the *communication payload* (payload), containing the actual radio communication equipment used for reception and transmission of radio signals, and the *spacecraft bus* (bus), which provides the supporting vehicle to house and operate the payload. It is critical that the payload and bus work hand in hand to establish a highly efficient radio repeater on a stable space platform. The end result is shown in Figure 5-1, which illustrates a typical geostationary communication satellite with a pencil beam serving a country or region of a continent. A beam with dimensions 3° by 8° would cover an area the size of the United States.

To visualize how complex a task this is, imagine that you are trying to keep a flashlight pointed at a distant spot on a wall. Make this more realistic by standing on a skateboard going down a smooth incline. The beam must always stay pointed at the spot, regardless of your motion. Similarly, the bus section of the satellite holds the narrow beam in tight alignment, while the payload efficiently receives, amplifies, and relays back the microwave radio signals coming from anywhere within the beam coverage area.

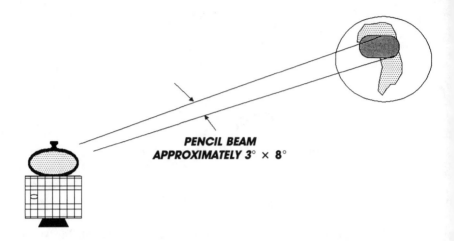

Fig. 5-1 Coverage of a Land Area from GEO Requires the Generation and Control of a Pencil Beam On-Board the Satellite

Figure 5-2 is a schematic drawing of a spacecraft showing the functions which are performed by the payload and bus. In fact, the drawing could represent any radio repeater (space or terrestrial) which is totally isolated from any means of support. The payload section consists of the microwave repeater connected to directional radio antennas for reception and transmission.

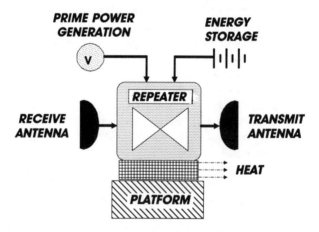

Fig. 5-2 Functional Diagram of an Independent Microwave Repeater Station for Use in Space or at an Isolated Location on the Ground

Obviously, the repeater will not operate on its own and needs the supporting functions illustrated around it. The electronics in the repeater need prime (electrical) power which in the case of commercial spacecraft is obtained by using a solar cell array to convert sunlight directly into electricity. An energy storage battery must be included to power the repeater when the prime source is not available, i.e., when the sun is eclipsed by the earth. For a satellite in geostationary orbit, eclipse occurs during a one-month period centered on the equinoxes lasting up to 70 minutes per day. Without batteries, the spacecraft would shut down entirely during eclipse and could lose all stability even after reentering sunlight.

The repeater will generate heat much like an operating television set or microwave oven. If not removed from the electronics, this heat will cause the temperature to rise sufficiently to affect or even damage the sensitive parts of the spacecraft, particularly the repeater electronics. The visible and invisible radiation from the sun also tends to raise the temperature of the spacecraft, while undesirably low temperatures can occur during eclipse. Therefore, the flow of heat from and to the spacecraft must be monitored and controlled. An important function of the spacecraft is to provide a stable platform throughout the life of the satellite. Precise pointing of the coverage beam, critical to the purpose of the satellite, is dependent on the stability of the control system which is integral to the spacecraft bus. Finally, remote control operation from the ground dictates that there must be a two-way radio link for maintenance of the payload and bus. All of these topics are explained in more detail further on in this chapter.

5.2 SPACECRAFT CONFIGURATIONS

Commercial aircraft essentially all take the same shape in order to be able to fly at high speed. Commercial communications spacecraft, however, can and do take on a variety of shapes and configurations, since the external forces in space are much weaker. There is, of course, the need to package the spacecraft for delivery to orbit by an earth-launched rocket. Once in space, the spacecraft is unfurled into one of three different configurations currently in use. Referred to as the *simple spinner*, the *dual spin*, and the *three axis*, these configurations and their attributes are discussed in the following paragraphs.

5.2.1 Simple Spinning Spacecraft

The original configuration to be employed for application as a geostationary communication satellite was the simple spinner. Figure 5-3 shows a simple spinner of modern design (the reason for the large reflector on top will be explained in a subsequent paragraph). Simplicity is very much a virtue in this

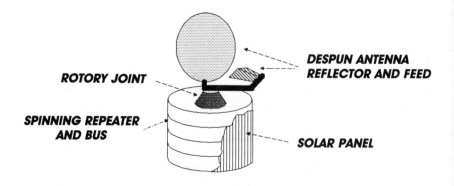

Fig. 5-3 General Arrangement of the Simple Spinning Spacecraft

very stable and reliable design, because, once set to spinning, the spacecraft will continue to rotate indefinitely about the spin axis without external control. The spinner is unconditionally stable, meaning that the spacecraft will stay erect and even correct itself if disturbed by an external force. In the design and construction of the simple spinner, the body and major components are arranged to provide maximum rotational inertia about the spin axis. This produces a drum shape more akin to that of a tuna can than to that of a pencil.

The configuration depicted in Figure 5-3 has greater communication capability that the first spinners because of the despun antenna mounted above the spinning body. With the payload repeater and spacecraft bus housed in the spinning section, the microwave signals pass through a waveguide rotary joint to reach the despun antenna. Before this critical piece of mechanical technology had been perfected, spacecraft antennas were nothing more than axial mounted rods which spewed microwave energy 360° around the satellite (only about 17° are occupied by the entire disk of the earth). Most despun antennas are composed of a parabolic reflector which is illuminated by a transmitting and receiving feed array, as discussed in detail in a subsequent section of this chapter.

All of the functions of the bus are contained within the spinning body. Electrical prime power is obtained from silicon solar cells which are mounted on the circumference of the drum. Batteries for energy storage are attached to the internal structure to give proper balance and are located to receive an even temperature environment. While spacecraft stability is guaranteed by its rate of spin, the despun antenna keeps its beam properly pointed by virtue of an active control system which is integral to the bus. A propulsion system provides pulses of thrust to maintain the proper orbit position (station-keeping) and spacecraft orientation. Again, all of these facilities are discussed in detail in applicable paragraphs of this chapter.

5.2.2   Dual Spin Spacecraft

This spacecraft design came out of continued research into spinning satellites at Hughes Aircraft Company, representing a major innovation in aerospace technology. The SBS spacecraft shown in Photo 5-A is typical of the dual spin design. The previous discussion for a simple spinner generally relates to the dual spinner, but with certain important distinctions. To get an appreciation for the enhancements that this configuration offers, examine Figure 5-4. Again, the bus section of the spacecraft spins to provide stability; the entire payload, however, (repeater and antenna) is despun. This gives greater flexibility in designing the payload for maximum communication performance. The mechanical interface between the bus and payload, called the *bearing and power transfer assembly* (BAPTA), also allows electrical power to reach the payload. In this case, microwave signals do not have to pass across the mechanical joint, since the repeater is physically connected to the antenna feeds. Note that there can be an unlimited number of feeds illuminating the reflector as compared to the simple spinner where the number of separate microwave paths is limited by the rotary joint to two or three concentric pipes.

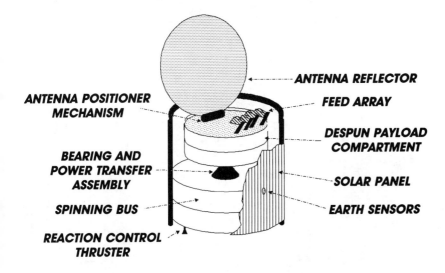

ANTENNA POSITIONER
MECHANISM

BEARING AND
POWER TRANSFER
ASSEMBLY

SPINNING BUS

REACTION CONTROL
THRUSTER

ANTENNA REFLECTOR

FEED ARRAY

DESPUN PAYLOAD
COMPARTMENT

SOLAR PANEL

EARTH SENSORS

Fig. 5-4 General Arrangement of the Dual Spin Spacecraft Identifying Major Components and Subsystems

From the standpoint of dynamic stability, the dual spinner is much more complex than the simple spinner. First, the fact that the despun section does not rotate reduces the gyroscopic stiffness of the spacecraft. Second, there is a

Photo 5-A. The SBS Spacecraft, Shown Undergoing a Prelaunch Test in the Factory, Was the First of the HS-376 Series of Dual Spin Spacecraft Developed by Hughes Aircraft Company (photograph courtesy of Hughes Aircraft Company)

dynamic interaction between the spun and despun sections which can cause the spacecraft to drift gradually out of proper alignment. This process, called *nutation*, can be observed in a spinning top as it slows down. The top develops a second sideways rotation at a slower rate than the spin rate. Gradually, the top leans over until it falls on its side. In a similar manner, an uncontrolled dual spinner will lose its vertical alignment and ultimately lean over and go into a "flat" spin, i.e., it will be spinning about an axis perpendicular to the spin axis. Said another way, the dual spin configuration is not unconditionally stable like a simple spinner.

The key to achieving stability in a dual spinner is to introduce a proper degree of nutation damping on the despun section. While the satellite is spinning normally without nutation, the damping should not be active. Just as soon as the angle of nutation (or spin axis tilt) increases to some detectable level, however, sufficient damping is automatically provided by the onboard control system to cause a counter dynamic force. An understanding of the physical principle is difficult to obtain without a review of rather complex mathematics, which is beyond the scope of this book. Stability can be maintained with mechanical viscus damping devices located on the despun section or with electromagnetic damping induced through the BAPTA. In emergency situations, the spacecraft can be kept from nutating into a flat spin by allowing the onboard control system to pulse fire a thruster.

The use of damping to stabilize the dual spinner was an important innovation in spacecraft design, producing spinning satellites with almost unlimited capability. Current designs are long and narrow with telescoping solar panels for increased power capability. The reflector, as shown in Figure 5-4, can be attached to a motor-driven antenna repositioner mechanism which both deploys the reflector and permits adjustment of the beam while on orbit. The advantages of a simple spinner cited at the end of the previous section also apply to the dual spinner.

5.2.3   Three Axis Spacecraft

Several innovations in electronics and mechanical devices have permitted the design of satellites which do not rely on rotation of the body to achieve stabilization. As shown in Figure 5-5, the three-axis spacecraft (also called *body stabilized*) is not drum shaped but rather takes on the most convenient form for providing and supporting the communication function. Photo 5-B is an artist's conception of the Inmarsat three axis spacecraft. Typically, the body is box shaped with one side pointing toward the earth at all times. Antennas can be mounted on the earth facing side or adjacent to it. The solar panels are flat and deployed above and below the body, with orientation mechanisms provided to

Photo 5-B. The Inmarsat Spacecraft is a Three-Axis Design Intended to Provide Maritime Mobile Satellite Communication Services (photograph courtesy of British Aerospace)

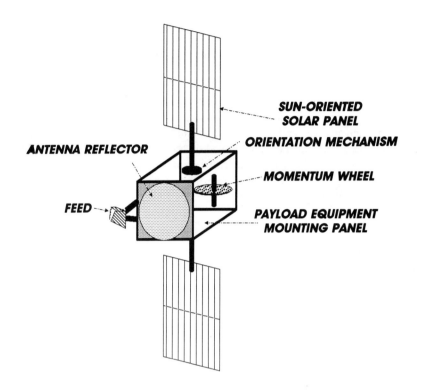

ANTENNA REFLECTOR

SUN-ORIENTED
SOLAR PANEL

ORIENTATION MECHANISM

MOMENTUM WHEEL

FEED

PAYLOAD EQUIPMENT
MOUNTING PANEL

Fig. 5-5 General Arrangement of the Three-Axis or Body Stabilized
Spacecraft Identifying Major Components and Subsystems

keep the panels pointed toward the sun as the satellite revolves around the earth.
The body makes one rotation per day relative to the earth; the solar panels,
however, make one rotation per day relative to the body.

Stability of the three-axis is assured through an active control system which
applies small forces to the body to correct for any undesired changes in spacecraft
attitude. The most common three-axis attitude control system (called *biased
momentum*) uses a high-speed gyro called a momentum wheel to provide some
stiffness and to act as an inertial reference. A basic control technique is either
to speed up or slow down the wheel to cause the body of the spacecraft to rotate
in the direction opposite to the speed change, which produces very precise east-
west adjustment of the platform. The momentum wheel can sense transverse
angular motion of the body (nutation) which causes a counter force on its support.
The momentum wheel can be twisted by gimbal (motor controlled pivot), placing
a precise dynamic force on the spacecraft. In an alternative approach called *zero*

bias, separate reaction wheels are provided for each of the three axes. Rather than spinning at a high rate in one direction, the reaction wheel can spin up and down and can actually reverse its spin and go in the opposite direction. This technique is extremely precise, since the axes are independently controlled and adjusted in orbit. Gyroscopic stiffness is nearly zero in comparison to the biased momentum and spinner designs.

The three-axis design has the obvious advantages of allowing the solar panel to reach any size and permitting convenient placement of antennas, which can either be rigidly attached or deployed on orbit. To provide these capabilities, it is necessary to package the spacecraft for launch and then deploy all of the appendages once orbit is reached. Furthermore, precise control of antenna beam pointing will rely on a fairly complex system of electromechanical devices and an onboard computer. Thermal and RF design are somewhat more difficult, while assembly of the spacecraft may be easier.

5.2.4   Configuration Summary

The previous discussion was meant to give the reader some appreciation for the major trade-offs in communication spacecraft design. Common features to both include attitude sensing, propulsion, and integration with the launch vehicle. Additional criteria are presented in the section on spacecraft bus subsystems. To select an appropriate spacecraft configuration, it is necessary to review all of the functional requirements and objectives for the service to be provided. Only then can the configuration be properly selected and optimized. Keep in mind also that each spacecraft manufacturer has its own particular experience and technology base, which often are the determining factors in the selection of a configuration. Consequently, experienced customers have learned not to attempt to specify configuration details to the contractor.

5.3   COMMUNICATION PAYLOAD

Consisting of the microwave repeater and the associated antenna system, the payload is the radio station that is maintained in orbit for the purpose of completing the communication links between and among earth stations. A complete flight model of the communication payload from the first Intelsat VI spacecraft is shown in Photo 5-C. The electronics which make up the repeater are reviewed in this section, emphasizing the impact of the elements on the microwave signals which pass through them. Some of this information supplements the discussion of impairments contained in Chapter 4. Spacecraft antenna systems are quite different from their terrestrial counterparts and are treated in their own section to follow.

Photo 5-C. The Communication Payload with Reflectors Deployed is Shown Positioned Above the Fuel Tanks of the Intelsat VI Spacecraft
(photograph courtesy of Hughes Aircraft Company)

5.3.1 Repeater Configuration

Modern microwave repeaters, be they terrestrial or space, are intended to carry several wideband channels of communication. As discussed in Chapter 4, the wideband nature of each channel allows it, in turn, to support a variety of individual signal types, such as television, high speed data, and bulk quantities of telephone conversations (e.g., multichannel voice). There is, however, a marked difference between the design of a satellite repeater as compared to the typical terrestrial repeater, as reviewed in the following paragraphs.

5.3.1.1 Terrestrial Repeater Configuration

Figure 5-6 gives a block diagram of a typical terrestrial repeater which provides a separate *receiver-transmitter* (RT unit) for each wideband channel. The terrestrial repeater illustrated can support up to eight RT units using one antenna transmit-receive pair. One or more spare RT units (not shown) can be switched in automatically to restore a failed or degraded channel.

The RT unit itself contains a single channel microwave receiver which is fixed-tuned prior to installation to the specific carrier frequency of the desired wideband channel. The transmitter is also fixed-tuned to a complementary non-interfering frequency. Terrestrial repeaters are usually located within 10 to 30 miles (16 to 48 kilometers) of each other. Path loss (discussed in Chapter 3) is small for such links and consequently the input-output connections between the antenna waveguide and the RT units need not be particularly low loss. For example, in Figure 5-6, the combined input from the antenna is passively divided N ways to enter the different RT units. In using passive power division, all of the wideband channels remain together on each output leg of the divider but at a level equal to $1/N$ of the power coming from the antenna. If $N = 10$, the effective loss is 10 dB. This amount of loss can be tolerated in terrestrial links, since it is compensated by short path lengths or where necessary by using slightly larger dishes.

On the transmitting side, loss can be minimized by using individual microwave filters which reactively combine the carriers. Reactive combining refers to the ability of the filters to reflect signals from the other channels back into the transmitting waveguide and thus forcing them up towards the antenna. A more detailed discussion of reactive combining as it relates to spacecraft repeaters can be found in a subsequent section on waveguide filters and multiplexers.

An important advantage of terrestrial repeaters is that they can be maintained and repaired even while they are operating. For example, if one of the RT units should fail, a backup channel is automatically switched in to maintain service. Then, a repairman is dispatched to the site to replace the failed RT unit

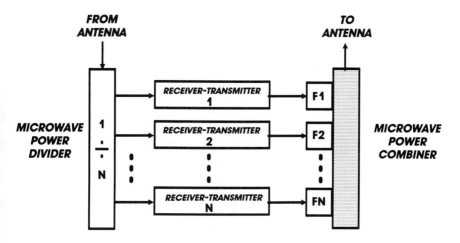

Fig. 5-6 Simplified Block Diagram of a Terrestrial Microwave Repeater Showing Separate Receiver-Transmitter Units for Each RF Channel

and switch the service back to it. The failed RT unit can be repaired later at a central depot. Service for the particular channel of communication can be maintained at all times, except possibly for very short interruptions, lasting seconds or perhaps milliseconds, when the RT units are switched.

5.3.1.2 Satellite Repeater Configuration

A satellite repeater also handles several broadband channels and includes extra equipment to restore failures. However, there are several important distinctions which come about because of the need to minimize weight and power and to operate the repeater for up to 10 years without hands-on maintenance. Shown in diagram form in Figure 5-7, the satellite repeater employs a series of microwave components in order to optimize the use of equipment. Each individual chain is referred to as a *transponder*, which is a contraction of two words: transmitter-responder. A detailed description of each of the components of the transponder is given in subsequent paragraphs. There is an obvious parallel between the transponder and the RT unit of a typical terrestrial repeater. Unlike the RT units, however, the payload repeater uses a single wideband receiver to accept all *N* channels from the receiving antenna. Typical receivers have an operating bandwidth of 500 MHz, which is sufficient to handle the 12 channels at 36 MHz each that can be found in most domestic C-band satellites. Modern commercial satellites employ frequency reuse, which requires that there be a receiver for each polarization or beam. The receiver amplifies the uplink frequency range and translates it to the downlink range without modification.

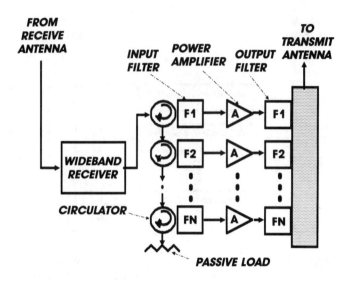

Fig. 5-7 Simplified Block Diagram of a Satellite Communications Repeater Showing a Common Wideband Receiver and a Power Amplifier for Each RF Channel

The term *multiplexer* in the context of the satellite repeater refers to a set of microwave filter hardware used to separate or combine RF channels, as distinct from the FDM and TDM multiplexer used to assemble a baseband at the transmitting earth station. Draw your attention in Figure 5-7 to the series of circles (*circulators*) and attached boxes (*input filters*) composing the input multiplexer. The circulator is nothing more than a microwave revolving door which causes any signal power entering a port to rotate in the direction of the arrow and exit at the next immediate port. Rotation is set up by a disk of ferromagnetic material which creates a magnetic field in a direction perpendicular to the paper. The polarity of the magnetic field determines the direction of rotation, which is fixed for a permanently magnetized disk.

Since all of the channels pass through the circulator together, it is the function of the bandpass filter to select only one channel for amplification by that particular transponder. Input filter F1 allows channel 1 to pass through and reflects all others back to the circulator. Thereafter, $N-1$ channels are routed down the circulator chain with one more channel being "dropped" in each subsequent bandpass filter. By the time channel N reaches its bandpass filter at the end of the chain, it has experienced the reflection process $N-1$ times. This reduces the power of channel N by a significant amount due to losses in the circulators and filter input sections. The amount of loss, however, is significantly less than $1/N$ (i.e., less than 10 log N in dB). At the final arm of the chain is found a passive load (called a *termination*) to absorb any remaining channel energy and prevent power from being reflected back up the chain. Circulator coupling is extremely effective for the purpose of separating channels, tending to minimize impairments while assuring that only one channel enters each transponder chain. Leakage of adjacent channels produces an undesired effect called *repeater multipath*, which is different from propagation multipath discussed in Chapter 3. Repeater multipath is reviewed in the section of this chapter on waveguide filters and multiplexers.

Power amplification is important to payload operation because of the long path length to the ground station. Traveling-wave tube amplifiers (TWTAs) remain the mainstay, particularly at higher frequencies (10 GHz and higher) and at higher power levels (10 watts and higher). Microwave power transistors are finding their way into commercial satellites for use in solid-state power amplifiers (SSPAs). Typical power levels of TWTAs and SSPAs are reviewed in Chapter 3. The particular power amplifier must be operable for essentially the entire life of the satellite and therefore only the most reliable devices can be selected; hence the preference for TWTAs and proven SSPAs. Also, the amplifier design must be lightweight, typically weighing under five pounds (two kilogram), and be capable of converting dc power into RF with efficiencies of 30 to 50%.

The last major component of the satellite repeater is the output multiplexer. This device works exactly the same as its terrestrial counterpart, using reactive combining to minimize the loss of valuable RF power. It makes no sense to generate power with solar arrays and convert it to RF in a TWTA or SSPA if it is wasted in a lossy power combiner. In addition to the functional components of the repeater, extra receivers and power amplifiers are provided to allow replacement of failed units by ground command. The RF switching necessary to accomplish this is described in a subsequent paragraph.

5.3.2 Wideband Receiver

The concept of using a single wideband receiver to amplify and translate the entire range of communication channels (typically covering 500 MHz) is unique to commercial satellite design. As shown in the block diagram in Figure 5-8, the range of channels in the uplink frequency band appears at the input; the same range appears at the output, but it has been translated to the downlink frequency band. In addition, the power level of the signals has been increased greatly—by the order of 50 to 60 dB (i.e., amplified in power by a factor of 10^5 to 10^6), depending on the particular design. Assume that F_u is the center frequency of the uplink band and F_d is the corresponding center frequency of the downlink band. The difference, $F_u - F_d$, is a fixed value or offset between uplink and downlink, having been specified by national and international regulatory authority. Allocation and assignment of frequency bands is discussed in

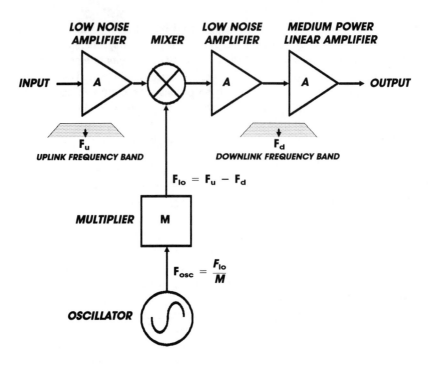

Fig. 5-8 Block Diagram of a Typical Wideband Communications Receiver Which Amplifies the 500 MHz Uplink Band and Translates it to the Downlink Frequency Range without Modification

Chapter 1. In C band, for example, F_u = 6175 MHz and F_d = 3950 MHz, giving a difference frequency of 2225 MHz. This same difference applies for every transponder of the repeater. Within the receiver, translation is produced through down conversion in the *mixer* (shown by the circle with an X through it). There are two inputs to the mixer: the uplink frequency range and a pure single carrier from the *local oscillator*. The frequency of the local oscillator, F_{LO}, is clearly the difference frequency. (This is similar to the operation of the earth station down converter, discussed in Chapter 3.) It is convenient to use a device called a frequency multiplier to generate F_{LO} as a harmonic from a crystal controlled oscillator operating at a much lower frequency (typically in the range of 100 to 200 MHz).

Because multipliers and mixers are nonlinear devices, they generate a variety of unwanted frequencies (harmonics and intermodulation products) in addition to those just described. Therefore, filters and frequency traps are inserted in the input and output legs of the mixer to preclude propagation of such spurious products (spurs) through the receiver or backward into its input. Spurs can interfere with the desired transmissions of this satellite and other satellites as well.

In addition to frequency translation, the receiver must provide a great deal of amplification to overcome the uplink path loss. Approximately 50 to 60 dB of gain is easily obtained with several transistor amplifier stages in tandem. An important consideration in satellite receiver design, however, is obviously thermal noise, which is produced in all active and passive microwave devices. The term *low noise* (discussed in Chapter 3) is used to describe an amplifier with specially designed and selected transistors which have the property of minimizing the generation of internal noise. Given the noise temperature and gain of each stage, it is a simple matter to calculate the overall noise temperature of the receiving system, as follows:

$$T_{sys} = T_a + T_l + \frac{T_{re}}{G}$$

where

T_{sys} is the total system noise temperature in K;

T_a is the antenna temperature, which is approximately equal to 270 K for the spacecraft viewing the "warm" earth;

T_l is the noise temperature of the first amplifier stage;

T_{re} is the equivalent noise temperature of the receiver stages following the first amplifier;

G is the gain of the first amplifier stage as a true power ratio (i.e., not in dB).

This type of analysis shows that the total system noise temperature is dominated by the noise contributions of the antenna and the first amplifier stage. The contribution of all the stages that follow is reduced by a factor equal to the gain of the input stage, expressed as a true ratio and not in dB. One particular offender is the mixer, which actually reduces the level of the signals that are translated in frequency. The *conversion loss*, as it is called, has the unfortunate effect of amplifying the noise power contribution of the subsequent stages. Thus, having adequate gain in the first stage (ahead of the mixer) is clearly important for minimizing T_{sys}.

Following the mixer are typically two separate transistor amplifiers, the first still being designed for low noise. The final stage brings the power level of each of the channels high enough to drive the input to the TWTAs or SSPAs, as appropriate. While these stages do not add significantly to system noise, the relatively high power level does place considerable demand for linearity on the last stage. The intermodulation products produced in this wideband stage, which increase as the output power demand increases, must be kept at a minimum or else the transponders will be subject to unwanted IMD interference. Because all carriers pass through this stage, it must have a power output capability considerably in excess of actual requirements. It is not unusual to have a one watt amplifier operating with a total output power for the sum of all channels of only 0.05 watts. Intermodulation distortion products (reviewed in Chapter 4) in the last wideband stage of the receiver must be added on a power basis to those generated in the transponder high-power amplifier. In a properly designed receiver, however, IMD from the transponder amplifier usually dominates, and that from the last receiver stage can be ignored in the link budget.

The elements of the receiver along with the associated power supplies are housed in a metal box to protect the components and facilitate placement on the repeater equipment shelf of the satellite. Because frequency translation is influenced by the stability of the internal local oscillator, the typical receiver includes a thermostatically controlled heater. This minimizes the variation of temperature directly affecting the crystal reference, particularly as the satellite passes into and out of eclipse. A properly designed and compensated receiver will produce a shift of five kilohertz or less during the eclipse cycle. Frequency stability of one kilohertz or less can be obtained at added cost and complexity by using a frequency reference of high accuracy on board the satellite or by way of ground commanded adjustment.

5.3.3   Redundancy Switching

Having described the first major active element in the repeater, it is necessary to review how redundancy can be provided effectively on the satellite. Techniques for switching active and spare units consider two important attributes: first, the switches must pass microwave signals with the minimum amount of loss and distortion; and, second, the switching scheme must permit the repeater to be reconfigured to allow access to spare units without disrupting the remaining operating equipment. Switches must also be reliable because a given switch often represents a potential single point failure mode (i.e., failure of a switch could render a transponder or group of transponders useless). Switches which use coaxial connectors (similar to those used for interconnecting video equipment) are appropriate for RF power levels under 10 watts and where some measurable loss is acceptable. Waveguide switches, although heavier and bulkier than coaxial switches, are necessary for high power levels and low loss applications, particularly at Ku band. Since waveguide dimensions and weight vary as the wavelength, the use of waveguides at the higher frequencies is advantageous.

The following paragraphs review the currently accepted switching devices and redundancy configurations. The discussion goes into considerable detail on different types of switches and how they are used in the repeater. Because this subject is important but usually ignored in the literature, readers may find the discussion valuable. The illustration that is provided with each switch shows the symbol, the schematic diagram, and a typical application of the particular switch in a repeater.

5.3.3.1   S Switch

As shown in Figure 5-9, the S switch is the simplest form of redundancy switch. The single coaxial input can be routed to either of two coaxial outputs, thus it is a single-pole, double-throw switch. The application drawing with two amplifiers (or perhaps receivers) shows how a backup unit can be used to replace a failed or degraded operating unit. This redundancy scheme is often called *two-for-one* redundancy, meaning that two identical units are carried to provide one operating channel of service. (This should not be confused with the designation *one for one* used in terrestrial systems for the same configuration.) Two-for-one redundancy with S switches is required whenever the devices must cover the same frequency range or when full redundancy is needed to meet reliability requirements.

The S switch can be implemented with two different technologies. The most common approach is to use coaxial input and output connections and a mechanical wiper arm, similar to the A-B switch used to interconnect video displays and televisions. Another type of S switch uses ferromagnetism to direct microwave energy from the input to the selected output. It operates similarly to the circulator which was described in a previous paragraph and is controlled by pulsing a magnetic coil to reverse the direction of the internal magnetic field. Ferrite switches are often used at the input to C and Ku-band receivers, because the ferrite cannot fail as an open circuit, even if the control circuit stops in mid-position.

5.3.3.2   2/3 Switch

As shown in Figure 5-10, two S switches can be packaged together to provide a versatile switch with two ports on one side and three on the other. If the two-port side is the input, it is called a 2/3 switch; with the three ports, it

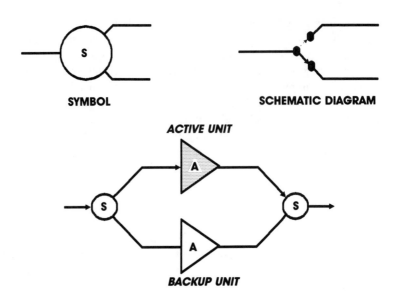

Fig. 5-9 Definition and Application of the S Switch Which Is Used to Switch in Redundant Equipment

is a 3/2 switch (it only depends on how the switch is used in the repeater). The fundamental application, shown at the bottom of Figure 5-10, is to allow three-for-two redundancy, where one spare unit can backup two operating units. Because of increased confidence gained by experience with amplifier and receiver reliability, this configuration has become both popular and effective. An extension of this method uses a pair of 2/3's and 3/2's along with a pair of S switches to implement a five-for-four redundancy scheme. Many current C-band satellites use five-for-four redundancy for sparing of TWTAs. The spare amplifier in such cases must be capable of operating over the bandwidth of each of the transponders that it is sparing.

5.3.3.3   C Switch

One of the more innovative arrangements is the C switch, shown in Figure 5-11. The schematic diagram in the upper left-hand corner shows how the two inputs and two outputs can be connected together. In the *straight-through* position, the upper input goes to the upper output and the lower input to the lower output. If the switch is commanded into the *cross* position, however, the upper input goes to the lower output and the lower input goes to the upper output.

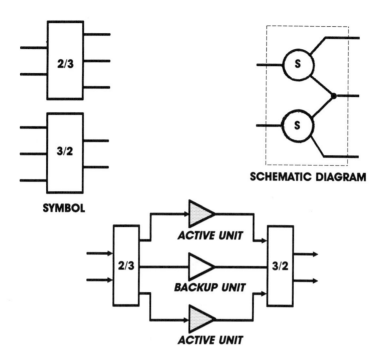

Fig. 5-10 Definition and Application of the 2/3 Switch Which Is Used to Share Redundant Equipment

These are the only two positions. This switch uses coaxial input and output ports and therefore is suitable for low-level signals (i.e., under 10 watts).

A typical application of the C switch, shown at the bottom of Figure 5-11, allows two operating units to be interchanged. If the upper amplifier were to fail, it would be possible to restore that particular channel of communication by commanding both C switches from *straight through* into *cross*. Obviously, communication capacity is lost, but at least there is the option of maintaining the more important of the two channels. This same switch can also be used as a routing device to rearrange communication paths within a repeater.

5.3.3.4   R Switch

The last switch to be described is designed to work with low-loss waveguide connections and is particularly suited to frequencies above 10 GHz. Called the *R* switch (for redundancy switch), it provides the means to interconnect four

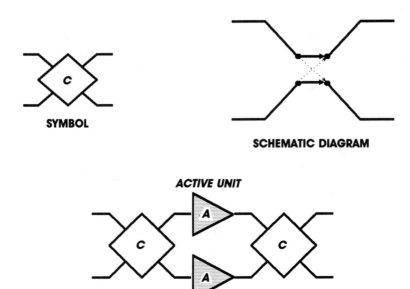

SYMBOL

SCHEMATIC DIAGRAM

ACTIVE UNIT

ACTIVE UNIT

Fig. 5-11 Definition and Application of the C Switch Which Is Used to Interchange Equipment or Switch Paths

separate waveguide ports, as shown in Figure 5-12. The schematic diagram of the switch is the same as its cross-sectional view, showing a metal disc having straight and curved channels carved in it. These channels provide waveguide paths inside the switch for microwave energy to pass between the four ports. It has been called a *baseball switch*, an obvious reference to the appearance of the cross-sectional view. The schematic diagram shows three possible positions: two *cross* positions and one *straight through*. A more common form of the baseball switch does not include the *straight-through* path. In some applications, one port is terminated with a resistive load to absorb the full power of an amplifier if the switch is commanded to disconnect the active element.

The R switch can handle power levels considerably in excess of 10 watts and is also useful at the input to the spacecraft receiver because of its low loss and wide bandwidth properties. Its size and weight, however, are roughly inversely proportional to frequency, making it practical for satellite installation at Ku band and higher frequencies.

The redundancy scheme shown in Figure 5-12 has been termed *ring* redundancy. A three-channel system is depicted with the darkened amplifiers operating. The R switches at the input and output of the operating amplifiers are

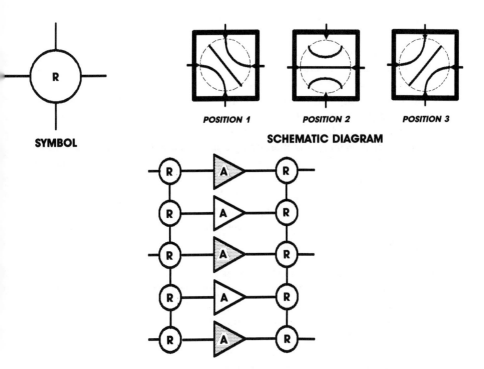

POSITION 1   POSITION 2   POSITION 3

SYMBOL   SCHEMATIC DIAGRAM

Fig. 5-12 Definition and Application of the R Switch or Baseball Switch Which Is Used to Switch in Redundant Units or Between Waveguide Connections

in the *straight-through* position (position 2 in the schematic diagram), placing the backup amplifiers completely out of the circuit. If the middle amplifier were to fail, then either of the two spare amplifiers could be used to restore service in the center channel. To use the upper spare, the input and output R switches for *both* amplifiers are put in positions 3 and 1, respectively. This causes microwave signals to be routed from the center channel away from the failed amplifier and into the upper spare. The ring is created by continuing the pattern of R switches and amplifiers upward and downward from the five sets shown in the diagram, until the chain connects back into itself. The scheme obviously works best on a circular equipment shelf, such as is found on a spinning spacecraft.

The redundancy switch designs and configurations are typical of what is used in the industry, but the discussion is not intended to be all inclusive. There are many variations to these schemes, and new switch technologies are appearing all the time. You may use this framework to understand the specifics of a given repeater and switch design.

5.3.4 Waveguide Filters and Multiplexers

Modern satellite repeaters can provide several wideband channels of communication (i.e., transponders) because the individual channels can be separated from each other on the basis of frequency. As was discussed in the section on repeater configurations, the input multiplexer separates the channels for amplification and the output multiplexer combines them again from transmission to the ground through the antenna. The multiplexer contains a microwave filter for each individual channel, the filter being tuned to pass the full bandwidth of that channel and to reject (or reflect) all others. As shown in Figure 5-7, an input multiplexer typically uses circulators to route the entire spectrum of channels to the filters in a sequential manner, each filter being used to drop off one of the channels. One nice feature of using circulators is that they essentially isolate the filters from each other, which from a technical standpoint tends to simplify their design and manufacture.

The output multiplexer is constructed a little differently and without the use of a lossy circulator chain. Each filter is attached to a section of waveguide called a *manifold*. Without circulators to provide isolation, the filters must be positioned in accordance with wavelength along the manifold and manually adjusted (tuned) as an integrated system. An example of a filter-manifold combination is shown in Figure 5.13, where frequency channels F_1 and F_2 are combined. The rectangular waveguide filter in this example has two waveguide cavities which are separated by a sheet of metal with a small opening called an *iris*. The combination of the two cavities and iris produce a tuned circuit with mutual coupling to enhance the shaping of the filter characteristic. More sections separated by additional irises would improve the shaping and rejection of adjacent frequency channels, but would also tend to increase the insertion loss experienced by signals which pass through. Channel F_2 is travelling along the manifold, having been applied through its own waveguide filter (not shown), while channel F_1 passes through its filter and enters the manifold through a coupling port. Because the F_1 filter appears to channel F_2 as a short circuit, energy in the F_2 bandwidth is reflected back into the manifold, as if the waveguide wall was solid metal. Energy in the F_1 band which reaches the manifold will likewise be reflected back by the F_2 filter as well as by the shorting plate mounted on the end of the waveguide (not shown). The combined action of the filters is to cause virtually all of the energy from both channels to appear at the output end of the manifold.

We have been describing the action of a microwave filter without being specific about the way it affects the signals that pass through it. Figure 5-14 gives a qualitative view of the frequency response of the filter by itself and of the combined action of filters in a multiplexer. The characteristic of a single filter (shown at the top of Figure 5-14) includes a passband of sufficient bandwidth to allow all of the signals within the particular transponder to be transmitted with minimal distortion. A perfect filter would have a flat passband and would have

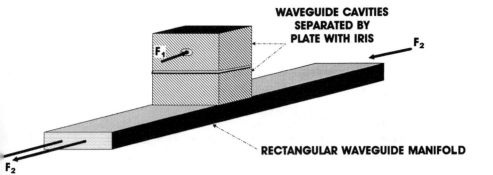

Fig. 5-13 Conceptual Drawing of a Two-Channel Output Multiplexer Composed of a Waveguide Cavity Filter Attached to a Waveguide Manifold

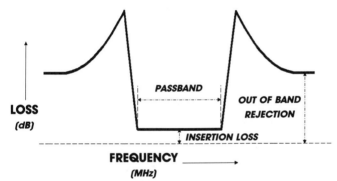

(A) LOSS VERSUS FREQUENCY FOR A SINGLE BANDPASS FILTER

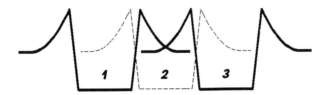

(B) LOSS CHARACTERISTICS OF TWO ODD- NUMBERED CHANNELS ON ONE MULTIPLEXER AND ONE EVEN-NUMBERED CHANNEL INTERLEAVED WITHIN THE OPEN GUARDBAND

Fig. 5-14 Characteristics of a Single Microwave Filter in Comparison to the Odd- and Even-Numbered Channels of an RF Multiplexer

infinite loss for all frequencies which are outside of the passband (*out-of-band*). As was mentioned earlier, there is some residual loss, called *insertion loss*, within the passband. The perfectly flat insertion loss characteristic shown is impossible to achieve and one must be satisfied with variations in loss of typically ± 0.5 to 1 dB across the passband. This variation can appear as a rounding of the edges of the passband, as a ripple within the passband, or as a combination of both. The out-of-band portion of characteristic shown in Figure 5-14 is more representative of real filters, where the loss increases rapidly starting at the edge of the passband until a point of maximum loss is reached. Beyond this point, the out-of-band loss can decrease, but will generally stay above some minimum level which is termed the *out-of-band rejection*.

A well-designed filter will have low insertion loss, a reasonably flat passband, rapidly increasing attenuation at the edge of the passband, and high out-of-band rejection. Another important property is *delay distortion*, which was mentioned as an impairment in Chapter 4. Unfortunately, these characteristics represent trade-offs in filter design and construction. For example, rapidly increasing attenuation at the edge of the passband requires that many filter sections (cavities) be used, which increases both the insertion loss and delay distortion.

Combining several filters into a multiplexer implies the overlaying of their individual frequency responses, as shown at the bottom of Figure 5-14. The three filters are each tuned to different center frequencies corresponding to three adjacent transponders. The slight gap between the passbands (guardband) is necessary to prevent repeater multipath, which occurs when a signal on the edge of one channel finds a second path through the adjacent channel equipment. If uncontrolled, repeater multipath can cause all kinds of problems in the operation of the communication payload, such as tilted transponder passbands and frequency selective valleys in the antenna coverage pattern. Another problem called *spurious response* is the leakage of power through a multiplexer on undesired frequencies.

Again referring to Figure 5-14, the amount of loss at the point where the filter skirts cross over is important to the design of the multiplexer. The greater the loss at this point, the easier it is to match the actual performance of the multiplexer to theory. The loss at the crossover can be significantly increased by splitting the channels into two groups with each group on one multiplexer having every other channel. For example, one group would consist of the odd-numbered frequency channels (the darkened curves at the bottom of Figure 5-14), while the other would consist of the even-numbered channels (the dotted curve). This greatly improves the cross-over performance of the multiplexer, since an entire empty channel now lies in the gap. Advances in filter technology have made adjacent-channel (called *contiguous*) multiplexing feasible, where steep filter skirts provide the needed cross-over loss without having to use an even-odd split. The benefits of the contiguous multiplexer are the elimination of repeater multipath and the simplification of the antenna interface so that a more optimum footprint can be obtained.

5.3.5 Traveling Wave-Tube Amplifiers

It is often said that the design of a traveling wave tube (TWT) is an art, which refers to the complexity of its internal structure and involved principles of design. However, the TWT has proven to be the workhorse of commercial satellite communication because of its track record of excellent, long-life service. A TWT is a sophisticated vacuum tube which uses a narrow electron beam guided by a shaped magnetic field. Amplification is achieved by transfering energy from this beam to a microwave signal as it enters at one end and exits at the other. Because of the high voltages needed to generate and control the beam, a TWT requires a fairly complex power supply to convert the dc voltage from the spacecraft electrical system. As a matter of definition, the tube by itself is called a TWT, while the tube with its associated power supply is called a *TWT amplifier* (TWTA).

To understand the operation and design of a typical space TWT, examine the schematic diagram in Figure 5-15. The electron beam is generated by the gun (shown at the left), which consists of the heater, cathode, and anode. The heater raises the temperature of the cathode to cause it to emit negatively charged electrons which are then drawn off by the positively charged anode. Like any electron tube, the cathode is the principle life-determining component, and great pains are taken in its design and manufacture. Also, the temperature must be selected and maintained by the heater so that the cathode will emit electrons at the proper rate without exhausting the material which it carries on its surfaces to enhance performance. Not shown in the figure is the focus electrode surrounding the cathode, which aims and compresses the beam much like a lens. This produces the high beam current density needed for efficient TWT operation from a much lower cathode current density.

Immediately following the gun is the *slow-wave structure* which allows the beam to interact with the microwave signal under amplification. The low-level input signal enters through the port at the left and encounters a long, tightly wound coil called the *helix*. Microwave energy in free space travels at the speed of light, which is considerably in excess of the speed of the electrons in the beam. The helix reduces the velocity of the microwave signal to approximately that of the electron beam. The beam is kept tightly formed within the helix by a string of permanent magnets. Electromagnetic interaction of the microwave signal, which is a wave phenomenon, with the beam causes bunching of the electrons as they move along. Ultimately, this bunching transfers energy back to the microwave signal, adding considerable power to it. When the signal reaches

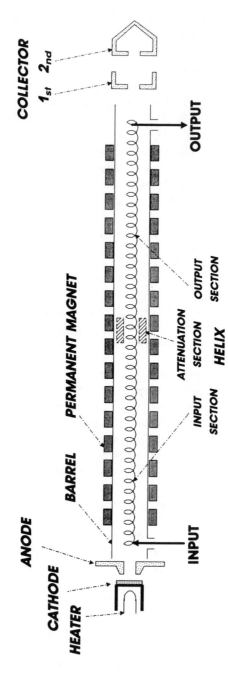

Fig. 5-15 Schematic Diagram of a Helix Traveling Wave Tube Intended for Space Applications Requiring High Efficiency and Long Life

the end of the tube, the electron beam has lost the majority of its energy of motion while the microwave signal has become greatly amplified in power. The amplification (gain) of the TWT is roughly proportional to its length, which is easy to see because the interaction and transfer of energy increases as the beam and signal travel along the slow-wave structure. The attenuation section at the center of the helix is an added feature to prevent self-oscillation and thereby stabilize TWT operation. An output port at the end of the helix allows the amplified signal to exit.

The collector, located at the end of the TWT, is critical to efficient operation. It is the objective of tube operation that energy be transferred from beam to signal, which implies that the velocity of the beam gradually reduces as it moves towards the output end. By the time the electrons reach the collector, they still possess considerable energy and are moving at only slightly less velocity than at the gun. Efficient operation is achieved if the electrons are collected in such a way that their velocity is reduced to near zero before they actually hit the collector. This is accomplished by placing a negative voltage on certain collector stages to repel the electrons and thereby slow them down. The use of negative voltage for this purpose is called *collector depression* and is done with a multiple-staged collector, as shown in Figure 5-15.

The previous discussion was by no means all inclusive, and the understanding of the detailed design and operation of space TWTs is beyond the scope of this book. It should, however, give the reader some idea of how a TWT works and generate an appreciation for the sophistication of the technology. Areas of critical importance include the materials and the manufacturing processing techniques used. These aspects determine the physical properties of the TWT (weight and ruggedness) as well as the lifetime and reliability of the amplifier when operating in orbit.

It is important to say a few words about the power supply which must accompany the TWT for the purpose of providing the various voltages and currents. Examine the typical TWT voltages in Table 5-1 to get an appreciation for the complexity of the design requirements. The circuitry to obtain these voltages usually consists of an ac oscillator, high voltage transformers, and capacitor-type voltage multipliers. To provide stable operation of the TWTA, it is vital that these voltages be held constant under all conditions of TWT signal loading and unit temperature, and throughout the lifetime of the repeater. Also, transient conditions on the power line coming into the power supply should also not be transmitted to the TWT because of the possibility for spurious phase modulation. A well designed TWT power supply will meet these stringent requirements and also have an efficiency (i.e., the ratio of power actually applied to the TWT to the dc input power from the spacecraft power system) in the range of 90 to 95%.

TWT ELECTRODE	TYPICAL VOLTAGE
HEATER	− 4000 (with − 5 volts across the heater)
FOCUS ELECTRODE	− 4000
ANODE	+ 200
SLOW WAVE STRUCTURE	0 (ground)
COLLECTOR	
FIRST STAGE	0 (ground)
SECOND STAGE	− 2500
THIRD STAGE	− 3200

Table 5-1 Typical Voltages Provided by the TWT Power Supply

5.3.6 Solid-State Power Amplifiers

Historically, the TWT has been the only nonsolid-state active device on commercial satellites. This is because while transistors have always been found in the digital circuitry used to control the various bus and payload elements, the TWT was the only practical device which could amplify microwave signals to power levels in excess of one watt with reasonable efficiency. Keep in mind that our context is the operation of a microwave repeater in the space environment for 10 years. You simply cannot afford to experiment with new or unproven technology under these conditions. The first solid-state amplifiers for C band were used in the mid-1970s for the medium power stage in the spacecraft wide-band receiver. In the early 1980s, the gallium arsenide field effect transistor (GaAs FET) established itself as a reliable and efficient power amplifier device and now is in use in a number of C-band satellites. The term *solid-state power amplifier* (SSPA) is used to refer to an amplifier using GaAs FET devices and providing an output power in the range of one to ten watts (higher power levels are coming on the horizon, as discussed in Chapter 3).

An SSPA is not a single amplifying device like a TWTA, but rather is built up from individual amplifier modules. The basic building block, shown at the top of Figure 5-16, is the single-stage microwave transistor power amplifier. The triangle symbol represents a GaAs FET and its associated bias circuitry. Circulators at the input and output provide considerable isolation (hence the term *isolator*) from the rest of the SSPA and repeater. Note how the third port of the circulator is connected to a dummy load, which catches any microwave energy which is reflected back into the circulator by the amplifier or output. Without the isolators, the GaAs FET would tend to produce unpredictable results and may even damage itself.

The basic module can have from six to ten dB of gain and a maximum power output of from one to five watts. Higher levels of gain or power out are obtained by combining stages, as illustrated in the rest of Figure 5-16. Gain is increased by adding stages in tandem, where the individual gains (in dB) are simply added algebraically. This will not increase the maximum output power capability, because all of the signal must still come from the last stage; the input level, however, can be reduced to a much lower level, corresponding to that which has passed through the input multiplexer. To achieve a total gain comparable to that of a TWT (roughly 50 dB), will take at least five stages in tandem.

The method of paralleling stages, shown at the bottom of Figure 5-16, will increase the maximum output capability in direct proportion to the number of stages in parallel. At the input, the signal power is split into two equal parts with a four-port device called a *hybrid*. Note that the fourth port of the hybrid is not required and is therefore terminated, i.e., it is connected to a passive load. Amplification is accomplished by a matched set of single-stage microwave transistor power amplifiers, whose outputs are combined by a second hybrid. The gain of the parallel combination is equal to that of a single stage, but it can output approximately twice the power since two amplifiers are working together. The key to successful operation is that the hybrids split and combine the signals precisely with the proper phasing and that the individual GaAs FET stages be nearly identical in their characteristics. Not shown in the figure are the circuit components which allow a technician to adjust the balance and phasing of the signals to achieve the desired performance. With everything properly aligned, virtually all of the output power will appear at the upper port of the hybrid on the right and none will appear at the terminated port.

With need to tandem and parallel stages, it is easy to see that the achievement of high power and high gain comes at a price in SSPAs. On the other hand, there are some unique benefits in using SSPAs as compared to TWTAs. GaAs FET devices, being solid state in nature, do not wear out like the cathode of a TWT, meaning that a well designed and constructed SSPA should last forever if its temperature is kept within the prescribed range. On the other hand, an SSPA is more complex in terms of the number of internal microwave connections, which can increase the chance of failure of a random nature. For example, the solder joints or welds where the GaAs FETs are connected into

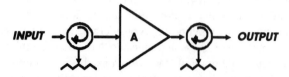

(A) SINGLE STAGE MICROWAVE TRANSISTOR POWER AMPLIFIER

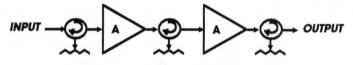

(B) TWO TRANSISTOR STAGES IN TANDEM

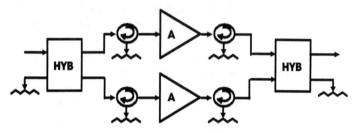

(C) TWO HYBRID COUPLED STAGES IN PARALLEL

Fig. 5-16 Solid-State Power Amplifiers for Microwave Transmission Employing Individual High Power Transistor Stages

their associated circuits can deteriorate and open up. On the performance side, the linearity of an SSPA generally tends to be superior to a TWT by itself, although this factor is now becoming moot with the advent of linearizers (discussed in Chapter 9).

The areas where the TWTA continues to shine are in power output and efficiency. The current maximum practical output for a C-band SSPA is approximately 10 watts while TWTs with powers in excess of 100 watts are being built. The efficiency of an SSPA tends to decrease as power is increased (because of the need to parallel and suffer losses through the hybrids that are required for each pair of stages) while just the opposite is true for a TWTA. In some applications, TWTAs have also been paralleled using commandable switches as this provides an added degree of flexibility. Why then use an SSPA? Clearly, the performance of GaAs FET devices will continue to improve and their cost will come down. These trends will eventually make SSPAs the best choice for many applications in satellite communication. The TWTA will probably remain as the front runner for high-power applications such as direct broadcasting satellites.

5.3.7 Transponder Gain Control

While earlier communication satellites generally employed fixed-gain repeaters, the trend has been towards providing each transponder with commandable gain control. A commandable gain step is useful to tailor the transponder to the particular earth station network. In some instances, interference can be rejected by reducing transponder gain and raising uplink EIRP accordingly. The most common technique is to include one or two switchable attenuators, each with three or six dB of attenuation, on the input side of the TWTA or SSPA. Such an attenuator consists of a ferrite switch with the third port connected to a termination with the desired amount of loss. Other types of gain control are being applied, such as PIN diode attenuators, limiters, and automatic gain control (AGC) circuits, although these are by no means standard equipment.

5.4 SPACECRAFT ANTENNA SYSTEMS

The spacecraft antenna system, which is often viewed as part of the communication payload, has many special and important characteristics and therefore is deserving of its own section of this chapter. Modern antenna systems provide a variety of communication coverage patterns such as domestic and spot beams, allowing the repeater to be utilized in an efficient and flexible manner. The following paragraphs explain how typical antennas are physically constructed and how they create the appropriate coverage patterns. An exact description of antenna operation would require the use of electromagnetic theory, which, while mentioned in Chapter 3, is beyond the scope of this book. The somewhat simplified explanations that follow, however, should provide a practical understanding of spacecraft antennas.

5.4.1 Reflector Arrangements

The majority of spacecraft antennas use an electrically conductive reflector pointed in the direction of propagation with one or more feed horns placed at the focus of the reflector. In the transmit mode, microwave energy enters the feed horn from a piece of waveguide which carries the output of the repeater. The feed horn radiates the energy into space in the direction of the reflector, causing electrical currents on its conductive surface. The combination of all of these currents reradiate the microwave energy in the direction of the earth and over an angular range corresponding to the desired coverage pattern. Viewed another way, the reflector intercepts the feed horn's radiated beam and forms a new collimated beam aimed towards the earth.

Reception works in the opposite direction, although with a much weaker signal. The energy arriving at the satellite produces very weak electrical currents on the surface of the reflector, which reradiates it towards the feed. In this case, the reflector acts as a gatherer of signal energy, focusing it on the feed. A nice feature of such passive antenna designs is that a single reflector with feed can function either for transmitting or receiving or both simultaneously. This property, called *reciprocity*, was mentioned in Chapter 3.

Two typical antenna geometries using parabolic reflectors are shown in Figure 5-17. In both cases, the reflector surface is formed by taking a parabola and rotating it about a line drawn from the focus to the center of the parabola. Shown at the top of Figure 5-17 is the prime-focus-fed parabola, which operates in principle like a reflecting mirror, producing a collimated beam of parallel rays from a source located at the focus. The prime focus approach is efficient and effective because of the ideal geometry that it possesses; it has, however, the drawback that the feedhorn (or system of feedhorns) can block and deflect a portion of the collimated beam. This is particularly troublesome in frequency reuse spacecraft antennas where feedhorn blockage can degrade cross-polarization isolation of the beam and scatter energy outside of the desired coverage region on the earth.

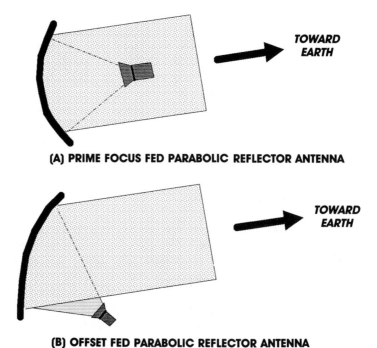

(A) PRIME FOCUS FED PARABOLIC REFLECTOR ANTENNA

(B) OFFSET FED PARABOLIC REFLECTOR ANTENNA

Fig. 5-17 The Prime-Focus-Fed Parabolic Reflector Antenna is Subject to Feed Blockage While the Offset-Fed Design Provides an Unobstructed Beam

The difficulties of blockage are effectively overcome be using a section of the parabolic reflector, as shown at the bottom of Figure 5-17. Notice that only the upper portion of the parabola is present and the feed is aimed to illuminate that portion. The resulting beam is offset slightly away from the center line of the parabola, thus entirely avoiding the feed. To obtain a horizontal beam without placing the feed in the beam's path requires that the entire antenna (reflector and feed) be tilted downward. The only technical drawback of the offset parabola is that some efficiency is lost by tilting the beam upward. However, the resulting loss (in the range of typically 0.5 to 1.0 dB) is compensated by the elimination of losses and beam distortion due to feed blockage.

Nonreflector types of antennas are also used on commercial satellites. For example, full earth (global) coverage, requiring a beamwidth of approximately 17^0, is efficiently achieved with a single horn pointed towards the earth. Omnidirectional antennas (similar in concept to an automobile radio rod antenna) are used for transfer orbit and emergency operations, as will be described later in this chapter. Another entirely different class of antenna which has been applied for a few specialized missions is the planar array. Its configuration is that of a flat metal plate with a series of slits cut into it. Each slit is fed through a power divider mounted behind the array, and the combination of the patterns of all the slits produces a narrow beam. The principal advantage of the planar array is that it occupies much less space than a comparable parabolic reflector antenna. The planar array, however, is limited in the bandwidth that it will operate over, which restricts its use to that of either a transmitting or a receiving antenna. Application of the planar array to the receive-only earth station is discussed in Chapter 9.

5.4.2 Antenna Patterns

For most spacecraft antenna systems, the feedhorn works together with a reflector of some sort to produce the desired coverage pattern. At the top of Figure 5-18, a reflector with diameter D is illuminated with microwave energy by a single feedhorn located at the focus. The feedhorn has a radiation pattern (indicated as the shaded area in front of the reflector) which has a maximum along the centerline and decreases in intensity towards the edge of the reflector. The specific manner in which the intensity is adjusted is called the *taper*. As you will recall from the previous discussion, the primary illumination produces a corresponding distribution of electrical currents across the reflector surface. These currents reradiate the energy towards the front of the reflector, resulting in the desired secondary pattern in the far field of the antenna. The far field is a region where the beam is completely formed, beginning at some considerable distance in front of the antenna.

An example of a secondary pattern is shown at the bottom of Figure 5-18. The main lobe in the center provides the desired coverage, a concept first

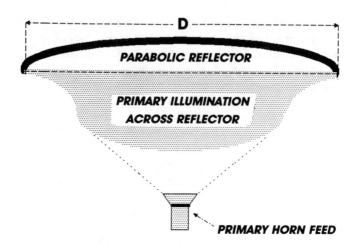

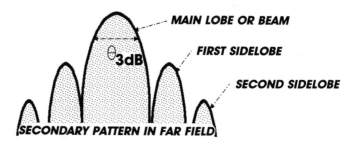

Fig. 5-18 Illumination of a Parabolic Reflector by a Waveguide Horn Producing a Secondary Pattern Which Contains a Main Beam and Sidelobes

introduced in Chapter 1. Visualize that the peak of this lobe is pointed at the center of a country to be covered. The main lobe extends across an angular dimension, Θ_{3dB}, which roughly corresponds to the width of that country. The parameter Θ_{3dB} is the 3-dB beamwidth, defining the point where the gain of the antenna is 3 dB down (i.e., one-half the power) from the peak. This natural characteristic of an antenna beam explains why reception from domestic satellites is generally better in the center of the country than at the borders.

The secondary pattern also shows side lobes, located on either side of the main lobe. The sidelobes represent signal energy taken from the main lobe which radiates into adjoining regions on the earth. Sidelobes of course are potential sources of radio interference to and from earth stations in the geographic regions where they fall. In satellites which use multiple beams to reuse frequency, it becomes particularly important to control the level and location of these side-lobes. This can be accomplished through the selection and location of feedhorns as well as the use of the proper taper of the primary pattern.

In rough terms, the 3-dB beamwidth (in degrees) of the far field pattern is related to the diameter of the reflector through the following approximation:

$$\theta_{3dB} = \frac{70}{FD}$$

where

D is the antenna diameter measured in feet,
F is the microwave frequency in GHz.

This formula shows that the beamwidth decreases as either the diameter or frequency are increased. The gain of the antenna, on the other hand, increases as the square of either the diameter or frequency. Also, the relationship between the 3-dB beamwidth (i.e., coverage area) and the gain of the antenna is independent of diameter and frequency.

At C-band frequencies and higher, it is practical to generate a beam which follows the contour of a country or region by combining the action of several individual feedhorns. Figure 5-19 shows how three feedhorns can be combined to produce a shaped beam. Horn B, located at the focus of the reflector, produces the expected main lobe labeled B. Now, examine the horn labeled A and its associated far-field main lobe. Shifting the horn to the left has caused the main lobe to be shifted to the right, much like what happens with a glass mirror. Similarly, shifting the horn C to the right causes the far-field pattern to shift to the left. The sum of the three patterns is illustrated by the wavy line labeled, *combined pattern in far field*. This is produced by a feed network which divides the signal three ways, reducing the power that reaches each feed. For example, an equal three-way split reduces the signal level by 10 log (3), which is approximately 5 dB. The power will recombine in the far field due to the overlapping of the individual secondary patterns. In the case of reception, the same signal coming from the three horns is summed in the feed network.

Beam shaping is a powerful technique for increasing the effectiveness of a communication satellite. In Figure 5-20, the coverage of Mexico provided by a single elliptical beam is compared with a shaped-beam coverage from combining four nearly circular beams (indicated as the shaded area). Both the single and shaped beams cover the entire Mexican land mass. The single beam, however, radiates a substantial fraction outside of Mexico, which represents a loss

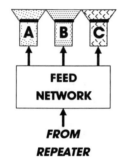

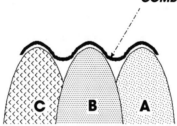

Fig. 5-19 Generation of a Shaped Beam Antenna Pattern Using Multiple Feed Horns and an Associated Feed Network

of about half of the available signal power. In comparison, the shaped beam provides a relatively tight fit of Mexico, giving as much as 3 dB more gain as compared to the single elliptical beam.

It is not sufficient to cover the area of interest. Some additional margin must be provided to allow for movement of the antenna caused by small changes in spacecraft attitude. This means that the actual gain which can be used effectively is somewhat reduced. This aspect of antenna performance will be covered in a subsequent section on attitude control.

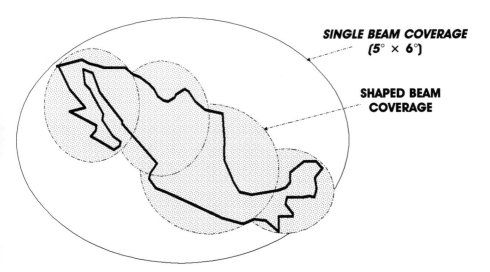

Fig. 5-20 Spacecraft Antenna Coverage of the Mexican Land Mass Demonstrating that a Shaped Beam Is More Efficient than an Elliptical Beam

5.5 SPACECRAFT BUS SUBSYSTEMS

The spacecraft bus encompasses those elements of the satellite which support the communication payload. As depicted in Figure 5-2, this support is multifaceted, involving the following functions: providing prime power; pointing the antenna beam precisely at all times; controlling temperature to maintain proper operation of electronics and mechanical devices; providing physical support during launch; maintaining the position of the satellite during its operating lifetime; and allowing ground personnel to have remote control of each subsystem. Each of these fuctions involve one or more of the bus subsystems, which are described in the following paragraphs.

5.5.1 Attitude Control Subsystem

An assumption was made in the previous discussion on antennas that the far-field pattern could be held perfectly on the geographical region being covered. In real life, there are several forces acting on the spacecraft which cause the platform and antenna to move away from optimum pointing. The *attitude control subsystem* (ACS) is that combination of elements which senses any change in pointing and then causes the spacecraft to realign itself. This type of function can be found on virtually every space vehicle, including guided rockets, scientific deep space probes, and, of course, geostationary satellites. Commercial satellites usually have some built in (*autonomous*) ACS capability, but manual intervention from the ground is often necessary during certain phases of orbital operations.

5.5.1.1 Attitude Control Loop

Shown in Figure 5-21 is a conceptual block diagram of an ACS control loop intended for autonomous operation. The *pointing sensor* (located at the upper left) is capable of precisely measuring the pointing angle with respect to some reference. Having the ability to detect changes along two axes (north-south and east-west), the sensor is a critical element because its measurement accuracy has a large impact on overall ACS pointing accuracy. Two sensing techniques are reviewed in a subsequent paragraph.

A typical ACS loop includes a sensor electronic unit to process the sensor's output signals and produce a properly calibrated error message. The *attitude control digital processor* is a fairly complicated box which in modern satellites contains a microcomputer. It accepts the error message for use in determining corrective action. Ground control of the processor can be exercised during spacecraft maneuvers and to update its programming.

The processor is connected directly to the electrical windings of the mechanical devices (drives) or other transducers which cause the spacecraft attitude actually to change. In the case of a spinning satellite, the east-west mechanical drive is the BAPTA, which controls the relative spin rate between the antenna and the bus. Three axis spacecraft typically use several mechanical drives and devices. For example, the speed and gimbal angle of the momentum wheel can be adjusted to cause small changes in spacecraft body orientation. To maintain a stable three axis platform, these forcing functions must be softly applied because of the small degree of gyroscopic stiffness as compared to the spinner. However, modern digital processors can be programmed to use *adaptive control laws* to minimize the extent and duration of transients during orientation changes.

The spacecraft is not a rigid body but actually has several parts such as the solar panels and antenna reflectors which are flexibly attached. Therefore, as shown at the bottom of Figure 5-21, the force for change from the mechanical drives is applied to the body through *spacecraft dynamics*. This simply means that some parts of the body will bend and vibrate when a force is applied to the spacecraft. This combined with the inertia of spacecraft mass produces *transients* in the pointing performance of the antenna beams which can last several seconds. It is important that the ACS prevent the peak value of the transient from exceeding the acceptable beam error and that transients are properly damped out without excessive overshoot.

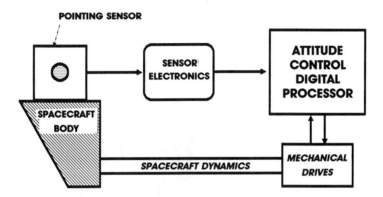

Fig. 5-21 Conceptual Block Diagram of the Attitude Control Subsystem
Showing the Arrangement of the Control Loop

The control loop in this description is now complete because the sensor is
mounted on the body and will also move when the attitude of the spacecraft
changes. The sensor transmits a new indication of orientation, which in turn is
fed into the digital processor. The active and adaptive nature of the control loop
allows it continuously to adjust the orientation of the spacecraft and to dampen
any transients.

5.5.1.2   Sensors

The two principle types of attitude sensor are the *earth sensor* and *RF
tracking*. At certain times in the mission, it is not possible to use the earth as a
reference due to interference from the sun or moon. This is usually overcome
with a *sun sensor* made up of a silicon solar cell and optical barrel.

Earth Sensor Tracking.

Depicted in Figures 5-22 and 5-23 are earth sensor concepts for a spinning
satellite and for a three axis satellite, respectively. Both use a narrow beam
optical device consisting of a small telescope with an infrared detector at the
viewing end. For the spinning bus (Figure 5-22(A)), it is a relatively simple
matter to attach two of these sensors to the rotating part of the spacecraft, allowing
them to scan past the earth. The north and south pointing earth sensors each
intersect a cord from the relatively warm earth's disk. The two cords will be
equal in length (and hence the time scans across the earth will be equal in
duration) only if the body is pointed towards the equator. If the body were

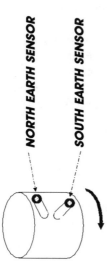

(A) ARRANGEMENT OF NORTH AND SOUTH EARTH SENSORS ON THE BODY OF A SPINNING SPACECRAFT

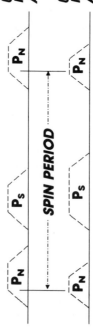

(i) Equal North and South Pulses Indicate that Spacecraft Spin Axis Is Aligned on the Equator.

(ii) Short Noth Pulse and Long South Pulse Indicate that Spacecraft Spin Axis Is Aligned to the North.

(B) EXAMPLES OF EARTH SENSOR PULSE TIMING WAVEFORMS

Fig. 5-22 Arrangement and Operation of Dual Fixed Earth Sensors on a Spinning Spacecraft

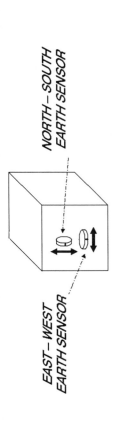

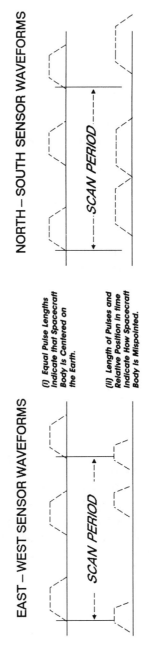

(A) ARRANGEMENT OF NORTH-SOUTH AND EAST-WEST EARTH SENSORS ON THE BODY OF A THREE-AXIS SPACECRAFT (DOUBLE HEADED ARROWS INDICATE SCANNING MOTION)

NORTH–SOUTH EARTH SENSOR

EAST–WEST EARTH SENSOR

NORTH–SOUTH SENSOR WAVEFORMS

EAST–WEST SENSOR WAVEFORMS

---- SCAN PERIOD ----

(i) Equal Pulse Lengths Indicate that Spacecraft Body Is Centered on the Earth.

(ii) Length of Pulses and Relative Position in time Indicate How Spacecraft Body Is Mispointed.

(B) EXAMPLES OF EARTH SENSOR PULSE TIMING WAVEFORMS

Fig. 5-23 Arrangement and Operation of Dual Scanning Earth Sensors on a Three-Axis Spacecraft

pointed north, then the duration of the north earth sensor pulse would be shorter than that of the south earth sensor, with the precise difference being a direct indication of the amount of misalignment.

The waveforms of Figure 5-22(B) depict the time relationship between the pulses coming from the two spinning earth sensors. The north sensor is pointed slightly ahead of the south sensor to prevent the pulses from overlapping in time. This allows the two pulses to be sent along the same signal path. The top line represents the pulses with the body properly aligned, while the set below it corresponds to the condition with the body pointed northward. Pointing along the east-west (rotational) direction is determined by comparing the start of the north pulse with respect to an index pulse generated within the BAPTA (or drive motor for the rotary joint in the case of a simple spinner). A ground commanded offset is stored in the attitude control digital processor to provide a reference for comparison with the measured offset between the north and index pulses. Using the earth pulses, the index pulses and the offset, it is possible to determine attitude along both pointing axes to within $\pm 0.05°$, which is adequate to maintain reasonably good pointing of an area coverage beam.

The type of earth sensor used on a three-axis must be different, because the body does not move regularly with respect to the earth. This problem is overcome by using an earth sensor assembly which does its own scanning, producing pulses with the appropriate type of information. In the simplest approach, two mirrors are mounted on a common torsion beam that scans back and forth. The mirrors are oriented north and south just like the respective fixed sensors on a spinning satellite. Infrared radiation from the earth is reflected by the mirrors onto separate IR sensors. Since the sensors output pulses of lengths proportional to earth chord widths, the technique operates essentially the same as described for the spinner.

Another more elaborate sensing system for three-axis spacecraft is illustrated in Figure 5-23. The box at the center represents the spacecraft body and the two small disks are sensors, one oriented for north-south motion and the other for east-west. The infrared detector is placed next to a rotating prism or oscillating mirror, causing the detector's output to be a cyclical sweep along one axis. To the left of the box is shown a set of waveforms for the east-west sensor, indicating that the scanning is periodic. The top waveform corresponds to the body pointed at the center of the earth while the waveform beneath shows what would happen with the body pointed to the east and either north or south of the equator. The north-south scanning sensor produces similar waveforms, the upper one corresponding to proper alignment with the earth. Below it, the waveform indicates that the body is pointed towards the south, resolving the ambiguity in the corresponding (lower) east-west waveform.

RF Tracking.

The RF tracking technique, depicted in Figure 5-24, is perhaps the most accurate system for sensing spacecraft attitude. Some of the same devices that are used for reception of the uplink microwave signals are applied to tracking. Each axis requires two receive horns and an associated hybrid. Out of the hybrid comes two ports, one containing the sum $(A + B)$ and the other the difference $(A - B)$. The sum signal represents the combination of the two beams, having a combined pattern similar to the one shown on the right. The difference signal, however, effectively passes through zero in its response precisely where the individual horn patterns overlap. The difference pattern, which has the appearance of a sinewave, is used to detect a null in signal energy corresponding to proper alignment of the antenna beam. This requires that a reference earth station be located where the null should be placed and that this station transmit a continuous signal called a *pilot carrier* or *beacon.*

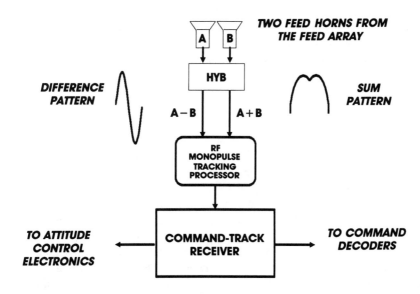

Fig. 5-24 Attitude Sensing by the Spacecraft Antenna and Command Receiver When Tracking an RF Pilot Signal Transmitted from the TTAC Earth Station

There remains the problem that the difference signal by itself does not provide a continuous error signal when the beacon enters the null. This is overcome by modulating the $A - B$ response onto the $A + B$ response, which is accomplished within the *RF monopulse tracking processor.* The modulation can then go through its zero point without introducing intolerable noise into the control loop. In most applications, the beacon signal is also used as the command uplink to the spacecraft. Separation of the attitude error signal from the command signal is usually accomplished within the *command-track receiver*, shown at the bottom of Figure 5-24. RF tracking systems have measurement accuracies in the range of ± 0.01 to 0.04°.

5.5.1.3   Antenna Pointing

The real measure of ACS performance is its effect on the stability of spacecraft antenna pointing. Sensor accuracy, discussed above, contributes approximately ten to twenty percent of the total accuracy of pointing. A second big contributor is the movement of parts of the physical antenna due to variations in solar heating of the reflector and feed supports. Referred to as *thermal distortion*, this effect can produce as much as one half of the total error, depending on the thermal stability of the material used in antenna construction. Another error is that due to the precision with which the antenna and sensor are attached to the spacecraft, a process which requires the use of optical alignment instruments during assembly on the ground. Finally, the transient behavior of the ACS during thruster firing will cause the antenna to be momentarily misdirected.

The error components cited in the previous paragraph result in a maximum value of total error which will occur at various times during the life of the satellite. The fixed and deterministic ones can to some extent be compensated for after placement in orbit. For a typical operating satellite, the overall pointing error of the antenna beam is in the range of ± 0.05 to 0.15 degrees in either the north-south or east-west directions. Motion about the third axis of the spacecraft (*yaw*) causes the antenna pattern to twist with respect to the earth and therefore represents a third error prone direction of motion. For coverage regions some distance from the equator, it can be nearly compensated by east-west and north-south ACS control. Larger yaw error, which is usually not measured directly by an onboard sensor, can be reduced to an acceptable value by appropriate thruster firings based upon analysis performed at the ground station.

Examine the antenna coverage of Mexico in Figure 5-25, which is based on the shaped beam antenna design described previously. This pattern provides 30 dB of gain (the black contour) over the Mexican landmass, and reaches 33.5 dB at the peak. The approach commonly used to evaluate antenna pointing error is to employ boxes whose sides have a dimension corresponding to the maximum value of pointing error anticipated. Because Mexico is considerably north of the equator, yaw error has been broken down into east-west and north-south components which are already included. In the example, the ACS pointing error is assumed to be ± 0.10° in both directions, which makes the error box 0.2° on each side. Boxes are then placed at critical locations such as key cities or at points along the border of the region or country being served. In Figure 5-25,

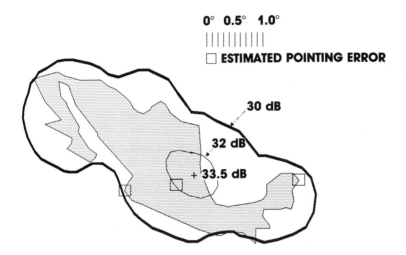

0° 0.5° 1.0°

||||||||||||

☐ **ESTIMATED POINTING ERROR**

30 dB

32 dB

+ 33.5 dB

Fig. 5-25 Spacecraft Antenna Gain Performance in dB Indicating How Pointing Error Is Taken into Account

error boxes have been placed at Mexico City as well as two points along Mexico's coast which protrude into the water. The Mexico City box shows that the gain at that point nominally will be 32 dB but can be expected at times to decrease as much as 0.5 dB (obtained by interpolation between the 32 and 30 dB contours). The lower-right box (located at the tip of the Yucatan Peninsula) shows that even with maximum error, a gain of 30 dB is maintained. The error box at the left (Pacific) coast, however, extends outside the contour and the gain will therefore at times drop below 30 dB. As an alternative to using boxes, the size of the map of Mexico can be increased by the extent of the maximum pointing error.

This procedure is used to compare the predicted performance of the spacecraft to the specification. While values of gain are shown in Figure 5-25, it is more appropriate to label the contours with EIRP and G/T, determined in accordance with the procedures given in Chapter 3. This ties together the performance of the communication payload and attitude control system.

5.5.2 Solar Power

All geostationary communication satellites use panels of silicon solar cells to provide prime power to the payload and bus. Shown in Figure 5-26 is a comparison of the two common panel forms: the cylindrical drum and the flat panel. The dimensions D and L define the effective area which is illuminated by the sun. The power output of a solar cell is proportional to the intensity of solar radiation reaching the cell. This intensity is maximum with the rays arriving perpendicular to the cell and decreases as the cosine of the angle of the ray with respect to the perpendicular. A condition of zero output occurs when the rays are parallel to the cell's surface. Note that this same principle applies to taking a sun tan.

In the case of the type of flat panel on a three axis spacecraft, a drive motor maintains the array in the direction of the sun and all cells receive identical illumination. For a cylindrical panel, the cells are connected in series strings running the length of the cylinder. The output of a string remains at zero as the string rotates from behind to a point at the left visible edge, and increases to a maximum as the strings rotate to be in direct line with the sun's rays. Stated another way, the useful output of a cylindrical solar panel is determined by the cross section (*projected area*) in the direction of the sun.

The mathematical relationship shown at the left side in Figure 5-26 indicates that a cylindrical panel would have π (3.14159) times as many solar cells as a comparable flat panel which is continuously oriented towards the sun. Mathematics, therefore, indicates that a flat panel of the type used in a three axis satellite is roughly three times as efficient as the cylindrical panel used in a spinner. Degradation of solar cells caused by free electrons, however, is greater for flat panels due to exposure of both sides of the array, reducing the performance advantage at end of life to some degree.

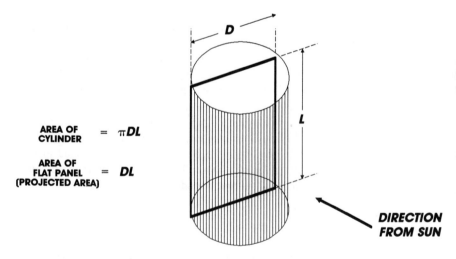

AREA OF CYLINDER = π*DL*

AREA OF FLAT PANEL (PROJECTED AREA) = *DL*

DIRECTION FROM SUN

Fig. 5-26 Comparison of Cylindrical and Flat Solar Panels from the Standpoint of the Effective Area in the Direction of the Sun

The output power from a solar panel, be it cylindrical or flat, does vary over the course of a year due to the orbital geometry. A simplified drawing of this geometry is shown in Figure 5-27, indicating that the equatorial plane is tilted approximately 23° with respect to the ecliptic plane (i.e., the plane of the orbit of the earth around the sun). This means that a satellite experiences the seasons just as we do on earth. (The figure uses summer and winter as seen from the northern latitudes.) In summer and winter, the sun's rays hit the panel at an angle, reducing the efficiency of the solar cells. The worst case occurs on the solstices, where the efficiency factor is equal to cos(23°), i.e., 92%. In the spring and fall, on the other hand, the sun provides better illumination of the panel and the cells give their maximum output at the equinoxes. It happens that the point of minimum panel output occurs at the summer solstice, where the distance between earth and sun is greater than in winter.

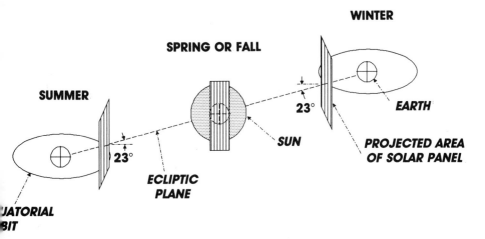

Fig. 5-27 Variation of the Illumination of the Solar Panel as the Earth and Satellite in GEO Revolve Around the Sun

These geometrical factors should provide some appreciation of the basic requirements for solar panel design. There are, however, many other factors to consider. It was mentioned earlier that electrons in the geostationary orbit region impinge on the solar panel and degrade the performance of solar cells. By proper cell and panel design, it is possible to reduce this degradation to the range of 15 to 20 percent over the life of the satellite. Most of this power loss occurs in the first few years of operation, while the loss in later years tapers off. Mechanisms and drive motors which are used to deploy and orient the panels must be very reliable with redundancy built in as much as possible.

5.5.3   Spacecraft Electrical System

The solar array described in the previous section is only a part of the spacecraft electrical power system which provides continuous power to all electrical loads. For one, there is the eclipse period during which the sun is concealed by the earth and the spacecraft must derive power from a battery system. Another consideration is voltage regulation, which is important to achieving stable electronic performance of the units onboard and to minimizing excess heat generation when large voltage swings from the solar panel must be absorbed throughout the spacecraft. The electrical system must not cause or propagate electrical transients which could affect payload or bus operation. Such dangerous transients are produced when electrostatic charge which has built up on surfaces of the spacecraft is allowed by faulty design to discharge into the electrical system.

5.5.3.1   Electrical Power Buss

Figure 5-28 is a simplified block diagram of a typical electrical system incorporating dual independent electrical busses (*buss* is spelled with a double *s* to differentiate it from the spacecraft bus). Separate busses provide redundancy and give assurance that a major failure (such as a short circuit) could only eliminate half of the system. This concept is extended to all electronic equipment, where units are paired so that they can be split with one-half on each buss. Alternatively, a single buss with redundant power electronics could be employed. To understand the construction of the electrical system, examine the arrangement of the upper half of Figure 5-28 (i.e., the part corresponding to buss 1 of a dual buss system.).

Prime power is generated in the main array and delivered to the buss. The limiter immediately to the right of the main array is provided to remove a segment of each string of cells to drop the voltage during periods of maximum solar illumination (during the equinoxes) or minimum power demand within the spacecraft. Switching in or out of the limiter is accomplished automatically by sensing the voltage on the buss (see the dashed line). The symbol composed of alternating short and long lines represents the battery composed of electrical cells used to store energy for eclipse operation. Nickel-cadmium cells have been used successfully for many years, but the more efficient nickel-hydrogen cells are now appearing in commercial satellites. Battery charge is maintained in these batteries by using separate charge arrays, indicated below the main arrays in Figure 5-28. The purpose of the battery controller is to switch the electrical buss from the array to the battery at the start of eclipse and back at the conclusion. This action can be automatic or by ground command, depending on the particular

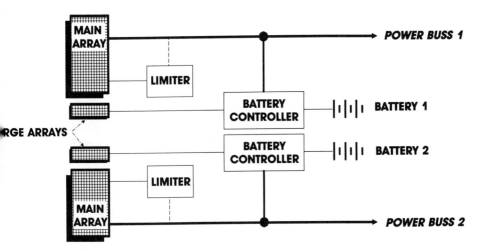

Fig. 5-28 Spacecraft Electrical Power System Including Solar Arrays and Batteries with Dual Independent Power Busses

approach taken in the design of the system. The battery controller is also used for ground-commanded maintenance of the batteries, which consists of maintaining a light "trickle" charge most of the time and periodically commanding a rapid discharge into resistors for cell reconditioning. Such maintenance procedures prolong cell life to ten years or more.

5.5.3.2   Electrostatic Discharge

The spacecraft electrical system provides conduction paths to every electronic and electrical unit within the spacecraft and can allow potentially damaging electrical transients to propagate through the system. Low-level transients which are generated aboard the satellite by normal operation of the payload can be rendered harmless by proper power supply design. It is possible, however, for spikes in the range of hundreds to thousands of volts to occur from *electrostatic discharge* (ESD), a phenomenon not unlike lightning.

ESD is the result of a buildup on external surfaces of the spacecraft of a static charge from electrons travelling in space. In a well-designed and constructed satellite, all conducting surfaces are electrically connected together to provide a common ground running through the spacecraft structure. This means that all points inside the spacecraft rise in voltage potential together. If any external surface (conducting or non-conducting) is not connected to ground, however, its voltage potential will differ from the rest of the spacecraft. An electrical arc could then leap across any gap that separates the external surface and another (grounded) element such as a piece of metal waveguide or structure. The large surge of electrical current that would ensue could pass from ground into the power system and be carried right into sensitive electronic equipment.

The effect of ESD has been experienced in the past, particularly on new spacecraft designs. A seemingly random shut down of an operating transmitter could be a symptom of ESD, as could a "glitch" (wild variation) in the telemetered output of a sensor. In some cases, ESD has been known to damage digital electronic equipment and power supplies permanently. It is therefore vital that ESD be carefully taken into account by using appropriate materials and by proper grounding.

5.5.4 Propulsion Systems

Commercial communication spacecraft typically control their orbital positions by using small liquid-fuel rocket engines. The amount of thrust is generally five pounds or less and depends on the needs of the spacecraft design. Large amounts of thrust required for major orbit changes can be provided either by solid rocket motors or by large liquid-fuel engines, as discussed in Chapter 7. The general arrangements of spinning and three axis spacecraft propulsion systems are compared in Figure 5-29.

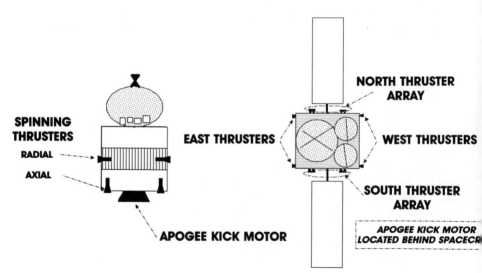

Fig. 5-29 General Arrangement of Propulsion Systems for Spinning and Three-Axis Spacecraft Configurations

Historically, the launch vehicle has provided the boost to place the space-craft into synchronous transfer orbit, an elliptical orbit with perigee at approx-imately 200 miles and an apogee at near-synchronous altitude (22,300 miles). Chapter 7 contains more background on launch and transfer orbit operations; suffice it to say, however, that geostationary orbit can be reached from the transfer orbit by firing an internal rocket motor when the spacecraft is nominally at apogee. The configurations in Figure 5-29 both assume the use of a solid-fuel *apogee kick motor* (AKM) which is permanently integrated into the spacecraft and fired by ground command. In the case of the spinner, there is a need for four liquid thrusters of approximately five pounds, all mounted on the rotating section. Either one of the *axial thrusters* when fired continuously will push the spacecraft upward, which is useful for north-south station-keeping. The spin axis can be moved to adjust spacecraft yaw attitude by pulsing one axial thruster in synchronization with the spin rate. Since the spacecraft is acting as one gigantic gyro, the pulsing must be done 90° ahead of the desired spin axis change. Pulsing of a *radial thruster* must also be synchronized with spin to move the spacecraft in the plane of the orbit. To prevent misaligning the spin axis, the direction of thrust passes through the center of mass of the spacecraft. Note that only two liquid thrusters are required (one axial and one radial) to satisfy requirements for attitude correction and station-keeping.

The fact that a three axis satellite does not spin to provide stability leads to the need for many more thrusters and for a much lower level of thrusting. As shown in Figure 5-29, the typical three axis uses 12 thrusters arranged in arrays on the north, south, east, and west faces. Thrust levels are measured in fractions of a pound to minimize disturbance of spacecraft attitude during thrusting. In comparison, the high gyroscopic stiffness of a spinner requires the use of rela-tively large thrust levels to correct spacecraft attitude. An evolving technique called *ion propulsion* is reviewed in Chapter 9.

5.5.4.1 Reaction Control System

The liquid fuel tanks, fuel lines, valves, and thrusters make up the *reaction control system* (RCS) which is an integral part of every commercial communi-cation satellite. Figure 5-30 shows a conceptual drawing of the spinner's RCS which uses a single liquid fuel called *hydrazine*. With the tanks having been pressurized prior to launch and with the spacecraft spinning on orbit, fuel exits the tanks and remains in the lines. The drawing is not accurate in that the lines are actually connected to the tanks on the side facing the exterior (solar panel) so that rotation forces the fuel out of the tanks.

The system is split into two redundant halves, either of which could support the mission with one axial and one radial thruster and a pair of tanks. An interconnect latch valve, which normally blocks connection between the two

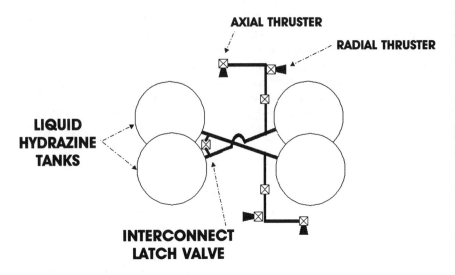

Fig. 5-30 Simplified Diagram of a Spinning Reaction Control Subsystem Employing Monopropellant Hydrazine Fuel

halves, can be commanded open to allow fuel from one side to move to the other. This is normally used during the mission to equalize fuel load and pressure but can also allow access to half the fuel in the event of a thruster failure. Note the use of an isolation valve in the line between the radial thruster and the tanks, which can be closed if a thruster should fail in the open position. Tanks and lines are typically made from welded titanium, which have been thoroughly tested on the ground to preclude even the slightest possibility of a leak.

In the case of a three axis satellite, the flow of fuel in the tank is controlled using a device within the tank rather than the force of rotation. One approach is to use a rubber diaphragm separating the fuel from the pressurant gas, allowing the gas to push the fuel out of the tank much the way we squeeze a tube of tooth paste. Another technique employs a spongelike device to direct liquid fuel toward the tank exit by capillary action.

Conventional liquid systems use hydrazine fuel alone, which decomposes into its constituents on contact with a catalyst. The process releases energy, resulting in high pressure gas at the thruster nozzle. Another important innovation in spacecraft RCS was the introduction of *bipropellant* technology, i.e., the use of a separate fuel and oxidizer. Monopropellant and bipropellant thrusters are compared in Figure 5-31. Having separate fuel and oxidizer produces greater thrust for the same weight of fuel, which will allow a bipropellant system to yield longer life (or conversely save fuel weight for the same life). Of necessity, bipropellant systems have more tanks, lines, and valves and therefore there is

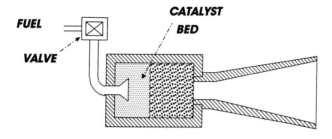

(A) MONOPROPELLANT THRUSTER

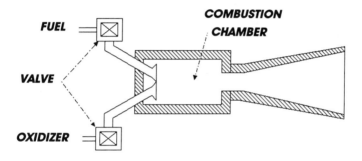

(B) BIPROPELLANT THRUSTER

Fig. 5-31 Liquid Propellant Thrusters Employing Monopropellant and Bipropellant Technologies

some penalty in cost and increased complexity. An improvement in monopropellant performance has been achieved with the *electrically heated thruster* (EHT) which increases thrust by heating the propellant with an electrical winding. Thrusting with the EHT would therefore have to be done in such a way as to use excess electrical power; otherwise, there would be a weight penalty for the additional solar cells. The benefits of bipropellant and EHT technology usually outweigh the costs for larger spacecraft and with missions that extend beyond 10 years.

5.5.4.2   Solid Rocket Motors

These rocket motors are filled with a relatively hard, rubbery combustible material (i.e., *solid fuel*) which when ignited by a pyrotechnic device within the motor case, burns rapidly producing intense thrust lasting one minute, more or less. Figure 5-32 shows a cross section of a typical small solid motor. This type of rocket motor can be fired only once and is ideal for major orbit changes, such as for apogee kick. Redundancy can really only be applied to the *igniter*, as shown. The case is constructed of titanium, although high strength fibers can also be used when wound in the proper shape. Attached at the exit is a *nozzle assembly* made of mixtures of carbon and other materials. During firing, the nozzle gets red hot from the heat of the expelled gasses. Nozzle design is as much an art as a science and the importance of quality control and testing cannot be overemphasized. Failures of such nozzles in the past have left satellites in unusable orbits.

As shown in subsequent spacecraft configuration drawings presented in Chapter 7, a single solid motor can be integrated into the spacecraft and the empty case carried for the remainder of the satellite lifetime after firing. Other solid motors can be attached at the bottom and discarded after use. There has been a recent trend to use relatively large liquid bipropellant motors which may or may not be part of the RCS because such a motor can be restarted and fired at successive apogees. Solid motors will, however, still find application during launch and orbit change because of their efficiency, simplicity, and shelf life.

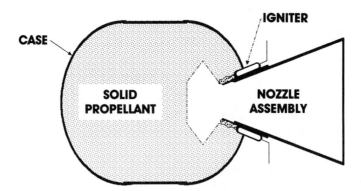

Fig. 5-32 Typical Solid Fuel Rocket Motor to Be Part of the Spacecraft for Use in Apogee Kick or Perigee Kick

5.5.5   Tracking, Telemetry, and Command

The communication payload and spacecraft bus, although designed to serve for a period of many years, require ground support and intervention even under normal circumstances. Consequently, there is need for a two-way system of radio communication to allow ground personnel to determine the status of the spacecraft and to control the various subsystems of the payload and bus. This is the purpose of the *tracking, telemetry, and command system* (TTAC), which, as illustrated in Figure 5-33, consists of both ground and space elements.

The TTAC ground station and its associated satellite control center (SCC) provide a sophisticated facility consisting of RF equipment, baseband, and digital processing equipment, computers, and operator display consoles. All aspects of the TTAC ground facilities are described in Chapter 6. The RF equipment is in the form of a fairly typical earth station with the exception that the antenna has the ability to track the satellite to help measure its position. Commands generated by operators or computers are sent to the satellite on the command uplink from the TTAC station. On board the satellite, these commands are decoded and activate some aspect of satellite operation. The telemetry downlink carries what is called housekeeping data, consisting of measurements of temperature, electrical voltage, RCS tank pressure, and other important parameters. Telemetry data is recovered in the ground facility and processed in the computer system to provide a current picture of satellite health and to be stored for evaluation of long term-performance.

Most communication spacecraft employ two different antenna systems for TTAC. As shown in Figure 5-33, an omnidirectional antenna (discussed later on in this section) is used during transfer orbit at which time the main reflector is not pointed toward the earth. The high-gain (main reflector) antenna is subsequently used, since it permits the TTAC station to reduce its power significantly. In the case of RF tracking (discussed earlier in this chapter in the section on sensors), the high-gain antenna includes the feed horns which simultaneously receive the command carrier and generate pointing error signals for use by the ACS.

5.5.5.1 Satellite Tracking and Ranging

It was mentioned that one function of the TTAC station is to provide for the measurement of satellite position. The specific techniques employed are called *tracking* and *ranging*, illustrated in Figure 5-34. Since it is known that the satellite is in the geostationary orbit, it is a relatively simple matter to fix its position by measuring the azimuth and elevation of the earth station antenna when its beam is aligned to receive the telemetry signal. Note also at the top of Figure 5.34 that there is only one unique value of range (distance to the satellite from the ground station) for a given geostationary satellite, once we know whether it lies to the east or west of the earth station's longitude. The precise range is obtained by measuring the time delay at the TTAC station between transmission of a reference signal (like the pulse in the bottom drawing) and its reception after being relayed by the satellite. Taking into account many factors in the link, the range can be calculated from this delay, since the speed of propagation is fixed at the speed of light. In actual operation, a series of measurements is taken over

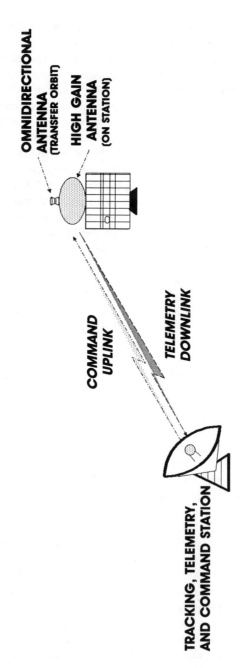

Fig. 5-33 Tracking, Telemetry, and Command (TTAC) Operations from the Ground Using the Omnidirectional and High Gain Antennas of the Satellite

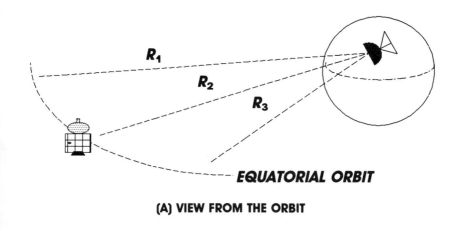

EQUATORIAL ORBIT

(A) VIEW FROM THE ORBIT

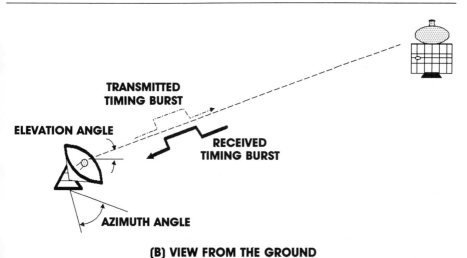

TRANSMITTED TIMING BURST

ELEVATION ANGLE

RECEIVED TIMING BURST

AZIMUTH ANGLE

(B) VIEW FROM THE GROUND

Fig. 5-34 A Single TTAC Earth Station Measures the Range and Direction to the Satellite so that its Position Can Be Computed

time as the satellite moves about its expected position in orbit. Noise in these measurements also requires data taken over a minimum time interval. The amount of time delay through the satellite and earth station equipment, which must be removed from the measurement, is determined by ground tests and by long-term analysis of ranging data. The combined accuracy of range measurement is typically 100 meters or less.

5.5.5.2   Spacecraft Telemetry System

It was mentioned previously that the telemetry link between the spacecraft and the ground station is used to provide data concerning the status and health of the payload and bus subsystems. To get a feel for how this data is gathered onboard the spacecraft and transmitted to the ground, examine Figure 5-35, which is a simplified block diagram of the telemetry system. At the left are examples of some of the critical elements of the spacecraft: a battery, a fuel tank, and an RF power amplifier. Measurement of a key parameter of each is made through a transducing device, which senses the parameter and produces a corresponding output voltage. Battery voltage is taken directly and adjusted to a standard level range with a set of voltage dropping resistors. A pressure transducer is connected into the fuel lines to provide information as to the amount of fuel and gas remaining. This device outputs a corresponding voltage which can be telemetered. The last example in Figure 5-35 is an SSPA for which we might wish to telemeter both the output power and the temperature of the baseplate to which the GaAs devices are attached. A power meter detects a small amount of RF output power taken from a 20-dB coupler (this steals only one percent of the total output of the amplifier, equivalent to an output loss of 0.04 dB) and again produces a corresponding voltage to be telemetered. Baseplate temperature can be measured with a temperature sensor of the thermistor type.

The simple system depicted in Figure 5-35 requires the transmission of four channels of telemetry. On a real spacecraft, several hundred separate channels could be involved, some being simple on-off indications and others being complex analog measurements like the four previously discussed. Therefore, time division multiplexing is used to combine the channels into a single stream for downlink transmission. While some of the early satellites transmitted the analog samples directly (i.e., pulse amplitude modulation), virtually all modern commercial telemetry systems encode the samples using pulse code modulation (PCM). This is the same technique used in digital telephone and data communication systems, described in Chapter 4.

The output at the right of Figure 5-35 is therefore a multiplexed stream of digitized telemetry samples repeated in intervals of typically one second or multiples of one second. In a real system, some of the bits of data will represent *status* (on-off) information.

All of the telemetry information is transmitted to the ground, where it is recovered by the baseband and digital processing equipment in the TTAC station. On ground command, continuous analog measurements can be substituted for the digital stream. An important example of this is the use of the telemetry downlink for ranging, as discussed in a previous paragraph. In the case of

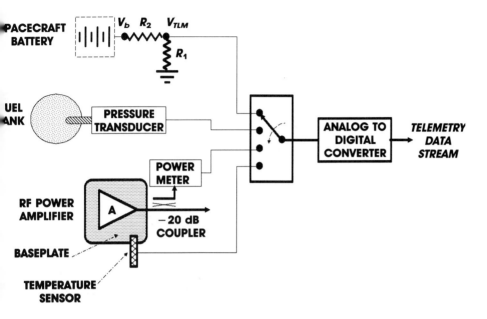

Fig. 5-35 The Spacecraft Telemetry Subsystem Makes Analog Measurements and Converts Them to Digital Data Before Transmission to the Ground

spinning satellites, measurements of spin rate are telemetered to be used to synchronize RCS thruster firing commands.

5.5.5.3 *Spacecraft Command System*

To control the spacecraft from the ground, a dedicated link is established from the TTAC station to the satellite. The link is received on board the satellite and processed by the spacecraft command system. Unlike the continuously operating telemetry system described above, the command link need only be transmitting when the spacecraft must be actively controlled. The one exception is the RF tracking system in which the command link is continuously on the air to provide the beacon. Modern command links incorporate various forms of protection to prevent the taking of control of the satellite by unauthorized parties.

Shown in the simplified diagram of Figure 5-36 is an example of how the command system actually controls some elements of the spacecraft (in this case, the payload). Each unit to be controlled has associated with it a *control driver*, which can be as simple as the single transistor circuit shown at the top. The control driver requires two inputs before it will activate the unit under control.

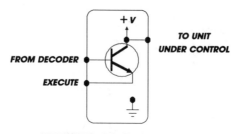

SIMPLIFIED CONTROL DRIVER

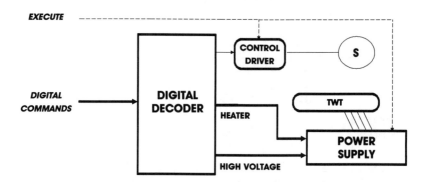

Fig. 5-36 Simplified Block Diagram of the Spacecraft Command Sub-system Showing How the COMMAND and EXECUTE Functions Are Used

First, the *command* line from the spacecraft command decoder must go "high" (meaning that a positive voltage must be applied to the base of the transistor). Then while *command* remains high, the *execute* line must be grounded so that the transistor will conduct. Under these circumstances, the output to the unit under control will change from the high voltage, *V*, to near ground potential. The unit would then be activated. The reason why this dual process is used is to provide an extra safeguard against operator mistakes and equipment anomalies.

Just how the *command* and *execute* signals are processed is depicted in the lower part of Figure 5-36. Each function to be controlled has assigned to it a unique digital command word, like a post-office box number. These are maintained in a list which is unique to the particular type of spacecraft. To protect against unauthorized access, these words are part of a coded structure. Commands are selected by the spacecraft control operator who sends them over the command link to the satellite. In the spacecraft, the specific command is identified by the command decoder, which has a direct and unique connection to each control driver. Three typical examples are shown at the right. An S switch can be commanded between its two positions using its control driver, and a TWTA can be turned on and off. Note that the TWTA requires two separate *on* commands, first for the heater and then (after a warm-up period) for the high voltage.

The procedure for commanding a unit *on* is as follows. First the command word is sent to the spacecraft, where it is received, decoded, and retransmitted to the ground via telemetry for verification. The ground station computer automatically checks to see that the received command word is the same as that which was sent. At this point, the operator can be sure that the spacecraft is ready for the *execute*, which is sent with an entirely different signal on the command link. Only that unit for which the proper command word was sent will respond to the *execute*.

5.5.5.4 TTAC Omnidirectional Antenna

It was mentioned previously that the TTAC system on the spacecraft uses two different antennas during the mission lifetime. For most of the initial operations in transfer orbit and before the main communication antenna is functional, the TTAC omnidirectional antenna provides all access to the spacecraft. Figure 5-37 presents a drawing of a common omni antenna design called a *bicone*, named for its composition of two truncated cones. Along the center band are slots which radiate in directions perpendicular to (radial from) the cone.

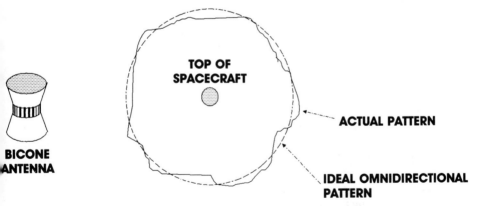

Fig. 5-37 The Bicone Antenna Is Nearly Omnidirectional to Provide a Circular Pattern About the Spin Axis of the Spacecraft

To the right is shown the combined antenna pattern in the form of a polar plot looking down from the top of the spacecraft and bicone. An ideal omnidirectional pattern would be perfectly circular so that an earth station could receive or transmit via the omni pattern, no matter what the spacecraft attitude happened to be. The actual pattern of the bicone, while being roughly circular, has imperfections due to electromagnetic interaction with metallic elements in the body of the spacecraft. Another consideration is that the bicone, or any real omnidirectional antenna, does not radiate efficiently out the top and bottom. This produces nulls in the omni pattern to be taken into account in the planning of TTAC operations during the transfer orbit.

5.5.6 Thermal Control

One of the little appreciated yet vital areas of spacecraft design is thermal control. As was mentioned at the beginning of this chapter, the temperature of each element of the bus and payload has a considerable impact on its performance, reliability, and operating lifetime. Therefore, the thermal control system represents a common denominator for all operating elements of the spacecraft. Often we hear about a satellite that has been successfully placed into service in geostationary orbit only to experience problems with unexpected high temperatures. This would cause great concern for such components as moving bearings and solid-state electronic devices, which may have been designed and tested for a more nominal temperature range. This would therefore be a failure of the thermal control system, possibly due to inaccurate analysis of heat generation and distribution. The difficulty of analyzing and testing the thermal control system during development, however, should not be underestimated.

To get an appreciation for the elements of the thermal control system, examine the cross section of a simplified spacecraft configuration shown in Figure 5-38. This picture does not represent a particular spacecraft design but shows the key components and their arrangement. *Passive thermal control* means that the desired temperature range is maintained using simple conduction and radiation, augmented by thermostatically controlled electrical heaters. This is the most reliable system, because it does not depend on active devices which are themselves subject to failure. An example of an active device is a *heat pipe*, which uses a gas-liquid thermal cycle to move heat from the interior to the exterior of the spacecraft. *Active thermal control* could be required for a very high-power payload such as that used in a direct broadcasting satellite or to cool sensitive instruments on a scientific satellite.

Reviewing the elements of a passive design, the heat producing components (TWTs and other electronics) are typically attached to a heat conducting surface such as an aluminum honeycomb equipment shelf. The primary source of external heat is the sun (shining on the spacecraft from the right in Figure 5-38), which must be precluded from raising the temperature within the compartment above acceptable limits. In addition, the heat generated within the compartment by the electronics must be transmitted to space or else it too will cause the internal temperature to rise. Both of these necessities can be accomplished with a quartz

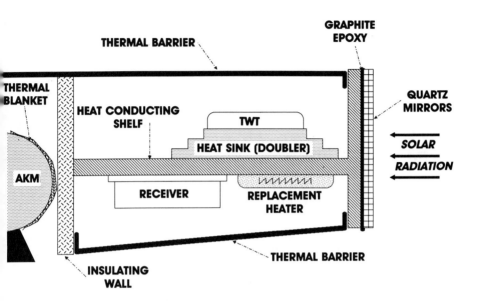

Fig. 5-38 Overview of Passive Thermal Control Techniques Which Rely on the Conduction and Radiation of Heat

mirror radiator located on the side facing the sun. This mirror acts like a filter, reflecting visible and ultraviolet radiation back towards the sun and transmitting infrared radiation from inside to outer space. Mirrors have to be placed carefully on the spacecraft because any contamination or clouding of their surfaces during the life of the satellite will reduce their effectiveness. It is normal for solar radiation and contamination buildup to degrade the effectiveness of such a mirror by as much as half or more during a ten-year lifetime. The obvious consequence is that the temperature within the spacecraft will gradually rise on a yearly basis, which must be taken into account in the overall design of the thermal control system.

If the spacecraft contains an apogee kick motor, it is necessary to provide considerable thermal control measures for it. As shown at the left of Figure 5-38, the AKM is surrounded by a *thermal blanket*. Electrical heater wires may be placed underneath the blanket if needed. The purpose of these measures is to keep the motor and propellant temperature above a prescribed minimum prior to its firing. To protect the rest of the spacecraft from the heat of the motor firing, an insulating wall and *thermal barriers* are placed between it and the sensitive components.

Within the thermally controlled compartment, the electronics receive and transmit heat during their normal operation. It becomes fairly difficult to achieve thermal balance in the desired temperature range during seasonal variations and when units are individually turned off and on. The TWT shown in Figure 5-38 can be a high localized source of heat which can be distributed more evenly using metallic heat sinking (this technique, unfortunately, adds considerable weight to the spacecraft). The term *doubler* is used to describe the added metal for this purpose. The receiver mounted below it is therefore heated by the TWT, aiding in its temperature control. If and when this TWT is not operating, the heat necessary to warm the receiver is provided by a *replacement heater* located in proximity to the units. Replacement heaters, operated either automatically or by ground command, would also be necessary to maintain an overall "bulk" temperature for the spacecraft.

The previous discussion dealt with limited aspects of thermal design and was only intended to provide an introduction. An important aspect of such study is the creation of analytical thermal models for use in predicting temperatures within the spacecraft at various critical points and times in the mission. These models must be verified by ground testing in simulated space environment. Once on orbit, it becomes very difficult to compensate for errors in analysis or design, although this happens all too frequently. This is why it is important to use telemetry to measure the temperature of critical elements after the satellite is operating in orbit and to maintain records throughout the mission lifetime. These data can then be fed back to the thermal designer to aid in the development of improvements and new vehicle designs.

5.5.7 Structural Arrangements

The last remaining area to discuss in spacecraft design is the structural arrangement or chassis. Figure 5-39 shows the common arrangements for the spinner and three axis. To provide rotational symmetry, the spinner uses a central cylinder or truncated cone. This type of structure, also called *monocoque*, is very rigid and strong along its axis, which is the direction of maximum force during launch of an expendable rocket. The monocoque can be replaced by a trusswork to provide greater strength in cross directions. Attached to this central structure are one or more equipment shelves, which allow placement of payload and bus electronic components. The cylindrical solar panel is attached around the circumference of the equipment shelf. In the case of a dual spinner, the spinning and despun sections are each constructed in this manner and brought together for testing as a system. The sections can be separated for shipment. The box structure of Figure 5-39(B) is most often used for three axis satellites, since it facilitates the attachment of solar panels and antennas. Note that a monocoque is still placed at the center to handle launch loads. Equipment is mounted on panels, which are then integrated with the spacecraft. Both arrangements are suitable for commercial communication spacecraft, allowing access to equipment, disassembly for shipment, and integration with the launch vehicle.

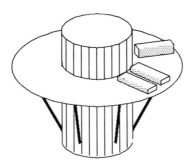

(A) THRUST TUBE AND SHELF OF A SPINNING SPACECRAFT

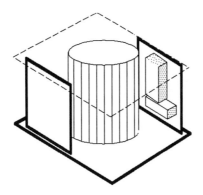

(B) THRUST TUBE AND PANELS OF A THREE AXIS SPACECRAFT

Fig. 5-39 Basic Structural Arrangements in Use with Spinning and Three-Axis Spacecraft Configurations

Chapter 6

Earth Stations and Terrestrial Technology

Earth stations provide access to the satellite, interconnecting users with one another and with the terrestrial network. The communication performance of the earth station has been covered in previous chapters. In this chapter, much more will be said about the various earth station architectures in relation to the types of services that are provided. Trade-offs in earth station design are also described. The terrestrial *tail* connecting the earth station with the outside world is reviewed, as are considerations for implementing the building and other support facilities.

6.1 BASIC EARTH STATION CONFIGURATION

For the purposes of this discussion, an earth station can be broken down into the following major elements: the RF terminal including the antenna, the baseband and control equipment, and the user interface. In addition to these electronic systems, every earth station must include a physical facility capable of housing the equipment, supplying reliable electrical power, and maintaining the temperature and humidity of the electronics within acceptable limits. These latter functions should be recognizable as being similar to those provided by the spacecraft bus, while the former are comparable to those of the communication payload, as discussed in Chapter 5. The key difference here is that the majority of operating earth stations can be serviced by maintenance personnel. This allows earth stations to be designed from building blocks which are for the most part easily repaired and changed.

The major elements of a generic earth station are illustrated in the block diagram in Figure 6-1. As indicated by the dotted box, a large portion of the station is called the *RF terminal*, encompassing the antenna, high-power amplifier (HPA) system, low-noise amplifier (LNA), and up and down converters. In this example, the LNA and HPA are connected to the antenna feed through the horizontally polarized downlink and vertically polarized uplink waveguide ports of the antenna feed. The operation and performance of these components were covered in Chapters 3 and 5. Where an earth station is used as a major hub of a network or is required to provide very reliable service, redundant or backup equipment is included in the RF terminal. The diagram is simplified in that the requisite redundancy switching is not shown; this will be covered in subsequent sections.

The *baseband equipment* performs the modulation-demodulation function along with baseband processing and interfacing with the terrestrial tail or network. The specific configuration of the baseband equipment depends upon the modulation and multiple access method employed (covered in Chapter 4). In Figure 6-1, a digital communication system with digital modems and time division multiplex (TDM) baseband equipment is assumed. Multiple lines are shown interconnecting these facilities, because there would be several independent data channels. Also, equipment redundancy in some form could be included.

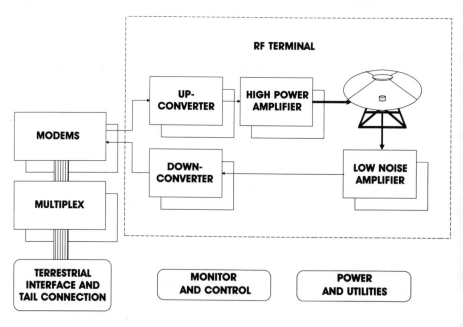

Fig. 6-1 Major Elements of an Earth Station Used to Provide Two-Way Digital Communications Links

The last electronic element of the station is the *terrestrial interface* along with the terminal end of a tail connection of some kind. Interfaces must be properly engineered and specified so that communication services can be carried over the satellite link without disrupting the operation of the overall network. Unfortunately, it is all too common for this interface to be left to the last minute, causing incompatibility problems that take a considerable amount of time and money to correct. The tail connection itself would be composed of a metallic or fiber optic cable link or a microwave link, extending to the point of service such as an office building, telephone switching office, or television studio. Tail connections deserve more attention than they usually get because they impact on quality and reliability in a direct and significant way. Poorly engineered or installed tails will introduce noise, distortion and, in the case of voice, echo. Furthermore, the high reliability of the satellite-to-earth station path is easily compromised by the susceptibility of buried cable tails to breakage and deterioration.

The power and building facilities for the earth station (analogous to the bus of the spacecraft), often get overlooked, but are important nevertheless. It is common to utilize battery backup for critical parts of a station providing vital communication service. To do this, a multiple sequence of ac to dc to ac conversion is followed. For example, in a typical *uninterruptable power system* (UPS), commercial power from a local power utility company (or a diesel generator in the case of a remote installation) is converted in a rectifier to dc and tied to a lead-acid battery system capable of powering the essential electronics (called the *critical load*) during an outage of up to approximately 30 minutes. The stable ac that is required to power the critical load is obtained by passing the stable dc through a dc to ac inverter. Critical loads which obtain their power in this manner are isolated from the commercial power source, protecting them from voltage drops and power surges. In addition, the batteries are always available to supply power automatically in the event of a short disruption. Backup diesel generators are also included, to be automatically started if the disruption lasts more than a few minutes (recall that battery capacity is only good for approximately 30 minutes). To minimize battery requirements, noncritical loads such as air conditioning and office lighting would not be tied to the UPS.

A properly engineered facility also provides heating and cooling to maintain the equipment within its prescribed operating temperature and humidity range. Electronic racks are often mounted on top of a raised floor (called *computer flooring*) so that conditioned air can be conveniently fed from below; this also allows cables and waveguides to be neatly routed between racks. When done properly, a large earth station facility will look attractive and will allow easy and convenient maintenance of the electronic equipment. A very small earth station such as a VSAT, on the other hand, can be treated like a single piece of telephone or data processing equipment installed in an ordinary building. Care must still be taken, however, because of the required environmental conditions of the station. Building modifications are usually needed to access the outdoor RF portion, often roof mounted, and reliable power with UPS provisions may still be required.

Monitoring and control (M&C) functions of an earth station, touched on in Chapter 2, allow local and remote control operation. In modern satellite networks, M&C capabilities are advancing rapidly and involve sophisticated networks of their own. Earth stations which incorporate digital switching (see the discussion on the IDNX in Chapter 2) and TDMA require a centralized system of control to ensure that the proper channel and data packet routing are correctly established. This may be done once or twice daily in a pre-programmed fashion, or may be changed on user demand (i.e., demand assignment). The operation and status of RF and baseband equipment can also be determined and, in the event of failure, redundant equipment can be switched by remote control. In principle, M&C is to an earth station what TTAC is to the satellite itself.

6.2   PRACTICAL CONSIDERATIONS

The following items are of particular relevance when the characteristics of an earth station need to be determined so that a ground system can be properly defined. Considered are trade-offs in the design of major parts of a station which are useful in minimizing costs.

6.2.1   Antenna Configurations

A considerable amount of technical information on the properties and performance of antennas was given in Chapters 1, 3, and 5. In this section, we focus on the physical characteristics of antennas specifically used in earth stations. These are the *prime-focus-fed parabola* and the *Cassegrain*. In the early days, earth stations were easily recognized by the large and obtrusive parabolic antennas which were required to operate with the relatively low-power C-band satellites of the late 1960s. An example of such an antenna with a diameter of 30 meters is shown in Figure 6-2. With the advent of higher powered satellites, the size of antennas has been significantly reduced. The 7-meter antenna presented in Figure 6-3 is typical of the smaller C-band antennas used for two-way communication services on a modern domestic satellite. Even smaller antennas are emphasized later in the chapter in discussions of TV receive-only (TVRO) stations and very small aperture terminals (VSATs).

Fig. 6-2 The First INTELSAT Earth Station Antenna in Brazil Was 30 Meters in Diameter to Be Able to Operate with Low Power C-Band Satellites such as Intelsat III
(photograph courtesy of Hughes Aircraft Company)

6.2.1.1   Prime-Focus-Fed Parabola

Two common earth station parabolic reflector antenna designs are compared in Figure 6-4. Antennas of diameter less than 15 feet (4.5 meters) and particularly those used in receive-only service employ the prime-focus-fed configuration shown at the left. A detailed discussion of the operation of this type of antenna can be found in Chapter 5. The cost is usually the lowest because of its simplicity and ease of installation. To minimize RF loss and noise, a compact LNA package is located directly on the waveguide port of the feed to minimize loss between LNA and feed. The RF cable to connect between LNA and indoor receiving equipment is attached to one of the struts, as shown. Unless the electronics can be fitted at the feed, the prime focus configuration is not attractive for transmit-receive applications.

Fig. 6-3 C Band Antenna using Modern Domestic Satellites such as Galaxy II Have Diameters in the Range of 5 to 7 Meters and are Capable of Providing the Full Range of Two-way Communications Services
(photograph courtesy of Hughes Communications, Inc.)

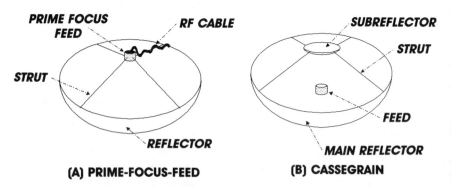

(A) PRIME-FOCUS-FEED   **(B) CASSEGRAIN**

Fig. 6-4 Earth Station Antenna Configurations Commonly Used for Receive-Only and Two-Way Communications Links

In a variant of the prime focus approach, the feed horn is at the end of a hook-shaped piece of waveguide which extends from the vertex of the parabolic reflector. The LNA is attached to the end of the waveguide behind the reflector and the assembly is supported at the feed horn with either struts or guy wires. This has the obvious advantage of allowing the electronics to be more easily accessed and provides placement out of the way of the main beam. The mechanical rigidity and thermal stability of the bent waveguide system are limited, but small diameter antennas used for TVRO purposes can get by with this approach.

6.2.1.2 Cassegrain Optics

Many of the shortcomings of the prime-focus-fed antenna are overcome with the Cassegrain system, shown at (B) in Figure 6-4. Using the folded optics principal of the reflector telescope, the focus of the parabola is directed back by a hyperbolic subreflector to a point at the vertex of the center of the main reflector. Proper illumination is still provided, but the feed and electronics can be joined together at an accessible point in the antenna structure. In large antennas, a hub enclosure is provided at the back for placement of essentially the entire RF terminal in close proximity to the feed. The Cassegrain system eliminates the cable or waveguide runs between RF electronics and feed, allowing the RF terminal to achieve its optimum performance.

As with the prime focus system, there is a variant of the Cassegrain which uses a piece of waveguide extending from the vertex of the reflector to the prime focus. Instead of a bent end with a horn, however, illumination is provided through a flat plate which functions like the subreflector of the Cassegrain. The waveguide may now be supported within a structurally sound hollow tube, eliminating the need for struts or guy wires. This type of system has become very popular in nearly all sizes and types of ground antennas, because it combines the benefits of the prime-focus-fed system with those of the Cassegrain.

Variants of the prime focus and Cassegrain systems were described in the previous paragraphs. The offset-fed geometry which was reviewed in Chapter 5 for spacecraft antennas has also been applied to earth stations. A main benefit of the offset approach is the elimination of main beam blockage by the feed and struts which tends to improve antenna efficiency and reduce sidelobe levels. In a particular design, there may be mechanical or cost advantages as well.

6.2.2 Antenna Beam Pointing

The relatively narrow beamwidth provided by an earth station antenna will result in some variation in signal strength as either the satellite or antenna physically move with respect to each other. As discussed in Chapter 3, the 3-dB beamwidth of an antenna defines the angle for which the gain will be one-half its peak value (or 3 dB down from maximum). Figure 6-5 compares main beam shaping for two separate antennas: a large antenna with a narrow 0.5-degree beamwidth (produced by a reflector of approximately 10 meters at 4 GHz) and an antenna of one-half the diameter yielding a beamwidth twice as wide.

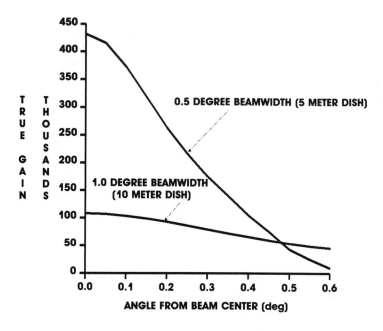

Fig. 6-5 The Effective Gain of an Earth Station Antenna Depends on the Beam Pointing Accuracy and the Beamwidth

The peak gain of the smaller antenna (i.e., the one with the wider beamwidth) is one-quarter of that of the larger antenna, since a factor of two decrease in diameter will reduce the gain by the square of two. It is interesting to note that the absolute gain of both antennas is equal at a point approximately 0.5 degrees from the peak.

For argument's sake, suppose that the satellite were to move back and forth over a 24-hour period due to orbit inclination by plus or minus 0.5 degrees (about ten times current practice). This would cause the received signal strength to have a comparable periodic variation, dropping by a factor of approximately eight for the large antenna and only a factor of two for the smaller one. The advantage of using the large-size reflector would be lost because of frequent mispointing. To get around this problem, the larger antenna would have to be repointed toward the satellite every so often during the day. Such pointing leads to the use of automatic satellite tracking systems, whereby the received signal is used as a reference to guide a control loop of some type. The beam of the smaller antenna, however, is so broad relative to the satellite's motion, that tracking provides little benefit and therefore is unnecessary.

Another aspect of pointing has to do with the alignment of the antenna on the nominal position of the satellite using the antenna's mount. Earlier mounts were configured like that of an artillery piece, with adjustments being provided for azimuth (0 to 360 degrees) and elevation (0 to 90 degrees). This is adequate if the antenna must be capable of pointing anywhere in the sky, which is the case for antennas used to track the satellite in transfer orbit. In moving the antenna between satellites in geostationary orbit, both the azimuth and elevation axis have to be adjusted, which can be time-consuming and cumbersome. The more common type of mount used to communicate with geostationary satellites is the polar mount, named for the fact that the main axis of rotation is aligned with that of the earth. The reflector can then be moved rapidly from satellite to satellite by one rotation. Polar mounts tend to be simpler in construction, are more compact, and allow greater flexibility in covering the orbital arc.

6.2.3   High-Power Amplifier Sizing

The performance of an earth station uplink is gauged by the EIRP, the same parameter which applies to the satellite downlink. As was discussed in Chapter 3, the EIRP is the product of the HPA output power, the loss of the waveguide between HPA and antenna, and the antenna gain. The result is expressed in dBW (dB relative to one watt), so it is also convenient to add the component performances in dB terms. For example, an EIRP of 80 dBW results from an HPA output of 30 dBW (i.e., 1000 watts), a waveguide loss of 2 dB and an antenna gain of 52 dB. Since the dimensions of an earth station antenna are not subject to the physical constraints of launch vehicle, the diameter and, consequently, the gain, can be set at a more convenient point. This could be the optimum which occurs where the cost of the antenna plus HPA is minimum.

Figure 6-6 presents a trade-off curve for the design of an earth station uplink for use in full transponder FM video service. To deliver an uplink C-band EIRP of 80 dBW, the curve gives the requisite antenna diameter and HPA power. An allowance of 2 dB for waveguide loss has been made in the curve. Relatively low HPA powers (less than 250 watts) are acceptable with antennas of 15 meters in diameter or greater. To be able to employ a more compact reflector of 6 meters in diameter (typical for a truck-mounted transportable earth station), the HPA must be capable of outputting over 1000 watts. The curve rises rapidly as the diameter tends towards the minimum 3-meter size indicated. There is an additional problem with the smaller diameter antennas, namely that the excessive power will also be radiated through the antenna sidelobes, producing unacceptable interference in the adjacent satellite. For that reason, video transmission from transportable and other small diameter antennas is subject to tighter control by the satellite operators and by the Federal Communications Commission in the United States. If such a station causes interference to services in an adjacent satellite, then it must upon notification remove such interference (i.e., reduce power or, if that doesn't solve the problem, shut down).

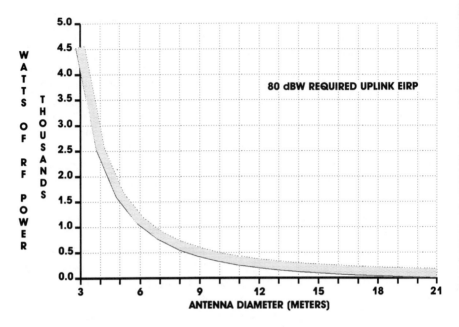

Fig. 6-6 Earth Station HPA Power versus Antenna Diameter for an FM Uplink at 6 GHz

The discussion of HPA technology in Chapter 3 provides another perspective with which to evaluate the trade-off in Figure 6-6. Sufficient antenna size will permit the use of lower powered, less expensive HPAs. In FDMA services, it is possible to use an SSPA to achieve the required earth station EIRP, provided that sufficient antenna gain is available. Likewise, a klystron HPA could be avoided if the power for video service is less than 600 watts, which is possible with a 10-meter antenna.

6.2.4 Earth Station Receiving-System Figure of Merit

As in the case of uplink power, there is a useful measure of overall earth station performance in the downlink called the figure of merit or G/T. This is the ratio, expressed in dB, of the antenna *gain* to the noise *temperature* of the receiving system. Higher antenna gain improves sensitivity as does lower noise, hence the use of a ratio. The G/T of the station can be used in link-budget calculations, discussed in Chapter 3, to compute the ratio of carrier to noise. In general, earth station downlink performance can be adequately measured and optimized by consideration of the G/T concept.

The figure of merit (G/T in dB/K) of a C-band earth station is plotted in Figure 6-7 as a function of antenna diameter for three levels of noise performance: 80 K, 120 K, and 160 K. These noise temperatures include the effects of the LNA along with the noise contributions of the environmental background. The lowest noise temperature corresponds to the use of a parametric amplifier, the next to the cooled FET, and finally the highest to a conventional uncooled FET.

Larger diameter antennas are expensive to build because of the structural strength needed to maintain reflector surface accuracy, particularly in high wind. Surface accuracy, which is the accuracy with which the surface fits a true parabola which has been rotated to produce a circular reflector, has a significant effect on the gain of the antenna. Likewise, the mount and motor drive must withstand greater antenna weight and wind load to keep the beam pointed in the proper direction. The cost of an antenna increases rapidly with the diameter, following an exponential relationship. For example, doubling of the diameter from 5 meters to 10 meters (a 6 dB increase in gain) increases cost by a factor of 10 or greater. This consideration generally encourages the system designer to use the smallest antenna with an appropriate LNA to achieve the necessary G/T. If the station is to transmit as well as receive, then there will be a lower limit on antenna size imposed by the practicality of HPA power as discussed in the previous section.

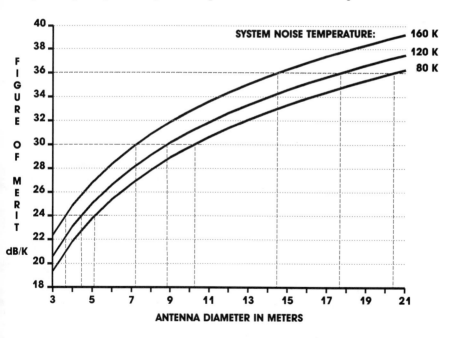

Fig. 6-7 C-Band Earth Station Receiving Figure of Merit (G/T) as a Function of Antenna Diameter and System Noise Temperature

The impact of system noise temperature on G/T is quite pronounced, particularly when you look at the size of antenna needed to maintain performance. Three levels of typical G/T performance are indicated in Figure 6-7 by dashed lines. At 24 dB/K, the station can receive commercial quality video programming. The required antenna diameter ranges from 3.6 meters for the PARAMP to 5 meters for a typical FET LNA. The lowest cost may be obtained with the 5-meter antenna, because parametric amplifiers are expensive and often difficult to maintain. A receiving site may have physical restrictions, however, which make the larger antenna impractical.

A G/T of 30 dB/K is typical of what is required for TDMA voice and data service on a domestic satellite. The range of antenna diameter indicated in Figure 6-7 is from 7 to 10 meters. The cost variation among these antennas is very significant, with the largest diameter being doubly penalized by the possible requirement for automatic tracking to compensate for the narrower beamwidth. Therefore, the lowest cost may be had with, say, the 9-meter antenna and the cooled FET. International satellites generally have less downlink EIRP for a given part of the footprint and therefore even higher values of G/T are needed. To obtain a G/T of 36 dB/K, antennas in the range of 14 to 20 meters are appropriate, making the LNA selection even more important. Automatic tracking on these antennas would be required in any case.

6.2.5   Earth Station Building and Equipment Arrangement

The last practical consideration to be covered is the physical installation of the earth station, i.e., the design of the building and arrangement of the equipment therein. It is instructive to take as an example the layout of the site and building for a major earth station, shown in Figure 6-8. The principles can be applied to smaller stations, including VSATs. Because it is assumed in the example that the station is located north of the equator, the antennas are aligned along the southern wall of the site to afford visibility of the GEO arc. This arrangement of the antennas is usually the most flexible, if there is sufficient space between the reflectors to allow independent pointing of each main beam to any orbit position. Care in placing the foundations must be taken so that antennas never touch each other during repointing and so that the beams do not overlap one another to a significant degree. The latter will minimize the interaction of the electromagnetic fields around the antennas, including the effects of diffraction. With proper isolation between antennas, the beams will be properly formed, giving the desired cross-polarization isolation and control of sidelobes.

The next important aspect is the location and arrangement of the RF equipment. As was described in the previous section, the low-noise amplifiers or low-noise converters should be mounted directly on the receive port of the feed horn to minimize noise and loss. This can also be done for the HPAs if the power level is in the range of 5 to 150 watts, because compact SSPAs and TWTAs can be mounted to the reflector within a temperature-controlled hub enclosure. Power levels in the hundreds to thousands of watts require high-power TWT and klystron amplifiers, respectively, which must be located inside the building, as illustrated in Figure 6-8. Operation in two or more transponders at the same time is accomplished with an RF combiner of the type described in Chapter 5. The RF combiner should be located as close as possible to the antenna to minimize waveguide losses.

The baseband and control equipment can be located anywhere within the building, since baseband and IF cable lengths are not critical to the performance of the earth station. Here, the main considerations deal with allowing station personnel to operate and maintain the equipment. The appearance of the equipment in the room is also important, both to the people who work there and to guests who may come to visit. Equipment which could be hazardous to humans, such as batteries, high voltage electrical equipment, and diesel generators, should be isolated from the general flow of people, as shown in the upper right of the drawing. A major earth station also deserves to have a front lobby to control access to the facility and office space for administration and management personnel. Test, calibration, and repair of electronic equipment can also be done in a small laboratory.

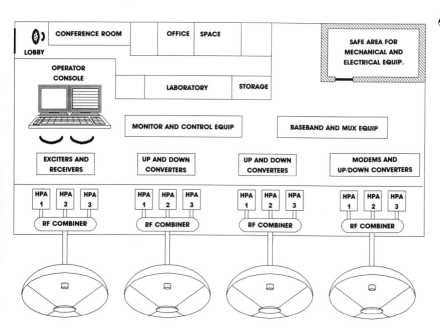

Fig. 6-8 Site Plan and Equipment Arrangement for a Typical Major Earth Station

The importance of providing adequate space between adjacent antennas to minimize RF interaction has already been stressed. Figure 6-9 illustrates another important aspect in antenna placement dealing with the protection of personnel on site and within the local community. The far-field pattern of the ground antenna contains the familiar main beam and sidelobes. The near field region, however, produces measurable levels of RF radiation with much greater intensity than would be predicted by following the far-field pattern shaping. Humans and other living beings which enter the near field can be subjected to excessive levels of microwave radiation. The normal practice is to fence in the site to prevent living things from ever reaching such close proximity; in crowded metropolitan areas, however, this may be impractical.

A shield wall of metal or concrete such as that shown in Figure 6-9 can greatly reduce the radiation exposure to humans in the surrounding area. The top of the wall must generally reach above the highest point on the antenna for any angle of elevation that it may take. Usually, the worst case occurs when the antenna is pointed essentially at the horizon, which also maximizes the absolute level of radiation along the particular azimuth. A high wall will minimize the diffraction over the top, which is the same consideration in using natural or man-made shielding to minimize RFI. There are analytical techniques using wave and diffraction theory which can predict radiation levels in the vicinity of the antenna and wall, provided that the detailed structure of the antenna and wall are included in the analysis.

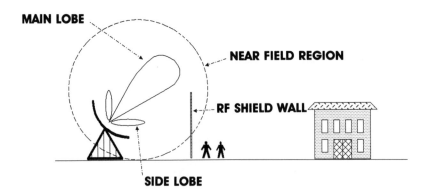

Fig. 6-9 Protection of Personnel and Buildings from Local RF Fields Around the Transmitting Earth Station Antenna

6.3   TERMINAL CLASSES

There is a unique class of earth station to be employed for each type of communication service being rendered. In addition, the size and complexity of the station will depend on the quantity of traffic and, if appropriate, the variety of services offered. The following paragraphs briefly review and describe some of the more common station configurations in use for domestic and international communications. To start off, the TTAC earth station and its associated satellite control center are presented to give the reader a feel for the scope of the ground facility used to operate the space segment. The remaining paragraphs cover stations ranging in size from the largest class used for television uplinking and bulk transmission down to the smallest VSAT and TVRO.

6.3.1   TTAC Ground Facilities

The TTAC ground facilities of a satellite operator cover a variety of functions and capabilities, as depicted in Figure 6-10. In some systems, all of the functions are centralized at one location to minimize capital and operating expense. This approach occupies the least land and building space and can economize on equipment. Additional savings accrue from minimizing expenses for running the buildings and by being efficient in the use of personnel. For example, a single maintenance team can service all of the electronic equipment. A second approach splits the facility between a TTAC earth station and a satellite control center (SCC), as indicated by the vertical broken line in Figure 6-10. Using a tail link such as microwave or leased private lines, the SCC is established at a distant point such as the headquarters of the satellite operator. This is advantageous where much of the business is carried out in a central city and the TTAC is located remotely to avoid RFI. The following paragraphs review the design and capability of each half in the TTAC facility.

6.3.1.1   TTAC Earth Station

The tracking, telemetry, and command (TTAC) station has essentially the same capability as the generic earth station given in Figure 6-1, i.e., incorporating the RF terminal, baseband equipment, and terrestrial interface (appropriate to a separated SCC). This is the part of the facility which communicates with the TTAC subsystem of the spacecraft bus by way of the satellite's command uplink and telemetry downlink. The antennas employed are usually 10 to 13 meters in diameter (whether C or Ku band) to provide the maximum possible link margin, since abnormal conditions need to be accommodated. In a typical TTAC station,

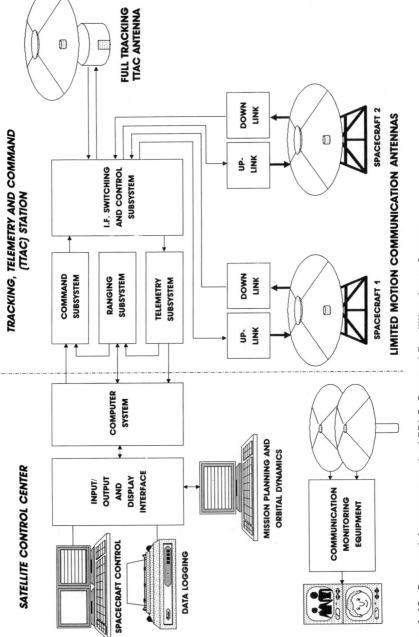

Fig. 6-10 General Arrangement of TTAC Ground Facilities for a Space Segment Consisting of Two Geostationary Satellites

there would be one *limited-motion* antenna pointed at each operational satellite (two are assumed in the illustration), while the *full-tracking* antenna would be used for transfer orbit operations and for testing purposes during the life of the satellites. An example of a TTAC station with full and limited-motion antennas is shown in Figure 6-11. All antennas aid in tracking the satellites by providing azimuth and elevation readouts from their respective mounts. The full-tracking and limited-motion RF terminals interface with the rest of the station at intermediate frequency.

Fig. 6-11 A Typical TTAC Earth Station with a Full Motion Antenna for Tracking and Testing as well as Several Limited Motion Antennas Used for Full-Time TTAC Links and Communications Services
(photograph courtesy of Hughes Communications, Inc.)

The baseband equipment is shown at the upper center of Figure 6-10. In the *command subsystem*, the actual digital commands are taken from the incoming data stream and modulated on the IF carrier using either FSK or PSK, depending on the design of the spacecraft command receiver. Other special features can be incorporated in the command subsystem, such as providing the pilot carrier modulation used by a spacecraft RF tracking system. For commanding purposes, the command carrier need only be on the air during the process of sending commands and for ranging, which is described in a subsequent paragraph. This could permit the uplink chain to be used on another satellite or for other purposes when commanding is not being performed.

The *telemetry subsystem* receives the telemetry carrier at IF from the downlink and demodulates the actual stream of telemetry data. This process is straightforward and directly analogous to the reception of data communication in a standard earth station. The third function of the baseband equipment is for ranging, which is the process outlined in Chapter 5 for measuring the position and velocity of the satellite. The *ranging subsystem* generates a baseband ranging signal which the command subsystem modulates on the uplink carrier. After passing over the TTAC link of the satellite, the ranging signal is received at the TTAC station, demodulated, and the baseband compared with what was transmitted. The measured time delay provides the basis for computing the range and range rate. In an alternative ranging approach, the ranging baseband signals are modulated on an independent carrier and uplinked to a frequency within one of the operating transponders of the communication payload. Referred to as *transponder ranging*, this technique eliminates the need to switch the command link between the commanding and ranging functions but consumes some of the communication bandwidth of the satellite repeater.

The interconnection and switching of command, telemetry, and ranging links between each other and among different satellites is facilitated by the *IF switching and control subsystem*. For example, during transfer orbit operations, the TTAC link to the satellite is established through the full tracking antenna. A switchover to the assigned limited-motion antenna is normally accomplished with the IF switching and control subsystem after the satellite is located in its assigned orbit slot and has been fully deployed and tested. The TTAC station must be capable, however, of switching the full-motion antenna back in line for testing purposes or in the event of an emergency situation which could happen at any time within the operating lifetime of the satellite.

6.3.1.2 Satellite Control Center

The SCC is the brain of the satellite operation, providing the computing power and human intelligence necessary to operate and control a system of several satellites and TTAC earth stations. Depicted in the left half of Figure 6-10 is the configuration of a typical SCC. The baseband signals between the TTAC and the SCC can interface directly with the computer system. Additional pieces of specialized digital processing equipment may be found between computer and baseband. An example of such a device is the *synchronous command generator*, used with spinning satellites, which synchronizes itself with the satellite spin rate. Thereafter, thruster firing commands generated by the unit will have the proper timing. The synchronous command generator, which is itself a small computer, also allows commands to be entered directly from its front panel. A complementary device called the *telemetry decomutator* accepts the telemetry TDM data stream and demultiplexes the telemetry channels. On a manual basis, individual telemetry channels can be examined on its front panel.

The single box labeled computer system in Figure 6-10 contains sufficient computing power and redundancy to support all requirements of the SCC including reliability. The computer system performs real-time functions of command generation, telemetry reception and processing, and ranging. Additionally, there are several SCC activities which are handled by the computer system in a batch mode. *Orbital dynamics* is the principal area using the batch mode, dealing with the determination of the satellite orbit and the planning of orbit correction maneuvers necessary to maintain satellite position. Using ranging data as an input to the program, the orbital dynamics personnel generate maneuver plans which are presented to the spacecraft controllers (i.e., the people who actually "fly" the satellites) for action by the command system. The orbital dynamics personnel and spacecraft controllers access the computer system with the terminals shown at the upper left of Figure 6-10. In the photograph in Figure 6-12, spacecraft controllers can enter spacecraft commands through the video display terminals in front of them. The computer system keeps an ever watchful eye over the telemetry data and compares the reading to previously stored threshold alarm values. The printout device indicated in Figure 6-10 logs every action taken by the controllers and records unusual spacecraft data identified by the computer.

The last function of the TTAC ground facility is the *monitoring* of the communication transmissions to and from the satellite. Prior to the start of service, the communication payload is thoroughly tested and every major component checked out from the TTAC earth station, usually using automatic test equipment associated with the full-tracking antenna. With commercial communication services being provided over the satellite, it is important that the satellite operator have a system to monitor the entire downlink spectrum of each satellite continuously. This is needed to insure that all RF carriers are set to their prescribed power levels and are located at their assigned frequencies. If the satellite employs dual polarization to achieve frequency reuse, then the purity of polarization of every carrier must also be checked prior to start of service and monitored during operation. Most of the transmissions to the satellite do not emanate from the TTAC station; therefore, the communication controllers must have telephone access to the uplinking earth stations, no matter where they may be located.

If the *communication control console* is located at the TTAC site, then the limited-motion antennas can receive the downlink spectrum and deliver it to the SCC for inspection with spectrum analyzers and video monitors. Figure 6-10 indicates the other approach where the communication control is colocated with the SCC some distance from the TTAC earth station. In such case, one or more

Fig. 6-12 The Satellite Control Console where the Galaxy Satellites
Are Controlled and Monitored through the Video Display Terminals
(photograph courtesy of Hughes Communications, Inc.)

separate receive-only antennas can be provided, but only if the satellite footprint
covers the location of the SCC. Satellites which provide frequency reuse using
narrow spot beams, such as applied at Ku band, do pose a bit of a problem in
downlink monitoring, since a separate earth station is required in each independent footprint. The communication console used to monitor transmissions from
the Galaxy satellites is shown in the photograph in Figure 6-13. Note the use
of video monitors to augment RF measurements and the availability of telephone
communication for contacting uplinking earth stations and other satellite operators.

6.3.2   Major Earth Station

A major earth station is a communication facility which is designed to
provide a large quantity of satellite transmission service, usually involving video,
voice, and data. The term *teleport* has been adopted to refer to a major earth

Fig. 6-13 The Downlinks of the Galaxy Satellites are Monitored on a 24-Hour Basis by Communications Controllers at the Galaxy Network Operations Center
(photograph courtesy of Hughes Communications, Inc.)

station which is open for business to serve the needs of a number of customers. In a dedicated satellite network, a major earth station would be the large central node for a city, government installation, or industrial building complex. Another example of a major earth station is the video uplink and downlink facility of a television network or cable TV programmer. Any major earth station has the full range of facilities discussed at the beginning of this chapter and shown in Figure 6-1, often including a full complement of redundant equipment.

The configuration of the electronic systems of a typical major earth station is shown in Figure 6-14. Video uplink and downlink service for full transponder analog FM TV is provided. In this example, digital communication service for voice and data using FDMA is accommodated at the same time in another copolarized transponder on the same satellite. Full duplex (transmit and receive) operation is established with the station being capable of receiving in both polarizations, vertical and horizontal, although only the vertical path is described herein.

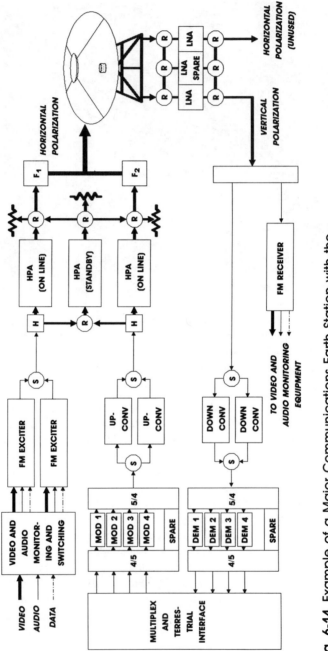

Fig. 6-14 Example of a Major Communications Earth Station with the Capability to Provide Full Duplex Analog Video and T-1 Digital Transmission

6.3.2.1 Video Equipment Chain

The analog video baseband covering a frequency range of 0 to 4 MHz is accepted from the terrestrial interface by the *video and audio monitoring and switching unit*, shown at the upper left of Figure 6-14. Along with the video would come one or more channels of high quality audio (monaural or stereo, with possibly additional channels for other languages) as well as data channels for use in the TV network. The data could also be provided as a separate transmission service, to be delivered along with the video carrier. The monitoring and switching equipment is used in both the transmit and receive directions to route the baseband signals between uplinks, downlinks, redundant equipment, and TV test equipment. Video quality is extremely important in television broadcasting, so earth station personnel must have the facilities and training to make standard video measurements and to help in troubleshooting technical problems.

The video uplink and downlink chains follow exactly the descriptions found in Chapter 3 and illustrated in Figures 3-14 and 3-16, respectively. This particular example shows the FM modulator and upconverter combined into an exciter and the complementary down converter and demodulator into a receiver. For video service, the HPA would have output power in the range of 400 watts (TWTA) to 1500 watts (KPA), depending on the size and gain of the ground antenna and the sensitivity of the satellite (refer to Figure 6-6). The configuration in Figure 6-14 shows a second HPA operating in another transponder; hence, the two HPA outputs are combined in a reactive power combiner. This is the same type of device used in the output of a satellite repeater, discussed in Chapter 5. The very high power levels involved demand the lowest possible RF loss and adequate cooling of the waveguide filters of the combiner. Redundancy switching is accomplished with waveguide rotary "baseball" switches (discussed in Chapter 5) to cross connect on-line and standby HPAs. The resistor symbols indicate high power dummy loads which absorb the output of an HPA when it is not switched into the operating chain.

The downlink equipment mirrors the uplink with the only difference being in the configuration of the LNAs. A separate operating LNA is provided for each polarization, although the station in Figure 6-14 is not using both simultaneously. When receiving a backhaul video point-to-point feed, either polarization may come into use. The LNA connected to the vertical antenna port provides sufficient gain to overcome the loss of a passive power splitter which feeds the entire frequency range to both the video exciter and the FDMA data communication equipment. The receiver can be tuned to any transponder in the downlink frequency range, including that of the uplink for monitoring purposes.

6.3.2.2   FDMA Digital Communication Service

A digital communication subsystem capable of transmitting four T-1 channels is shown at the left of Figure 6-14. Each T-1 has its own modulator-demodulator (modem), tuned to a separate frequency within the transponder. Redundancy is provided for the modems on a five-for-four basis using an integrated switching system. The T-1 channels interface with the terrestrial network through a TDM multiplexer which combines the four streams into one 6 Mbps (T-2) channel.

In a star network using FDMA, this major station transmits one T-1 to each of four different destination stations, which in turn transmit back one T-1 each. The transponder contains eight carriers: four uplinked from this station and one each from the four other stations. Operation in a single transponder allows the use of one operating upconverter and one operating down converter, there being full redundancy provided to maintain high reliability.

FDMA service may involve multiple transponders, in which case there would be a separate down converter for each transponder accessed. To include redundancy, it may be necessary to increase the ratio of spares to operating equipment. This is because the down converters would operate on different frequencies and because there would have to be individual modem banks. Equipment which is capable of remote control permits the use of nonspecific spare units which can be set to the proper channel at the time of replacement, thus saving on equipment expense.

Because earth station transmissions must be on different frequencies, FDMA can be complicated to arrange and even more difficult to change once the network goes into operation. This aspect was covered in Chapter 4. One inherent advantage, however, is that the transmit power of the station can be tailored to its traffic requirement (i.e., the total number of carriers and channel capacity). In the previous example, a remote station could employ a 10-watt SSPA to uplink its single T-1, while the major station may require more than 100 watts to transmit four carriers. This is because the higher powered amplifier (probably a TWTA) would need to be operated with backoff to control intermodulation distortion. Aside from the aspect of transmit power, the complexities of FDMA are essentially overcome with TDMA, which is discussed in the next section.

6.3.3   TDMA Earth Station

TDMA earth stations were developed to use an entire transponder in the most efficient manner, transmitting at 60 to 120 Mb/s to squeeze in the maximum number of voice channels possible. Over the years, digital technology has developed to the point that the principal advantage of TDMA now lies in its flexibility. This is because the digital elements of a TDMA terminal can be configured to provide any type of transmission or service and can be reprogrammed at any time. Computer techniques allow the station to work efficiently in a digital network, adapting to the user requirements and demands to alter routing. TDMA is not only used for high capacity trunking systems but also for low-cost thin-route networks involving VSATs. Figure 6-15 presents a simplified block diagram of a typical TDMA earth station. The following discussion relates to the type of major earth station used for full-transponder TDMA, while the approach for VSATs is covered in a later section.

6.3.3.1 RF Equipment for TDMA Service

The configuration of an RF terminal designed for TDMA service, shown in Figure 6-15, is similar to that of the video uplink. In full transponder TDMA service, the figure of merit and EIRP of this type of station usually demand an antenna of 10 or 7 meters, for C or Ku-band service, respectively. Along with this, the HPA must have an output power in the range of 400 to 1000 watts to saturate the transponder. The up and down converters are typical "off the shelf" items.

6.3.3.2 TDMA Terminal

Moving to the left half of Figure 6-15, the TDMA terminal section consists of the modems, baseband equipment, multiplex, and monitor and control (M&C) equipment. It is customary to purchase the terminal as an integrated subsystem from a TDMA manufacturer. Ignoring the fact that the interface with the RF terminal is at IF, the TDMA terminal performs the same functions as an intelligent T-1 multiplex such as the IDNX discussed in Chapter 2. A typical TDMA terminal is shown in the photograph in Figure 6-16. The computer terminal connected to the M&C equipment is used to program the terminal for the required traffic arrangement or routing. Usually, one station acts as the network master and is used to create the overall traffic routing pattern. Called the *network map*, this routing pattern is stored in each TDMA terminal and used to direct individual TDM communication channels to the proper destination. Depending on the time of day or traffic demand, the network map is modified by appropriate programming of the central M&C computer. Central control for the network can actually be exercised from a location not at an earth station, since the computer terminal can be connected through a voice-grade line (terrestrial or satellite).

The design and control of the TDMA modem are critical to the operation of the terminal. This type of modem is intended for burst operation, i.e., where the carrier must be turned on and off in rapid succession. Transmitting of bursts

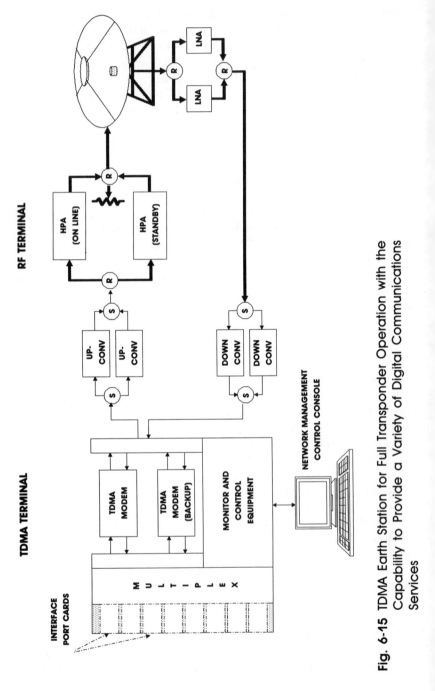

Fig. 6-15 TDMA Earth Station for Full Transponder Operation with the Capability to Provide a Variety of Digital Communications Services

Fig. 6-16 A TDMA Terminal Capable of Full Transponder Operation with Burst Transmission at Either 60 or 120 Megabits per Second (photograph courtesy of Hughes Network Systems)

via the modulator is simplified primarily because only an on-off switching function is required. The demodulator, however, has the difficult task of locking onto the incoming carrier at IF and synchronizing with its modulated digital information stream. This dual process must be accomplished for each received burst before the useful data can actually be recovered. Burst modem design has matured over the last two decades so that extremely efficient and reliable units are now available. Typical burst transmission rates are 15, 45, 60, 120, and 240 Mb/s; since a full transponder could be employed, these are referred to as wide band TDMA. Rates below 15 Mb/s (called narrow band TDMA) allow several TDMA carriers to be placed in the same transponder, sharing its power and bandwidth. On the other end of the scale, experimental burst modems have been demonstrated for rates around 1 Gb/s although there are currently no commercial satellite applications for such high rates and bandwidths. These high rates are, or course, useful for the continuous transmission of digital information on fiber optic cable systems.

The terrestrial interface is illustrated at the left of the figure, with an arrangement similar to that of the smart multiplexer. Within the multiplex section, buffering of the burst-rate digital stream adjusts the speed to a continuous rate typically matching the standard digital hierarchy (T-1 or T-3, depending on the requirements). *Port cards* are plug-in circuit boards used to configure the terrestrial interface for specific user applications. For example, if only T-1 channels

channels are desired, then there would be sufficient port cards to support a specific number of 1.544 Mb/s streams. Other port card options include 56, 64, or 256 kb/s (often a common port card design is used with the unit "strapped" for the desired channel rate); ADPCM or PCM voice; T-3; or other specialized interface conditions. Adaptive features such as reprogrammable rates and statistical multiplexing are also available. The type of statistical multiplexing used for voice is called *digital speech interpolation* (DSI), which transmits digitized voice samples over the satellite only when there is actually an active talker on the line.

6.3.3.3   Carrier Hopping

The capacity of a given TDMA carrier, which is transmitted sequentially from several earth stations, is limited by its bandwidth and power. When the sum of the channel requirements of the individual stations is greater than the capacity of the carrier, than additional carriers must be provided. Carrier hopping is the technique whereby stations can switch between several such carriers in order to pick out traffic destined to them. Carrier hopping in wide-band TDMA must be done between transponders; hence, the RF terminal is equipped with a separate down converter for each transponder so accessed. Narrow-band TDMA is usually done within the same transponder, eliminating the need for multiple down converters. The demodulator is capable of changing its frequency, however, within the IF range. Multiple demodulators, each pretuned to a frequency in use, are an alternate way of providing the necessary connectivity for a particular earth station.

The technique of carrier hopping is particularly well suited to VSAT applications, since the capacity of each carrier is held to a relatively low value such as 120 kb/s. With each carrier handling a small VSAT network, it will take 50 to 100 carriers to fill a transponder. Larger networks will therefore require that some of the VSATs be capable of moving to other carrier frequencies to reach destinations not on a particular frequency. This principle applies to wideband TDMA networks such as those of INTELSAT, which utilize carrier hopping between transponders to allow any station to be interconnected with any other. With the large traffic requirements of such major earth station nodes, the extra equipment (including proper redundancy) is easily justified.

6.3.4   TV Receive-Only Earth Stations

A TV receive-only (TVRO) earth station can actually take on one of a number of possible configurations, depending upon the particular application. An installation used for a cable TV head end must be capable of receiving several channels at the same time. For a home installation, only one receiver is required;

that receiver, however, should permit the viewer to change transponder channels conveniently. The following paragraphs review the sizing of the antenna and equipment configurations of TVRO stations.

6.3.4.1 TVRO Antenna Sizing

It was emphasized in Chapter 3 that the size of receiving antenna is determined primarily by the RF power (i.e., the EIRP) of the transmitting source. It was also mentioned in Chapter 1 that international and domestic regulations limit C-band EIRP because of the possibility of RFI between satellites and terrestrial microwave services which share this band. No terrestrial sharing is required for much of the Ku-band frequency range. As a consequence, the power level of C-band satellites is considerably lower than that of Ku-band satellites. This, of course, is the result of the regulatory limit on the design of the satellite transponder and has nothing to do with the physics of propagation.

Figure 6-17 presents in graphical form a summary of TVRO antenna sizing for parabolic reflectors in the range of 2 to 16 feet (shown along the X axis). A system noise temperature of 100 K has been assumed. Satellite EIRP values between 30 and 55 dBW (shown along the Y axis) cover the typical ranges for C band, Ku-band FSS, and Ku-band BSS, indicated by the shaded areas. Based on power alone, there should only be one curve; the factor of rain attenuation, however, forces the curve for Ku band to move up the power range. As discussed in Chapter 1, the microwave path will experience some loss of signal strength during heavy rainfall and that additional power margin should be provided to maintain adequate signal strength. The upper curve includes 4 dB of additional power to provide the same link reliability in the Ku-band range (FSS and BSS), which would be sufficient for temperate climates such as in the northeastern United States, Japan, or Europe, and with an elevation angle greater than about 30 degrees. Tropical regions with heavy thunderstorm activity and frequent torrential rains would require even greater incremental power margin. The C-band curve begins at a diameter of 6 feet and an EIRP of approximately 38 dBW because of the aforementioned international limitations on power flux density. With the rain effect, it takes approximately 42 dBW at Ku band to achieve the same link performance with the 6-foot antenna. In the Ku-FSS range, an antenna diameter as small as 3 feet (approximately one meter) is adequate with an EIRP of 48 dBW. Because FSS satellites are not intended for broadcast video services exclusively, however, the satellites may be spaced so closely together that ground antennas smaller than 3 feet will be subject to unacceptable interference. Also, in the United States the FCC has not authorized any satellite operator to use more than approximately 48 dBW in the FSS portion of the Ku-band range.

The Ku-BSS range is available for truly high power direct-to-home broadcasting, as shown in Figure 6-17. Satellites using the same frequency channels

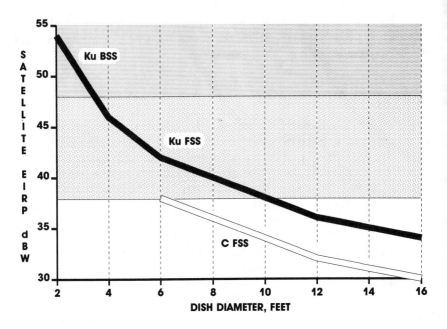

Fig. 6-17 Antenna Diameter of a TV Receive-Only Home Earth Station versus the EIRP of the Satellite at C and Ku Bands

and polarization are to be separated in orbit sufficiently to allow the use of antennas as small as two feet in diameter. To achieve this at Ku band (with rain attenuation), the satellite must be capable of delivering an EIRP of approximately 54 dBW or higher. The power output of the appropriate transponder amplifier is usually more than 100 watts, which is double that used in the FSS segment of Ku band.

6.3.4.2 Cable Head End TVRO Configuration

The most elaborate TVRO system, illustrated in Figure 6-18, is used to receive several wideband video channels simultaneously for distribution in a cable TV system. Four such channels are equipped in the figure; in an actual CATV head end, however, there would be up to 24 channels per C-band downlink. The antenna used to gather the downlink is of sufficient diameter to assure good signal to noise quality over expected link conditions, as discussed in previous paragraphs. While a single low-noise block converter (LNB) is shown, it is more common to find two units: one for the vertical and one for the horizontal

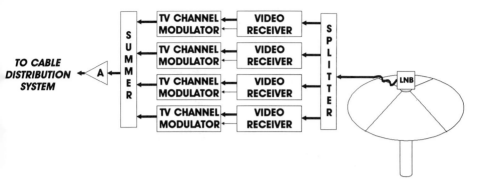

Fig. 6-18 Configuration of a Cable TV Receive-Only Earth Station of the Type Located at a Cable Head End

polarization. On-line redundancy is typically not provided because of the high reliability that solid-state LNBs usually provide. In the event of failure, the bad LNB can be rapidly changed out by technical personnel at the head end. The dc power for the LNC is usually carried over the conductors of the same coaxial cable used to bring the RF signals back to the receivers.

The wideband output of the LNB is divided on a power basis to provide the entire spectrum to the video receivers. Each of the receivers, tuned to a different transponder channel, delivers a video baseband with its associated audio to a TV channel modulator. A power summer and amplifier combine the several TV channels which now lie within the receiving frequency range of normal television sets. The cable distribution system spreads the ensemble of channels out to cable TV subscribers. Modern cable systems provide each home with a *converter unit* which allows the viewer to select from over 40 separate TV channels all delivered over the cable without touching the channel selecter of the TV set. Because pay channels may be involved, the converter unit has the capability to be programmed to allow the viewer to watch only those channels which have been authorized by the cable company (and for which the subscriber is presumably paying).

In data broadcasting applications, a stream of digital data is recovered from the receiver baseband and subsequently processed for transmission over the cable network. Some cable systems deliver the data directly to the subscriber for use with a personal computer, while others produce a normal video signal which can be viewed on the subscriber's TV set.

6.3.4.3   Direct-to-Home TVRO

The current direct-to-home installation at C or Ku band is the forerunner to the home DBS receiver. In a direct-to-home installation, there is one video receiver which also incorporates the TV channel modulator. A low-noise converter could be used in lieu of the LNB, since only one channel is being received at a time. Provision is made for convenient tuning of the LNC and receiver to any desired channel that the viewer wishes to watch, and the antenna itself would probably have a motor-driven mount and polarizer. Such receiving systems are made "user friendly" by microprocessor control, allowing the viewer to key in the desired satellite and channel with a wireless remote control unit. The intelligence within the receiver causes the antenna to move over to the general position of the desired satellite, adjust the alignment automatically for maximum signal power, and then display the correct channel on the video monitor.

6.3.4.4   Receiving Scrambled Programming

The TVRO must include a descrambler for each channel which has been scrambled at the uplink source. There are several scrambling systems in use in North America and Europe, each differing in the degree of disruption of the video and audio and in the degree of difficulty of unauthorized receiving of the signal. The most common system in North America for scrambling cable TV programming is Video Cypher II, developed by M/A-Com and manufactured by General Instruments. In Europe and for industrial applications in the United States, systems based on the *multiplex analog component* (MAC) technique have been adopted. Several other techniques have been developed and applied on satellite and terrestrial links at one time or other. Depending on the scrambling system, the descrambler would be placed at either the input side or the output of the video receiver. The direct-to-home type of descrambler, unlike the cable head end model, can be switched between transponder channels fairly rapidly. Another type of unit called an *integrated receiver descrambler* (IRD) combines both of those functions and offers the prospect of reducing the cost of home TVRO equipment.

6.3.5   VSAT Configurations

Very small aperture terminal (VSAT) technology brings all of the features and benefits of satellite communication down to an extremely economical and usable form. As discussed in Chapters 1 and 2, VSATs provide efficient bypass of terrestrial networks for voice, data, and video services. The favorable economics result from sophisticated digital technology and advanced communication network protocols. In a typical network, a VSAT provides one or more 56 kb/s data channels, each of which can be subdivided or applied directly. Voice communication is also possible using 16 or 32 kb/s, depending on the compression algorithm. The use of Ku band (in the FSS portion of the spectrum) simplifies earth station siting by eliminating the need for terrestrial frequency coordination and the higher power satellites permit more services to be carried, including analog video, with antenna diameters in the range of 4 to 6 feet (1.2 to 1.8 meters). Implementation of a VSAT network is practical at C band with spread spectrum coding for transmission rates up to 19.2 kb/s. Although transponder capacity is relatively low, the spread spectrum technique and superior propagation characteristics of C band permit the use of antennas in the range of 2 to 4 feet (0.6 to 1.2 meters).

The configuration of a typical VSAT with full-service capability, shown in Figure 6-19, is reviewed in the following paragraphs. This should be taken as an example, since VSAT technology is constantly evolving. Photographs of Ku-band and C-band VSATs are presented in Figures 6-20 and 6-21, respectively.

6.3.5.1 Outdoor Equipment

The RF terminal of a VSAT is extremely compact and often attached to the antenna itself. As shown at the right of Figure 6-19, the RF equipment is composed of a LNB for reception and an upconverter and SSPA for transmission. Highly reliable solid-state electronics are used and so a single nonredundant string is usually adequate. Redundancy could be added for applications demanding greatest reliability and where the VSAT might be difficult to reach by maintenance personnel. The antenna in the illustration is the combination of an offset-fed parabola (discussed in Chapter 5) and a Cassegrain, which permits the feed and electronics to be mounted below the reflector and out of the path of the main beam. In comparison, the antenna in the photograph of the Ku-band VSAT (Figure 6-20) is a prime-focus-fed parabola with electronics mounted directly to the feed. A fixed mount is normally provided, since operation is only necessary with a single satellite. Ability to repoint the antenna to another orbit position is desirable if a change of satellite is ever contemplated.

6.3.5.2 Indoor Equipment

The remainder of the VSAT indoor equipment, consisting of one or more compact electronic boxes about the size of a personal computer, would be located in the building to which service is provided. As shown in Figure 6-19, the elements are functionally the same as those provided in the major earth station described earlier in this chapter. The capabilities assumed for this station included

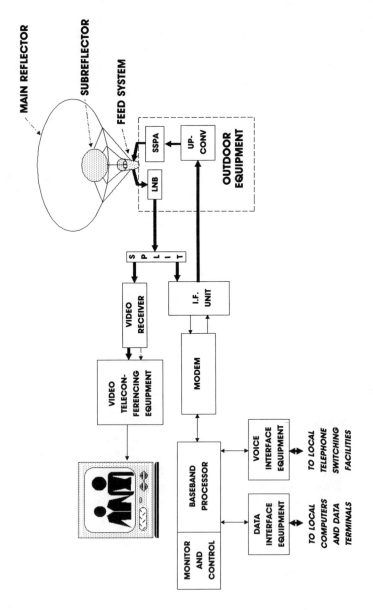

Fig. 6-19 Configuration of a Very Small Aperture Terminal (VSAT) Which Combines Two-Way Voice and Data with One-Way Video

Fig. 6-20 RF Terminal Portion of a Ku Band VSAT Employing a 1.2 Meter
Offset-Fed Parabolic Reflector
(photograph courtesy of Hughes Network Systems)

digital voice and data transmission as well as analog FM video reception. Because
of the low transmit power and small diameter of the RF terminal, a VSAT
typically would not be capable of transmitting video. A way to get around this
limitation would be to employ compressed digital video operating at 56 kb/s.
The quality of such a two-way link is significantly poorer than analog FM in
terms of its response to rapid picture motion, but could be acceptable for meetings
and pictoral information.

The techniques for transmitting and receiving data, both on a broadcast
and interactive basis, involve the use of random-access packet transmission (e.g.,
Aloha) as well as TDMA. Both modes are necessary, because most VSATs in
a network receive more data than they send. The modem illustrated in Figure
6-19 is therefore a burst modem, operating in the range of 56 to 256 kb/s
(depending on the particular network design). For the first transmission from
VSAT to hub, a packet would normally be uplinked. Many messages are short,
such as one line of a keyboard entry, a request to the hub for a file transfer, or

Fig. 6-21 Data Broadcast Receive-Only Terminal at C Band Employing Spread Spectrum Coding and a 0.6 Meter Antenna; Below— Two way Interative Terminal with 1.2 Meter Antenna (photographs courtesy of Equatorial Communications Company)

a brief report requested by the hub. The TDMA mode is effective for long or relatively frequent transmissions from several VSATs, and for voice and video communication. Switching between random access and TDMA would be in response to local traffic demands, activated either by the centralized network management system or automatically by the VSAT itself.

The star network structure is assumed for the example in Figure 6-19. If the network is to be used extensively for switched telephone service, then the configuration of the mesh is going to be far more effective. By allowing direct links between VSATs, the system will avoid double hops or multiple hub stations interconnected by expensive terrestrial links. This can be achieved with FDMA where each VSAT has one or more demand assigned SCPC modems which are used to set up point-to-point links during calls. In a more or less traditional demand assigned scheme, a request for service enters the VSAT over the telephone interface and is transmitted over the star network to a hub where the set up of the link is directed. The hub responds with digital instructions to the VSATs on both ends of the intended circuit to tune their SCPC modems to a frequency pair assigned for the duration of the call. Through this hub, the network management system monitors the use of the network and accomplishes such tasks as data traffic routing and billing. The combination of the star and mesh networks allows a system of VSATs to achieve the objectives of ISDN using satellite communication.

The voice and data interface equipment is needed to make the VSAT appear to be the same as any telephone or data communication circuit. For example, the VSAT network may use a proprietary protocol to carry and process signalling information which the user's PABX does not understand. The voice interface would then convert standard telephone signalling into the network protocol. Likewise, data protocols such as IBM SDLC and packet X.25 are converted to the VSAT network protocol in the data interface equipment. In addition to signalling and protocols, the interface equipment can provide signal conditioning such as bandwidth compression and S/N enhancement.

Video teleconference services on a point-to-multipoint basis are well within the capabilities of VSATs. As shown at the upper left of Figure 6-19, a standard video receiver provides a baseband signal to a teleconference unit. The picture could then be carried to a conference room or theatre. In addition to the video, the equipment might provide a voice interface for interactive "question and answer" service, using the VSAT to provide the reverse audio link.

6.4 TERRESTRIAL INTERFACES AND LINKS

Earth stations are a means of providing access to a satellite communication network of some type. An important part of their design deals with the interface between the station and the user, illustrated as the last box at the lower left of Figure 6-1. It was emphasized at the beginning of this chapter that an improperly designed or installed interface or tail will seriously degrade the quality of service. Often access to the satellite network will be blocked entirely, particularly in the case of digital traffic and signalling. The following paragraphs review general criteria for these interfaces as they relate to voice, data, and video information. At the conclusion of the chapter is a discussion of the types of terrestrial tails that may be utilized at a noncollocated earth station to extend this interface over some distance.

6.4.1 Typical Interface Requirements

The most common interfaces used in communication services carried both by satellite links and terrestrial systems are described in Figure 6-22. Each line and arrow indicates an independent signal path, required to interconnect the communication equipment with the user properly. Since this is an overview chart, many of the physical details such as voltage level, timing requirements, and connector type are missing. Detailed information of that type can be obtained from technical specifications of equipment and international standards such as those promulgated by the technical consultative committees of the ITU.

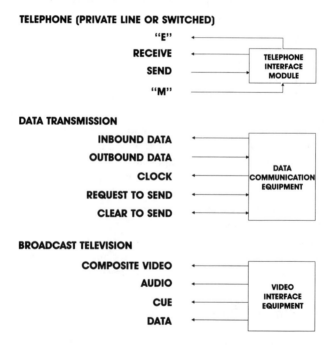

Fig. 6-22 Overview of Terrestrial Interface Alternatives for Telephone, Data, and Broadcast Television Service

6.4.1.1   Telephone Interface

The type of telephone interface illustrated at the top of Figure 6-22 inter-connects analog voice circuits in either private line or switched service. A detailed explanation of telephone service can be found in Chapter 2. Separate directions for send and receive (i.e., four wires) are normally provided since the conversion to two wires for the subscriber loop is accomplished by a telephone hybrid located within the telephone switching equipment. It is important to note that the audio voltage levels, which are measured in dBm (dB relative to 1 milliwatt), must be adjusted to the values prescribed in a system-wide plan and maintained at those levels by periodic testing and adjustment. The method of measuring the levels is by inserting a 1 kHz audio tone into the send side of the transmitting end and measuring the level of that tone on the receive side of the receiving end of the link. After amplification in the terminal equipment, the receive level is several dB greater than the send level; therefore, tandeming of receive to send and *vice versa* requires that resistive attenuators called *pads* be inserted in the connecting cables to ensure that correct levels pass through the link.

Circuit control is exercised by *supervisory signalling* over the E (ear) and M (mouth) wires. The telephone switch at the near end alerts the distant end that a call is about to come through by transmitting an inaudible signal over the M lead. At the distant end, the signal arrives over the E lead. Unlike the receive and send lines which are each a pair of wires, the E and M leads are single wires which indicate either a voltage different from zero (5 volts, for example) or zero volts (i.e., ground potential). When an earth station is connected to a terrestrial tail at voice frequency, the E lead of the station is connected to the M lead of the tail and *vice versa*.

6.4.1.2   Data Transmission Interface

Data transmission links at digital baseband require a pair of two-way wire lines much like telephone. The difference, however, is that protocols and timing references must also be considered. The information shown at the center of Figure 6-22 is an example of one arrangement for low-speed data communication equipment using an interface such as the common RS-232 standard. The inbound and outbound data lines are essentially the same as their counterparts in telephone. Since data communications require precise timing, a clock output is provided to synchronize the receiving side (the *slave*) with the sending side (the *master*). If the illustrated end were the master, then the clock would be sent in the opposite direction.

The *request to send* (RTS) and *clear to send* (CTS or CLS) amount to a form of supervisory signalling. When the transmitting end wishes to send data, the RTS line is activated much like the M lead. The receiving end, if operating and not occupied by some other task, responds by activating its CLS line. Digital communication equipment has more capability than historical telephone equipment, hence the CLS and RTS are bidirectional.

Numerous other interface arrangements have been specified and are available for data transmission. There has been much effort to develop international standards under ISDN and OSI so that digital systems will interconnect with one another and be capable of passing the maximum amount of data.

6.4.1.3   Television Interface

The last example in Figure 6-22 presents the terrestrial interface for video reception, where the transmit side would have exactly the same lines. *Composite video* is the term for the complete color TV baseband signal with its luminance (black and white) and *chromanance* (color) components. It is customary to measure the time waveform of the output in terms of the peak-to-peak voltage swing of the luminance signal, which extends from the tip of the sync pulse (called *blacker than black*) to the maximum possible white level. The value will be specified for the particular video format which has been dictated for the country of operation. Other such standards apply to the chromanance signal and to the line and frame repetition rates. All of these interface parameters for video are specified in engineering documents available to the domestic broadcasting industry. The composite video signal can only be viewed on a video monitor and is intended to be transmitted from a VHF or UHF broadcast station.

The audio portion of the broadcast video signal is sent separately, since broadcast stations have individual video and audio transmitters which are RF combined on the same antenna tower. (Normal home TV receivers have the capability to separate the audio from the video.) At the audio interface in Figure 6-22, the baseband channel covers a bandwidth of 20 Hz to 10 kHz, providing a high fidelity program channel. It is important that audio levels be set according to a common interface standard to prevent wide changes in volume as one tunes between television channels. An additional audio channel called a *cue* channel is provided for network control purposes and is not intended for broadcasting. As discussed in Chapter 2, each audio channel is modulated on a separate FM subcarrier and placed above the video baseband at a center frequency between 6 and 8 MHz.

The last interface in Figure 6-22 provides a one-way (point-to-multipoint) data broadcast channel extracted from the baseband. Assuming that digital modulation such as QPSK was used in the subcarrier, the video interface equipment includes the demodulator section of a digital modem. The interface of the demodulator would be that illustrated for data transmission at the center of Figure

6-22. Although only one direction of transmission is possible, the digital interface would still provide all of the interface lines and functions with the demodulator exercising appropriate control of data flow.

6.4.2   Terrestrial Tails

A terrestrial tail is a dedicated link between a communication earth station and one or more user locations. The distance to be covered can range from hundreds of feet to hundreds of miles. In C-band satellite systems, the earth station is often isolated from a city to reduce RFI difficulties, in which case an elaborate tail is required. On the other hand, terrestrial interference is not present in most Ku-band systems, and tails can therefore be relatively short. An exception is the case where a large earth station (i.e., a teleport) is shared by several users each of which must be reached by local terrestrial transmission links.

6.4.2.1   Purposes for Using Terrestrial Tails

The overall tail configuration for a major earth station is illustrated in Figure 6-23. In this example which is not to scale, any connection between facilities is referred to as a tail. A cable *interfacility link* (IFL) connects each of two RF terminals (lower left of the figure) to the main earth station building. Within this building can be found the baseband and interface equipment appropriate for the types of service being provided. It is assumed that all of the traffic (voice, data, and video) is to be transported to a switching office in the nearest city. These transmission requirements are met in the example with a single-hop terrestrial microwave link, equipped with sufficient receiver-transmitter units to carry the video, voice, and data traffic. The customer location or locations access the switching office through either public or private local loops consisting of fiber optic cable and conventional multiple pair cable.

The switching office and local loops can be bypassed (the dotted line between the customer location and the major earth station) with another private tail fitting the requirement. The reason for bypassing can be based on economics, it possibly being less expensive to own the tail facility rather than leasing capacity from the local telephone utility. The private bypass, which permits the user to maintain control of these resources, eliminates some of the time necessary to implement new public facilities. Reliability can be greatly improved with the path diversity of using both the public access lines and the private bypass link. This also happens to be a valid basis for using satellite transmission in the first place, providing a parallel path to existing terrestrial systems.

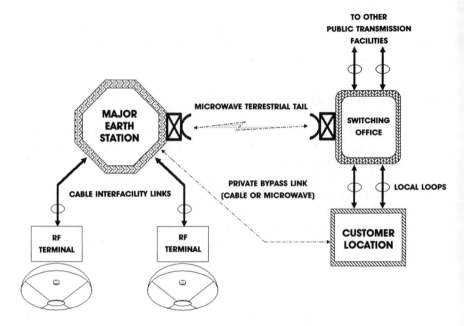

Fig. 6-23 Use of Terrestrial Tails Between Earth Station Facilities, Switching Offices, and Customer Locations

6.4.2.2 Terrestrial Tail Alternatives

The two principal types of terrestrial tail for bulk transmission purposes are line-of-microwave and fiber-optic cable. Both are effective and reliable and can be economical when applied properly. Short distances between buildings, such as for the IFL within an earth station site or when connecting a VSAT to one or more users, are best traversed with copper cable. Prime examples of this type of cable include coaxial cable and multiple pair cable. Waveguide can be used where minimum RF loss is needed.

Focusing in on large capacity terrestrial tails, Figure 6-24 compares fiber optic with microwave on the basis of investment cost. A fiber-optic link is relative costly per mile of construction, particularly within a metropolitan area. The black line of constant slope is the cost of the cable, electronics, and installation for a basic point-to-point link, assuming that the right-of-way is already available at essentially no cost. Most of the expense is for the repeater and terminal electronics and for installation, which is labor intensive. Fiber-optic cable itself is a small part of the cost, and hence it is usually wise to include many more fiber pairs than are necessary for the current demand.

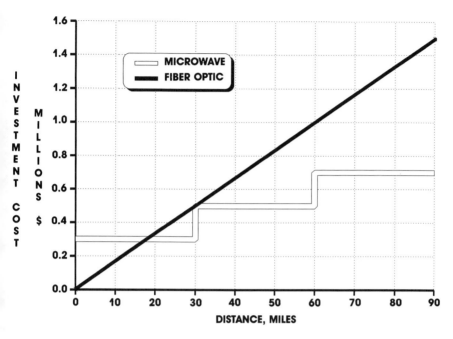

Fig. 6-24 Comparison of Fiber Optic and Terrestrial Microwave Links on the Basis of Investment Cost for a Terrestrial Tail (excluding Land and Right-of-Way)

The cost of putting in a high capacity terrestrial microwave system including receiver-transmitter units, towers, and antennas, is shown with the stair step, where the step occurs at the assumed repeater spacing of 30 miles. In comparing the two technologies, it is clear that fiber optic is attractive for relatively short tail lengths, i.e., less than the extent of one microwave hop. On the other hand, the fiber system can be expanded in capacity after initial installation to have many times the traffic capacity of the microwave system. This is because the cable contains extra fiber pairs which are available for expansion (and which were included in the original cable at little extra cost). In addition, transmission rates on a given fiber pair can be increased as newer optical modems and electronics are introduced.

It should be kept in mind that any real world situation should be examined in detail before the tail technology is selected. This is because installation and right-of-way costs can vary widely, as can the cost of the equipment itself. Figure 6-24, however, illustrates a valid framework for making such a comparison.

Chapter 7

Launch Systems and Orbital Operations

The technologies which make it possible to put a communication spacecraft into GEO and maintain its position over a lifetime of ten years or more are the result of rocket science and astrodynamics. Rather than attempt to cover these very specialized fields, we have taken a practical approach in providing a basic understanding. Needless to say, the necessary systems work quite well, and, although significant risks are involved in launching satellites, spacecraft have been placed into orbit, have landed on the moon, and are visiting faraway planets in our solar system. Twenty or more years of experience with satellite operations have reduced these technologies to commercial practice, although one must never lose sight of the sophistication which lies below the surface. For this reason, satellite operators rely heavily on the specialized capabilities of spacecraft manufacturers and the organizations which build and launch the rockets.

In addition to a review of the technologies, this chapter also presents a summary of usable launch systems. This should not be taken as the final word, because the particular set of usable launch vehicles will continuously change over time, both in terms of the particular rockets and in terms of their specific capabilities. For example, many of the older US expendable rockets were to be retired as the space shuttle went into full-scale commercial operation. With shuttle service being cut back, however, the older rockets are now being modernized and upgraded to the point where their capabilities and costs will continue to be attractive in the future.

7.1 THE LAUNCH MISSION AND ORBITAL OPERATIONS

An overview of the process through which a commercial communication satellite reaches GEO is presented in Figure 7-1. Major changes in the trajectory and orbit of the vehicle are provided by powerful liquid-fuel or solid-fuel rocket engines which increase the velocity of the vehicle by the amounts indicated in the figure. Generally speaking, the first booster stages lift off from the launch site and deliver the vehicle to an altitude of between 100 and 200 miles. At this altitude, the spacecraft follows a circular orbital path which is used in many LV systems as a *parking orbit*. This distance is exaggerated in the figure, since 200 miles would appear like the thickness of a pencil line if shown properly to scale. Another rocket stage is then used to kick the vehicle into the elliptical *geostationary transfer orbit* (GTO), where the farthest point (apogee) is at geosynchronous altitude and the closest point (perigee) is still at 100 to 200 miles. Once the spacecraft is in transfer orbit, all control is exercised through the TTAC station and the satellite control center. At a subsequent apogee, the last rocket stage provides sufficient boost to circularize the orbit by raising the perigee to 22,300 miles. Other initial touch-up maneuvers and orbit corrections during the life of the satellite are made using the spacecraft's propulsion system, discussed in Chapter 5. These phases of the launch mission are reviewed in more detail in the following paragraphs. Table 7-1 lists the events in a typical launch mission beginning with lift-off and ending with the start of operations in geostationary orbit. A graphic example of a mission on an expendable LV (i.e., the Delta rocket) is shown in Figure 7-2 for the HS-376 dual spin spacecraft.

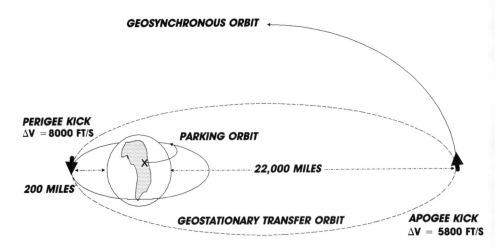

Fig. 7-1 Major Orbit Changes to Reach Geosynchronous Orbit

7.1.1 Delivery to Low Earth Orbit

To reach low earth (parking) orbit, an object must be elevated high enough above the earth to escape the drag of the atmosphere. This is done with a ballistic rocket stage which lofts the payload, following a path that would return to earth some distance from the launch site. In Figure 7-3, the ballistic trajectory brings

EVENT
1. **LIFTOFF OF MAIN BOOSTER**
2. **PARKING ORBIT ACHIEVED**
3. **TRANSFER ORBIT INJECTION**
4. **TT&C LINK ESTABLISHED WITH GROUND**
5. **REORIENTATION TO AMF ATTITUDE**
6. **PREBURN RCS MANEUVER**
7. **APOGEE MOTOR FIRING**
8. **ORBITAL ADJUSTMENTS**
9. **DRIFT TO ASSIGNED STATION**
10. **ORBIT AND ATTITUDE ADJUSTMENTS**
11. **DESPIN OF PLATFORM**
12. **SPACECRAFT DEPLOYMENTS**
13. **BUS TESTING**
14. **PAYLOAD TESTING**
15. **START OPERATIONS**

Table 7-1 Launch Sequence for a Geostationary Orbit Mission Identifying Key Events and Ground Support Activities

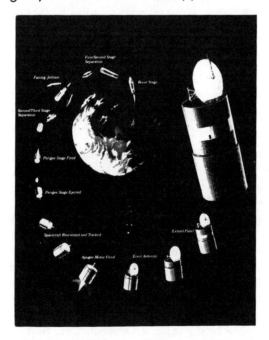

Fig. 7-2 Geostationary Orbit Mission Sequence for Launch by the Delta Rocket of an HS-376 Dual Spin Spacecraft (photograph courtesy of Hughes Aircraft Company)

the LV above the atmosphere and allows the second rocket stage to push the LV into an orbit around the earth. Kepler's first law governs the motion of the vehicle in orbit, wherein the satellite follows an elliptical path with the earth centered at one focus. The satellite stays up in orbit because the force produced by centripetal acceleration is equal to the gravitational pull of the earth.

Because the mass of the satellite is insignificant compared to that of the earth, the time period of the orbit is completely determined by the velocity of the satellite. The second stage of the booster is pointed along the tangent to the desired orbit, and the total thrust increases the velocity of the vehicle to the required value. In the parking orbit, the vehicle makes one revolution around the earth in approximately one and a half hours. Since this is too fast for conventional TTAC stations to track the LV, operation of the first, second, and third stages is automatically controlled by an on-board computer.

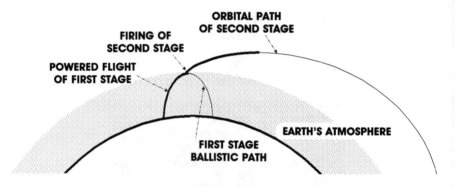

Fig. 7-3 Two-Stage Launch into Low Earth (Parking) Orbit

The thin atmosphere that extends to the parking orbit is very minute, but there is sufficient drag to cause some slowing of the vehicle. As this friction drag reduces velocity, the orbit gradually decays, and eventually the vehicle will reenter and burn up. Since this can take from months to years, there is little risk to the satellite between the time it reaches the parking orbit and when the third stage propels it to geosynchronous altitude. There can be circumstances where the second stage does not provide its full increment of velocity, and the vehicle is then on an orbital or even ballistic path back into the denser atmosphere. Timely firing of the third stage would then be extremely important in order to prevent loss of the mission.

There is an issue which relates to the geographical latitude of the launch site. Nearly every launch site is located some distance from the equator, while the geostationary orbit is in the plane of the equator. The parking orbit produced by the second stage will be at an angle with the equatorial plane; this is referred to as *inclination* of the orbit. The inclination, which is approximately equal to the latitude of the launch site, must be removed using rocket energy at some point during the mission prior to putting the satellite into commercial service. This aspect is discussed in more detail in the next section. Obviously, the closer the launch is to the equator, the less additional rocket energy is needed to correct for inclination.

7.1.2 Transfer Orbit

As discussed in a previous paragraph, geostationary orbit is reached by first placing the satellite into GTO with apogee at 22,300 miles and perigee at the altitude of the parking orbit (100 to 200 miles). The term *perigee kick* is used to describe the action of the third rocket stage, which may either be part of the LV or provided separately for the spacecraft. The mechanical aspects of these alternatives are reviewed later in this chapter. Perigee kick is designed to increase the velocity of the vehicle by approximately 8000 feet per second, which produces the desired elliptical orbit.

Figure 7-1 shows how transfer orbit is initiated from parking orbit wherein the perigee kick stage is fired at the point opposite from where apogee is to occur. The mission plan usually specifies that the first apogee after injection into GTO must be in view of a TTAC station at a specific location. Conversely, the firing position may be fixed for the particular launch site and LV, forcing the location of the TTAC station to be in view of the resulting first apogee. The period of GTO is approximately 12 hours and the satellite is easy to track near apogee when its motion is slowed considerably. Because each successive apogee occurs at a different longitude on the earth, it is advantageous to have TTAC stations in the eastern and western hemispheres. This can be accomplished without owning additional sites by contracting with a satellite operator in the opposite hemisphere for the use of their TTAC station during the transfer orbit phase of the mission.

The transfer orbit will normally retain the inclination of the parking orbit, although some of the energy of the second stage can be expended for the correction of inclination by redirecting the velocity of the vehicle during firing. It is usually more efficient to delay this type of maneuver until apogee kick, which happens also to be when better tracking data is available from the TTAC station in view of the satellite.

The final phase of transfer orbit operations is the injection into geosynchronous orbit, illustrated in Figure 7-4. At the right of the figure is shown the vector representation of the velocities before and after injection, looking toward the point of *apogee motor firing* (AMF) from the right. The satellite velocity vector in the inclined transfer orbit at the point in question is at the angle i with respect to the geostationary orbit plane. To cause the final synchronous orbit velocity to be in the equatorial plane, the spacecraft is oriented so that the apogee kick motor will fire along the vector direction shown pointed upward at angle *a*. The thrust increment at AMF is sufficiently greater than that required to produce synchronous orbit speed to correct for inclination. Therefore, the resultant velocity is in the equatorial plane (i.e., horizontal in the vector diagram) and its magnitude is the 8500 feet per second needed to circularize the orbit at 22,300 miles altitude.

The durations of the required rocket burns and their orientations are never perfect; consequently, the orbits produced will be slightly off. The first step in correction is to determine the orbit after injection using the TTAC station and orbital dynamics capabilities at the SCC. Touch-up maneuvers are then performed with the spacecraft reaction control system. As was mentioned previously, the particular transfer orbit where AMF is accomplished is selected for operational reasons. For example, it is desirable (but not always possible) to fire the AKM at an apogee which is as close as possible to the final orbital longitude of the satellite and thus minimize the time for movement from AMF longitude.

7.1.3   Drift Orbit and Initial Checkout

Following injection from transfer orbit, the satellite is in a near synchronous orbit and drifting either towards or away from its assigned longitude, depending on the magnitude and direction of the injection errors. Since the detailed parameters of the initial drift orbit are unknown after AKM firing, the first priority of TTAC operations is to determine the orbit as accurately as possible. The next step is to make the necessary velocity corrections to cause the satellite to drift in the correct direction. Figure 7-4 shows how a satellite in drift orbit is actually at a different altitude than the geostationary orbit, which is a consequence of Keplar's second law. This limits the possibility of a drifting satellite bumping

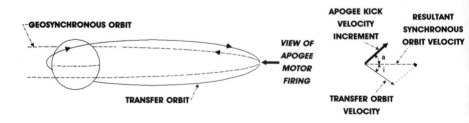

Fig. 7-4 Injection from Transfer Orbit into Geosynchronous Orbit Using the Apogee Kick Maneuver

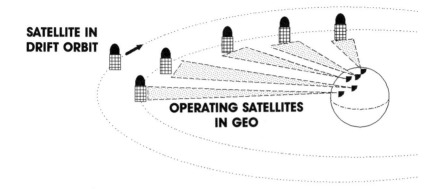

Fig. 7-5 Drifting of a Geosynchronous Satellite from the AKM Injection Longitude to the Final Longitude Position

into a stationary one. A satellite drifting westward is above the geostationary orbit, while one drifting eastward is below. There still remains, however, the possibility of RF interference and disruption of TTAC as the drifting satellite passes through the antenna beams of the TTAC and communication earth stations which point at their respective geostationary satellite longitudes.

Potential problems with RFI in drift orbit are overcome through detailed coordination between satellite operators. Without this, some serious consequences could occur for the drifting and stationary satellites alike. This is the motivation for the needed cooperation between operators, some of whom are potentially competitors in business. International regulations, on the other hand, only pertain to the operation at the final longitude. As shown in Figure 7-5, the ground station antenna beams which radiate toward fixed orbit positions prevent continuous TTAC operations with the drifting satellite. The mission plan for the drift orbit includes information regarding the other operating satellite networks. Spacecraft command receivers are never turned off, and hence the other satellite operators are requested not to command during a period of overlap. Spacecraft deployments and testing can be conducted when the satellite is definitely out of view of operating ground stations, but it is usually best to defer such activities until the satellite reaches its assigned orbit position.

A predetermined amount of RCS fuel is consumed in order to stop the satellite from drifting. Final touch-up maneuvers with the spacecraft RCS bring the velocity and altitude into alignment with the geostationary orbit. From this point forward, the station-keeping phase of the mission begins and lasts through the rest of the satellite lifetime. Relocation of the satellite to another longitude can be initiated by first pushing the satellite into a higher or lower orbit, as appropriate, and allowing the satellite to drift again. This requires two equal amounts of fuel: one to start the drift and the other to stop it when the final longitude is reached. Because the duration of thrusting determines the speed of relative motion, the amount of fuel consumed is roughly inversely proportional to the time allotted for the relocation drift maneuver.

7.1.4 Geostationary Orbit Operations

Achievement of a geostationary orbit with the satellite at its assigned longitude usually starts the operational stage. If the earth was the only source of gravitational pull, and if its mass could be represented by a sphere of uniform mass density (or at least composed on concentric spherical shells of uniform mass), then the satellite would stay put at this longitude indefinitely. The real situation differs on both counts, as diagrammed from above the orbit in Figure 7-6. The sun and the moon exert significant gravitational attraction (as in ocean tides), pulling the orbit of the satellite along the line of force and out of its equatorial plane. The shape of the orbit becomes somewhat elliptical, a property called *eccentricity*, and the plane of the orbit tends to become inclined. Eccentricity is not particularly troublesome and is easily corrected along with the primary orbital adjustments.

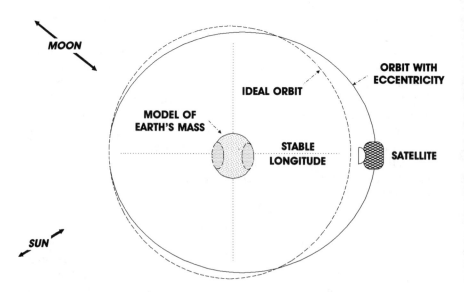

Fig. 7-6 Variations in the Geostationary Orbit in the Plane of the Equator

Figure 7-6 shows two bulges in the earth, representing the irregular quality of the mass of the earth. The consequence of this is that the earth's gravitational field is nonuniform at synchronous altitude. With the satellite as shown in line with the bulges, the gravity acting on it is in balance and the satellite tends to stay put. Likewise, positions 90 degrees away in the orbit have equal pull from each bulge, and no force acts to move the satellite. Intermediary positions experience a force which tends to drift the satellite towards an equilibrium longitude. The actual physical and mathematical relationships are much more complex than this; this simple model, however, can be a way of visualizing the natural east-west drifting of a geostationary satellite not located at one of the four equilbrium points. Fuel usage for a satellite positioned at the worst longitudes is still a small fraction of the total budget, which is dominated by that required to remove inclination (north-south station-keeping).

Properties of the inclined orbit are shown in Figure 7-7, which has been exaggerated for clarity. Gravity from the moon and to some extent from the sun cause the plane of the satellite's orbit to become inclined, increasing by approximately one degree per year. For a given amount of inclination (say 0.1 degrees), the satellite will be below the equator at one point in time and then be above the equator precisely 12 hours later. A satellite when viewed from the ground will appear to move north and then south over a 24-hour period. This topic was covered in Chapter 6 in connection with the possible need for ground antenna tracking in the event that the beamwidth is narrower than the north-south motion of the satellite. For optimum communication performance, the spacecraft antenna direction can be adjusted north or south over the 24-hour period to compensate for instantaneous position in the orbit as suggested by Figure 7-7.

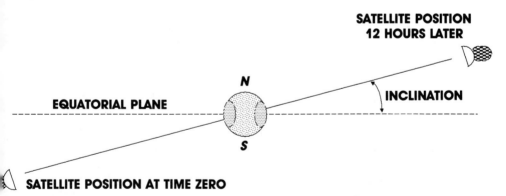

Fig. 7-7 Relative Position of a Satellite in an Inclined Geostationary Orbit as Seen Over a 24-Hour Period

7.1.5 RCS Fuel Allocation

The reaction control system of the spacecraft is used to provide several of the preoperational velocity increments as well as all of those necessary for station-keeping. Figure 7-8 presents an approximate allocation of RCS fuel for an entire satellite mission from transfer orbit to end of life. In this example, the RCS does not provide the bulk of the velocity increment for perigee kick nor apogee kick. The allocation for error removal has to do with orbit changes which are needed to correct for LV, PKM, and AKM injection errors. This is because no injection is perfect, and some RCS fuel must be expended to remove velocity and angular errors which would otherwise cause the satellite to end up in an unusable orbit.

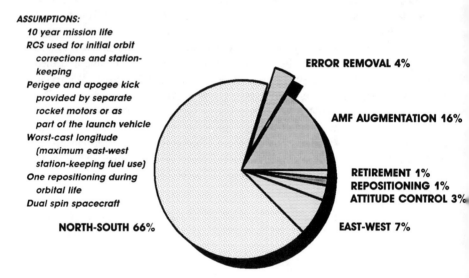

ASSUMPTIONS:
10 year mission life
RCS used for initial orbit
corrections and station-
keeping
Perigee and apogee kick
provided by separate
rocket motors or as
part of the launch vehicle
Worst-cast longitude
(maximum east-west
station-keeping fuel use)
One repositioning during
orbital life
Dual spin spacecraft

ERROR REMOVAL 4%

AMF AUGMENTATION 16%

RETIREMENT 1%
REPOSITIONING 1%
ATTITUDE CONTROL 3%

NORTH-SOUTH 66%

EAST-WEST 7%

Fig. 7-8 Allocation of RCS Fuel Usage for a Typical Geostationary Satellite Over a Ten-Year Mission Life

Once on station, the orbit is corrected during station-keeping, introducing velocity changes (increments) which are numerically determined by the orbit and not by the spacecraft mass. The amount of fuel consumed in station-keeping to produce the necessary velocity increments over a certain period, however, is proportional to the average total mass of the satellite. In Figure 7-9, the total mass of the satellite on an annual basis is plotted in relative terms. This could, for example, represent a satellite of 1000 kg at beginning of life (*dry* weight plus fuel). Each year, a steadily decreasing amount of fuel is used for station-keeping, as shown in Figure 7-10. These graphs use a simplified mathematical

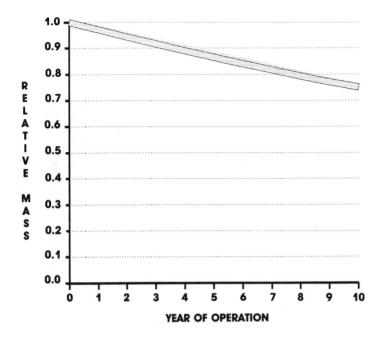

Fig. 7-9 Total Satellite Mass as a Function of Time over a Ten-Year Orbital Life Showing the Decrease due to Consumption of Station-Keeping Fuel

model, and a more accurate analysis would consider many other variables which have a measurable impact (plus and minus).

As is evident from Figure 7-8, approximately two-thirds of the fuel is required for north-south station-keeping (correction of geostationary orbit inclination). East-west station-keeping, while critical to every geostationary satellite, requires from zero to a maximum of ten percent of total RCS fuel. Both of these usages are predictable, and little can be done to extend the mission, once geostationary orbit is reached. One exception is the use of a storage orbit to conserve fuel before the satellite is placed into service. This involves injecting the spacecraft into an inclined geosynchronous orbit, where the orbit moves naturally towards the equatorial plane at the rate of approximately one degree per year. A satellite can be brought out of storage prematurely by consuming fuel to remove the remaining inclination.

Most of the attention of SCC personnel is directed towards accuracy in orbit determination and fuel use during routine station-keeping maneuvers. A small reserve for repositioning provides for moving the satellite to a new longitude, if required for some reason. Recall that half of this fuel would be used

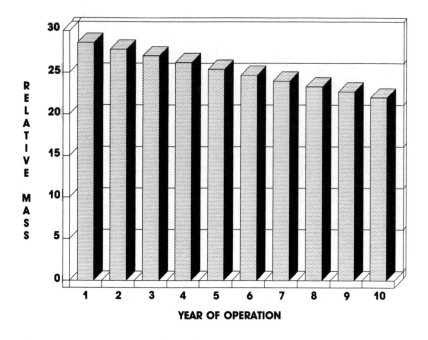

Fig. 7-10 Decreasing Annual Fuel Use for Station-Keeping as a Function of the Year of Life for a Ten-Year Mission

to start the drift and the other to stop when the desired position is reached. A final budget allocation is used at end of life to accelerate the satellite into a higher drift orbit where it will be left off and cannot interfere either physically or electrically with operating satellites.

7.2 LAUNCH TECHNOLOGY AND SYSTEMS

The launch vehicle situation is an ever-changing scene, as new rocket designs replace their older counterparts. Because of the complexities and risks associated with launching satellites, however, it is often the rule that the newer vehicles are merely modified versions of their predecessors. The one exception is the space shuttle which revolutionized space operations. Lately, the whole concept of a reusable space vehicle for commercial launching has even come into question. It is likely that future commercial launches will rely upon expendable rockets of improved design, many of which have familiar names like Ariane, Delta, and Titan.

The following paragraphs review the evolution of commercially available launch vehicles suitable for placing a spacecraft into geostationary transfer orbit

(GTO). As discussed in the previous section, this involves three stages: a first and second booster and a perigee kick stage. In some systems, the perigee kick stage is part of the LV, while in others, the spacecraft provides its own integral perigee kick. The discussion begins with an overview of the technology and evolution of current LVs.

7.2.1 Launch System Design

While the details of rocket technology are beyond the scope of this book, the basic alternatives are relatively easy to understand. A liquid-fueled first stage uses separate fuel and oxidizer supplies which are burned to produce the necessary thrust. The engine uses pumps to maintain constant fluid pressure, and temperature is controlled by piping the cooler liquids around the hotter parts of the engine. Typical fuel-oxidizer combinations include hydrazine-nitrogen tetroxide (i.e., bipropellant approach described in Chapter 5), kerosene-liquid oxygen (used by the Saturn 5 rocket of the Apollo Program), and cryogenic liquid hydrogen-liquid oxygen (used in the main engines of the space shuttle). For simplicity's sake, the name *hydrazine* is used herein to refer to compounds such as *unsymmetrical dimethylhydrazine* (UDMH) and *monomethylhydrazine* (MMH) which contain hydrazine as a component. Cryogenic propellants must be kept at an extremely low temperature so that they remain in liquid form and do not revert to a gaseous state. The trade-off between high energy cryogenic fuel and the others which can exist at room temperature is that the latter can be stored for long periods of time (i.e., in a missile silo or in space). An active control system causes the rocket to fly along a predetermined path to a point where separation occurs and the next stage ignites. Augmenting the thrust of the first stage are often "strap-on" rockets which employ either solid or liquid fuel.

Solid fuel rocket motors offer a convenient alternative to liquid because of the simplicity of design and integration, and because they may be stored for years at a time. This is the same technology as that used in the AKM of the spacecraft. The two large rockets attached aside the space shuttle are *solid rocket motors* (SRMs) which are filled with highly combustible propellant material. The thrust obtained is much higher than that of liquid rockets of the same weight; hence, solids offer a great deal of boost during critical parts of the launch sequence. Solid rocket motors burn rapidly and at a high temperature, requiring that great precautions be taken with their exit nozzles, cases, and attachments to the vehicle.

The second and third stages of the booster can take the form of solid or bipropellant liquid-fueled rockets. As explained in the previous section, the second stage is ignited after the LV is above the denser part of the atmosphere, propelling the vehicle into the parking orbit. Separation of the stages involves the firing of small explosives which sever bolts holding specifically designed fittings together. Clearly, the sequence of ignition, burn, and velocity control, separation and ignition again is vital to the achievement of mission success. Much of the attention and concern of launch operation personnel is focused on this critical sequence, which occurs automatically without ground control.

Preparation of the LV and spacecraft is another vital area and one often overlooked. Many of the modern LVs are capable of launching two or more payloads at the same time. Even with a single payload, the preparations at the launch site take one or more months, since the spacecraft must be checked and then properly integrated with the LV. The launch agency, rocket manufacturer, and spacecraft supplier work essentially around the clock during this period to assemble the LV, install the payload or payloads, check and fuel the system, and conduct various prelaunch tests and rehearsals. The facilities involved are extensive, and there are only a few qualified launch sites in existence. It was also mentioned in previous chapters that tracking sites are required during each phase of the launch and transfer orbit, and all must be prepared and checked out prior to lift-off.

7.2.2 Typical Launch Vehicles

Before describing the currently available commercial LVs and their capabilities, it is instructive to review the evolution of these systems. Table 7-2 presents three timeframes for commercial launch systems, beginning in the decade of the 1970s and moving through the 1980s into the 1990s. Because of emphasis by the United States government on the space shuttle during the mid-1970s, only the Delta and Atlas Centaur were operational for commercial launches. The situation continued into the 1980s as shuttle operations went into full swing. Under the plan at the time, all expendable LVs were to be phased out and production of the Delta, Atlas Centaur, and Titan was nearly halted. Meanwhile, the European Ariane system became available, and some commercial satellite operators took advantage of attractive rates and convenient schedules. The introduction of Ariane is fortunate for the satellite industry, now that the shuttle has been shifted away from commercial service, a situation which is expected to persist into the 1990s.

Beginning in the mid-1980s, the expendable LV market opened up to even greater competition. Encouraged by the new policies and buying practices of the US government, several commercial LVs have been advanced. In particular, the Titan rocket has always been used by the US government for military and scientific launches. As discussed in a subsequent paragraph, its lift capability and success records are both very good; commercial Titan launches, however, have only been made available in the late 1980s. The Japanese and Chinese have significant launch capabilities, and some commercial activity by them is anticipated. The Soviet Union has indicated its interest in launching commercial

1970 TIMEFRAME

DELTA 2914

ATLAS CENTAUR

1980 TIMEFRAME

ARIANE 1, 2, 3

ATLAS CENTAUR

DELTA 3914, 3920

JAPANESE N-1, 2

LONG MARCH 1, 3

SPACE SHUTTLE

TITAN 3

1990 TIMEFRAME

ARIANE 3, 4, 5

ATLAS CENTAUR

DELTA II

JAPANESE N-2, H-1

LONG MARCH 2, 3

PROTON

SPACE SHUTTLE (pending)

TITAN 3, 4

Table 7-2 Review of Commercial Launch Vehicles (Past, Present, and Future) Capable of Supporting Geosynchronous Orbit Missions

payloads using the Proton LV, a rocket which has been used extensively for a quarter century. Other Soviet rockets could also perform the LV role for the commercial market.

The impression one should take away from this discussion and Table 7-2 is that the LV lineup is constantly evolving and that the situation with regard to any specific rocket will not remain constant very long. The best choice is usually a system which is based on an experienced rocket with a good success record. This goes without saying because of the expense and business risk which are involved with implementing and operating a communication satellite system. These factors and others are reviewed in the following detailed comments on the LVs of the 1990 timeframe. The various systems are listed for convenience in alphabetical order and their nominal characteristics and success records (as of October 1987) are compared in Table 7-3.

7.2.2.1   Ariane

The European commercial expendable LV, Ariane, was developed by the *European Space Agency* (ESA) and the French *Centre d' Etudes Spatiales* (CNES) and is now manufactured, operated and marketed by a French-led consortium called Arianespace. Being liquid fueled, the first and second stages use hydrazine-nitrogen tetroxide and the cryogenic third stage uses liquid hydrogen-liquid oxygen. Solid or liquid strap-ons may be combined with the first stage. Ariane 2, configured to be competitive with the Atlas Centaur, had the capability to lift an INTELSAT spacecraft or two smaller domestic spacecraft into GTO. The dual launch capability was proven in US Government programs; it was applied for the first time, however, in commercial service for Ariane. Another important feature of the program is the use of the Kourou launch site in French Guiana at a latitude very close to the equator. As discussed in a previous section, this reduces the inclination of the transfer orbit and offers the capability to save fuel or extend life. The Ariane rocket is a derivative of earlier European rocket programs from the French, British, and German governments and hence has the type of history needed for success. On the other hand, the concept of a commercial company, i.e., Arianespace, was totally new and has become the pattern that several others are following.

The principal commercial vehicles are the Ariane 3 and Ariane 4, while Ariane 5 would appear to be a developmental concept geared towards very heavy payloads such as the Hermes reusable "spaceplane." Ariane 3, shown in the photograph in Figure 7-11, has the capability to place two satellites of the Delta 3920 class into GTO, using a structural casing called the SYLDA. GTE was the first US company to chose the dual launch Ariane system to place their Spacenet and GStar satellites into GEO. For very heavy payloads such as Intelsat VI, the Ariane 4 is available. The Ariane record of 12 successes out of 15 attempts (not including Ariane 4) is acceptable, and further success is anticipated as the LV manufacturer continues to improve component and subsystem design. In the future, many commercial organizations as well as government satellite operators will use the Ariane vehicle, because the capabilities appear to be well matched to needs.

LAUNCH VEHICLE	POUNDS TO GTO	AGENCY	USAGE	SUCCESS/ ATTEMPTS
ARIANE 3	5,689	ARIANESPACE	SPACENET/GSTAR	12/15
ARIANE 4	9,482	ARIANESPACE	INTELSAT VI	
ARIANE 5	12,789	ARIANESPACE	HERMES	
ATLAS CENTAUR	5,200	GEN DYNAMICS	INTELSAT V	33/37
DELTA 3920	2,830	M-DAC	GALAXY	73/79
DELTA II	3,560	M-DAC	GPSS	
JAPANESE N-2	1,500	NASDA	GMS	9/9
JAPANESE H-1	2,200	NASDA	BS-3	1/1
LONG MARCH 2	4,630	CHINA GW		7/8
LONG MARCH 3	3,087	CHINA GW	WESTAR 6S	2/3
PROTON	9,420	SOVIET UNION		113/124
SPACE SHUTTLE	17,000	NASA	LEASAT	24/27
TITAN 3	4,100	MARTIN MARIETTA	JC-SAT	31/34
TITAN 4	9,900	MARTIN MARIETTA		

Table 7-3 Comparison of Commercial Launch Vehicles in Synchronous Orbit Missions for the 1990s Timeframe

Fig. 7-11 The Ariane 3 Rocket Lifting off from the Kourou Launch Site
and Carrying Arabsat and Brazilsat (SBTS)
(photograph courtesy of Arianespace)

7.2.2.2 Atlas Centaur

Having been around for three decades, the Atlas Centaur has played an
important role in lifting medium payloads into GTO and other orbits. The liquid-
fueled rocket is built by the Convair Division of General Dynamics. The Atlas
first stage was originally a ballistic missile and employs a liquid kerosene-liquid
oxygen system. The second stage, called the Centaur, was the first high-energy
cryogenic liquid hydrogen-liquid oxygen engine developed in the United States.
Delivery to GTO is provided by the Centaur stage, since the Atlas (acting
effectively as one and a half stages) performs a portion of the injection into
parking orbit. Intelsat IV, aboard the Atlas Centaur in Figure 7-12, required
greater lift capability than Delta because it was heavier than previous INTELSAT
designs. Many military geosynchronous satellites such as Fleetsat have used this

Fig. 7-12 The Launch of an Atlas Centaur Rocket from the Kennedy
Space Center at Cape Canaveral, Florida, with an Intelsat IV
Spacecraft On-Board
(photograph courtesy of Hughes Aircraft Company)

LV extensively and it has a good overall success record. All launches into GTO
are conducted from NASA's *Kennedy Space Center* (KSC) at Cape Canaveral,
Florida.

General Dynamics has announced its intention to offer the Atlas Centaur
for commercial launches in the future. The US Government has examined making
additional purchases of the Atlas Centaur, which, if made, would assure the
long-term availability of this rocket. An advanced configuration of the Atlas
Centaur has been proposed with a capability to lift approximately 9,600 pounds
into GTO, which is comparable to that of the Ariane 4. This would be a welcome
addition to the lineup because of the largely successful record that Atlas Centaur
has built up.

7.2.2.3 Delta

Referred to as the workhorse of NASA, the Delta rocket has established an impressive track record since the first US launches of geosynchronous satellites. McDonnell Douglas Astronautics Company (M-DAC) is the manufacturer and now operator of the Delta, which employs a kerosene-liquid oxygen first stage and a hydrazine-nitrogen tetroxide second stage. Up to nine solid rocket motors are strapped onto the side of the first stage for added lift. To propel the spacecraft from low-earth orbit into GTO, a solid rocket motor called the *payload assist module* (PAM) can be provided by M-DAC. Earlier versions of the Delta included a solid third stage as part of the LV, but the advent of the space shuttle led to the development of the PAM as a generic perigee kick stage usable with either LV. All launches to GTO are conducted from NASA's KSC facility.

The most common version of the Delta has been the 3920, shown in Figure 7-13, which has the capability to place a 2700 pound domestic spacecraft into GTO. It was mentioned previously that the Delta with its excellent success record was planned to be phased out in conjunction with the expansion of space shuttle service. Under the latest US-government policy, LV manufacturers are being encouraged to offer their services directly to spacecraft operators and to compete with one another. M-DAC is in a strong position, since it will provide an upgraded Delta rocket called the Delta II to the US Air Force for the purpose of launching medium payloads including those for the *global positioning satellite system* (GPSS). The Delta II has significantly greater lift capability than the 3920 and in addition has a *fairing* (spacecraft enclosure) diameter of 9.3 feet *versus* the 8 feet of the earlier design. Being built on the earlier success record, having greater capabilities, and being in large-scale production for the US government, the Delta II is an attractive alternative for medium-sized spacecraft such as those used for domestic satellite communication.

7.2.2.4 Japanese Launch Vehicles

The Japanese government entered the field of launching geosynchronous satellites by employing a version of the Delta under license from M-DAC. The particular government agency in Japan responsible for launch and other space programs is the *National Space Development Agency* (NASDA). As shown in Table 7-3, the N-2 rocket is only capable of putting the smallest payload into GTO, although it has the best record of essentially 100% success for nine launches. The first stage is a kerosene-liquid oxygen stage with solid strap-ons (similar to the Delta), while the second is a liquid hydrazine-nitrogen tetroxide rocket engine built in Japan. Perigee kick is provided by a Thiokol solid rocket motor. Launches take place on the Japanese island of Tanegashima.

Fig. 7-13 The Launch of the Galaxy III Spacecraft with the PAM Aboard
the Delta 3920 Rocket
(photograph courtesy of Hughes Communications, Inc.)

The upgraded H-1 rocket draws heavily from the N-2/Delta design, but
has more Japanese technical and manufacturing content. Favorable comparisons

can be made with the N-2, but the lift capability of the H-1 is still well short of that of the Delta 3920. NASDA has plans to develop the H-2 rocket with a Japanese liquid hydrogen-liquid oxygen first stage and the ability to place approximately 9000 pounds into GTO. Such an LV would clearly place Japan in the running for any of the larger class of commercial spacecraft. The Japanese launch capability is currently limited, however, by use restrictions at the launch site, which can only be operated for a few months of the year. This can obviously be remedied by moving launch operations to a remote site not on Japanese territory, possibly very close to the equator. Alternatively, rocket engines or other major components could be exported for sale in the United States or other countries. The essentially perfect success record makes the Japanese capability worthy of careful consideration once they make their services or hardware available to the international market.

7.2.2.5   Long March

With decades of experience in missile and launch-vehicle development, the Chinese government has now made available the Long March to the commercial market. The contracting authority, called the China Great Wall Industrial Company, has entered into launch discussions with several satellite operators, including American companies like Western Union and Hughes Communications. Lift capability is in the low to middle range, making the Long March suitable for many commercial spacecraft such as those used for domestic communication. In terms of rocket design, the first and second stages employ liquid engines using hydrazine-nitrogen tetroxide propellant. A cryogenic third stage with liquid hydrogen-liquid oxygen is provided. To employ the system, foreign spacecraft must be delivered to the Chinese launch site at Xichang. The experience to date indicates a relatively small number of publicized launches and a reasonably good success record, and attractive pricing has made this Chinese system quite alluring to foreign buyers.

7.2.2.6   Soviet Proton

The Soviet Union has launched more payloads than any other country in the world and has recently made overtures to the west to provide commercial launch services. An American company called Space Commerce Corporation of Houston, Texas, is representing the Soviet government in marketing the Proton and associated launch services at the Russian launch site. Table 7-3 provides an example of a configuration with substantial lift capability and also indicates that the success record according to the marketing organization is good. A unique feature of Proton is that direct injection into geosynchronous orbit is offered as an optional service. The types of liquid fuels utilized in the four-stage rocket have not been publicized.

7.2.2.7 Space Shuttle

The *Space Transportation System* (STS), the official NASA name for the space shuttle, was developed for the purpose of inexpensively placing payloads into earth orbit. While it failed to achieve its objective for economy, there can be no doubt that the space shuttle was and remains an outstanding accomplishment in space hardware development. The main engines of the shuttle employ cryogenic liquid hydrogen-liquid oxygen propellants contained in the large external tank to which both the orbiter spaceplane and the twin SRMs are attached. Only the Saturn rocket of the Apollo program had greater lift capability. The shuttle actually delivers its payloads to low earth orbit (in the same manner as the first two stages of a conventional rocket) and a perigee kick stage is relied upon to take the spacecraft to GTO.

The orbiter of the STS performs several functions, including those of a payload carrier and airplane. Mentioned previously was the external tank, which delivers the propellants to the main engines of the orbiter. The major elements are clearly visible in the photograph of an STS launch in Figure 7-14. In addition, the orbiter has *orbital maneuvering engines* which are fueled by hydrazine-nitrogen tetroxide. The cargo bay of the orbiter can hold the payloads to be delivered to orbit (deployed); and other payloads can remain fixed to the orbiter for return to earth. As many as three payloads have been deployed on one mission, although a theoretical maximum of seven PAM-D spacecraft is possible. Deployment schemes are covered later in this chapter. An added feature of the STS is its demonstrated ability to support repair operations and to recover spacecraft for return to earth. The orbiter is, however, restricted to low earth orbit and cannot itself reach GEO. The concept of a *space tug* has been advanced wherein a separate orbital vehicle would bring payloads, fuel, etc., back and forth between GEO and the shuttle orbiter.

It has long been the assumption that manned launch missions are more reliable than unmanned from the standpoint of reaching low earth orbit. The basis for this is that the vehicle is designed to include many safeguards and backup systems which would be uneconomic for expendable LVs. In addition, the payloads themselves must be protected in such a way that there is little chance of explosion in the shuttle bay. The disaster which destroyed the shuttle Challenger and killed the seven crew members, however, again revealed that launch operations involve great complexity and risk. Expendable LVs would therefore appear to be essential to an overall space program.

Fig. 7-14 The Space Transportation System (Space Shuttle) Lifting off from the Kennedy Space Center with the Leasat Spacecraft On-board
(photograph courtesy of the National Aeronautics and Space Administration)

7.2.2.8 Titan

The military side of US launch operations has relied heavily on the Titan 3 launch vehicle, developed from the Titan 2 intercontinental ballistic missile. As indicated in Table 7-3, the lift capability and success record are both good, making the system attractive for larger domestic and international communication satellites. Martin Marietta, the manufacturer, has been awarded the contract to develop the upgraded Titan 4, which provides a massive lift capability comparable to that of the space shuttle. Commercial launches with the Titan 3 are being made available by Martin Marietta to satellite operators such as JC-Sat in Japan and INTELSAT. A photograph of a Titan 3 launch is presented in Figure 7-15.

The first stage consists of a hydrazine-nitrogen tetroxide fueled rocket engine augmented by two large solid strap-on motors. To reach low earth orbit,

Fig. 7-15 The Launch of a Titan 3 Rocket
(photograph courtesy of Martin Marietta)

the second stage employs the same hydrazine-nitrogen tetroxide combination. The final phase to reach GTO can be provided by any of several different perigee kick systems. For example, in a dual launch arrangement similar to Ariane, each spacecraft could employ either a PAM solid rocket motor or an integral propulsion system. The IUS and TOS are two solid rocket systems for perigee kick, manufactured by Boeing and Martin Marietta, respectively. It is also possible to use the Centaur upper stage for this function, particularly for NASA's deep space missions.

7.3 LAUNCH INTERFACES

Part of the task of launching a spacecraft is the definition and design of the physical interfaces between the payload and the launch vehicle. From the previous section, it should be clear that there is a wide variety of LV arrangements and capabilities. This is reflected to some extent in the interface with the spacecraft to be launched. Many modern spacecraft designs incorporate features which permit the use of different LVs, allowing the satellite operator to obtain the best possible arrangement for launch. Beyond the physical interfaces between the spacecraft and LV, there are the management interfaces which require a continuing process of coordination among the manufacturer of the spacecraft, the purchaser, and the launch agency.

7.3.1 Physical Launch Interfaces

The communication spacecraft that is to be launched must be designed and tested in such a way that it can be properly attached to the LV. In addition, the spacecraft must withstand the expected acceleration, shock, and vibration of rocket flight. An important consideration is that the spacecraft fit within the dimensions of the LV. The electrical connections between spacecraft and LV, which must be severed at time of separation, are primarily for the purpose of activating the separation system and the ignition sequence of the AKM. In general, the spacecraft is self-powered through its internal batteries.

7.3.1.1 Expendable LV Interfaces

Figure 7-16 presents in simplified form the physical interface for two typical expendable LVs: the Delta and the Ariane. The fairing is the outer shell of the LV which contains the spacecraft, constraining its height and width. In the illustration at the left in (A), the spacecraft is shown attached to the PAM with an adaptor ring. The use of an adaptor ring allows the spacecraft and LV manufacturers to build their respective attachment systems ahead of time without having to bring the two parts together prior to integration at the launch site. Even with this technique, integration tests are still performed on the first sample of any new combination of spacecraft and LV.

The interfaces in the Ariane are compatible with the dual launch feature. In Figure 7-16 (B), one spacecraft is mounted on top of a structural casing within which the second spacecraft is contained. The terms SYLDA and SPELDA are abbreviations in French for two different arrangements for dual launch. Once in transfer orbit, the spacecraft are sequentially released for subsequent injection

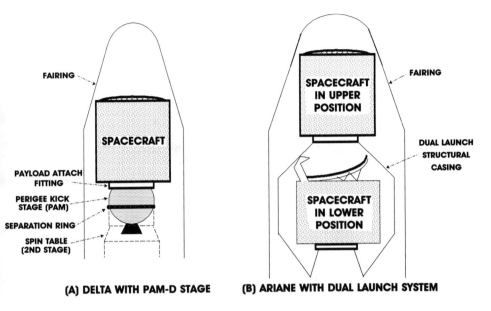

FAIRING

SPACECRAFT

PAYLOAD ATTACH FITTING

PERIGEE KICK STAGE (PAM)

SEPARATION RING

SPIN TABLE (2ND STAGE)

SPACECRAFT IN UPPER POSITION

FAIRING

DUAL LAUNCH STRUCTURAL CASING

SPACECRAFT IN LOWER POSITION

(A) DELTA WITH PAM-D STAGE   **(B) ARIANE WITH DUAL LAUNCH SYSTEM**

Fig. 7-16 Payload Integration Arrangements for the Delta and Ariane Expendable Launch Vehicles

into GEO by their respective AKMs. Arianespace uses an enlarged three-meter diameter fairing which makes possible the launch of relatively large spacecraft like Intelsat VI. The trend in other expendable LVs is now towards such enlarged fairings because of the flexibility afforded to the spacecraft designer.

7.3.1.2 Space Shuttle Interface

Integration with and deployment from the space shuttle orbiter involves interfaces which are considerably more complex than those for the expendables. Most readers have seen TV coverage of deployment from the orbiter of satellites such as AUSSAT K-1, shown in Figure 7-17. This spacecraft was designed for launch by either the Delta 3920 or STS; hence, it was attached to the PAM perigee kick stage (referred to as the PAM-D) and was spun up prior to ejection from the cargo bay. The basic physical installation of such a PAM-D payload in the orbiter cargo bay is illustrated by the cross-sectional view in Figure 7-18. The spacecraft and PAM are attached to the spin table of the cradle, which is horizontally oriented at time of launch. This is actually at right angles with the orientation for a Delta launch. Once the orbiter is in parking orbit, the doors are

Fig. 7-17 AUSSAT K-1 Spacecraft and PAM-D Stage Being Ejected from the Orbiter Cargo Bay of the Shuttle
(photograph courtesy of the National Aeronautics and Space Administration)

opened and a sun shield is closed over the spacecraft to protect it from direct sunlight. To deploy the payload, the sun shield is opened, the spacecraft and PAM are spun up to 60 revolutions per minute (i.e., one revolution each second) by the spin table, and the spacecraft is released from the cradle. Springs push the payload out and away from the orbiter and, after a predetermined delay, the PAM fires, propelling the spacecraft into GTO.

All of the actions described in the previous paragraph, except for PAM firing, are commanded by members of the orbiter crew. Both computer-driven and manual controls are located on various control panels with an appropriate electrical path provided to the cradle and spin table. The provisions which prevent PAM firing until the spacecraft is free of the orbiter are called *inhibits*, there being a NASA requirement for three such inhibits for any hazardous commands. Since it is possible that the payload cannot be deployed due to difficulties with the STS system or with the payload, provisions are made to allow the payloads to be brought back to earth while still inside the orbiter bay. The orbiter usually lands at a primary landing site, but contingency plans are made for possible landings at backup sites located around the world.

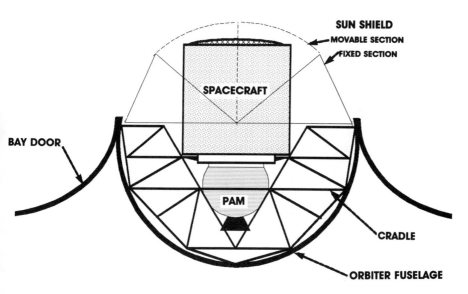

Fig. 7-18 Cross Section of the Shuttle Orbiter Showing a PAM-D Class Spacecraft and Supporting Cradle

A unique integration and deployment scheme developed only for use with the space shuttle by Hughes Aircraft Company is illustrated in Figure 7-19. By positioning the cylindrical payload along the same dimension of the orbiter, the maximum diameter can be employed. The payload is deployed using the FRIS-BEE technique, wherein the spacecraft is pushed out from one side with springs, while the other side acts as a nonattached pivot point. Because of Newton's First Law, the force exerted by the springs is countered by an equal force at the pivot, causing the payload to move directly out and away from the orbiter. This is shown in the photograph of a Leasat deployment in Figure 7-20. A slow spin which is imparted to the spacecraft also stabilizes it during the first minutes after deployment. The type of cradle used in the FRISBEE technique is completely rigid, except for the ejection spring.

The previous discussion of launch interfaces had to do with deployment of payloads into low earth orbit. The orbiter has proven effective, however, as a system for servicing spacecraft already in orbit. In 1984, the Palapa B2 and Westar 6 spacecraft were recovered by astronauts and then brought back to earth in the orbiter for refurbishment and subsequent relaunch. The interface in this case involved a special fitting which an astronaut could attach to the burned out AKM of the spacecraft and then to the cargo bay. Before either spacecraft was touched, the AKM had been fired and all of the RCS hydrazine fuel was expended. An interesting sidelight of the recovery mission is that it was the first

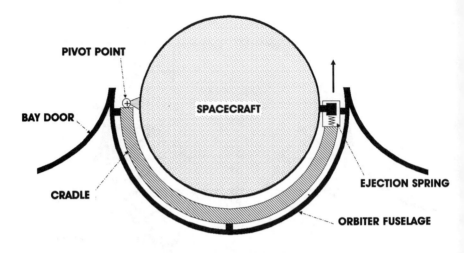

Fig. 7-19 Payload Deployment System from the Shuttle Orbiter Using the FRISBEE Ejection Technique

time that commercial spacecraft experienced the reentry and landing of the orbiter.

7.3.2 Integration with Orbit Transfer Stages

As discussed earlier in this chapter and illustrated in Figure 7-1, the spacecraft requires two major orbit changes to reach GEO from the parking orbit. The second, called the apogee kick, is usually provided by a rocket engine internal to the spacecraft, such as a solid AKM or a high thrust liquid engine which is part of the spacecraft RCS. Perigee kick may be provided either by the third stage of the LV or by a separate rocket engine attached to the spacecraft. The spacecraft buyer would not need to be concerned with the perigee kick stage if its function is provided by the LV agency (as is the case with Ariane and Atlas-Centaur).

Three alternatives for separate perigee kick are shown in Figure 7-21. At (A) is the more conventional scheme of using a solid PKM which is ejected from the spacecraft after the burn is complete. The PAM is a clear example of such a solid PKM, available from M-DAC for Delta or STS launch. The spacecraft manufacturer could incorporate it in the design and thereafter be responsible for carrying out the interface task.

At (B) in the center of Figure 7-13 is the concept of integral propulsion, wherein the spacecraft liquid RCS acts as the AKM to raise perigee to synchronous altitude. The spacecraft is put into GTO by an ejectable PKM in the form

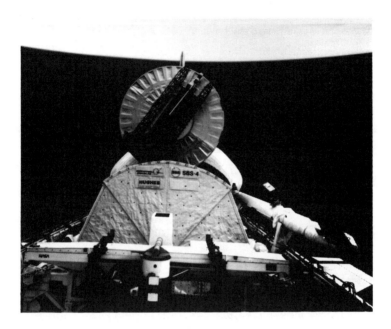

Fig. 7-20 Leasat Drifting Away After FRISBEE Deployment from the Orbiter
Prior to Firing of its Perigee Kick Motor
(photograph courtesy of Hughes Aircraft Company)

of a solid rocket motor such as the PAM or IUS. Because the liquid engines
cannot deliver the thrust of a solid, the perigee is raised in successive steps each
time the satellite is near apogee. It may take anywhere from four to twenty orbits
before the velocity and perigee altitude are at their synchronous orbit values.
An added benefit of this technique is that injection error is all but eliminated
since each step is under direct ground control and can be verified by tracking
and ranging.

A liquid perigee kick stage could possibly be used along with a solid AKM,
as illustrated in (C) of Figure 7-6. Using the liquid system to reach GTO would
involve a great deal of ground control and monitoring, making the approach
quite cumbersome. Another approach would be to use a liquid perigee kick stage
which would be ejected after GTO is achieved. This is preferable because the

tanks and engines are quite heavy and the dead weight would have a diminishing effect on fuel life.

These various alternatives have to be considered carefully, both by the spacecraft manufacturer and by the satellite operator. A spacecraft which is designed for launch on several different LVs, including those which deliver the spacecraft to GTO and those which leave it in low earth orbit, could take either form of an ejectable-optional PKM, shown in Figure 7-21 (A) and (B).

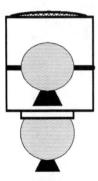 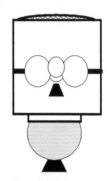 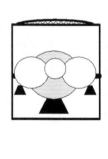

(A) SOLID ROCKET MOTORS FOR PERIGEE AND APOGEE KICK   **(B) SOLID ROCKET MOTOR FOR PERIGEE KICK WITH LIQUID APOGEE STAGE**   **(C) LIQUID PERIGEE STAGE SOLID ROCKET MOTOR APOGEE KICK**

Fig. 7-21 Spacecraft Integration with Three Configurations of Orbit Transfer Stages

7.3.3   Management Interfaces

While not all-inclusive, the following paragraphs provide a brief overview of the plans and activities carried out by organizations involved in launching commercial communication satellites.

7.3.3.1   Launch Services Agreement

The first step in arranging a commercial LV is to enter into a *launch services agreement* (LSA) with a launch agency such as Arianespace, McDonnell Douglas, or Martin Marietta. Because the LSA is a legal document, it is usually prepared and negotiated like any other contract. In addition to laying out the schedule for payments to the launch agency, the LSA delineates major responsibilities including those shared by the buyer of the services, who could be either the satellite manufacturer or the intended operator of the satellite. There would be a technical appendix to provide specifications for the rocket and its interfaces with the payload. One of the most important specifications is the maximum payload weight which the LV is capable of placing into parking orbit, GTO, or GEO, as appropriate for the particular LV. Another LSA would be required for a transfer stage obtained separately from the LV service.

7.3.3.2 Payload Integration Plan

While the technical appendix to the LSA covers physical interfaces and requirements, it still may be necessary and desirable to prepare a document after the launch agency is under contract to define precisely every aspect of the integration of the payload with the LV. NASA has coined the term *payload integration plan* (PIP) as the name for the particular document, which is prepared jointly by the agency and the buyer of the service. Often most of the information is provided by the spacecraft manufacturer, since that organization is the most knowledgeable about the physical and electrical characteristics and constraints of the payload. All parties have a great deal at stake in the launch process, however, and therefore need to take an active interest in the preparation of an accurate PIP. From a contractual standpoint, the requirements of the PIP need to stay within the limits of the LSA, so that the buyer is not subject to increased cost and to insure that the capabilities of the LV are not exceeded.

7.3.3.3 Program Plan

While the technical specifications of the previous documents and agreements cover the physical interfaces, there is a vital need for a comprehensive plan and time schedule for all of the activities leading up to lift-off. The manufacture of the spacecraft and LV are the responsibilities of the respective contractors, but delivery of the hardware from the factories must be consistent with the overall project schedule. Prior to the start of launch site activities, there are usually compatibility tests and rehearsals carried out to verify that things will fit together and that the launch itself will go smoothly.

A very detailed schedule is generated for the activities at the launch site. The spacecraft contractor working at the site performs a series of checks and tests to prepare the spacecraft for integration with the LV. Meanwhile, the launch agency and LV manufacturer assemble the LV and begin the process of payload integration. In the case of the shuttle, integration is done in a special building off of the launch pad. After the complete STS is assembled and the payloads integrated, the entire vehicle is moved to the pad on the *mobile launcher*, a gigantic tractor. Most of the expendable LVs are integrated with their payloads right on the launch pad.

The program plan must deal with the availability of support services and facilities at the launch site, since the spacecraft contractor will usually not have a facility of his own nearby. The launch agency which operates the site may provide these services as part of the cost of the launch itself; otherwise a separate agreement must be entered into with whatever organization happens to have the ability to provide this support. One of the more critical activities at the site is the fueling of the spacecraft RCS and the attachment of the AKM, both of which are hazardous.

7.3.3.4 Mission Direction

While many of the responsibilities can be delegated to the spacecraft manufacturer, the ultimate responsibility for the mission direction lies with the buyer of the launch service, who is often the prospective satellite operator. The *mission director*, working for the launch services buyer, is positioned at the launch and is consulted by the launch agency and its launch team. The *launch director* (also called the test director, a throwback to the days of missile testing) works for the launch agency and commands the team which executes the actual launch. This individual will not agree to launch, however, without the consent of the mission director.

Following lift-off and after the spacecraft separates from the LV, all control reverts to the buyer and his subcontractors. This is the transfer orbit phase, described in detail at the beginning of this chapter. As part of the program plan and preparation, the mission direction and TTAC support around the world should have been tested by rehearsals and simulations well ahead of the actual mission. It is also a good idea to have *contingency plans* to deal with the unexpected. For example, a TTAC site in a remote part of the world may experience an equipment failure just prior to the time of need. Contingency plans can be incorporated into the mission analysis performed by the orbital dynamics group so that tracking and commanding could be accomplished in a number of different ways. In any case, it is important to have the full operational and analytical capability available at all times during the initial phases of the mission.

Chapter 8
Economics of Satellite Systems

The successful implementation of a system or network is as much dependent on economics as it is on technology. Commercial satellite systems have reached a stage of maturity similar to that of other industries, particularly the telecommunication service industry, and therefore it is possible to make reasonably accurate predictions of what it will cost to implement and operate a system. Unknown factors in system economics often have to do with new technology which must be developed and introduced for commercial service. Another set of unknowns involves the expected amount of traffic that the system could carry and the prices that users are willing to pay. Competition, such as exists in the United States, is an extremely strong factor which can render even the best system implementation concept uneconomic.

A satellite system in its entirety is costly to implement but the technology provides versatility and flexibility which are far greater than that of any other telecommunication technology. As was discussed in Chapter 2, a single communication satellite delivers any combination of voice, data, and video services between any set of earth stations located within the footprint. A comparable terrestrial network must be implemented on a wide-scale basis and rapid relocation is virtually impossible. Therefore a communication satellite is attractive from an economic standpoint because the particular mix of services can be altered rapidly and the value of the investment not lost due to changing demand. A satellite that has been launched will see its use increase over time even to the end of orbital life when it must be retired from service. NASA's ATS 3 satellite, launched in November 1967, is an interesting exception. It was retired but has continued to provide service to remote Pacific islands for more than a decade after exhausting its fuel supply.

The nominal ten-year lifetime of an operating earth station is relatively short compared to that of telecommunication equipment used by telephone companies for switching and terrestrial transmission. Part of the reason for this short economic life is the trend towards ground equipment obsolescence as newer satellite services are introduced. The advent of microelectronics has greatly increased the versatility of ground equipment at the same time that unit costs have decreased. Also higher powered satellites permit a significant reduction in ground antenna size and RF electronics costs. These mitigating factors encourage the replacement of functional but obsolete earth station equipment.

The approach that follows is meant as a framework for understanding the underlying economics of a satellite system. It should be possible to use this framework to create a specific economic model of any system so that the detailed costs can be determined. As a general rule, the economics of the system go hand in hand with the functions that it is required to perform. The investment costs are embodied in the block diagrams of the elements and for the system as a whole. On the other hand, the annual costs are usually more difficult to assess, involving labor and other expenses for managing and operating the system. Typical studies of system economics consider the recovery of the original investment by including the time value of money and computing equivalent annual payments.

8.1 SYSTEM DEVELOPMENT METHODOLOGY

The basic approach for evaluating system economics is to view the system as an investment. When in operation, the system produces services which can be sold to customers, providing revenues to recover all costs and potentially yielding excess revenue or profit. Figure 8-1 presents a simplified flow chart which identifies the various stages of system implementation and operation. Financial inputs are required for each aspect of system evolution, i.e., investment to create the system and service revenues from users (e.g., customers, subscribers, et cetera). The objective is to end up with an operational system which is self-sustaining in an economic sense.

Beginning at the top of Figure 8-1, a telecommunication organization begins the process of planning for the construction of a system. The first step is to determine the service requirements or needs which the system is to satisfy. Research into the needs of potential users is performed over some period of time either by investigating historical patterns of telecommunication usage (satellite and terrestrial) or by conducting surveys among the prospective users. Such a project represents a one-time cost, being the first fixed expense in system development. This may be considered part of the investment in the system, or it may come under the normal operating budget of the private company or government agency doing the research.

With the requirements more or less quantified, the next step is to use the process of systems engineering to determine the system concept. This is a major planning project and is best performed by an organization which is very familiar

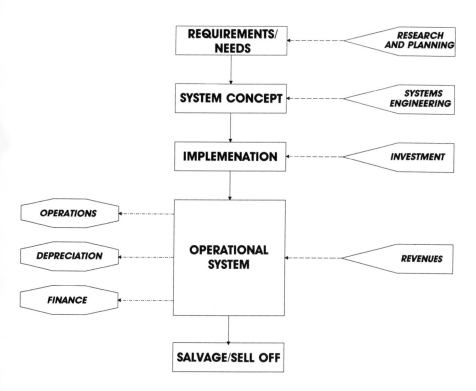

Fig. 8-1 Flow Chart Illustrating the Economics of Implementation and Operation of a Commercial Communications Satellite System

with the technology and economics of satellite communication. The final product of such an effort is a system design document which lists performance requirements for the major elements of the system. For example, the system concept would identify the type of satellite, its frequency band, number of tranponders, and their specific characteristics. The locations and service capabilities of earth stations would also be identified as well as their multiple access and signal processing concepts. Using current information from equipment suppliers, the cost of system implementation would be estimated. A thorough systems engineering study includes trade-off analyses of various alternatives, yielding an approach which is nearly optimum for the particular set of user requirements. Another important aspect of this process is the consideration of how the system can be expanded or modified after it has gone into operation. This can have a decided effect on the approach taken with the initial system design.

Perhaps the most dynamic phase of the process is system implementation, during which most of the investment is made. Before construction begins, the

functional requirements from the system concept are turned into detailed hardware specifications. The earth station locations around the service area are firmly
established with consideration given to the footprint of the satellite antenna.
Contractors and subcontractors are selected and schedules set for construction
of all of the elements of the system. The system operator may perform the role
of system implementation manager, but in many instances another experienced
system integrator is selected. Depending on the type of facility involved and
whether a new spacecraft must be constructed, system implementation can take
anywhere from one to three years. Essentially all of the expenses incurred during
implementation become the investment in the system itself and are recoverable
mainly through collecting revenues during its useful life.

After the system is implemented, the operational phase begins and lasts
as long as useful services can be provided. The economic input to the operating
system is usually in the form of service revenues from users, as indicated at the
right of Figure 8-1. Revenues may be collected monthly, yearly, or in a lump
sum before service is even rendered. An example of the former is the monthly
telephone bill that most all of us pay, while the latter would be the up-front
payment for a transponder on a condominium satellite. The system must be
operated and maintained by ground personnel over its useful life, indicated at
the left of the figure.

Recovery of the initial investment is accomplished by setting revenue
money aside for depreciation. In other words, users pay back to the operator the
investment over time so that when the system is retired, there is a pool of money
at least equal to the total used in construction. Another expense which must be
covered is the financing of the system, since the investors and lenders who
provided the investment money in the first place must be compensated in some
way. The two types of finance include interest and profit.

Additional investment would be made over the useful life of the system
to add access for new users and to provide new services. Any proposal for new
facilities would go through the entire process described above, although on a
smaller scale. Repair of existing facilities associated with current services comes
under the expense of operating the system and would not be a new investment.
When the system or element has reached the end of its useful life, either due to
wearout or to obsolescence, then it is disposed of. If it can be sold, then some
additional recovery of investment money is possible. Otherwise it is disposed
of in a manner which cannot interfere with continued operations or future activity.

The previous was a generic discussion of the evolution and economics of
a system used to provide telecommunication services, or any services for which
users pay. In the following paragraphs, the particular aspects of satellite communication are discussed using this framework.

8.2   SPACE SEGMENT ECONOMICS

The economics of implementing and operating the space segment of a satellite system are dominated by the initial cost of manufacturing the spacecraft and placing them in orbit. Figure 8-2 reviews the main elements of a space segment, including initial investment as well as operating costs. Under a fixed price contract with a spacecraft manufacturer, one or more communication satellites are designed, built, and tested. The same manufacturer could provide either or both of the perigee kick and apogee kick rocket stages. A separate contract is usually required with the launch agency, which in turn pays for the LV hardware and then provides the integration and launch direction services at the launch site. Following injection into GTO, either the satellite operator or the spacecraft manufacturer takes over tracking and control of the satellite, performing the transfer orbit services indicated by the circle in Figure 8-2. While these expenses are for operating the tracking stations and satellite, they are usually considered part of the initial investment in the system. Prior to the start of revenue producing service, the satellite is drifted into its final position, configured for operation, and tested to ensure that the launch environment has not damaged any of the subsystems. An ever-increasing element of space segment cost is the launch insurance which provides coverage for a possible launch or injection failure. Premiums for such insurance have become extremely costly, running between 20 and 30% of the cost of spacecraft plus LV. This is roughly equivalent to holding a financial reserve based on one failure in four attempts, which is extremely conservative in comparison to actual experience. Insurance has become nearly essential, however, because of financial commitments to other parties often made by the satellite operator.

The TTAC ground facilities shown at the left of Figure 8-2 are the part of the space segment investment which is continuously manned and maintained during the life of the satellite. Due to the close tie to the particular satellite design, it is a common practice to procure most of the electronic equipment and software from the spacecraft manufacturer. Also, by doing so, the manufacturer can demonstrate prior to launch that all of the ground and space components will work together properly.

The annual costs associated with operating the space segment, indicated in the diamond-shaped element in Figure 8-2, include expenses for the personnel who perform the technical and administrative functions at the satellite control center and TTAC station. The cost of training the technical staff is high and many personnel are required to be available around the clock. Fortunately, only one or two facilities are needed to operate a space segment consisting of several communication satellites. The efficiency of using these personnel is excellent

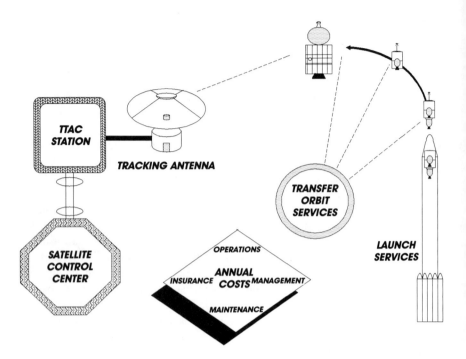

Fig. 8-2 Major Elements of the Investment and Operations Expense of the Space Segment of a Commercial Satellite System

and probably much greater than can be expected in most other capital-intensive activities. The expenses of maintaining the ground facilities are usually fairly small, due to their compact nature. An ongoing relationship with the spacecraft and ground equipment suppliers is essential to be able to maintain and expand the system over time. Management of the space segment is not particularly complex for these same reasons. Perhaps the most difficult task in a commercial environment is the marketing of the services on the system. This can involve a large staff of sales engineers and service representatives, organized in teams to cover different user groups and applications.

Another annual expense that is indicated is that of on-orbit insurance. This type of coverage was introduced in the late 1970s, which allowed satellite operators to protect their investments. Later, purchasers of transponders needed this insurance coverage, because it was demanded by the banks which provided the funds necessary to purchase the transponders in the first place. It could be argued that on-orbit insurance (also called life insurance) provides little benefit, because there have been few significant commercial satellite losses once satellites were successfully placed into service. On the other hand, the financial loss is great in the event of a total failure of a satellite, which could justify the coverage.

The relative magnitude of each of these major cost elements for a two-satellite system is shown in the pie chart in Figure 8-3. Annual costs have been considered by taking the simple sum of such costs over an assumed five-year period which is one-half of the actual life of the space segment. This takes account of the time value of money, i.e., money spent several years in the future is worth less than money spent in the current year. The most costly single element is for spacecraft, representing approximately one-quarter of the total. The sum of the cost of launch, transfer stage, and launch insurance, however, is significantly greater and represents approximately one-third. Investment in ground facilities for the TTAC station and satellite control center is relatively small (5%). Operating expense over the five-year period takes another relatively large chunk, i.e., approximately one-quarter of the total expense. In the following paragraphs, the investment and annual expense elements are reviewed in more detail.

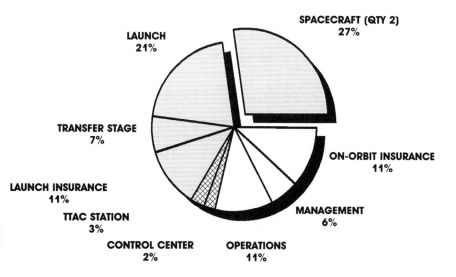

Fig. 8-3 Allocation of the Cost of a Space Segment Composed of Two Satellites Including the Initial Investment and Five Years of Operations Support

8.2.1   Investment Cost Elements

As discussed at the beginning of this chapter, the investment cost elements of the space segment are purchased prior to the initiation of operation and are intended to last through the end of life of the satellites. These elements are indicated in Figure 8-3 by the shaded areas, and discussed below.

8.2.1.1   Spacecraft

A communication spacecraft is designed and built as an integrated system, as presented in Chapter 5. Upon delivery to the launch site, it is capable of being placed in orbit and operated for its useful life without direct servicing. Any repairs or adjustments must be made by ground command and with test and redundancy capabilities which are already built in. Also, once a satellite is placed into service 22,300 miles away in orbit, it generally cannot be removed from service or stored for later use. If the initial injection is into an inclined storage orbit (as discussed in Chapter 7) and the plane of the orbit allowed to move into that of the equator over an inactive period of a few years (determined by the particular mission plan), however, then the operating life can be delayed. Once a satellite is actually placed into service, its cost is completely "sunk," meaning that it cannot be recovered except by selling services to users or by selling the entire satellite to another operator. At any time in its orbital lifetime, a satellite can be repointed or moved to a new longitude to provide service in a different manner or to a different region.

It should be evident from the discussion in Chapter 5 that a communication spacecraft is a complex and therefore costly item. As reviewed in Chapter 1, the historical trend has been from small spacecraft with few transponders to larger spacecraft with many transponders and even multiple frequency bands of operation. Also, the power levels of the individual transponders have been increased over the years. Ignoring inflation, the cost of a spacecraft has continued to increase in line with spacecraft weight and complexity. Communication payload weight increases because the quantity of repeater electronics and size of the antenna have increased. Providing more payload power expands the quantity of solar cells and batteries; this along with the enlarged propulsion system and fuel supply increases the weight of the spacecraft bus. The weight of the structure would also have to increase to provide the volume and physical strength to support the expanded payload and bus.

As a general rule, it is possible to view the cost of a spacecraft as being directly related to its weight. Therefore, the heavier the spacecraft, the more it will cost. The relationship is perhaps not linear, so that there is an economy of scale (i.e., a decrease in the relative cost in terms of some monetary unit such as dollars per pound) as one moves towards larger spacecraft with more communication capability. Components of a spacecraft such as battery cells, solar cells, and electronic amplifiers can be manufactured with modern automation techniques, which tends to reduce cost. Larger elements of the spacecraft, however, are typically custom-made by highly skilled technicians whose time expended tends to increase as complexity increases. This aspect is difficult to change because all work is of the highest quality to assure proper operation during orbital lifetime.

An area where automation has played an important role is in the testing of subsystems and the entire spacecraft. Digital computers programmed to control modern test equipment can perform the testing during each phase of manufacture and at the launch site. This increases the accuracy and amount of data and can decrease the number of personnel on test teams. The primary benefit of using this form of automation, however, is the improvement in reliability that comes from being able to spot potential problems before they occur. Once on orbit, this data base becomes very useful during initial testing to see if there has been any detrimental change after launch and for aiding in trouble shooting during the life of the satellite.

8.2.1.2 Launch and Transfer Stage

As evidenced by Figure 8-3, the fixed cost of placing a spacecraft in orbit is comparable to the cost of the spacecraft itself. A satellite operator does not purchase LV hardware, but rather purchases the services of a launching agency which is then responsible for the manufacture and performance of the rocket system. Whether or not the transfer stage is part of the launch service depends on the particular LV and mission, as discussed in Chapter 7. An LV, such as Ariane 3 or Atlas Centaur, will inject the spacecraft into GTO, where a normal AKM firing is all that is required to reach geosynchronous orbit. The Delta 3920 and Titan 3 would typically deliver the spacecraft to low earth orbit and a separate transfer stage would be used for perigee kick. Direct injection into geosynchronous orbit is possible with the Proton rocket, obviating the need for both the transfer stage and apogee kick motor.

The total cost of the launch mission, just like the spacecraft, is directly related to spacecraft weight. It is easy to see why it is important to design the spacecraft for minimum weight consistent with the communication requirements. Smaller satellites are less expensive than larger ones to build and launch. On the other hand, larger satellites tend to have significantly greater service capability and even offer the possibility of an economy of scale, as discussed in the previous section. The availability of a large LV that can place multiple payloads in orbit can also make an economy of scale available to smaller spacecraft (refer to the discussion of Ariane and the dual launch in Chapter 7).

Some additional expenses associated with the launch mission involve the support services at the launch site and during the transfer and drift orbit phases. The spacecraft contractor can bundle the launch site (launch prep) expenses into the price of the spacecraft, as may the launch agency. Transfer orbit services are fixed and independent of the particular satellite design and can be purchased from another satellite operator. The spacecraft contractor will normally direct the AMF, drift orbit, and initial checkout activities and turn the tested satellite over to the satellite operator. The communications payload, however, would normally be tested by the satellite operator to determine the fitness for service. The cost of all of these services, while essential, is relatively low compared to the costs of the spacecraft and LV.

8.2.1.3   Launch Insurance

Launch insurance has been an important element of satellite system implementation, particularly when the system is operated as a commercial business and requires outside financing. The general trend toward higher insurance premiums for all kinds of coverage (not just for satellites) has also contributed to the problem. The risks associated with launch have always been very high but a nearly perfect commercial launch record between 1970 and 1980 made the risks appear to be diminishing. Consequently, launch insurance premiums during that decade were low enough to encourage satellite operators not only to insure their investment but their expected revenues as well. This removed all of the technical risk from the satellite operator and placed it in the hands of the major insurance underwriters, notably Lloyds of London.

The costly launch failures that occurred in the 1980s nearly caused the elimination of launch insurance at any price, although some underwriters continue to write policies at much higher premium rates. It is anticipated that premiums in the range of 20 to 30% of the insured value will continue to be available, with the possibility that these rates will drop by five percentage points as LV reliability perceptibly improves. With these higher rates, most satellite operators are limiting coverage to the cost of replacing the LV and spacecraft.

8.2.1.4   TTAC Ground Facilities

As discussed at the beginning of this chapter, the investment cost of TTAC ground facilities is primarily tied to the equipment block diagram and facilities layout. It is a fairly straight forward matter to identify all of the equipment necessary to perform the TTAC functions as well as those associated with system management. The buildings are designed so that the equipment is properly housed and environmentally controlled. It is also important that human factors be taken into account, since operations are conducted around the clock throughout the life of the satellites.

The relative cost of implementing the ground facilities (indicated in Figure 8-3) is small in comparison with that of any other single element. Designing and implementing a proper ground environment would therefore be a wise measure, even considering the extra cost of doing the job right. Placement of equipment for convenient access and the provision of well-designed operator consoles and support software will tend to reduce personnel costs. This can also result in more reliable operation of the satellites themselves, as the proper resolution of problems will depend on the capability of the people who man the SCC and TTAC station.

Particular attention should be focused on the computer system used to monitor and control the satellites, perform orbital and engineering analyses, and operate other parts of the TTAC facilities. Having excess computing power and backup computer equipment will almost always prove to be of significant value during the life of the system. Another area is in the monitoring of the transponders and signals within them. This can be important in providing services to users, who rely upon the SCC to control access to the communication payload and to resolve interference problems as quickly as possible. Photographs of well-designed facilities are shown in Figures 6-11, 6-12 and 6-13.

There is an important issue as to whether the SCC and TTAC station should be split apart or be located at the same site. Historically, the TTAC station has been remotely located to avoid terrestrial interference or to satisfy restrictive zoning regulations. This puts the SCC away from the management center of the satellite operator. The needs of users could better be served by locating the SCC and its communication monitoring console at the headquarters of the satellite operator, thus increasing both investment and operation costs. Depending on many detailed factors, this may ultimately improve the overall economic performance of the space segment (i.e., in the marketplace).

8.2.2   Annual Space Segment Costs

The following paragraphs review the main annual costs of operating the space segment. In addition, the financing of the investment in the space segment usually results in an annual expense to the satellite operator for interest, depreciation, and return on investment. Because of the wide variety of ways for financing a system and the different circumstances that satellite operators are under, these aspects are not covered in this chapter. A financial text is listed in the bibliography for reference.

8.2.2.1 Satellite Operations

The performance of satellite control and network management is by the team at the TTAC station and satellite control center. These personnel include engineers, computer scientists, and technicians, many of whom hold advanced degrees. Training in specialties such as spacecraft engineering, orbital dynamics, and communication systems is often provided by the spacecraft manufacturer, since the knowledge can be specific to the particular satellite design. The operations personnel who perform the ongoing tasks at the spacecraft and communication consoles need to be on duty 24 hours a day, seven days a week. As shown in Figure 8-3, the expense for this labor is substantial, amounting to approximately one-tenth of total system cost, assuming a five-year period. The quality and experience of this staff is vital to the successful operation of the space segment and the quality of services rendered; therefore, it would not be wise to economize in this area.

8.2.2.2 Equipment Operations and Maintenance

The ground equipment and facilities, which allow the operations personnel to perform their tasks, must be maintained properly during the useful lifetime. These expenses, while significant, are relatively small in comparison to the annual operations costs reviewed in the previous section. Allowance is made for the utilities and maintenance on the buildings housing the SCC and TTAC stations. The electronic and computer equipment will usually be fairly costly to maintain, due to its complexity. There is a trade-off between hiring a full-time staff to perform electronic maintenance *versus* contracting for such services with the original suppliers of the equipment. Even if outside services are used, a skeleton crew of electronic technicians is still needed to respond to emergency situations at the SCC and TTAC station.

8.2.2.3 In-Orbit Insurance

Insurance taken out on the performance of the satellite after it has been placed into service is called either in orbit insurance or life insurance. The need for this type of coverage depends very much on the circumstances of the particular satellite operator. For example, life insurance proceeds would compensate the satellite operator for lost revenues in the event of a loss of satellite capability. In the absence of such a need and if the satellite operator has sufficient on-orbit capacity to deal with any contingency, then life insurance would probably not be worth the expense. The significant amount shown in Figure 8-3 is based on the assumption that the insurance is to cover the cost of replacing the satellites in orbit (i.e., including the cost of the LVs).

8.2.2.4 Management and Marketing

The nonoperations functions of management and marketing might be viewed as unnecessary overhead. From an economic standpoint, however, a space segment cannot become self-supporting, unless these critical functions are provided for. Management organizes the various personnel resources of the system and arranges for hiring, training, and administrative support. In the case of a commercial system, management is responsible for operating the system at a profit in the face of internal technical and administrative problems and external difficulties with suppliers, customers, and competitors.

The role of marketing is to provide a continuing flow of new customers and revenues, without which the transponders on board the satellites will remain empty. In this context, the sales function (i.e., locating prospective customers and executing service agreements with them) is part of marketing. New applications for the space segment should continually be examined by the marketing staff so that services can be adapted to changing user needs. Marketing will usually be responsible for estimating the future loading of the current space segment and for the preparation of plans for replacement satellites.

8.3 EARTH STATION ECONOMICS

The ideal way to evaluate the economics of an earth station is to identify each major element and relate its technical performance to the associated cost. Such a detailed approach will give assurance of realism in determining network cost, even if the implementing organization purchases complete stations from a contractor. Purchase of stations on a ''turn key'' basis indicates that the contractor designs, installs, and tests the complete station, and simply turns the keys over to the buyer. This approach can be taken on an entire network, a single station, or on one or more major elements of a station. An alternative approach which puts more control in the hands of the system operator is to build up an internal staff of engineers and installation people who can procure the individual elements and then perform the integration themselves.

The economics of a single earth station are reasonably simple to consider, once the elements and their costs have been identified. The investment costs and annual expenses of individual stations can be added together for the network and then analyzed as a system. To be useful in network design and optimization, the analysis must consider the relationship between the performance of the earth stations and that of the space segment. This brings into play the requirements of the microwave links to and from the satellite and the technical parameters of modulation and multiple access, reviewed in Chapters 3 and 4. If the price of using the space segment is determined by public tariffs, then the analysis is simplified because the number of possibilities is reduced. A satellite operator who can design the entire network from the ground up (no pun intended) can perform optimization studies which allow the characteristics of the satellite to vary along with those of the ground stations. As discussed at the end of this chapter, there are useful trade-offs which can help define an optimum space segment design that provides the desired capability for the least cost.

8.3.1   Earth Station Investment Cost Elements

The major elements of a communication station were reviewed from a technical standpoint in Chapter 6 and are illustrated in block diagram form in Figure 8-4. The RF terminal provides the actual uplink and downlink paths to the satellite, while the baseband equipment arranges the information (video, voice, and data channels) for efficient access. Interfacing of services with users is by way of the terrestrial interface and tail (if required). Indicated at the bottom of the figure are categories of expenses for monitor and control, power and utilities, as well as annual expenses for operations and maintenance. Economic aspects of each of these sections are reviewed in the following paragraphs.

8.3.1.1   RF Terminal

The two essential characteristics of the RF terminal are the transmit EIRP and the receive figure of merit (G/T), reviewed in Chapters 3 and 6. These two parameters have a direct impact on the investment cost of the earth station. In Figure 6-6, it is shown that the power output of the high-power amplifier and the gain of the transmitting antenna combine with each other to produce the specified value of EIRP. Also, Figure 6-7 presents receive G/T as a function of the antenna size and LNA noise temperature.

The relationship of performance to cost of these elements is highly non-linear and should be considered on a case by case basis using the most recent information from equipment suppliers. For example, the investment cost of an antenna increases at an increasing rate with diameter. Doubling the diameter from 5 to 10 meters increases cost not by a factor of two but by more like a factor of ten. A power increase from 10 to 20 watts (within the typical range for C-band SSPAs) may only increase cost by a factor of two, but increasing from 20 to 40 watts (requiring a TWTA instead of an SSPA) could increase cost by a factor of four. The use of a small antenna (with a relatively low value of gain) requires that the HPA deliver a relatively high power output. On the other hand, increasing the size of the antenna permits the use of a lower powered HPA at reduced cost. There is typically an optimum point where the sum of HPA cost and antenna cost is minimum. If this occurs under the condition of a relatively large antenna, there will be the benefit of improved receive gain and G/T as

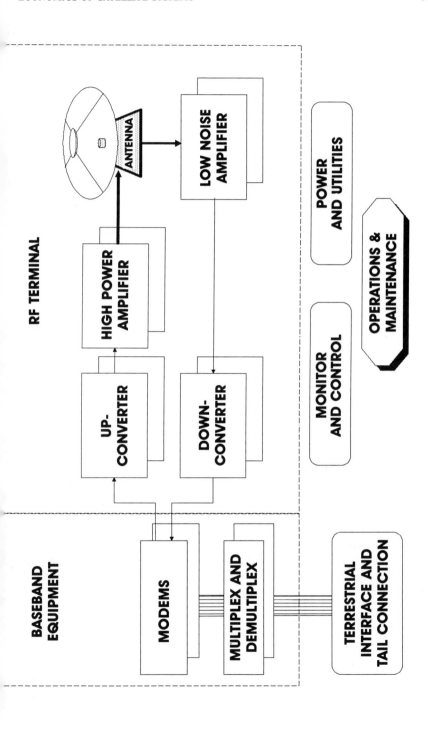

Fig. 8-4 Typical Earth Station Configuration Which Identifies the Major Elements of Investment and Operations Expense

well. A nonoptimum combination with a small antenna may be forced by the need to minimize the physical size of the installation due to local zoning restrictions.

The up converter and down converter are essentially fixed cost items not dependent upon the RF performance of the station. As discussed in Chapter 6, some of the investment expense can be reduced by obtaining integrated electronic units called exciters and receivers which combine the functions of modulation with up conversion and down conversion with demodulation, respectively. The availability of such multifunctional elements will depend on the service application. While a reduction in investment cost is possible, the combining of elements makes it more difficult to reconfigure these parts of the earth station in response to changing requirements.

A major factor in the cost of the RF terminal is the quantity of redundant electronic equipment and the degree of automation with which it can be controlled. In terms of overall network economics, the ultimate cost of outage of a critical service could far outweigh the initial cost of providing sufficient redundancy. Ignoring the antenna, a full set of redundancy (i.e., 100% or two-for-one backup) will more than double the investment cost in electronics. This is usually justified in a major earth station serving as a heavy node or hub in a network. A VSAT or TVRO may have a single string of RF components (without redundancy) under the assumption that alternate means of communication would be available in case of electronic failure.

8.3.1.2 Baseband Equipment

The modulators, demodulators, and multiplex equipment which make up the baseband section of an earth station often represent a significant portion of the investment and operation expense. More modern stations employ digital processing, notably TDMA and packet data, providing significant flexibility in the manner in which the station is used. On the other hand, digital technology is constantly evolving and, as mentioned in Chapter 2, few systems have been standardized. An earth station may be designed in such a way that the RF terminal can be retained, even if the baseband equipment is changed out. In VSATs or TVROs, on the other hand, the baseband portion may even be integrated into the RF terminal, precluding such retention.

8.3.1.3 Terrestrial Interface and Tail

The manner in which the user is connected to the earth station as well as the physical distances involved will have a large impact on station investment cost. Minimum cost goes along with tying the station directly to the user, which is the concept behind the use of VSATs for private networks and TVROs for direct-to-home service. However, a major earth station would serve several users or user locations, requiring that local access or tail facilities be included. If an extended distance is involved, then the choice must be made between renting this tail link from the local telephone company or installing a private link or bypass.

8.3.1.4 Monitor and Control

The traditional method of monitoring network performance is to rely upon users to complain when they experience problems. While this simple approach may have worked in the early days of satellite communication, the expectations of today's users cannot be met without continuous monitoring and extensive maintenance capabilities in the hands of the satellite operator or network service organization.

Having an automated system of monitor and control will reduce or eliminate the need for on-site maintenance or operations personnel. This is clearly preferred in a large network, where labor costs could be extremely high. Such a specialized network capability will raise the initial investment in the network. If not incorporated in the beginning, an automated capability will be extremely costly to add, since the electronic equipment at remote sites would not have been designed for remote control and monitoring. Personnel at the centralized control site will need to be trained in network management. They should be able to dispatch resources to expedite corrective actions, once problems have been uncovered and isolated to a particular location or piece of equipment.

8.3.2 Annual Costs for Earth Station Networks

Two areas of annual expenses for earth stations are shown in Figure 8-4. Power and utilities simply refers to the cost of operating the building which houses the earth station electronics and personnel (if appropriate). This particular expense is significant in the case of a major earth station. Operations and maintenance expenses, however, are very significant in almost all cases, since it is anticipated that electronic and mechanical equipment will demand servicing and repair during its operating lifetime. Reliability of solid state electronics continues to improve, even with the trend towards greater complexity. Incorporating the M&C capabilities cited in the previous paragraph often provides the means to detect and deal with problems before they affect the network services.

While the cost of maintaining a single station may be manageable, the issue of supporting a nationwide network of hundreds or even thousands of remote sites, major uplinks, hubs, etc., can be particularly challenging. For this reason, the services of an existing maintenance organization would be attractive, provided that the service personnel can be trained to maintain the type of electronic equipment employed. Providing sufficient redundant units at the remote sites could eliminate the need for a widespread service capability, relying instead on returning failed units to the manufacturer or a centralized depot.

8.4   ANALYSIS OF NETWORK ECONOMICS

The overall economics of a satellite network can be analyzed by building as complete a model as possible and evaluating the costs as a function of various performance parameters. This can use the techniques of financial modeling and operations research, aided by the use of a digital computer. It is particularly convenient to develop the model on a personal computer, using conventional spreadsheet software. Once the model is entered into the computer, it is relatively simple to change some aspect of the performance of the network, such as the traffic loading or microwave characteristics (EIRP or G/T) of the earth stations. A simple arithmetic model can be used to estimate system investment cost and annual expense for one specific configuration. More complex modeling incorporates mathematical search and optimization algorithms which look at many possible network arrangements for satisfying a variety of traffic requirements. A particular network design would then be selected for detailed analysis and specification.

The basic outline of the analysis procedure is shown in Table 8-1. The steps involve gathering traffic data, formulating network models, and evaluating alternatives for network implementation, as discussed in the following paragraphs.

8.4.1   Determination of Traffic Requirements

The first stage reflects the starting point at the top of Figure 8-1. The term *traffic* actually refers to the quantity of information flow and its distribution over time. For example, telephone traffic is expressed in call attempts and in call minutes, i.e., durations of telephone conversations measured in minutes. Existing telephone switching equipment can measure telephone traffic between various destinations within an existing terrestrial network, thus providing the traffic data needed to design a new satellite network.

I. DETERMINE TRAFFIC REQUIREMENTS
    a. COLLECT CURRENT USAGE DATA
    b. MAP THE NETWORK
    c. DETERMINE CHANNEL REQUIREMENTS
        i. VIDEO
        ii. VOICE
        iii. DATA

II. MODEL EARTH STATION ELEMENTS
    a. DETERMINE STATION CATEGORIES
        i. MAJOR EARTH STATION
        ii. VSAT
        iii. TVRO
    b. FORMULATE EARTH STATION COST MODELS

III. EVALUATE THE TOTAL NETWORK
    a. CONFIGURE EARTH STATIONS
        i. INSTALL TRAFFIC CAPABILITIES
        ii. DETERMINE REDUNDANCY, ETC.
    b. PERFORM TRADEOFFS FOR NETWORK
        i. SUM TOTAL COSTS
        ii. TEST SENSITIVITY
        iii. CONSIDER SPACE SEGMENT

Table 8-1 Outline of an Analysis Procedure for Determining the Economic Performance of a Satellite Network

For video distribution, the usage is usually predetermined by the TV programmer and can be specified as a requirement which is fixed for a period of time. A cable TV programming service may specify a total of four full-time video distribution channels split equally between two different time zones of a country. One type of video traffic which is variable in nature is backhaul for news and sports events, discussed in Chapter 2. Such requirements would have a seasonal element (baseball, football, *et cetera*) as well as a component which is entirely random (news events, Olympic games, *et cetera*).

Data communication traffic has traditionally been treated like telephone traffic. The difficulty has been that telephone calls used for dial-up data links cannot be isolated from normal voice conversations. With the advent of public packet data networks and switched high speed digital links (56 kb/s, for example), the direct measurement of data traffic has become possible.

An example of the expected flow of traffic between the geographic nodes of a network is plotted in Figure 8-5. Primary locations such as corporate and division headquarters of a multinational corporation would have large traffic requirements, justifying the use of a mesh of major trunking paths (shown as diamonds connected by heavy lines). Regional centers, indicated by shaded squares, have significant full-time communication requirements with the primary locations. The smallest predictable traffic requirements are between remote sites such as branch offices and customer locations. These thin routes have occasional demand for service over the course of a day to pass data and voice traffic with the regional centers and possibly with the primary locations. Using terrestrial technology, each location on the map is a node which can be expected to generate and accept traffic. It is usually desirable, however, to bring closely spaced nodes together through a process called *bundling*. Many alternative arrangements of nodes which satisfy the traffic requirements can be analyzed with the overall economic model when it is complete, yielding the network configuration which is truly the most economical to implement. The disadvantage of reducing the number of nodes is that it will increase the length and quantity of local access lines and tails, since user locations will often be some distance from the closest node.

The last step in determining the traffic requirements is to convert traffic flows into full-time communication channels. This is necessary because an earth station includes a specific quantity of interface ports to deliver the required video, voice, or data to the terrestrial interface. Devices which respond to the time varying traffic flow can be installed, but there still is an upper limit to port capabilities. The model should allow the temporary selection of channel capacities and the testing of these assumptions to see if the projected traffic can be supported. Insufficient channel capacity between two nodes causes blockage, meaning that attempts to place calls or use the link will receive a "busy" signal. In a terrestrial version of the network, traffic from a remote site can reach a primary location by passing through a regional center node. This can pose a problem for a satellite network, since such connections involve a double hop. Direct point-to-point connections are possible over the satellite, if the demand

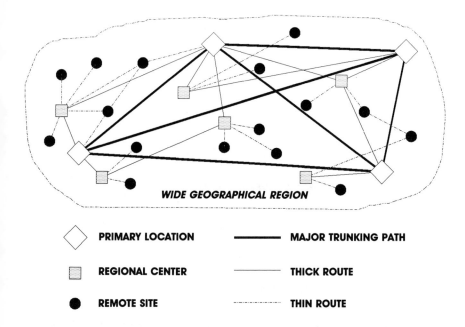

Fig. 8-5 Interconnection of User Locations in a Private Wide Area Communications Network Based on a Terrestrial Implementation

assignment feature is included in the network architecture. Otherwise a quantity of terrestrial circuits should be retained as part of the backbone to prevent a double hop when a circuit connection must pass through another node. A version of the wide-area network employing three classes of earth station is illustrated in Figure 8-6.

8.4.2 Modeling of Earth Station Elements

The first priority in earth station modeling is to select the various categories of stations and their capabilities. As suggested in Table 8-1, there might be three different classes of earth station in the network. A site would receive the type of station and quantity of channels which match the local traffic needs. Figure 8-6 suggests the deployment of three classes of earth station for the network previously discussed. In this ''first cut,'' the traffic has not been bundled, meaning that there is one earth station for each node in the network. Subsequent study of the network would consider reducing the number of earth stations and providing terrestrial tail circuits where required.

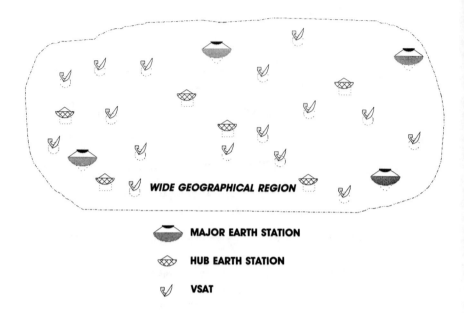

MAJOR EARTH STATION

HUB EARTH STATION

VSAT

Fig. 8-6 Configuration of a Private Satellite Network to Satisfy Requirements for Interconnectivity Between Points in a Wide Geographical Region

A previous section of this chapter reviewed the main elements in the earth station from an economic standpoint. Figures 8-7, 8-8, and 8-9 present the relative investment and annual costs for three examples: a major or hub earth station, a VSAT, and a TVRO, respectively. The annual expenses for operations and maintenance and utilities have been assumed for a five-year time period. Relative contributions are indicated as a percent of the total station cost. The major station costs are dominated by the investment in electronics and facilities, with annual expenses being reasonably contained. A VSAT, on the other hand, would require more attention as to its annual expenses, mainly because the electronics are not particularly costly and placement in an existing building is assumed. A TVRO station would appear to represent an extreme case where the cost of power for the electronics over a five-year period is comparable in cost to the initial expense for the antenna and LNA. Expenses for O&M are small because of the simplicity of the design of the TVRO and because repairs are typically accomplished by sending the failed unit back to the factory. To compare the three stations to each other, the relative magnitude of total cost (i.e., the size of the individual pies) would approximate 1000 to 10 to 1 for the major station, VSAT, and TVRO, respectively.

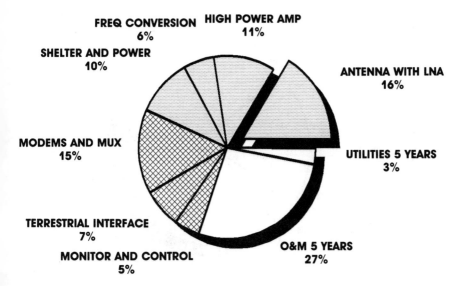

Fig. 8-7 Allocation of Investment and Operating Expenses Among Elements in a Major or Hub Earth Station

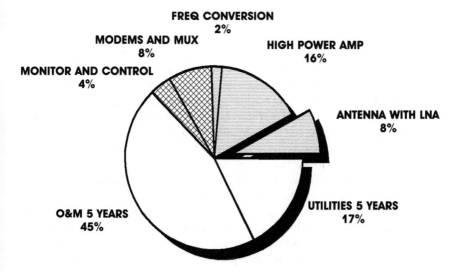

Fig. 8-8 Allocation of Investment and Operating Expenses Among Elements in a Very Small Aperture Terminal for Interactive Two-Way Communication

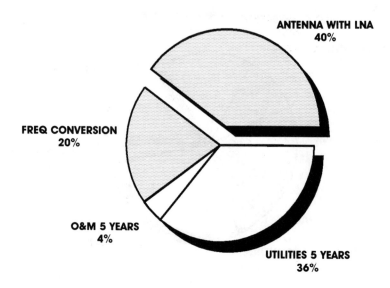

Fig. 8-9 Allocation of Investment and Operating Expenses Among Elements in a TV Receive-Only Terminal for Direct-to-Home Service

8.4.3 Total Network Evaluation

In the last phase of the study, the constituents of the network traffic arrangement, earth station deployment, and element cost are brought together for an integrated analysis. The stations are configured as nodes in the network such as that shown in Figure 8-6, incorporating the channel capacities determined in the first phase. As indicated in Table 8-1, it is important that redundancy be considered as appropriate for the particular applications. This can be accomplished by providing backup equipment in the individual earth station or by adding alternative communication paths in the network.

The complete economic model on a computer can automatically sum up costs for the network and compute useful indices such as cost per channel or per minute of service. In a commercial system, it would be important to determine the projected profit (or loss) which would result under various assumptions for system traffic loading and pricing to users. Various tests of sensitivity to key parameters can be made after the accuracy of the model has been established.

8.4.4 Optimization of Space and Earth Segments

As was mentioned previously, it is desirable to bring the economic aspects of the space segment into the analysis. One of the more interesting trade-offs is the determination of the optimum earth station *G/T*. The results of such a trade-off for TVRO service using the Ku-band broadcasting satellite service (BSS) are presented in Figure 8-10, where the underlying assumptions are indicated at the upper left. The cost of a certain quantity of satellite bandwidth will usually depend on the amount of RF power (EIRP) delivered in that bandwidth. In this example, it is assumed that the total weight and cost of the satellite are fixed, but the power per transponder and number of transponders are varied (i.e., doubling of TWT output power will halve the total number of transponders on the satellite). The benefit of more power is that the diameter of the receiving earth station antenna can be reduced, saving ground total investment cost. In the case of the satellite, however, the cost of the single transponder assumed in the trade-off increases because fewer transponders will be accommodated by the spacecraft. For a fixed system noise temperature such as 150 K, the *G/T* is entirely determined by antenna gain. Consequently, the trade-off is presented in terms of receiving dish size.

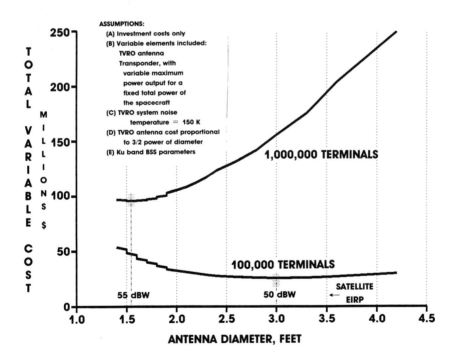

Fig. 8-10 Determination of the Optimum Antenna Size for a Direct-to-Home TVRO Terminal In the Ku-Band Broadcasting Satellite Service

There will be a combination of satellite power and antenna diameter which minimizes the sum of the costs of these two elements for all stations of the network. It usually turns out that the more earth stations there are in the network, the lower is the optimum antenna size (corresponding to a higher value of satellite EIRP). In terms of a nominal design point for the satellite, the number of transponders is 16 and their individual power is 100 watts, corresponding to a typical BSS satellite design with a per transponder EIRP of 52 dBW. Investment costs are estimated for the satellite in orbit and for the receiving dish without electronics, since these are the only variable elements of costs which are affected by the trade-off of dish size and satellite EIRP.

The curves in Figure 8-10 indicate that in the broadcasting application using a very high powered satellite transponder, the minimum cost occurs at approximately 3 feet for a system of 100,000 terminals while the corresponding minimum for 1,000,000 antennas is approximately half of that diameter. To allow the diameter to be decreased, the satellite EIRP should increase from approximately 50 dBW to 55 dBW, as indicated along the X axis of Figure 8-10. The BSS approach with relatively wide spacing between satellites is favored in these results because of the small dish size used to achieve optimum. Both of the minimum cost conditions in the figure are within flat bottoms of the respective curves, demonstrating that the sensitivity of the optimum to the selected antenna size is not particularly strong.

This particular trade-off and optimization study has been simplified to some extent, and the results should not be taken as conclusive. The power of the technique, however, is clearly evident. To be able to perform studies of this type, it is absolutely essential that accurate performance and cost data be used and that the model be properly constructed.

Chapter 9
Future Directions for Satellite Communication

Advances in satellite communication systems and applications have always been evolutionary in nature. The beginning of the industry was technology driven, with the development of the spacecraft design and the proving of its feasibility in the early 1960s. Favorable economics in comparison to terrestrial alternatives gave satellites a needed boost to get them literally off the ground and to expand. More recent innovations in fiber optic transmission, discussed later in this chapter, are seen in some ways as a response to the advances made by satellite communication in reducing transmission cost. The versatility of satellites should allow them to fill important and even vital needs, even as long distance fiber optic networks become widespread. At the same time that satellite applications are evolving in response to competition from terrestrial systems, the technology base is also undergoing evolutionary change. There is every reason to expect that the capability and versatility of satellites and earth stations will improve significantly over the coming years. This provides a technology push all over again, allowing system designers and operators to approach the new applications and markets with powerful hardware and software capabilities.

In the following paragraphs, an attempt is made to project into the future using the current shape of the industry as a starting point. Much of this should be viewed as conceptual and possible, since the precise makeup of the applications and technology is impossible to predict. Even the most conservative projection would show satellites having a significant role in the future telecommunication picture. Since unpredictable advances will occur, the future for satellites will probably be even brighter than is painted here.

9.1 EVOLUTION OF NEW SATELLITE APPLICATIONS

The changing nature of the uses to which communication satellites have been economically put is reviewed in Table 9-1. Prior to and during the 1970s the predominant applications were in telephone communication, a use which

1970s
LONG DISTANCE TELEPHONE **VIDEO POINT-TO-POINT**
1980s
VIDEO AND AUDIO DISTRIBUTION **POINT TO POINT DATA** **BROADCAST DATA** **PRIVATE NETWORKS**
1990s
VIDEO BROADCAST **INTERACTIVE DATA AND VOICE** **MOBILE COMMUNICATIONS** **ALTERNATE ROUTES AND BACKUP**

Table 9-1 Evolutionary Trends in the Applications of Satellite Communications Systems

employed 80 to 90% of the available capacity on domestic and international satellites. Video applications were primarily in point-to-point transmission across oceans and continents. At the time, the TV Networks continued their reliance on terrestrial microwave to distribute programming to their affiliates. Towards the end of the decade, point-to-multipoint distribution of cable TV and radio programming grew rapidly.

During the 1980s the combined mass of all video transmission consumed approximately one-half of total domestic satellite capacity serving the United States. This occurred because the cable TV programmers were finally joined by the TV Networks to take advantage of low cost and reliable satellite signal distribution. The 1980s also saw the explosive growth of private communication networks which use satellite transmission as an integral part. The quality and reliability of the satellite link made data transmission attractive for both point-to-point and point-to-multipoint (broadcast) transmission.

Projecting this into the decade of the 1990s, it seems reasonable to expect a continuation of the heavy dependence on satellite delivery of TV and radio programming. The advent of high powered DBS systems should greatly increase the quantity of TVRO dishes found at homes, principally because of diminished size and cost. As indicated in Table 9-1, small dishes would also prove valuable for interactive voice and data services in the environment of Ku band and VSATs. Mobile satellite services are also on the horizon, wherein users in vehicles and remote locations can access the public network for voice and data services. Satellites and earth stations should also continue to play an important role in backing up the transcontinental and transoceanic cable systems, and in providing alternative routing for maximum reliability.

This evolutionary picture provides an introduction to the following discussion of the lineup of valuable services which satellites can be expected to provide in the decades ahead. Keep in mind that applications often appear out of nowhere, and some of the more important ones to come have not even been thought of yet.

9.1.1 Emphasis on Broadcast Applications

The point frequently made in previous chapters is that one of the satellite's principle advantages is its wide area coverage capability. In broadcasting, the downlink signal is available everywhere within the footprint. This capability would continue to be attractive for video, audio, and data delivery purposes, as discussed in the following paragraphs.

9.1.1.1 Direct Broadcast Satellite

The decade of the 1980s has not really seen the introduction of true DBS service, although a number of experiments and trials are underway. Problems in the past have had less to do with technology than with market confusion. Current C-band direct-to-home service offerings from the cable TV programmers could be the precursor to similar services offered from high powered direct broadcast satellites. The type of home receiver required will use a dish between one and two feet in diameter, permitting the homeowner to locate the dish conveniently (even inside the building looking through a window). In Figure 9-1, the size of a current C-band dish is compared to that of the Ku-band dish that could be used with a true high powered DBS satellite.

The technology is feasible, even existing at the time of the writing of this book. It is a truism, however, that DBS will never be successful without programming, which happens to be the most costly element of such an endeavor. One opinion is that some type of new programming will need to appear before viewers will be willing to buy and install the dishes. This is made even more

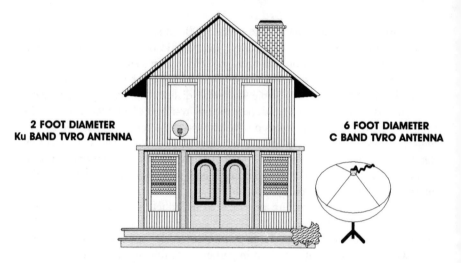

**2 FOOT DIAMETER
Ku BAND TVRO ANTENNA**

**6 FOOT DIAMETER
C BAND TVRO ANTENNA**

Fig. 9-1 Comparison of Home TVRO Antennas for C-Band and High Power Ku-Band Reception

difficult by the likelihood that viewers would need to subscribe to the service and ultimately pay money for the programming. Cable TV already represents a fertile environment for selling programming and testing new services in an existing market. One aspect of DBS that could prove useful is its ability to reach a segment of users dispersed throughout a nation. Programs in a particular foreign language such as Spanish, Japanese, or Chinese can be sent directly to the home for convenient viewing by families. This greatly simplifies the logistics of delivering the programming which otherwise would have to come by way of the local cable TV system or UHF station, both of which may be unavailable due to limited channel capacity.

Another possibility for DBS is in the delivery of high definition TV (HDTV) programming. There is currently no means of broadcasting HDTV to the home. The DBS satellite can easily transmit such a signal, which also happens to occupy approximately twice the baseband bandwidth of a standard color TV signal. While this is an attractive idea, it still rests on the assumption that enough viewers will purchase the more expensive HDTV receivers when they do appear on the market. The "chicken and the egg" problem exists, i.e., which comes first, the DBS satellite or the millions of HDTV receivers?

Probably the most encouraging trend for DBS is the growth in the number of backyard C-band dishes, reaching into the millions. As was mentioned previously, many cable programmers, including premium (pay) services, have scrambled their signals and are now offering their programming directly to home subscribers for a monthly or annual fee. A significant fraction of backyard dish owners have already purchased both the descramblers and programming, clearly indicating that there is a market for a DBS type of service. Backyard dish owners fall into two categories: those who live outside of the service area of their local cable company and those who live inside such areas. The former represent a reasonably easy target for DBS, since the current mix of satellite delivered programming is enough incentive for them to buy the somewhat expensive receiving systems now on the market. The latter, on the other hand, are attracted by other than the most basic motivations for purchasing the C-band receiving systems (before scrambling was introduced, the purchase of a TVRO was viewed as the only expenditure that was necessary to gain access to all basic and premium channels). Perhaps the ultimate size of both groups can grow to the necessary critical mass for true DBS when the really inexpensive and small DBS dishes become a reality. Clearly, the technology for both space and ground systems is currently available, making implementation possible in North American, Europe, and Japan before the end of the decade of the 1980s.

9.1.1.2 Broadcast Data

The broadcast of low and medium speed data to very small antennas (illustrated in Figure 2-10) is based on existing technology and should continue as an important satellite application. The consumer market has so far remained untapped because of the relatively high cost of the receiving equipment. Data broadcasting is currently available at reasonable cost through local FM radio stations using the SCA subcarrier technique mentioned in Chapter 2 and some services are offered over cable TV systems. Another data broadcast service called Videotex provides consumers with information in graphic and character form through the video channel for display on their TV sets. As more Videotex services become available and begin to prove themselves as viable businesses, the groundwork will become firmly established for the direct delivery of the same types of information from the satellite.

Increasing the data rate from a few thousand bits per second to perhaps a million bits per second would greatly improve the visual quality of digitized images. Also, such high data rates would increase the amount of information that could be downloaded into an internal database within the receiving equipment, allowing the subscriber to select for viewing only the portion of interest. This application is similar in concept to the use of laser disks which hold information for access by a computer terminal, although the satellite version has the important benefit of being able to provide information in real time. If access is to be controlled, the use of the digital information can be restricted by addressing packets of data for specific terminals.

9.1.2 Paralleling the Terrestrial Network

The evolution of satellite applications illustrated in Table 9-1 clearly shows that while satellite transmission was at first attractive for long-distance links, the situation has shifted significantly since the advent of fiber optics. Satellite links, however, will continue to be useful as diverse and alternate routes. Private networks employ satellites because of the flexibility of the services offered and the ability of the user to own the ground equipment and exercise nearly total control of the network.

9.1.2.1 Interplay of Terrestrial and Satellite Communication

In Figure 9-2, the shifting nature of the competition between terrestrial communication and satellite communication is illustrated. The first innovations in high capacity long distance transmission were in the terrestrial area. These developments included analog frequency division multiplex (FDM) and microwave radio. Satellite transmission took off next, relying upon these developments but greatly reducing the cost of transmission by eliminating the unnecessary microwave repeater sites. Satellites became well established and new technologies in digital processing and transmission, notably time division multiple access (TDMA), began to bleed over to the terrestrial side. This provided some of the basis for advances in terrestrial communication such as digital switching and high speed digital transmission. These digital technologies are essential to the effective use of fiber optic cables, and now the terrestrial side of Figure 9-2 is becoming dominant again. Quite logically, forthcoming innovations on the terrestrial side will aid in the redefinition of telecommunication services that can be provided conveniently by the next generations of satellites.

9.1.2.2 Satellites Versus Fiber Optics

It is anticipated that while fiber optic networks will become firmly established in the developed world, satellite communication will play a complementary and therefore important role. Conceptually, a fiber optic network in a given country provides the backbone of transmission between major cities and user locations. The economics of fiber are very favorable as long as the fibers and digital transmission groups within them can be adequately loaded with paying traffic. An unloaded fiber optic cable is not attractive economically, compounded by the fact that once the link is installed between two points it cannot conveniently be moved for deployment elsewhere.

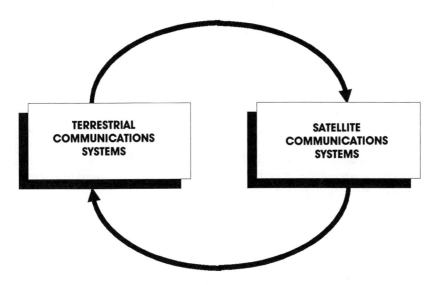

Fig. 9-2 Cyclical Nature of the Dominance of Satellite Communications versus Terrestrial Communications due to Technical Innovation and Competition

The obvious role of satellite transmission is to provide the flexibility that point-to-point cables cannot. Thin-route applications will always be attractive by satellite. A hybrid network of heavily loaded fiber and diverse satellite links can produce the lowest cost per call where service is to be provided on a widespread basis. The type of satellite that is called for would operate in the FSS portion of the Ku band, taking advantage of the ability to locate uplinks anywhere in the satellite footprint. A high capacity Ku-band satellite can achieve cost per call for thin-route service which is competitive with conventional service over the public network, even with low cost fiber optic transmission between major nodes.

9.1.2.3 International Communication

Satellites will continue to provide a cost effective means of spanning oceans and continental distances between countries. A high capacity satellite operated by INTELSAT provides a valuable point of central interconnectivity for the widest variety of traffic between dozens of international gateway stations within a hemisphere. On the other hand, it is possible that a specifically designed heavy trunking satellite can effectively parallel fiber optic cables in the heavy route marketplace. This will permit satellite to continue to play the role of provider of alternate routes and backup. An important implication of this is that the ISDN and OSI standards being developed must tolerate satellite time delay so that circuits and messages can take either a terrestrial or satellite routing.

The use of international satellites to provide telecommunication services within domestic borders should continue to be viable into the future. A developing country which wishes to upgrade the quality and reliability of domestic telephone and television service by installing a satellite network would find that transponder leasing is an economical way of getting started. This type of business is attracting organizations other than INTELSAT who intend to aggregate several such customers and operate the satellite on a condominium basis.

9.1.2.4   Expansion of Business Video

The development of video communication for private and business use has largely been made possible by advances in satellite transmission. Whether the signal is transmitted in analog or digital form, the application represents a new development in business communication. Point-to-multipoint broadcast as well as point-to-point teleconferencing are both growing quickly in use within the developed world. The service is easily added to VSAT networks operating at Ku band since the relatively high power of the satellite permits the direct reception of the video signal. An interactive service is possible with the transmit capability of the VSAT.

Business video is beneficial both in domestic and international satellite systems, where a significant reduction in travel time and expense is possible. Perhaps even more important is the increase in person-to-person communication with the added visual dimension. Business travel allows a few to meet, but business video increases the number of participants, since those who would not have traveled can now participate. The technology of video transmission for business applications is expected to reduce the cost of providing the service, leading to even greater use in the future. Bandwidth compression will make terrestrial transmission attractive for point-to-point teleconferencing, but broadcast usage will rely heavily on satellite well into the future.

9.1.3   Mobile Communication Services

Communication with and between vehicles, ships, and aircraft has been an important facet of radio. The use of satellites for such purposes has developed somewhat slowly because of the cost of providing the satellite capacity in orbit and the lack of sufficiently advanced signal processing technology for the mobile terminals. During the 1990s, these technical deficiencies in all likelihood will be overcome.

9.1.3.1 Maritime and Aeronautical Mobile

The Marisat system described in Chapter 1 and illustrated in Figure 1-15 is an excellent example of the potential that satellite communication has for providing reliable communication to points on the move. Building upon Marisat, the Inmarsat system is establishing a long-term maritime mobile capability worldwide and operating well into the next century. A similar system is being planned for aeronautical communication.

9.1.3.2 Land Mobile

Land mobile satellite communication represents a significant opportunity within the developed and developing worlds. From a technical standpoint, the system operates similarly to Marisat, shown in Figure 1-15. Mobile terminals communicate with the satellite at L band, while either C or Ku band (FSS) links the satellite to fixed hub stations. The latter provide access to the public telephone and data networks. The associated mobile antennas will be mounted directly on vehicles and therefore must be extremely compact. In addition, the coverage will be limited to a single orbit position within a geographical region because the vehicular antennas will not be able to discriminate between satellites. The types of services that are contemplated are illustrated in Figure 9-3. Two-way voice communication (D) represents the most attractive application, because much of the interior of a large country often does not have ready access to mobile cellular telephone service. From a business and economic standpoint, commercial vehicles represent one of the best markets for MSS. As illustrated at (C), contact can be maintained with heavy trucks which carry cargo between cities. Drivers could report their positions and receive instructions from their dispatcher along the route. A truck which is lost (or highjacked) can be quickly located. The same principle would apply to unmanned railcars (B).

Mobile communication by satellite would reduce the time to reach and control disasters, as illustrated for a fire at (A) in Figure 9-3. The service can be provided in unpopulated regions, since it does not rely on wireline or line of sight transmission. Public services, including police, fire, rescue, and national defense, would find MSS offers the potential to save significant sums if several manned facilities could be replaced by fewer centralized control points.

(A) EMERGENCY COMMUNICATIONS   **(B) RAILCAR LOCATION AND TRACKING**

(C) TRUCKING DISPATCH AND TRACKING   **(D) VEHICULAR TELEPHONE**

Fig. 9-3 A Mobile Satellite Communication System Will Provide New Services for Vehicles and Remote Locations

9.2 EVOLUTION OF TECHNOLOGY

While satellite communication began through the technology push of the space program, satellite applications and markets have motivated the expansion of the industry. The decade of the 1990s should witness the introduction of new technologies which can again play a leading role. The paragraphs that follow review a number of these evolving technologies, many of which have already been applied in government and commercial programs. What cannot be discussed are those technologies which are yet to be proven feasible, a dimension that provides for exciting possibilities far beyond those discussed anywhere in this book. As a matter of convenience, the following discussion is divided into separate sections on the space and ground segments.

9.2.1 Space Segment Technology Development

Significant advances in spacecraft design and manufacturing technology will have a profound impact on satellites of the coming decades. Figure 9-4 presents an overview of the evolving technologies for three axis (body stabilized) and dual spin configurations, where both are expected to play appropriate roles into the future.

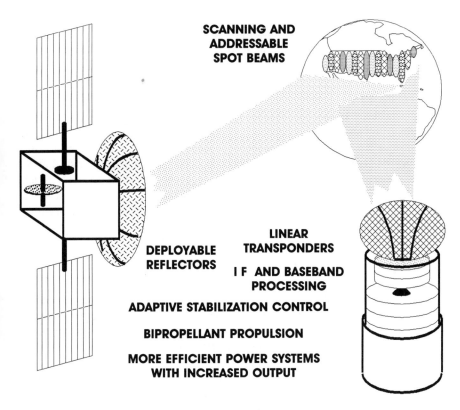

SCANNING AND ADDRESSABLE SPOT BEAMS

DEPLOYABLE REFLECTORS

LINEAR TRANSPONDERS

I F AND BASEBAND PROCESSING

ADAPTIVE STABILIZATION CONTROL

BIPROPELLANT PROPULSION

MORE EFFICIENT POWER SYSTEMS WITH INCREASED OUTPUT

Fig. 9-4 Examples of Evolving Technologies for Commercial Communications Satellites with the Three-Axis (Body Stabilized) and Dual Spin Configurations

9.2.1.1 *Advanced Spacecraft Antenna Designs*

The high gain antenna system strongly influences the capacity and versatility of a communication satellite. Coming generations will employ highly shaped beams and sophisticated RF networks to increase bandwidth through frequency reuse techniques. Figure 9-4 illustrates frequency reuse from scanning and addressable spot beams. The technology is best applied in the Ku band and eventually the Ka band, because the higher frequencies generate smaller spots for the same size of spacecraft antenna reflector. Each vertical slice of the coverage is tied to a selected portion of the total frequency band; the assignment of each portion repeats according to the sequence of shading. In this example at Ku band, the single allocation of 500 MHz is used a total of four times, yielding an effective bandwidth of 2000 MHz. Because of the narrowness of the spot beams, cross-polarization need not be used to isolate beams on the same frequency. Hence, the second polarization can be reserved for another service entirely or to permit colocation of a second satellite at the same orbital longitude.

The physical antenna which produces this capability would consist of a very complex feed system and a large diameter reflector or group of reflectors. A deployable or unfurlable reflector is shown mounted on the body stabilized satellite in the figure. This approach has already been demonstrated in space on a number of US-government satellites. A fixed reflector (as illustrated for the spinning satellite) usually performs better because the surface accuracy can be rigidly maintained. With a slightly smaller diameter, it is still possible for such a rigid antenna system to reach a level of performance comparable to that of the larger deployable. Ultimately, unfurlable reflectors will be as rigid and accurate as today's fixed reflectors.

9.2.1.2   Communication Payload Technology

The elements of the communication payload have undergone a transformation over the years, with newer equipment providing improved performance for lighter weight. Most of the emphasis is on increasing the power output of RF amplifiers which determine satellite EIRP. The TWT amplifier plays the key role in delivering powers in the range of 50 to 150 watts with efficiency of conversion (dc to RF) in the range of 40 to 50%. Therefore, TWT amplifiers will continue to be used in satellites with high-power transponders, particularly at higher frequencies like Ku band for BSS and Ka band for FSS applications. Transistorized SSPAs will improve in power output and efficiency, with units ranging up to 20 watts of output becoming available. The size of the spacecraft has grown to accommodate the larger and heavier electrical power system (solar cells and batteries) needed to provide the raw dc power for the payload.

The effectiveness of the transponder RF channel can be improved by the technique of linearization, which is particularly beneficial for FDMA and TDMA transmission systems. Nonlinear amplitude and phase distortion, which affect signals which vary in power level, are caused by active elements like the TWT and SSPA. Frequency distortion, which affects all wideband carriers, is produced by the passive microwave filters used to separate and combine the RF channels (as discussed in Chapter 5). The nonlinear distortion of the amplifier can be nearly removed with a linearizer which predistorts the spectrum of signals before amplification. The linearizer can be remotely controlled to set up the transponder for a particular type of operation and to adapt the link to power fluctuations from rain attenuation.

Improvements are continually being made in the microwave filters which define the transponder channels within the repeater. Typically, a filter will distort the spectral shape of the signal and introduce a time delay which is not constant over its bandwidth. An *equalizer* is a microwave device which inserts a complimentary frequency response into the channel to eliminate most of the distortion. Modern filter designs include equalization as an integral part of the device. Future improvements will be in better *selectivity* (the ability to pass only the desired RF channel and reject all others) and reduced frequency distortion. Weight and size should also diminish, allowing the inclusion of more elaborate multiplexing arrangements without increasing the weight of the repeater.

The typical repeater design of the 1970s and 1980s could be called a *bent pipe*, since it connects each uplink RF channel directly to the associated downlink channel. Innovations have already been made to provide more flexible interconnection of uplink to downlink, particularly in Ku-band satellites with multiple spot beams. As discussed in Chapter 4, this is called space division multiple access (SDMA). The conceptual arrangement of time division SDMA is illustrated in the block diagram in Figure 9-5. A carrier entering an uplink on the left is connected within the switch matrix to one selected downlink beam. For simplicity, the frequency translation in the wideband receiver has been left out of the figure. The connection paths within the matrix are shown with solid, broken, and dotted lines to distinguish between the uplink (origin) beams. At the particular instant of the illustration, earth stations in beam 1 can transmit TDMA bursts to stations in beam 2 and *vice versa*. Similar connectivity between beams 3 and 4 is also indicated. An on-board controller would alter the connectivity according to a stored program, permitting each beam to be connected with every other beam at some preassigned time. The programmed sequence would repeat at TDMA rates to allow voice, data, and digitized video traffic to be passed through the network. At any predetermined time, the programmed sequence can be changed to alter the connectivity pattern (or network map, in TDMA terminology).

This simplified picture of SDMA is meant only to provide an example of a manner in which multiple spot beams can be flexibly connected. Satellite switching has already been demonstrated in the TDRS satellites, built for NASA by TRW, and is also incorporated in the Intelsat VI spacecraft. Within the repeater, the interconnection would be accomplished at a relatively low frequency like an IF and the actual switching done with diode elements rather than one by four rotary switches. Future SDMA systems will use more sophisticated techniques to process and switch the carriers between beams. For example, each uplink can be converted to baseband and processed to allow the data rates on the uplink to differ from the downlink. This would be advantageous for VSAT applications, where the transmit power of the VSAT would only have to support

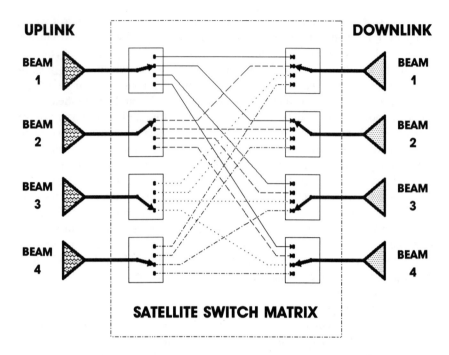

UPLINK   **DOWNLINK**

BEAM 1   BEAM 1

BEAM 2   BEAM 2

BEAM 3   BEAM 3

BEAM 4   BEAM 4

SATELLITE SWITCH MATRIX

Fig. 9-5 Space Division Multiple Access Using a Time Division Satellite Switching Matrix Located within the Satellite Repeater

a low data rate on the uplink, while the receive side of the VSAT could accept a much higher rate. All time division processing and switching systems require that the network have a common timing reference, which could be difficult to maintain in a large and diverse ground segment. On the other hand, the flexible traffic routing capability of any such TDMA-based network is a very attractive feature in the ISDN applications of the future.

An effective SDMA system can also be implemented using FDMA for the earth stations within a particular beam. The interconnection between beams is selected according to the specific frequency of the uplink carrier, as illustrated in Figure 9-4. In earlier multibeam satellites like Intelsat IV-A and Intelsat V, the beam to beam routing within the repeater was fixed for all time, having been established by the particular microwave filters and coaxial cable lines installed in the spacecraft. Future satellites could use frequency selective beam forming networks which can be rearranged by ground command. The technologies for this have been applied in radar systems, but not as yet in commercial spacecraft. It is advantageous to use frequency selective beams rather than time division switching because it simplifies the design and operation of the earth stations. Also, there is no need to maintain synchronization of timing throughout the network.

Systems of the future which employ scanning beams could make effective usage of Ka band, which has not as yet gained acceptance for commercial applications. Experiments in Japan, the United States, and Europe show that the ample allocated bandwidth could be used if the substantial rain attenuation can be tolerated by users. Antenna systems at Ku band appear to offer the capability to direct narrow spot beams and achieve the potential of SDMA. The power capability and efficiency of amplifiers, essential to dealing effectively with rain attenuation, tend to diminish as frequency is increased from Ku to Ka. Perhaps the primary motivation to move up to Ka band will be that the orbital slots and spectrum at Ku band will at some point be used up.

9.2.1.3 Spacecraft Bus Technologies

One of the more apparent trends in the spacecraft bus has been towards greater capability and larger size. The objective, of course, is to be able to support the more powerful payloads demanded by Ku-band applications. With its ability to deploy and maintain large sun-oriented solar panels, the three axis or body stabilized configuration continues to play a leading role in the future. Spinning satellites, being simpler in design and operation than body stabilized, should find an important place in small-to-medium class satellites, particularly at C band.

Some of the key bus technologies are indicated in the lower center of Figure 9-4. Adaptive stabilization control within the ACS is particularly important to the body stabilized configuration because of its relative lack of gyroscopic stiffness, discussed in Chapter 5. Any physical action, particularly the firing of an RCS thruster, causes the body and antenna to move. Beam pointing will then be altered, sacrificing communication performance. Any such disturbance can be corrected without degrading beam pointing if the on-board ACS has total knowledge of the static and dynamic characteristics of the satellite. As a practical matter, this type of knowledge cannot be preprogrammed into the ACS electronics before launch. The advanced adaptive technique allows the on-board control processor (a computer) to learn on its own precisely how the satellite behaves. During the life of the satellite, the characteristics change due to fuel consumption and so the adaptive process is continuous.

The adaptive control system will permit a body stabilized satellite to achieve more stable pointing performance than the current generation of spinners and three axis satellites. The sophistication lies both in the computer and sensor hardware on board as well as on the mathematical algorithms which cause the computer to perform its intelligent role.

Propulsion systems of the future will integrate the station-keeping function with apogee kick. Applying bipropellant technology, the efficiency and accuracy of the system will both improve. It was mentioned in Chapter 7 that a bipropellant AKM system has the benefit of being able to place the satellite precisely into geostationary orbit, avoiding the injection errors associated with solid rocket AKMs. Also, being able to perform the injection with a redundant system and with multiple burns should increase the overall confidence of reaching GEO. In total, bipropellant technology should produce a more reliable system with the capability to extend orbital lifetime beyond 12 years.

Since satellites of the future will provide more RF and dc power, the demands on the electrical power system will increase. Until some new technology for prime power generation is proven out for long-term use in space, solar cells will continue to be relied upon. The efficiency of the individual cells has improved over the years, with a movement from silicon to gallium-arsenide semiconductors on the horizon. Some increase in output is possible by adopting special geometries of the cells and panels, directing more sunlight onto the active cell surface.

Power during eclipse will still need to be provided by a battery system on board the satellite. Nickel-cadmium cells are continuing to improve in capacity and lifetime; nickel-hydrogen cells, however, are preferable for very high power applications. Intelsat VI is one of the first commercial satellites to include nickel-hydrogen batteries and the coming generation of true DBS satellites will no doubt take advantage of the same technology. Since batteries make up a significant fraction of power system weight, improvements in cell efficiency are particularly important.

The final category of bus technology improvements is referred to as *technology streamlining*, indicating that many diverse innovations often combine in a beneficial way. As new spacecraft are designed and built, numerous small weight reductions are introduced in the various subsystems. A lighter weight material might be found for the thermal blankets, the wiring might be simplified by using remote digital multiplexers, and advanced composites containing graphite might be used in parts of the structure to add strength at the same time that weight is reduced. The individual weight saving per item would be small (a few pounds here or there) but in aggregate, the reduction can represent several percentage points of the total spacecraft weight.

9.2.1.4 Future Launch System Technology

Chapter 7 provides an overview of launch vehicles which will be available in the 1980s and 1990s. It is difficult to make projections of major innovative technology before the next century. A significant problem is the escalating cost per pound of placing spacecraft mass into GTO. The space shuttle was to have greatly reduced this cost by employing a reusable vehicle with the capability to place several spacecraft into parking orbit at the same time. With much of the true cost of operating the STS now accountable, however, the shuttle seems no more cost effective than current expendable LVs.

A concept on the drawing boards (but not as yet heavily funded) is NASA's spaceplane, which would take off and land like a commercial jet liner. The European Space Agency and the Soviet government are also working on space-plane concepts. It will take more than a decade before the true capability of any such advanced system is comprehended by potential users and several years thereafter before the launch capability would be available. In the meantime, implementers of commercial satellite systems must proceed with what they know, that is, that expendable LVs are the best available means.

One of the benefits of the space shuttle is its ability to support the servicing of satellites in low earth orbit. This was tried successfully on an STS mission in 1984 when a scientific satellite was actually repaired. In 1985 shuttle astronauts revived the Leasat 3 satellite which had failed to activate after deployment from a previous shuttle mission. Recovery of the Westar 6 and Palapa B2 satellites, discussed in Chapter 7, was also performed successfully. These activities have raised the question of whether satellites in GEO might be serviced to extend their useful lives. A previous international space development project was to have created the space tug, an unmanned vehicle capable of carrying payloads between the orbiter's parking orbit and GEO. The project has not as yet gotten past the conceptual stage.

The trade-offs in mission planning which determine lifetime effect the possibility of bringing a satellite down from GEO for servicing. The apogee kick and perigee kick velocity changes indicated in Figure 7-1 would have to be reversed. The amount of fuel consumed, whether solid or liquid, is determined by the required velocity change and the mass of the satellite. To be able to perform these maneuvers at the planned end of life, the satellite would have to carry substantial excess propellant throughout its useful life. This would increase the cost of launch by a substantial factor, rendering the process uneconomic. Therefore, it will continue to be more favorable to launch a new satellite with only the fuel necessary to support the desired orbital lifetime. Perhaps a more economic approach would be to refuel satellites while they are still in GEO with an unmanned space tanker operating much like the space tug.

There is an extremely efficient propulsion technology which has been around for several years and has been demonstrated in orbit on an experimental basis. Called *ion propulsion* or *electric propulsion*, it uses the impulse of elec-trically charged particles ejected at very high velocity from an ion thruster. Electrical power from the solar array provides the energy to accelerate the par-ticles of a liquid material which is brought up with the satellite much like fuel. Unlike normal fuel, however, the total mass of the material is a small fraction of that required with conventional propulsion. A 10-year mission would only require a few pounds of material, leaving ample margin for other functions. The difficulty of using ion propulsion is that the thrust levels are so low that the thruster would need to operate nearly continuously. Lifetime is also a question, since the thruster uses technology similar to that of the traveling wave tube and is therefore subject to wearing out.

A final possibility for launch operations in the future is the space station or platform, which is under active study in the United States. It would be extremely costly and probably unattractive to attempt to put a space station into GEO. A space station at the altitude of the parking orbit, however, could prove useful as a staging area for subsequent unmanned missions. It has been suggested that large spacecraft can be brought to the space station for final assembly and test in space under realistic conditions. Then, a space tug or other propulsion system would move the satellite out to the desired orbit. Assembly in space represents an interesting possibility for the communication satellites of the next century.

9.2.2   Ground Segment Technology Development

The direction of technological innovation in earth stations and networks will almost certainly involve miniaturization and cost reduction. This tends to push VSAT and DBS applications downward towards individual users. On the other hand, the network, which has grown in size and diversity, must be managed effectively. This will demand advanced network management systems, such as are under development for terrestrial data communication networks which interconnect terminals, mainframes, and personal computers. The technology of digital signal processing and compression will continue to advance, making possible the integration of voice, data, and video communication. The following paragraphs review these possibilities in more detail.

9.2.2.1   VSAT Technology Extension

The impressive gains in the price and capability of small computers will in all likelihood be transferred to the VSAT of the future. Basic to understanding the effective use of VSATs are the star and mesh architectures, first discussed in Chapter 2 and illustrated in Figure 9-6. The principle benefit of VSAT networks is that they can bypass the terrestrial network, particularly the expensive local loops normally provided by the local telephone company. The first VSAT networks to appear were designed primarily for data communication and applied the star architecture, shown in Figure 9-6 (A). With the hub station colocated with the central computer to be accessed, the star provides sufficient benefit to be competitive with multidrop private line telephone service. Telephone traffic could also pass over the link from VSAT to hub; it is not advisable, however, to use another satellite hop to reach the final destination. The star architecture,

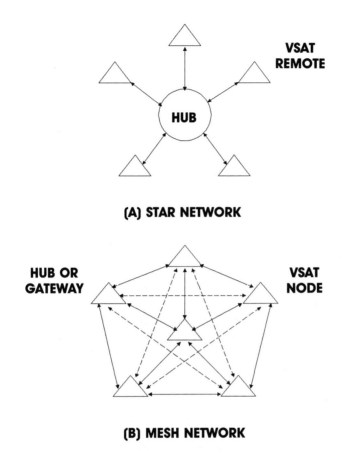

(A) STAR NETWORK

(B) MESH NETWORK

Fig. 9-6 VSAT Star Networks Currently in Use Will Give Way to VSATs in the Fully Interconnected Mesh Network Architecture

therefore, precludes VSAT to VSAT telephone communications, an application which on its own could pay for the network. Point-to-point connections are also beneficial for high-speed data transmission between mainframe computers. The only other practical way to include point-to-point service for voice or data is to use the hub as a gateway to the terrestrial network, provided that adequate terrestrial transmission is available at the hub. The cost of the call would rise because of the charge for using the terrestrial network (cancelling much of the advantage of having the satellite network available in the first place).

Point-to-point satellite links between VSATs require that each VSAT have the capability to transmit sufficient uplink power to be received with a small diameter antenna. Current VSATs operate with low power because the receiving antenna at a hub is typically considerably larger. Therefore, a critical technology is the reliable solid-state power amplifier which is part of the VSAT outdoor equipment. Amplifiers with sufficient output power are currently available, although the cost of these units will have to come down substantially before this type of VSAT would be affordable. Operation at Ku band places the additional burden that high rain attenuation on the uplink should be overcome to provide satisfactory overall reliability. A useful feature of the VSAT would be to include automatic uplink power control to boost the level when the uplink is experiencing heavy rainfall.

Full interconnectivity is possible with the mesh architecture, illustrated in Figure 9-6 (B). To use the mesh effectively, the individual links should be established only when needed to satisfy a demand for service. When using FDMA, each link represents one circuit or channel of communication, employing a single frequency pair from the pool of available frequencies in the transponder. This technique is also referred to as demand assignment multiple access (DAMA). Conceptually, the DAMA system makes the satellite a telephone switch in the sky, allowing calls to be set up between the earth station pairs only when required to satisfy a demand for service.

Mesh networks using DAMA are nothing new in satellite communications. INTELSAT has operated a fully automated DAMA system called SPADE for two decades. Each of approximately 100 international earth stations has its own SPADE terminal containing a computer and a quantity of digital SCPC modems. In the Palapa satellite system in the Republic of Indonesia, the DAMA facilities installed by Hughes Aircraft Company in 1977 employ a central computer to respond to the traffic demands of a network of earth stations in approximately 50 different cities throughout this archipelago nation.

These previous mesh networks provide the desired function, but the associated earth stations are too large and expensive for widespread use. The keys to the success of a VSAT mesh network are low equipment and installation cost, and the availability of centralized control through an advanced network management system. Conceptually, the network would appear as illustrated in Figure 9-7. Each remote VSAT communicates routinely with the network control station, indicating the occurrence and nature of a demand for service. The control station commands the earth station equipment into the proper configuration to complete the circuit over the satellite. Much of the traffic would be between remote terminal and major location such as the headquarters hub. On the other hand, communication directly between VSATs at branch offices and customer locations would occur frequently. This is consistent with a trend in business where suppliers are in nearly constant communication with their customers. Access to the public network, which is probably digital and fiber based, can be through a gateway hub station accessable from any VSAT or other hub. Gateways could be located at strategic points so as to minimize the cost of accessing and using the terrestrial network.

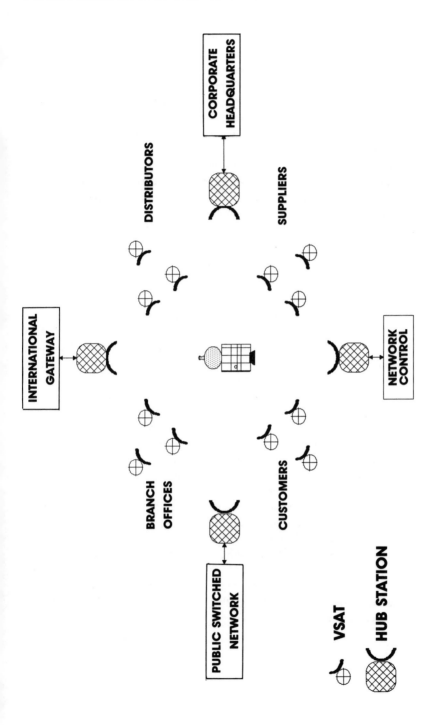

Fig. 9-7 An Example of an Advanced Satellite Network Using VSATs, Hubs, and Gateways to the Terrestrial Network

9.2.2.2   Inexpensive TVROs for DBS Service

The importance of reducing the cost of the terminal in broadcast receiving is just as vital as it is in two way VSAT applications. Fortunately, the simplicity of the video receive function makes cost reduction more a matter of manufacturing volume than technology innovation. The emphasis now is on using the smallest possible receiving dish to reduce cost and simplify installation, as illustrated in Figure 9-1.

The first way to reduce electronics costs is to put as many functions as possible into one unit. For example, the integrated receiver-descrambler (IRD) has already appeared on the market for use with US domestic C-band satellites. As production quantities increase, the price of one IRD will be nearly equal to that of a consumer VCR. From that point, emphasis will be on the antenna and LNC.

9.2.2.3   Flat Plate Antenna Technology

Illustrated in Figure 9-8 is a type of receiving antenna which offers significant benefits for Ku-band TVRO use. The front of the plate contains a matrix of narrow slots, where each individual slot has the radiation pattern of a dipole antenna element. Behind the matrix of slots is a combining network which sums up the received power of the individual slot elements. Referred to as a planar array in antenna engineering, the flat plate uses its area more efficiently than a parabolic reflector and hence can be smaller in size for the same receive gain. In order to reduce the cost of current designs, a fixed combining network is used. This requires that the plate be oriented perpendicular to the direction of the satellite and that the long dimension of the slots be oriented at a 90 degree angle with respect to the receive polarization. The example in the figure is set to receive horizontal polarization.

An important technological innovation in the flat plate will be to provide a variable combining network so that the antenna beam can be repointed without moving the plate itself. This allows the plate to be attached against a roof with the beam moved electrically by adjusting the combining network. Such an antenna would be very easy to install and would not disturb the appearance of a home or building. Some antenna efficiency is lost when the beam is scanned away from the perpendicular, requiring that the size of the plate be increased to restore the required gain.

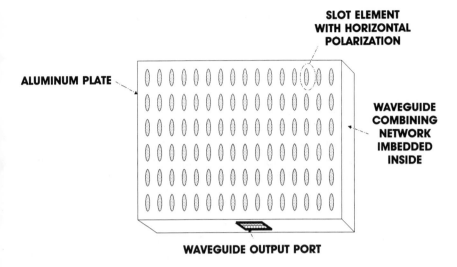

Fig. 9-8 The Flat Plate Receiving Antenna Using Planar Array Technology Is Applicable to Ku-Band TVRO Terminals

9.2.2.4 *Digital Compression of Video and Voice*

Development of digital compression for communication has been advancing at an accelerating rate. There are three parts to the problem, however: the mathematical algorithms which are used to digitize the analog signal and compress its bandwidth; the processing hardware which performs the algorithm; and the quality resulting after it has been restored to analog form. The last factor involves the perception of human subjects, i.e., the quality of the signal is in the eyes or ears of the beholder. Obviously the economics of how much capability can be obtained in a piece of processing equipment must be traded off against user acceptance of the quality of the result. New high-speed semiconductor memories and microprocessors are now available to push the trade-off in the direction of greater compression for the same expense. The other benefit of compression is the reduction in transmission rate which reduces the cost of providing the service.

In the area of video teleconferencing, current compression equipment operating at 1.544 Mb/s (i.e., T1 rate) is generally accepted by users while 56 kb/s quality is viewed as substandard. The equipment to produce either compressed video format is still too costly to allow widespread use, even if the cost of transmission were essentially zero. It is likely that the quality of 56 kb/s compression will improve to the point where it is equal to the current 1.544 system (of course, the 1.544 system will improve also). Equipment costs will come down significantly as the market develops and larger manufacturing volumes are possible.

The cost of transmission is also coming down, both because a lower rate is possible and because of the ability to use VSATs and advancing ISDN transmission systems. It would not be surprising to see 56 kb/s video teleconferencing achieve the dream of the picture telephone exhibited by AT&T at the 1964 New York World's Fair. That particular system would have required a 6 Mb/s link into every establishment, 100 times the bandwidth of today's technology. The ultimate video teleconferencing terminal will provide quality full-motion video at 56 kb/s or less and incorporate the features of a personal computer and telephone.

Compression of voice signals is always the subject of investigation because of applications in secure communication. Today, 64 kb/s PCM voice at eight bits per sample is no longer demanded, with 32 kb/s ADPCM being adopted as the international standard. Further reduction has been hampered by the use of telephone channels for low-speed data transmission on an analog basis. With the advent of ISDN networks, data transmission will be provided over separate facilities using packet switching. Therefore, telephone channels of the future can be optimized for voice. There is already a 16 kb/s transmission technology using a predictive algorithm which provides voice quality nearly indistinguishable from either 32 or 64 kb/s. Compression down to 4800 b/s has already been demonstrated at low quality but with acceptable intelligibility. When acceptable quality will be possible at this low speed, satellite applications will include both conventional telephone (particularly with encryption) as well as the mobile satellite service discussed earlier in this chapter.

9.3 SATELLITE COMMUNICATION INTO THE TWENTY-FIRST CENTURY

In approximately 25 years the satellite communication industry has clearly come a long way. Once seen as a technical feat and curiosity, the geostationary communication satellite is now commonplace and indispensable in many sectors. There has been a maturation process at work: first the technology had to be made economical, and, second, the applications for satellite communication had to prove themselves in a competitive marketplace. Clearly these have been accomplished with greater rapidity than anyone could have imagined.

Satellite communication is the foundation for, and now defines, certain industries. Cable TV in North America could never have become an $8 billion industry without satellites' reliable and low cost delivery of programming. Trans-oceanic communication would still be limited to only those heavy routes which would justify the investment in undersea cable. Numerous other uses, which are yet to become industries in themselves, are establishing themselves through access to C- and Ku-band space segment. Whether it be video shopping at home, broadcasting of financial news directly to stock brokers' offices, or the possibility of mobile communication by satellite with vehicles on the go anywhere in the nation, this developmental and evolutionary process is constantly going on.

The technology of the satellite itself is also advancing, although the changes now tend to be less dramatic. Essentially, the applications now drive the design of the satellites to be launched in the future. It is not uncommon for a technology to be developed specifically to provide a certain capability required for an application.

Satellite communication at the end of this century and in that coming will provide many services currently available. For example, the distribution of TV programming will certainly be by way of satellites. It is the new applications, not yet introduced, which will be the most exciting, providing the base for expansion of the industry in new directions. Satellite communication will be an important part of the evolving picture of the twenty-first century.

Glossary

Acronym	Definition
ACK	Acknowledgement of Error-Free Reception
ACS	Attitude Control Subsystem
ACTS	Advanced Communications Technology Satellite
ADPCM	Adaptive-Differential PCM
AGC	Automatic Gain Control
AKM	Apogee Kick Motor
AM	Amplitude Modulation
AMF	Apogee Motor Firing
AOR	Atlantic Ocean Region
ASK	Amplitude Shift Keying
ATS	Advanced Technology Satellite
BAPTA	Bearing and Power Transfer Assembly
BPSK	Biphase PSK
BSS	Broadcasting Satellite Service
CATV	Community Antenna Television
CDMA	Code Division Multiple Access
CNES	Centre d'Etudes Spatiales
CNN	Cable News Network
CP	Circular Polarization
CLS	Clear to Send
CTS	Communications Technology Satellite
COMSAT	Communications Satellite Corporation
CS	Communications Satellite (Japan)
DBS	Direct Broadcast Satellite
DCU	Delay Compensation Unit
DAMA	Demand Assignment Multiple Access
DNR	Dolby Noise Reduction

DSI	Digital Speech Interpolation
EHT	Electrically Heated Thruster
EIRP	Effective Isotropic Radiated Power
ESA	European Space Agency
ESD	Electrostatic Discharge
FCC	Federal Communications Commission
FDM	Frequency Division Multiplex
FDMA	Frequency Division Multiple Access
FET	Field-Effect Transistor
FM	Frequency Modulation
FSS	Fixed Satellite Service
FSK	Frequency-Shift Keying
GaAs FET	Gallium Arsenide Field-Effect Transistor
GEO	Geostationary Earth Orbit
GPSS	Global Positioning Satellite System
GSO	Geostationary Satellite Orbit
GTE	General Telephone and Electronics
GTO	Geostationary Transfer Orbit
HBO	Home Box Office
HDTV	High Definition TV
HPA	High-Power Amplifier
IBM	International Business Machines Corporation
IDNX	Integrated Digital Network Exchange
IF	Intermediate Frequency
IFL	Interfacility Link
IMD	Intermodulation Distortion
INTELSAT	International Telecommunications Satellite Organization
IRD	Integrated Receiver Descrambler
ISDN	Integrated Services Digital Network
ITU	International Telecommunication Union
KPA	Klystron Power Amplifier
KSC	Kennedy Space Center
LAN	Local Area Networks
LNA	Low-Noise Amplifier
LNB	Low-Noise Block Converter
LNC	Low-Noise Converter
LO	Local Oscillator
LP	Linear Polarization
LSA	Launch Services Agreement
LV	Launch Vehicle
MAC	Multiplex Analog Component
M&C	Monitoring and Control
M-DAC	McDonnell Douglas Astronautics Company

MIF	Modulation Improvement Factor
MMH	Monomethylhydrazine
MTS	Message Telephone Service
NAK	Negative Acknowledgement—Reception in Error
NASA	National Aeronautics and Space Administration
NASDA	National Space Development Agency
NMS	Network Management System
OCC	Operations Control Center
OSI	Open Systems Interconnection
OTS	Orbital Test Satellite
PAM	Payload Assist Module
PARAMP	Parametric Amplifier
PBS	Public Broadcasting Service
PBX	Private Branch Exchange
PCM	Pulse Code Modulation
PIP	Payload Integration Plan
PLL	Phase-Locked Loop
POR	Pacific Operating Region
PRN	Pseudorandom Noise
PSK	Phase-Shift Keying
PTT	Post, Telephone, and Telegraph
QPSK	Quadraphase PSK
RCS	Reaction Control System
RF	Radio Frequency
RFI	Radio Frequency Interference
RO	Receive-Only
RT	Receiver Transmitter
RTS	Request to Send
SBS	Satellite Business Systems
SCA	Subcarrier Channel Authorization
SCC	Satellite Control Center
SCF	Satellite Control Facility
SCPC	Single Channel Per Carrier
SDLC	Synchronous Data Link Control
SDMA	Space Division Multiple Access
SHF	Super High Frequency
SNA	System Network Architecture
SNG	Satellite News Gathering
SPADE	Single Channel per Carrier PCM Multiple Access Demand Assignment Equipment
SRM	Solid Rocket Motor
SRN	Supermarket Radio Network
SSB	Single Sideband

SSPA	Solid-State Power Amplifier
STS	Space Transportation System
STV	Subscription Television
SYNCOM	Synchronous Orbit Communications Satellite
TDM	Time Division Multiplex
TDMA	Time Division Multiple Access
TTAC	Tracking, Telemetry, and Command
TVRO	TV Receive-Only
TWT	Traveling Wave Tube
TWTA	Traveling Wave Tube Amplifier
UDMH	Unsymmetrical Dimethylhydrazine
UHF	Ultra High Frequency
UPS	Uninterruptable Power System
VHF	Very High Frequency
VSAT	Very Small Aperture Terminal
WATS	Wide Area Telecommunication Service

Bibliography

W. S. Cheung and F. H. Levien, eds., *Microwaves Made Simple*, Artech House, Norwood, MA, 1985.

International Radio Consultative Committee (CCIR), *Handbook on Satellite Communications*, International Telecommunication Union, Geneva, Switzerland, 1985.

D. M. Jansky, ed., *World Atlas of Satellites*, Artech House, Norwood, MA, 1983.

J. D. Kiesling, B. R. Elbert, W. B. Garner, and W. L. Morgan, "A Technique for Modeling Communications Satellites," *COMSAT Technical Review*, Vol. 2, No. 1, Communications Satellite Corporation, Clarksburg, MD, Spring 1972.

A. M. Noll, *Introduction to Telephones and Telephone Systems*, Artech House, Norwood, MA, 1986.

M. E. Porter, *Competitive Strategy*, Free Press, New York, 1980.

H. A. Rosen, "Spacecraft Design for the SBS System," *Conference Record*, AIAA Communications Satellite Systems Conference, San Diego, CA, American Institute of Aeronautics and Astronautics, 1982.

R. J. Saunders, J. J. Warford, and B. Wellenius, *Telecommunications and Economic Development*, World Bank publication, Johns Hopkins University Press, Baltimore, Maryland, 1983.

M. Schwartz, *Information Transmission, Modulation, and Noise*, 3rd Ed., McGraw-Hill, New York, 1980.

M. Schwartz, *Telecommunication Networks*, Addison-Wesley, Reading, MA, 1987.

J. R. Wertz, *Spacecraft Attitude Determination and Control*, D. Reidel, Dordrecht, The Netherlands, 1980.

J. F. Weston and E. F. Brigham, *Managerial Finance*, 7th Ed., Dryden Press, Hinsdale, IL, 1981.

Index

ABC Television Network, 56
Abramson, Norman, 55
Absorption of RF carrier power, 15, 97
Acceleration, 284, 286
Active thermal control, 212
Adaptive stabilization control, 188, 335
Adaptive-differential PCM (ADPCM), 131,
    344
Adaptor ring, 286
Adjacent satellite interference, 18, 73
Administrative support for satellite operators,
    307
ADPCM, *see* Adaptive-differential PCM
Advanced Communications Technology
    Satellite (ACTS), 23
Advanced network management systems, 338
Advanced spacecraft antenna designs, 331
Advanced Technology Satellite (ATS), 37
Advertising, 57, 62
Aeronautical Mobile Satellite, 9
Aerospatiale, 39
Aetna Life and Casualty Company, 40
Affiliates, 56
Africa, 18, 30
Aggregation of users, 78
Air and Space Museum of the Smithsonian
    Institution, 27
Air conditioning, 219
Airlines usage of data communications, 71
Airplanes, 9, 22
AKM, *see* Apogee kick motor
Algeria, 40
Algorithm, 79, 131, 134
Alignment, 88, 92

Allocated frequency bands, 11, 17, 23, 30, 64
Allocation for DBS, 17, 18
Aloha protocol, 55, 121, 251
Alternative routing by satellite, 323
Americom, *see* GE Americom
AMF, *see* Apogee motor firing
Amplification, 100, 104, 114, 255
Amplifier backoff, 145, 240
Amplifiers, 13, 28, 69, 126, 163, 217, 218,
    225, 227-229, 240, 303, 332
Amplitude modulation (AM), 126, 141
Amplitude nonlinearity (AM-to-AM
    distortion), 142, 147
Amplitude-shift keying (ASK), 141
AM-to-PM conversion, *see* Phase nonlinearity
Analog information, 124
Analog-to-digital conversion (A/D conversion),
    103, 130
Analog transmission, 115
Analog TV, 127
Andover, Maine, international earth station, 27
Anik satellite, 34
Annual costs, 296
Anode, 175
Antenna beam coverage, 2, 31, 152, 175, 183,
    187, 228, 295, 323
Antenna beam pointing, 223
Antenna beam, 21, 333
Antenna efficiency, 86, 223
Antenna gain, 86, 87
Antenna gain contour, *see* Antenna beam
    coverage
Antenna pattern, 87
Antenna pointing accuracy, 88, 194

353

Spot beam antenna, 149, 181, 331, 333, 335
Spread spectrum, 73, 133, 249
Spreading loss, 83
Spreadsheet, 312
Spun section, 155
Spurious products (spurs), 164
Spurious response of RF multiplexer, 174
Sputnik satellite, 24
SSPA, *see* Solid-state power amplifier
Stability, 24, 223
Stabilization, 35, 155, 177
Star network using FDMA, 240
Star networks, 69, 99, 253, 338-339
Stationkeeping, 152, 201, 267, 270, 335
Statistical multiplexing, 77, 78
Statsionar, 33
Stereo, 81, 127, 239
Storage orbit, 271, 302
Strap-on rockets, 273, 280
Structural arrangement, 214
Structure, 152, 175, 177, 199, 214
Studio, 51, 58, 82, 219
Studio-to-television transmitter links, 23
STV, *see* Subscription television
Subcarrier, 74, 127, 256
Subcontractors, 294, 298
Subreflector, 223
Subscriber loop, 64
Subscriber units, 64
Subscribers, 9, 26, 46, 61, 64, 79, 247, 255, 296, 325
Subscription television (STV), 57
Subsynchronous, 26, 33
Successors, 64
Suharto, 35
Sun sensor, 189
Sunk cost of a satellite, 302
Sunlight, 151
Sun-oriented solar panel, 335
Supermarket Radio Network (SRN), 82
Supergroup, 127, 134
SuperStation WTBS, 62
Supervisory signalling, 255
Suppliers, 47, 81
Support services and facilities at the launch site, 294
Support services at the launch site, 304
Suppressor, *see* Echo suppressor
Surface accuracy, 227
Switch matix, 333

Switched telephone service, 64, 253
Switches, 103
Switching, 163, 166, 198, 295
Switching office, 257
Switzerland, 11
SYLDA, 276, 286
Synchronization, 95, 121, 131, 201
Synchronous command generator, 234
SYNCOM, 23, 37, 51
Syndication, 56
System development, 296
System economics, 296
System implementation, 298
System integrator, 298
System Network Architecture (SNA), 54
System noise temperature, 165
Systems engineering, 296
S/N enhancement, 253

T-1 channel, 134
Tacsat, 28
Tail, 217, 231, 254, 255, 257
Talking heads, 80
Tandem, 79
Tandem connection of amplifiers, 165, 179
Tanegashima, Japan, launch site, 280
TDM, *see* Time division multiplex
TDM data stream, 235
TDMA, *see* Time division multiple access
TDMA burst operation, 241
TDMA earth station, 240
TDMA network of INTELSAT, 244
TDMA terminal, 241
TDRS system (SDMA), 333
Technology streamlining, 336
Telecast, 1, 58
Telecom, 38
Telecommunications equipment, 295
Teleconferencing, *see* Video teleconferencing
Telemarketing, 66
Telemetry alarm, 235
Telemetry decomutator, 235
Telemetry downlink, 231
Telemetry subsystem, 233
Telephone interface, 253, 255
Telephone local loop, 70
Telephone switching equipment, 312
Teleports, 41, 236, 257
Telesat Canada, 6, 34
Telescope optics for antennas, 189

The Author

Bruce R. Elbert is Director of Galaxy Systems at Hughes Communications, Inc., the satellite operating subsidiary of Hughes Aircraft Company. Mr. Elbert is currently responsible for marketing and program management of communication services via the Galaxy satellites and a nationwide earth station network. He has more than 20 years of experience in the satellite and telecommunication industries, having been technical director and proposal manager for several of the HS-376 spacecraft manufactured by Hughes. During the Palapa A program in the mid-1970s, Mr. Elbert led the communication engineering team which designed the first Indonesian domestic satellite network and personally directed the successful cut-over of service. In addition to his 13 years of Hughes experience, he worked for COMSAT and Western Union, and served a four-year tour in the US Army as a radio communications officer.

Mr. Elbert earned his BEE and MSEE degrees from the City College of New York and the University of Maryland, respectively, and recently graduated from Pepperdine University's Presidential/Key Executive MBA program. Mr. Elbert is active in the IEEE and AIAA, and has conducted seminars on satellite communication at AIAA conferences and at the Satellite Communication Users Conference. He resides with his wife and two daughters on the Palos Verdes Peninsula in California.

The Artech House Telecommunications Library

Vinton G. Cerf, Series Editor

Telecommuting, Osman Eldib and Daniel Minoli

Telephone Company and Cable Television Competition, Stuart N. Brotman

Teletraffic Technologies in ATM Networks, Hiroshi Saito

Terrestrial Digital Microwave Communciations, Ferdo Ivanek, editor

Transmission Networking: SONET and the SDH, Mike Sexton and Andy Reid

Transmission Performance of Evolving Telecommunications Networks, John Gruber and Godfrey Williams

Troposcatter Radio Links, G. Roda

UNIX Internetworking, Uday O. Pabrai

Virtual Networks: A Buyer's Guide, Daniel D. Briere

Voice Processing, Second Edition, Walt Tetschner

Voice Teletraffic System Engineering, James R. Boucher

Wireless Access and the Local Telephone Network, George Calhoun

Wireless Data Networking, Nathan J. Muller

Wireless LAN Systems, A. Santamaría and F. J. López-Hernández

Writing Disaster Recovery Plans for Telecommunications Networks and LANs, Leo A. Wrobel

X Window System User's Guide, Uday O. Pabrai

For further information on these and other Artech House titles, contact:

Artech House
685 Canton Street
Norwood, MA 02062
617-769-9750
Fax: 617-769-6334
Telex: 951-659
email: artech@world.std.com

Artech House
Portland House, Stag Place
London SW1E 5XA England
+44 (0) 171-973-8077
Fax: +44 (0) 171-630-0166
Telex: 951-659
email: bookco@artech.demon.co.uk